Residential Building Codes Illustrated

A Guide to Understanding the 2009 International Residential Code®

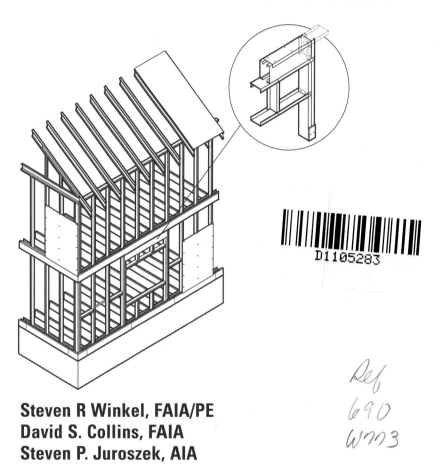

Steven R Winkel, FAIA/PE
David S. Collins, FAIA
Steven P. Juroszek, AIA

Building Codes Illustrated Series Advisor
Francis D.K. Ching

WILEY
John Wiley & Sons, Inc.

This book is printed on acid-free paper. ∞

Published by John Wiley & Sons, Inc., Hoboken, New Jersey
Published simultaneously in Canada

For general information about our other products and services, please contact our Customer Care Department within the United States at (800) 762-2974, outside the United States at (317) 572-3993 or fax (317) 572-4002.

Wiley also publishes its books in a variety of electronic formats. Some content that appears in print may not be available in electronic books. For more information about Wiley products, visit our web site at www.wiley.com.

Winkel, Steven, 1948-
  Residential building codes illustrated: a guide to understanding the 2009 international residential code
/ Steven R Winkel, David S. Collins, Steven P. Juroszek.
    p. cm. -- (Building codes illustrated series)
Includes bibliographical references and index.
ISBN 978-0-470-17359-6 (cloth)
1. Building-Standards. 2. Buildings—Specifications. I. Winkel, Steven R. II. Title
TH420 .C49 2003
690'.02'18--dc21
                                2002193364

Printed in the United States of America.

10 9 8 7 6 5 4 3 2 1

Disclaimer

The book contains the authors' analyses and illustrations of the intent and potential interpretations of the building construction provisions of the 2009 International Residential Code® (IRC) for the design of one- and two-family dwellings and townhouses. The illustrations and examples are general in nature and not intended to apply to any specific project without a detailed analysis of the unique nature of the project. As with any code document, the IRC is subject to interpretation by the Authorities Having Jurisdiction (AHJ) for their application to a specific project. Designers should consult the local Building Official early in project design if there are questions or concerns about the meaning or application of code sections in relation to specific design projects.

The interpretations and illustrations in the book are those of the authors. The authors do not represent that the illustrations, analyses, or interpretations in this book are definitive. They are not intended to take the place of detailed code analyses of a project, the exercise of professional judgment by the reader, or interpretive application of the code to any project by permitting authorities. While this publication is designed to provide accurate and authoritative information regarding the subject matter covered, it is sold with the understanding that neither the publisher nor the authors are engaged in rendering professional services. If professional advice or other expert assistance is required, the services of a competent professional person should be sought.

The authors and John Wiley & Sons would like to thank Peter Kulczyk of the International Code Council for his thorough review of the manuscript and illustrations in this book. This review does reflect in any way the official position of the International Code Council. Any errors in the interpretatons or illustrations in the book are solely those of the authors and are in no way the responsibility of the Interntional Code Council.

Acknowledgments

The authors would like to acknowledge the contributions of Francis D.K. Ching, whose drawings in *Building Codes Illustrated* provided the foundation and standard for the illustrations in this book. Finally, the authors would like to thank Barbara Sahm, Sarah Rice, and Sheri Juroszek for their support and encouragement throughout the process of producing this book.

Contents

Preface

The primary purpose of this book is to familiarize code users with the use of the *2009 International Residential Code®* (IRC) with a focus on the code provisions related to building construction. It is intended as an instructional text on how the code was developed and how it is organized, as well as a reference document on how to use the code for the design of one- and two-family dwellings. It is intended to be a companion to the IRC, not a substitute for it. This book must be read in concert with the IRC.

This book is designed to give an understanding of how the International Residential Code was developed, and how it is likely to be interpreted when applied to the design and construction of single family houses, two-family houses and townhouses no more than three stories high and with separate entries for each townhouse. The intent of this book is to give a fundamental understanding of the relationship of codes to practice for design professionals, especially those licensed or desiring to become licensed as architects, engineers or other related design professionals. Code knowledge is among the fundamental reasons for licensing design professionals, for the protection of public health, safety and welfare. It is our goal to make the acquisition and use of code knowledge easier and clearer for code users.

Many designers feel intimidated by building codes. Codes can seem daunting and complex at first glance. It is important to know that they are a product of years of accretion and evolution. Sections start simply and become more complex as they are modified, and new material is added to address additional concerns or to address interpretation issues from previous code editions. The complexity of a building code often comes from this layering of new information upon old without regard to overall continuity. Building codes are living documents, constantly under review and modification. It is vital to an understanding of codes to keep in mind that they are a human institution, written by ordinary people with specific issues in mind or specific agendas they wish to advance.

BUILDING CODE

Webster's Third New International Dictionary defines a building code as: "A set of rules of procedure and standards of materials designed to secure uniformity and protect the public interest in such matters as building construction and public health, established usually by a public agency and commonly having the force of law in a particular jurisdiction."

How This Book Is Organized

The first two chapters of this book give background and context regarding the development, organization and use of the IRC. Chapters 3 through 10 are organized and numbered the same as the corresponding subject-matter chapters in the IRC.

• *Page headings refer to major sections within each chapter of the code.*

• *Text is arranged in columns, typically on the left side of a single page or of two facing pages.*

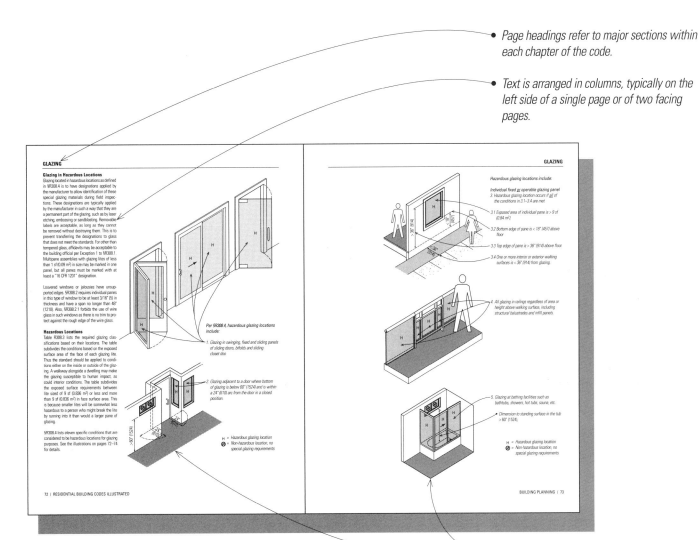

• *Drawings are typically to the right, accompanied by captions or explanatory notes. The illustrations are intended to help the reader visualize what is described in the text. They should therefore be considered to be diagrams that explain and clarify design relationships rather than representing specific design solutions.*

Target Audiences

This book addresses code issues specific to the design and construction of dwellings. It accompanies and expands upon the basic principles addressed in the *2009 International Residential Code®* (IRC).

For Emerging Professionals

Whether encountered during the design, production, management or construction administration phases for construction of one- and two-family dwellings and townhouses, codes and standards are an integral and inescapable part of the practice of architecture and engineering. New practitioners need to refine their skills and knowledge of codes to make their projects safe and buildable with few costly changes. The more practitioners know about the code the more it can become a tool for design rather than an impediment. The better the underlying criteria for code development and the reasons for code provisions are understood the easier it is to create code-compliant designs. Early understanding and incorporation of code-compliant design provisions in a project reduces the necessity for costly and time-consuming rework or awkward rationalizations to justify dubious code decisions late in project documentation, or even during construction. Code use and understanding should be part of accepted knowledge for professionals, so that it becomes a part of the vocabulary of design.

For Experienced Practitioners

The greatest value of this book is that it is based upon the broadly adopted International Residential Code. This is a code that is similar but by no means identical to the old Council of American Building Officials (CABO) One- and Two-Family Dwelling Code that many experienced practitioners have used in the past. New state and federal standards have been developed using the IRC and the new requirements, while similar, are by no means identical to those in prior codes. This book will guide experienced practitioners out of the old grooves of code use they may have fallen into with the old codes. The code-analysis methods and outcomes will vary between the old codes and the new IRC. While there are seemingly familiar aspects from each code interspersed throughout the new code, the actual allowable criteria and how they are determined are often quite different. It is likely that the illustrations and the underlying reasons for the development of each code section will look familiar to experienced practitioners. The experienced practitioner must not rely on memory or old habits of picking construction types or assemblies based on prior practice. Each dwelling must be looked at anew until the similarities and sometimes-critical differences between the new code and old habits are understood and acknowledged.

It is also worth remembering that building officials and plan checkers are now becoming more familiar with these codes as well. We are still in a period of transition during which dialogue between designers and plan reviewers will be essential. The precedents that people on each side of the plan-review counter in the building department are most familiar with may no longer apply. Designers and building officials must arrive at new consensus interpretations together as they use the new codes for specific projects.

How to Use This Book

This book focuses on the use and interpretation of the provisions of the *2009 International Residential Code*® (IRC). There are references to basic structural requirements, but this book does not attempt to go into the derivation of the structural requirements in depth. That is a subject for another volume. This book does discuss and illustrate the prescriptive structural requirements contained in the IRC. This book covers the first 10 chapters of the IRC. These chapters are the core of the provisions related to building planning and building structure. These chapters cover requirements for the major components of the building envelope: foundations, floors, walls and roofs. This volume does not address provisions for energy efficiency or requirements for mechanical, electrical or plumbing work.

The organization of this book presumes that the reader has a copy of the latest version of the IRC itself as a companion document to this book. The book is intended to expand upon, interpret and illustrate various provisions of the code. The IRC has been adopted in many jurisdictions. It is now being extensively applied, and while there is not yet a large body of precedent in application and interpretation, code users do have a history of prior use to draw upon. It is our hope that the analysis and illustrations in the book will aid the designer and the Authorities Having Jurisdiction (AHJ) in clarifying their own interpretations of the application of code sections to projects.

The book is not intended to take the place of the *2009 International Residential Code*® in any way. The many detailed tables and criteria contained in the IRC are partially restated in the book for illustrative purposes only. For example, we show how various tables are meant to be used and how we presume certain parts will be interpreted. When performing a code analysis for a specific project, we anticipate the reader will use our book to understand the intent of the applicable code section and then use the code itself to find the detailed criteria to apply. One can, however, start with either the IRC or this book in researching a specific topic:

Beginning with the *2009 International Residential Code*®
- Search Contents or Index.
- Read relevant section(s).
- For further explanation and/or clarification, refer to this book.

Beginning with *Residential Building Codes Illustrated*
- Search Code Index for section number or Subject Index for topic.
- Refer back to specific text of *2009 International Residential Code*®.

The text is based upon the language of the code and interprets it to enhance the understanding of the user. The interpretations are those of the authors and may not correspond to those rendered by the AHJ. We would encourage the users of the book to confer with the AHJ early in the design process, using the illustrations from this book to validate interpretations. Reconciling text with construction drawings often benefits from additional illustrations. We trust that this will be the case with the explanations and graphics in this book.

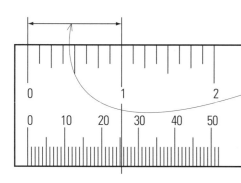

Metric Equivalencies

The *2009 International Residential Code®* uses the following SI units.

Length
- 1 inch = 25.4 mm
- 1 foot = 304.8 mm
- All whole numbers in parentheses are millimeters unless otherwise noted.

Area
- 1 square inch = 645.2 mm^2
- 1 square foot (sf) = 0.0929 m^2

Volume
- 1 cubic foot (cf) = 0.028 m^3
- 1 gallon (gal) = 3.785 L

Angle
- 1 radian = 360/2π = 57.3°; 1 degree = 0.01745 radian (rad)

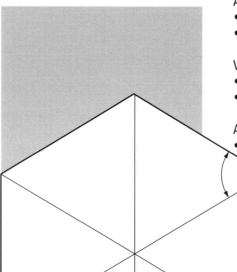

Weight
- 1 ounce = 28.35 g
- 1 pound = 0.454 kg = 0.004448 kN

Force
- 1 pound per square inch (psi) = 6.9 kPa
- 1 pound per linear foot (plf) = 1.4882 kg/m = 0.01459 kN/m
- 1 pound per square foot (psf) = 4.882 kg/m^2 = 0.0479 kN/m^2 = 0.0479 kPa
- 1 pound per cubic foot (pcf) = 16.02 kg/m^3

Light
- 1 foot-candle = 10.76 lux

Speed
- 1 mile per hour (mph) = 0.44 m/s = 1.609 km/h

Heat
- 1 British thermal unit (Btu) = 0.293 watts (w)
- °C = [(°F)-32]/1.8

1
Building Codes

The existence of building regulations goes back almost 4,000 years. The Babylonian Code of Hammurabi decreed the death penalty for a builder if a house he constructed collapsed and killed the owner. If the collapse killed the owner's son, then the son of the builder would be put to death; if goods were damaged then the contractor must repay the owner, and so on. This precedent is worth keeping in mind as you contemplate the potential legal ramifications of your actions in designing and constructing a building in accordance with the code. The protection of the health, safety and welfare of the public is the basis for professional licensure and the reason that building regulations exist.

Various civilizations over the centuries have developed building codes. The origins of the codes we use today lie in the great fires that swept cities regularly in the 1800s. Concerns about fire regulations in urban areas can even be seen dating as far back as the Great Fire of London in 1666. Chicago developed a building code in 1875 to placate the National Board of Fire Underwriters who threatened to cut off insurance for businesses after the fire of 1871. It is essential to keep the fire-based origins of the codes in mind when trying to understand the reasoning behind many code requirements.

"If a builder build a house for some one, and does not construct it properly, and the house which he built fall in and kill its owner, then that builder shall be put to death.

If it kill the son of the owner, the son of that builder shall be put to death.

If it kill a slave of the owner, then he shall pay slave for slave to the owner of the house.

If it ruin goods, he shall make compensation for all that has been ruined, and inasmuch as he did not construct properly this house which he built and it fell, he shall re-erect the house from his own means.

If a builder build a house for some one, even though he has not yet completed it; if then the walls seem toppling, the builder must make the walls solid from his own means."

Laws 229-233
Hammurabi's Code of Laws
(ca.1780 BC)

From a stone slab discovered in 1901 and preserved in the Louvre, Paris.

The various and often conflicting city codes were refined over the years and began to be brought together by regional nongovernmental organizations to develop so-called "model codes." These model codes were developed and written by members of the code organizations. The codes were then published by those code organizations. Model codes are developed by private code groups for subsequent adoption by local and state government agencies as legally enforceable regulations. The first major model-code group was the Building Officials and Code Administrators (BOCA), founded in 1915. They published the *BOCA National Building Code*. Next was the International Conference of Building Officials (ICBO), formed in 1922. The first edition of their *Uniform Building Code* was published in 1927. The Southern Building Code Congress, founded in 1940, published the *Standard (Southern) Building Code*.

These three model-code groups published the three different building codes previously in widespread use in the United States. These codes were developed by regional organizations of building officials, building materials experts, design professionals and life safety experts to provide communities and governments with standard construction criteria for uniform application and enforcement. The ICBO *Uniform Building Code* was used primarily west of the Mississippi River and was the most widely applied of the model codes. The BOCA *National Building Code* was used primarily in the north-central and northeastern states. The SBCCI *Standard Building Code* was used primarily in the Southeast. The model-code groups have merged together to form the International Code Council and have ceased maintaining and publishing their own codes. Also included in this merger was the incorporation of the Council of American Building Officials (CABO) into the International Code Council. CABO published the *One- and Two- Family Dwelling Code*. This code, which was limited in coverage to the types of occupancies noted in its title, was the closest thing to a national model building code in the decades preceding the development of the *International Building Code*.

The International Building Code

Over the past few years a real revolution has taken place in the development of model codes. There was recognition in the early 1990s that the nation would be best served by comprehensive, coordinated national model building codes developed through a general consensus of code writers. There was also recognition that it would take time to reconcile the differences between the existing codes. To begin the reconciliation process, the three model codes were reformatted into a common format. The International Code Council, made up of representatives from the three model-code groups, was formed in 1994 to develop a single model code using the information contained in the three current model codes. While detailed requirements still varied from code to code, the organization of each code became essentially the same after the mid-1990s. This allowed direct comparison of requirements in each code for similar design situations. Numerous drafts of the new *International Building Code* were reviewed by the model-code agencies along with code users. From that multiyear review grew the *International Building Code* (IBC), first published in 2000. There is now a single national model building code, maintained by a group composed of representatives of the three prior model-code agencies, the International Code Council, headquartered in Washington, D.C. This group was formed from a merger of the three model-code groups and CABO into a single agency to update and maintain the "I Code" family, which includes the *International Building Code* and the *International Residential Code*.

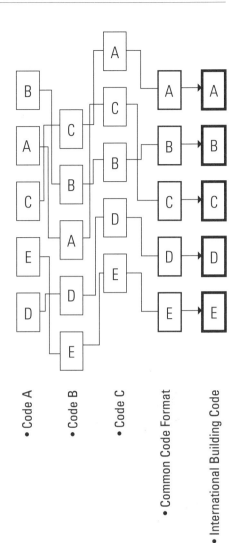

• Code A • Code B • Code C • Common Code Format • International Building Code

The International Residential Code

In addition to the *International Building Code* (IBC) there is the *International Residential Code* (IRC). This stand-alone code is meant to regulate construction of detached one- and two-family dwellings and townhouses that are not more than three stories in height with a separate means of egress. This code is designed to supplant residential requirements contained in the IBC in jurisdictions where the IRC is adopted.

The IRC is derived from a predecessor residential building code published by the Council of American Building Officials (CABO), the *One- and Two-Family Dwelling Code.* In 1996 CABO and the predecessor code organizations that ultimately became the International Code Council agreed to begin development of an updated stand-alone national model residential building code. This resulted in the first publication of the *International Residential Code* in 2000. This code includes provisions that replace the requirements of the *International Building Code* with requirements specific to buildings within the scope of the IRC. The IRC includes provisions for code requirements for all the systems typically contained in the one- and two-family buildings and townhouses regulated by the IRC. Among these "external" codes are the electrical sections of the IRC, which are taken from NFPA 70: *National Electrical Code.* The electrical chapters are produced under the auspices of the National Fire Protection Association (NFPA), which produces and copyrights the *National Electrical Code.* The IRC also contains materials regarding fuel gas provisions included through an agreement with the American Gas Association (AGA). [Note this book focuses on the first 10 chapters of the IRC, the requirements related to building design and construction, and does not address IRC requirements for such things as electrical or plumbing work.]

Note also that many local jurisdictions make other modifications to the codes in use in their communities. For example, many jurisdictions make amendments to require fire sprinkler systems, even in single-family residences, where they may be optional, or not even required, in the model codes. In such cases mandatory sprinkler requirements may change the design options offered in the model code for inclusion of sprinklers where not otherwise required by the code. It is imperative that the designer determines what local adoptions and amendments have been made in order to be certain which codes apply to a specific project.

There are also specific federal requirements that may need to be considered in design and construction in addition to the locally adopted version of the model codes. Among these are the Americans with Disabilities Act of 1990 and the Federal Fair Housing Act of 1988. While knowledge of these regulations will promote universal design for access to housing for persons with disabilities, note that these regulations typically do not apply to the types of buildings regulated by the *International Residential Code.* Accordingly they will not be discussed in any detail in this book.

State Building Codes

Each state has a separate and distinct code adoption process. Many states may have adopted one of the three previous model codes and perhaps the CABO *One- and Two-Family Dwelling Code* in the past but some states have their own building codes. The geographic areas for current state model-code adoptions correspond roughly to the areas of influence of the three previous model codes as noted previously on page 3. The BOCA *National Building Code* predominated in the northeastern United States. The *Standard (Southern) Building Code* was adopted throughout the southeastern United States. West of the Mississippi River, the *Uniform Building Code* was adopted in most states. These adoption-area boundaries were loosely defined and flexible. Note also that the predecessor document to the IRC, the CABO *One- and Two-Family Dwelling Code* had a broader national adoption than the three predecessor model building codes. Many states allow local adoption of codes so that in some states, such as Texas, adjacent jurisdictions in the same state may have different building codes based on different model codes. State processes often defer completely to local adoption. Make certain you know what code you are working with at the permitting level.

Local Building Codes

Many localities adopt model-code documents with little modification except for the administrative chapters that relate to local operations of the building department. Larger cities such as Los Angeles, New York, Chicago and San Francisco adopt much more sweeping revisions to the model codes. In the past, codes in such large cities were often not based on model codes and bore little resemblance to them. Many cities make local amendments to the model codes due to local conditions or building traditions. Also, since codes are general and building projects occur in specific places, the codes must be interpreted by both the designer and by code officials to apply the intent of the code to the project at hand. Coupled to local modifications, the need to interpret how the code applies to a specific project should be expected as part of the code review process. Be aware of local modifications and be prepared for varying interpretations of the same code sections among various jurisdictions. Do not

proceed too far in the design process based on review of similar designs in another jurisdiction without verification of the code interpretation in the jurisdiction where the project is located. Similarly, although this book offers opinions of what code sections mean, all such opinions are subject to interpretation by local authorities as they are applied to specific projects.

The IRC is much more than just a "building" code. It contains code requirements taken from various codes for other design and construction disciplines beyond architecture and structural engineering. The Building Code regulations are usually the

focus of interest for architectural and structural work and as noted above are the focus of this book, but you need to be aware of the existence of additional requirements in the IRC for such work as electrical plumbing, mechanical, fire sprinklers and fire alarms. Each of these may impact the work of design consultants and in turn the work of the architect. While these other requirements are contained in separate stand-alone codes for buildings other than those regulated by the IRC, the intent of the IRC is to provide a single source for all construction regulations related to one- and two-family dwellings and townhouses as defined in the IRC scope descriptions.

Code Interactions

The Authorities Having Jurisdiction (AHJ)—a catch-all phrase for all planning, zoning, fire and building officials having something to say about buildings—may not inform the designer of overlapping jurisdictions or duplicate regulations. Fire departments often do not check plan drawings at the time building permit documents are reviewed by the building department. Fire and life-safety deficiencies are often discovered at the time of field inspections by fire officials, usually at a time when additional cost and time is required to fix these deficiencies. The costs of tearing out noncomplying work and replacing it may be considered a designer's error. Whenever starting a project, it is therefore incumbent upon the designer to determine exactly which codes and standards are to be enforced for the project and by which agency. It is also imperative to obtain copies of any revisions or modifications made to model codes by local or state agencies. This must be assured for all AHJs.

The model codes have no force of law unto themselves. Only after adoption by a governmental agency are they enforceable under the police powers of the state. Enforcement powers are delegated by state or local statutes to officials in various levels of government. Designers must verify local amendments to model codes to be certain which code provisions apply to specific projects.

There are many different codes that may apply to various aspects of construction projects. Typically the first question to be asked is whether the project requires a permit. There are typically cost thresholds for when permits are required. These are usually set by local amendments to model code provisions. Certain projects, such as interior work for movable furniture or finishes, are usually exempt. Carpeting may be replaced and walls painted without a permit, but moving walls, relocating doors, or doing plumbing and electrical work will require a permit in most jurisdictions.

Traditionally, codes have been written with new construction in mind. In recent years more and more provisions have been made applicable to alteration, repair and renovation of existing facilities. For renovation work it is critical to define the scope of alteration or addition work to be able to define the area where the code applies to the work. The code does not come

into effect in those areas not impacted by the work. The code requires new work to meet the current code, but does not require remedial work in those areas not affected by the new work. It is typically not required to bring a whole house up to the new code in those areas not impacted by new work. Again, this should be verified against local code requirements.

Standard of Care

The designer should always remember that codes are legally and ethically considered to be the minimum criteria that must be met by the design and construction community. The protection of health, safety and welfare is the goal of these minimum standards. Registered design professionals and licensed contractors will be held by legal and ethical precedents to a much higher standard than the code minimum.

This concept is best described by the legal term "Standard of Care," which holds that the code is the minimum standard for practitioners, but that they also must respond to all of the other conditions affecting the project at hand. This is higher than the minimum standard defined by the code. The code is the level that a practitioner must never go below. Because professional work involves judgment, perfection is not expected of a design professional. The standard of care is defined for an individual designer as being those actions that any other well-informed practitioner would have taken given the same level of knowledge in the same situation. It is a relative measure, not an absolute one.

Life Safety vs. Property Protection

The basis for building-code development is to safeguard the health, safety and welfare of the public. The first and foremost goal of building codes is the protection of human life from the failure of building life safety provisions or from structural collapse. There is also a strong component of property protection contained in code requirements. Sprinkler provisions can serve both purposes. When buildings are occupied, sprinklers can contain or extinguish a fire, allowing the building occupants to escape. The same sprinkler system can protect a structure from loss if a fire occurs when the structure is not occupied. While many systems may perform both life safety and property protection functions, it is essential that code developers keep the issue of life safety versus property protection in mind. Security measures to prevent

intrusion into a structure may become hazards to life safety. A prime example of this is burglar bars on the exterior of ground-floor windows that can trap inhabitants of the building in an emergency if there is not an interior release to allow occupants to escape while still maintaining the desired security. In no case should property-protection considerations ever have primacy over life safety.

The Code Development Process

As described above, the three previously existing model-code development agencies and CABO have merged into one organization. These agencies modified their code development processes into a unified national format. This new format has been modified slightly over the past few years as it had been developed, but it now seems well settled.

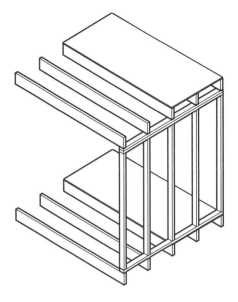

As in the past, any person may propose a code revision. Any designer, material supplier, code official or interested member of the public who feels they have a better way to describe code requirements or to accommodate new life safety developments or new technology may prepare revised code language for consideration. Proposed code changes are published for review by all interested parties. They are then categorized, based on what section of the code is being revised and assigned to a committee of people experienced in those matters for review and consideration. Committees are typically organized around specific issues such as means of egress, fire safety, structural, general, plumbing, mechanical and so forth. Anyone may testify at these committee hearings regarding the merits or demerits of the code change. The committee then votes to make its recommendation to the ICC annual business meeting. At the annual business meeting, testimony will be heard from interested parties, both from non-voting industry representatives and building officials who are given voting privileges. Only governmental members of the organization—typically public employees serving as building officials, fire officials or mechanical and plumbing officials—are allowed to vote on the proposed changes. This is described by the ICC as a "governmental consensus process."

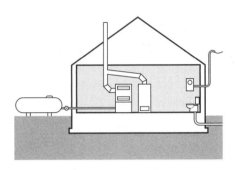

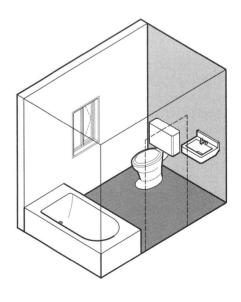

The *International Residential Code* is a living document. It is subject to yearly review and comment cycles. A new code is published at regular intervals, usually every three years. This publication cycle gives some measure of certainty for building designers that the code will remain constant during the design-and-construction process. The code development cycle allows the code to respond to new information, growing by accretion and adaptation.

Performance vs. Prescriptive Codes

The *International Residential Code* is, as were the codes that preceded it, "prescriptive" in nature. It is developed to mitigate concerns by creating specific and prescribed responses to problems that have been identified. Designers identify the problem to be addressed, such as the size of egress windows, and then they look up the prescribed response in the applicable code section. For example, guard heights are prescribed to be 42" (1067) high in non-residential buildings and 36" (914) high in residential buildings and are required when adjacent changes in grade exceed 30" (762). The designer follows the prescribed requirements to avoid the problem the code has identified—that is, preventing falls over an edge higher than 30" (762). The code provides a defined solution to an identified problem. We will discuss briefly the distinctions between prescriptive and performance codes.

Performance codes define the problem and allow the designer to devise the solution. The word *performance* in this context refers to the problem definition and to the setting of parameters for deciding if the proposed solution solves the problem adequately. These standards define the problem, but do not define, describe or predetermine the solution.

The use of performance codes has been increasing in the past few years, due in large part to the development of new modeling techniques for predicting how a building will react under certain fire, earthquake or other stimuli. Performance codes are used in many countries around the world. Their requirements may be as broad as "the building shall allow all of its prospective occupants to safely leave the building in the event of a fire." Most performance codes in reality have much more tightly defined requirements, but the guard requirements stat-

ed above are a good example of the essence of what performance-code requirements can be.

The basic form of modern performance-code language can be described as objective-based. Each code requirement is broken into three sections. We will use fall prevention as our example. Note that provision of guard rails is only one example of many solutions to the performance objective, not the only solution.

Objective: What is to be accomplished? In this case, the prevention of falls from heights of more than 30" (762).

Functional Statement: Why do we want to accomplish this? We wish to safeguard building occupants by preventing them from accidentally falling from a height great enough to result in an injury.

Performance Requirement: How is this to be accomplished? Performance codes could become prescriptive at this juncture, mandating a guard rail. More likely, such a performance standard would require that the barrier be high enough, strong enough and continuous enough to prevent falls under the objective circumstances. Note that a guard rail meeting current code standards would be deemed to satisfy those requirements, but alternate means and methods could also achieve the same ends. For example, landscaping could prevent access to the grade change, or innovative railing substitutes could be designed to function like automobile air bags to catch falling persons without having a visible rail present in most conditions. Let your imagination provide other alternatives.

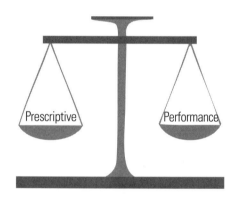

Performance codes give designers more freedom to comply with the stated goals. They also require the designer to take on more responsibility for knowing the consequences of their design actions. We anticipate that performance codes will be used in limited ways for innovative projects, but that many typical, repetitive designs will continue to use prescriptive code for speed, clarity and assurance of compliance during design review. Also, given the current legal climate, designers are often reluctant to assume the responsibility for long-term code compliance for innovative systems.

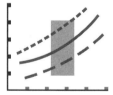

2
Navigating the Code, Administrative Procedures, Definitions

Navigation and Administrative Procedures

The key word to remember about how all building codes are developed and how they all work is *intent*. The intent of the author of a building code section in the *International Residential Code* (IRC) is to solve a specific design problem with prescriptive language. Designers are usually trying to measure the appearance and spatial arrangements of their projects against the language of the code. Builders try to determine the physical constraints dictated by the code to be certain they provide the materials and assemblies dictated by the code. During this process the designer or builder should ask themselves what problem, or performance criteria, the code section is addressing. The language may start to make more sense as one tries to go beyond the specific language to determine why the words say what they say.

Designers and builders also have intent. They are trying to achieve certain functional or appearance goals in the design of the building. Designers and builders should measure their own intent for the design against their interpretations of the intent of the code. When examined together, the intent of the code and that of the design or construction solution should be concurrent. It is also important to understand that the true intent of the original code writer will be subject to later interpretation both by the designer and builder as code users and by the authorities having jurisdiction as code administrators. The understanding of the code intent is filtered through the experiences, needs and wishes of each of the code users. It should therefore not be surprising that the "obvious" meaning of a code requirement can come to be so different for various parties in the construction process. When there is a misunderstanding or a disagreement about what the code requires, trying to determine the original intent of the code section in question is always a valuable way to have a productive dialogue rather than a non-productive argument between the parties to the construction process.

It is critical to understand that each section of the code was developed to solve a certain problem. The code is typically written in relatively short sections, by many different authors, generally working independently of each other. There is no single "author" of the code. There are literally thousands of authors: among them are code officials, fire officials, design professionals and construction professionals. We suggest that readers visit the ICC website for a detailed description of the code development process. The International Code Council is the *publisher* of the IRC, not the *author*. Sections are organized into chapters based on common themes, but sections in each chapter are often developed in isolation from one another with little attention to continuity of the entire document. As you look at the code, try and visualize the intent of the writer of that section and try to understand the problem they are addressing. Code language usually arises from a specific issue the code writer wishes to address based on experience, or on a construction or life safety issue. The writer then makes the requirements general so that they apply to more typical conditions than the specific instance that generated the concern.

The intent of the code is a crucial idea to understand. *Why* is a much more important question than *what* when you are puzzled by the actual language of a code passage. The code is a general document that must then be interpreted for its specific application to a specific project. If you know the code in general and think about its intent, you will be in a better position to formulate your own interpretation of code sections as they apply to your specific project. You will thus be in a position to help building officials see the validity of your opinion when interpretation of the code is required for a specific design condition. Confidence will come with experience in use of the code. Learning the code is vital to the success of a well-rounded designer or builder.

Learn the table of contents and use the index. It is very useful to get a copy of the CD-ROM of the code for use in your practice. This allows key word searches. Don't try and memorize passages of the code, as the code is a living document, and these will likely change over time as the code is amended. Learn the organization of the code and learn where to find things in that fashion. Use the index if the table of contents doesn't get you where you want to be. Think of synonyms for the topic you are researching to facilitate key word or index searches. Remember to try both singular and plural words when using key word searches in the CD-ROM. If you don't find *"handrail,"* try *"handrails."* You may have to scan large portions of the index to locate potential items. Remember also that the model code is often amended during adoption by state and local agencies. Be certain to know what local code amendments to the code apply to your projects. Also determine if the local AHJ has published written opinions regarding their interpretation of the code in their jurisdiction.

intent

+

interpretation

=

- intent

-

- *intent*

- **intent**

- intent

Scope, Purpose and Intent

§R101.1 states that the IRC shall "apply to the construction, alteration, movement, enlargement, replacement, repair, equipment, use and occupancy, location, removal and demolition of detached one- and two-family dwellings and townhouses not more than three stories above-grade in height with a separate means of egress and their accessory structures." Therefore, just about any activity on a dwelling or townhouse that fits within this scope definition will require a permit. The intent of the code is that any work on a dwelling will be done under permit so that the housing stock will become more code compliant with contemporary codes as work is done on them.

From our analysis of the code text and its definitions, we believe that the intent of the code is that the three-story maximum apply to both one- and two-family dwellings and to townhouses. Per §R105.2, certain activities are exempt from building permit requirements. These include items such as: work on small sheds or playhouses smaller than 120 square feet (11.15 m^2); fences under 6 feet (1829) high; short retaining walls less than 4 feet (1219) high; sidewalks and driveways; painting, wallpapering, carpeting and similar finish work; prefab swimming pools less than 24 inches (610) deep; swings and similar playground equipment or small window awnings. Similarly, maintenance items are exempt from mechanical, gas, or electrical permits. These include items such as: lamp replacement, portable gas heating equipment; portable fans and portable cooling units.

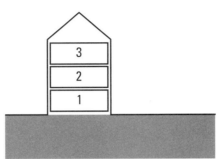

- *One-family dwelling*

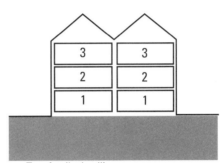

- *Two-family dwelling*

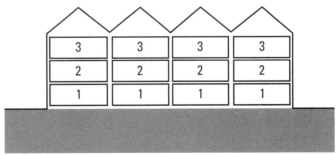

- *Townhouses*

DOCUMENTS

Construction Documents

Construction documents are defined in IRC §R202 as: "Written, graphic and pictorial documents prepared or assembled for describing the design, location and physical characteristics of the elements of a project necessary for obtaining a building permit. Construction drawings shall be drawn to an appropriate scale to be submitted." They are to be submitted per §R106. The building official may waive the requirement for construction documents for minor work where review of such documents would not be necessary to be sure that code compliance is obtained by the proposed work. The proponent for the proposed work must verify with the AHJ to what extent the design work needs to be done by a registered design professional in the locality where the work is to occur. Different jurisdictions have widely varying thresholds for when a registered design professional is to be utilized. Note also that the size and complexity of the proposed project may move the AHJ to require that the construction documents be prepared by a registered design professional. This is within the purview of the building official per §R106.1.

As noted above, the drawings should be to scale so that parts of the building are depicted in the proper graphic relationships for sizes and configurations. Details should be clear and sufficient to allow the building official to verify code compliance. If the dwelling is in a flood hazard area the requirements of §R106.1.3 should be noted for location in flood hazard areas and the elevations of such elements as finished floor elevations at the lowest level should be shown to allow verification of compliance with code requirements. The construction documents should have a site plan showing the proposed new construction in relation to existing structures. Existing structures should be described as to what portions are to be demolished and which are to remain. Lot lines should be shown and the distances from the lot lines to new and existing structures should be shown. The construction documents should graphically verify the code compliance of the proposed project without requiring the building official to request additional information to determine code compliance. The quantity and complexity of contract documents is directly related to the size, scope and complexity of the proposed work. We recommend the following minimum contents for the contract documents for any

project. The minimum drawing sizes are often dictated by local code requirements. Verify with the AHJ what their minimum size requirements are for drawings. Recommended document contents for a typical new dwelling or alteration, all drawn to scale, are:

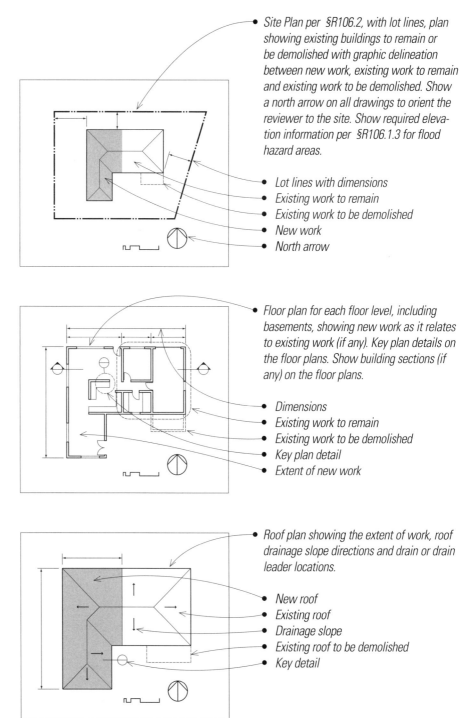

Site Plan per §R106.2, with lot lines, plan showing existing buildings to remain or be demolished with graphic delineation between new work, existing work to remain and existing work to be demolished. Show a north arrow on all drawings to orient the reviewer to the site. Show required elevation information per §R106.1.3 for flood hazard areas.

- *Lot lines with dimensions*
- *Existing work to remain*
- *Existing work to be demolished*
- *New work*
- *North arrow*

Floor plan for each floor level, including basements, showing new work as it relates to existing work (if any). Key plan details on the floor plans. Show building sections (if any) on the floor plans.

- *Dimensions*
- *Existing work to remain*
- *Existing work to be demolished*
- *Key plan detail*
- *Extent of new work*

Roof plan showing the extent of work, roof drainage slope directions and drain or drain leader locations.

- *New roof*
- *Existing roof*
- *Drainage slope*
- *Existing roof to be demolished*
- *Key detail*

The AHJ will review the submitted permit documents and when they are deemed satisfactory will issue a permit and mark the drawings as approved per §R106.3.1. The permit set is to be kept on the work site and available for use by the building official or by the field inspector. If amendments are made to the construction documents during the construction process the documents should be resubmitted for approval by the AHJ per the amended document provisions contained in §R106.4.

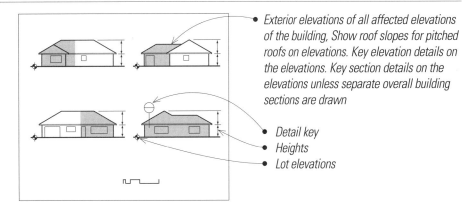

- *Exterior elevations of all affected elevations of the building, Show roof slopes for pitched roofs on elevations. Key elevation details on the elevations. Key section details on the elevations unless separate overall building sections are drawn*
- *Detail key*
- *Heights*
- *Lot elevations*

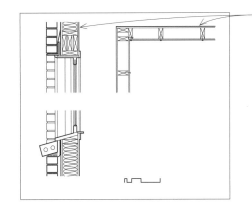

- *Building sections (if required to describe the work) with section details keyed here instead of on the elevations. If wall sections are drawn, key wall section on the building sections.*
- *Wall sections (if appropriate to the proposed work). Key details on wall sections.*
- *Detail key*

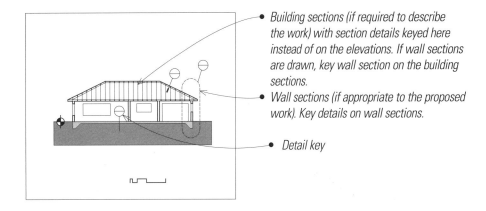

- *Details, as necessary to describe structural, fire protection and water protection. Enlarged scale as necessary to describe the work proposed.*

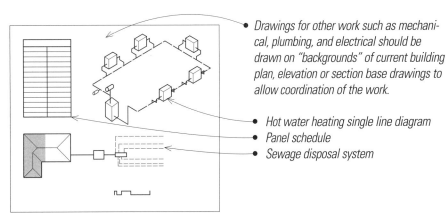

- *Drawings for other work such as mechanical, plumbing, and electrical should be drawn on "backgrounds" of current building plan, elevation or section base drawings to allow coordination of the work.*
- *Hot water heating single line diagram*
- *Panel schedule*
- *Sewage disposal system*

Inspections

Work done under a building permit is subject to periodic inspection by the building official or other persons designated to perform inspections. The inspections are to verify that the work is being installed in the field in accordance with both the requirements of the code and the criteria stated in the approved permit documents. The inspections are to occur at designated phases of the work which are required to occur at times when the work to be inspected is complete enough to determine code compliance, but still visible for observation prior to covering up with subsequent construction. It is the responsibility of the person holding the permit to request inspections in a timely manner, to allow access to the work so it can be inspected and to uncover any work not done in a timely sequence to allow it to be adequately inspected. The code allows the AHJ to allow inspections to be done by pre-approved outside agencies and to accept inspection reports from them. Work is not to proceed beyond permit milestones without approval of the prior work subject to inspection. Project milestones as noted in §R109 are:

- Foundation inspection,
- Plumbing, mechanical, gas and electrical systems inspection,
- Floodplain inspections,
- Frame and masonry inspection,
- Other inspections,
  - Fire-resistance-rated construction inspection,
  - Final inspection

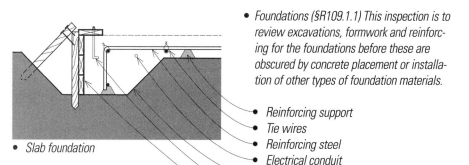

- Slab foundation

- Foundations (§R109.1.1) This inspection is to review excavations, formwork and reinforcing for the foundations before these are obscured by concrete placement or installation of other types of foundation materials.

- Reinforcing support
- Tie wires
- Reinforcing steel
- Electrical conduit
- Excavation for thickened slab
- Anchor bolts
- Formwork

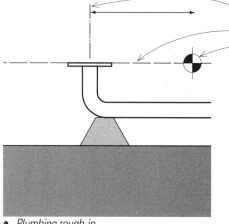

- Electrical rough-in

- Plumbing, mechanical and electrical systems (§R109.1.2) Rough installation of these systems is to be inspected when the work is done, but prior to being enclosed in foundations of walls.

- Switch box
- Conduit

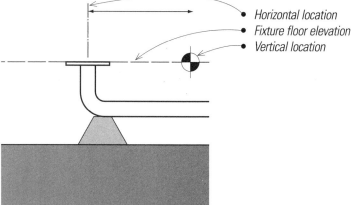

- Horizontal location
- Fixture floor elevation
- Vertical location

- Plumbing rough-in

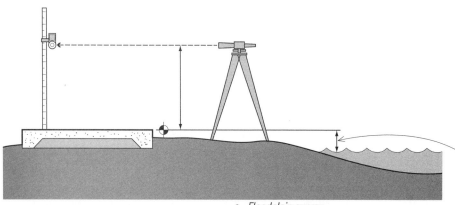

- Floodplain inspections (§R109.1.3) In flood-prone areas, as determined by Table R301.2(1) upon placement of the lowest floor level, which may be a basement level, a survey is to be made by a registered design professional verifying the actual elevation of that level and is to be submitted to the building department.

- Required height above maximum flood elevation

- Floodplain survey

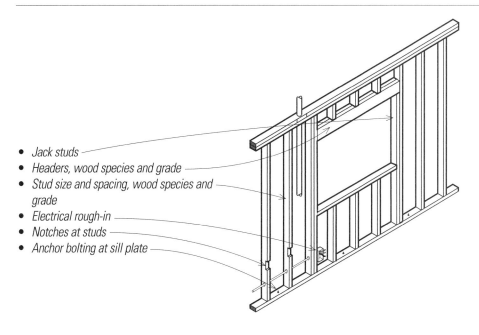

- Jack studs
- Headers, wood species and grade
- Stud size and spacing, wood species and grade
- Electrical rough-in
- Notches at studs
- Anchor bolting at sill plate

• *Framing and masonry inspection (§R109.1.4) After the wall framing and roof framing, including bracing, firestopping and draftstopping and all masonry is complete, the work shall be inspected for completeness and code compliance before the inspected systems are closed in by wall or roof coverings. This is to occur after the mechanical, plumbing and electrical inspections are complete.*

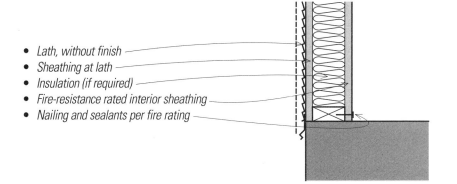

- Lath, without finish
- Sheathing at lath
- Insulation (if required)
- Fire-resistance rated interior sheathing
- Nailing and sealants per fire rating

• *Fire-resistance-rated construction (§R109.1.5.1) When fire-resistance-rated construction is required by the code, fire-resistive materials, such as lathing or wallboard, are to be inspected prior to installation of wall finishes.*

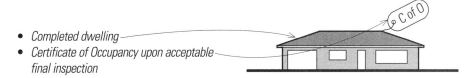

- Completed dwelling
- Certificate of Occupancy upon acceptable final inspection

• *Final inspection (§R109.1.6) The project is to be inspected when all of the permitted work is completed prior to occupancy. Upon successful completion of the final inspection the AHJ will issue a Certificate of Occupancy. No building or structure is to be used or occupied until the certificate is issued.*

Alternate Means and Methods

§R104.11 states that the provisions of this code are not intended to prevent the installation of any material or to prohibit any design or method of construction not specifically prescribed by this code. While written around prescriptive descriptions of tested assemblies and rated construction, the code recognizes that there may be many different ways of solving the same design problems. It recognizes that there will be innovations in building construction means and methods that do not fit neatly into prescribed classifications. New technologies may dictate new construction requirements. The code recognizes that there will be innovations in materials and construction technology that may happen faster than code revisions are made. Thus the code sets up a method for the building official to approve proposed alternative designs. Deviations from prescribed standards must be submitted for review and approval of the building official. The criteria they are to use are spelled out in the code. We have highlighted some of the key provisions of the approval in *bold italics*. The alternative is to be approved when "the proposed design is satisfactory and complies with the intent of the provisions of this code, and that the material, method or work offered is, for the purpose intended, at least the *equivalent* of that *prescribed in this code*" (emphasis added). These words are also the fundamental criteria for why each and every code section is included in the basic code.

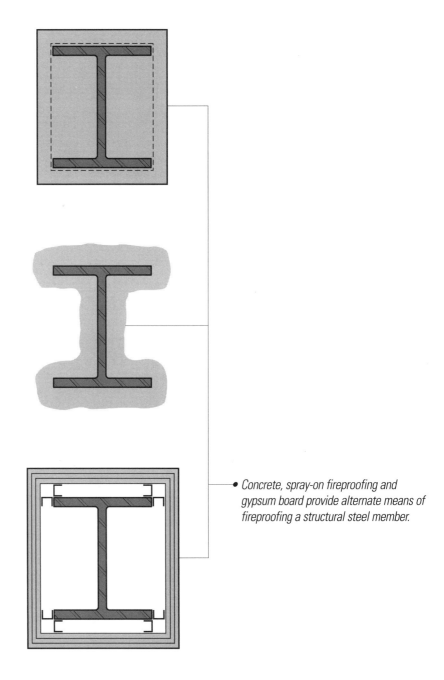

• *Concrete, spray-on fireproofing and gypsum board provide alternate means of fireproofing a structural steel member.*

Code Interpretations

Designers, builders and code officials approach interpretations from quite different perspectives. The designer or builder is trying to make a functional design code compliant while satisfying project requirements in an aesthetic, economical and practical way. The AHJ examines completed drawings for compliance with code requirements. While the AHJ is not unaware of the practical requirements contained in the building design, they are charged first and foremost with verifying code compliance. It is the responsibility of the designer to demonstrate code compliance and to modify noncompliant areas while continuing to meet the project requirements.

Both the designer and the AHJ are working to apply generalized code provisions to a specific project. It is differences in opinion about the application of the general to the specific that most often give rise to differences in interpretation. Code officials also see many more similar examples of the relationship of code sections to various designs. Thus they may generalize interpretations from one project to another even though the projects may be different in significant ways. On the other hand, designers may find that similar designs receive quite different interpretations by the AHJ in different jurisdictions. When differences of opinion about interpretation occur, the designer must work with the AHJ to reconcile the intent of the design to the interpretations of the intent of the code. If reconciliation cannot be reached, the designer must decide whether to revise the project to obtain approval or appeal the ruling of the AHJ to some civic body prescribed in the jurisdiction for hearing appeals. Often the AHJ can be requested to apply to the model-code agency that published the code for a ruling as to the publisher's opinion of the intent of the code section in question.

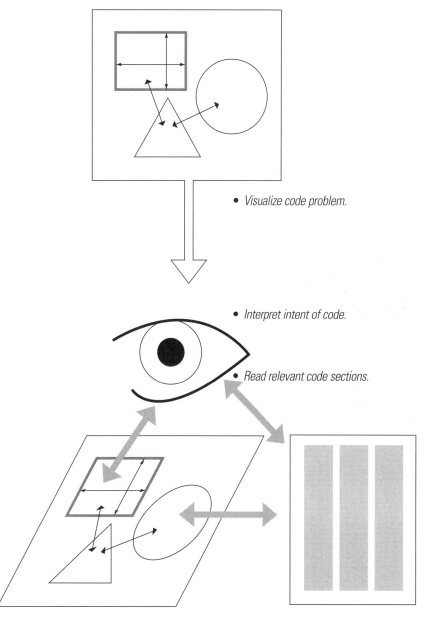

- *Visualize code problem.*

- *Interpret intent of code.*

- *Read relevant code sections.*

- *Re-visualize possible solution that satisfies both design intent and intent of the code.*

CODE COMPONENTS AND ANALYSIS

Documenting Code Interpretations

Every project, including residential projects designed and permitted under the IRC, should receive a basic code analysis that is recorded as a permanent part of the permit documents. All code interpretations and citations should have a reference to the code section in question to allow retracing steps in the code analysis. There is nothing more maddening than to have a statement in a code analysis upon which the design rests without any citation as to where it resides in the code.

The primary contents of the code analysis for residential construction are related to the following decisions:

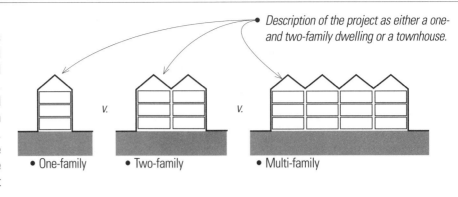

- Description of the project as either a one- and two-family dwelling or a townhouse.

v.   v.

- One-family
- Two-family
- Multi-family

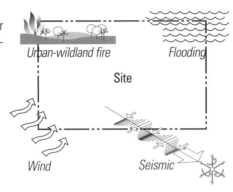

Urban-wildland fire   Flooding

Site

Wind   Seismic

- Site location to determine special requirements for wind design, seismic design, floodplain design or urban-wildland fire design criteria.

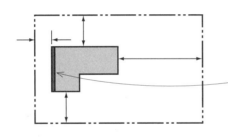

- Location of the project on the property, for determination of fire-resistance-rated construction requirements.
  - Fire-resistance-rated construction requirements

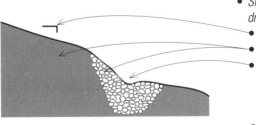

- Site conditions relative to soils, slopes and drainage requirements.
  - Slope
  - Soil conditions
  - Drainage

- Selection of foundation system(s), including subsurface systems such as excavations, fills and foundation piles.

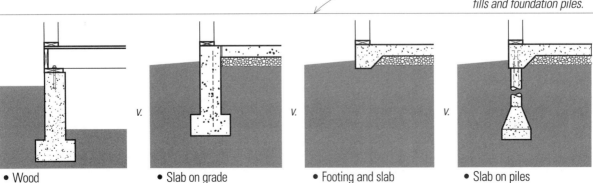

- Wood
  v.
- Slab on grade
  v.
- Footing and slab
  v.
- Slab on piles

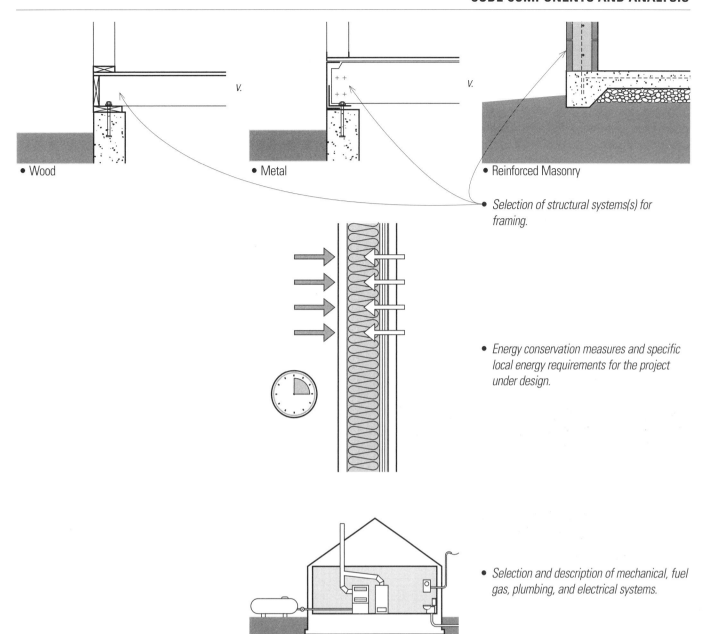

• Wood

• Metal

• Reinforced Masonry

• *Selection of structural systems(s) for framing.*

• *Energy conservation measures and specific local energy requirements for the project under design.*

• *Selection and description of mechanical, fuel gas, plumbing, and electrical systems.*

Early Meetings

One advantage of larger projects is that they are often large enough to warrant pre-review and consultation with the building department prior to finalizing design. No matter what size your project is, we recommend consulting with the applicable AHJ early in the process wherever possible, prior to commencing detailed design, even if a fee is charged. Do not expect the code official to do your work for you. Compliance is the responsibility of the designer. However, codes are subject to interpretation, and it is almost always in your best interest to determine what, if any, interpretations will be needed for any project. This should be done prior to expend-

ing a lot of time and energy designing a project that may be deemed not in compliance during plan review.

As noted before, don't be shy about using the table of contents and index to locate sections of the code. DO NOT TRY AND MEMORIZE PARTS OF THE CODE! As sections change and interpretations alter meanings, this is a recipe for trouble in the future. Clients may expect you to be able to rattle off requirements at a moment's notice, but it is not in the best interest of the project to be able to make snap code decisions. Remember where to look up information and check your decisions each time you apply them;

do not proceed on memory or analogy from other jobs. With the code reorganization that has been taking place over the past decade and with constantly evolving new code language, even seasoned code professionals use the index to locate familiar phrases in new locations as we all keep abreast of the new codes. It is worthwhile for designers to remember that in many jurisdictions local code officials will have little more experience with the evolving IRC language than design professionals. This should allow a dialogue to occur in a constructive atmosphere about code interpretations and applications

DEFINITIONS

Per §R201, where specific definitions appear in the IRC, they are to have the meanings indicated in the code definition. It is also acceptable to use definitions that occur in other International codes as published by the International Code Council. Where terms are not defined they are to have the "ordinarily accepted meanings such as the context implies."

We will discuss several definitions here where they have very specific meanings related to use of the IRC. We have selected these definitions as examples of the need to understand the code-specific nature of some of the definitions. Do not jump to using commonly accepted meanings until you have determined that there is not a specific definition for the term under consideration contained in the text of the IRC. When in doubt—look it up. Do not assume that a term is undefined until you have searched the code to determine that it does not have a special meaning in the IRC. The following definitions taken from Chapter 2 of the IRC, are meant to be representative, and were selected because they lend themselves to better understanding through an illustration. This is by no means an exhaustive list of specialized definitions. See Chapter 2 of the IRC for the full list of code-specific definitions.

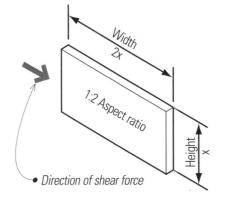

- Direction of shear force

- **Aspect Ratio**
The ratio of the height to width (h/w) of a shear wall. The shear wall height is the maximum clear height from top of foundation or diaphragm to bottom of diaphragm framing above and the shear wall width is the sheathed dimension in the direction of applied force on the shear wall.

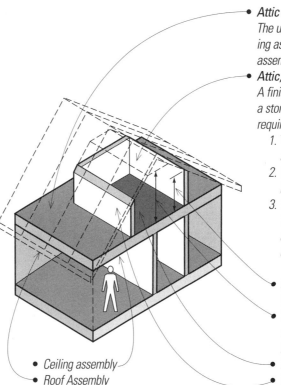

- Ceiling assembly
- Roof Assembly

- **Attic**
The unfinished space between the ceiling assembly of the top story and the roof assembly.
- **Attic, Habitable**
A finished or unfinished area, not considered a story, complying with all of the following requirements
    1. The occupiable floor area is at least 70 sf (6.5 m²), in accordance with §R304.
    2. The occupiable floor area has a ceiling height in accordance with §R305.
    3. The occupiable space is enclosed by the roof assembly above, knee walls [if applicable] on the sides and the floor-ceiling assembly below.

- 5' (1525) minimum height to count as floor area per §R304.4 and §R305.1
- 7' (2314) minimum ceiling height. At least 50% of ceiling must be above this height or above per §R305.1
- Floor area at least 70 sf (6.5 m²)
- Knee wall enclosure [optional], note that attic areas with ceiling heights less than 5' (1525) are not considered habitable floor area

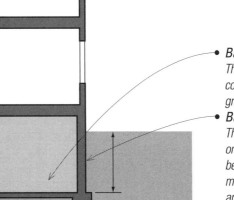

- **Basement**
That portion of a building that is partly or completely below grade (see "Story above grade").
- **Basement Wall**
The opaque portion of a wall that encloses one side of a basement and has an average below-grade wall area that is 50 percent or more of the total opaque and non-opaque area of that enclosing side.

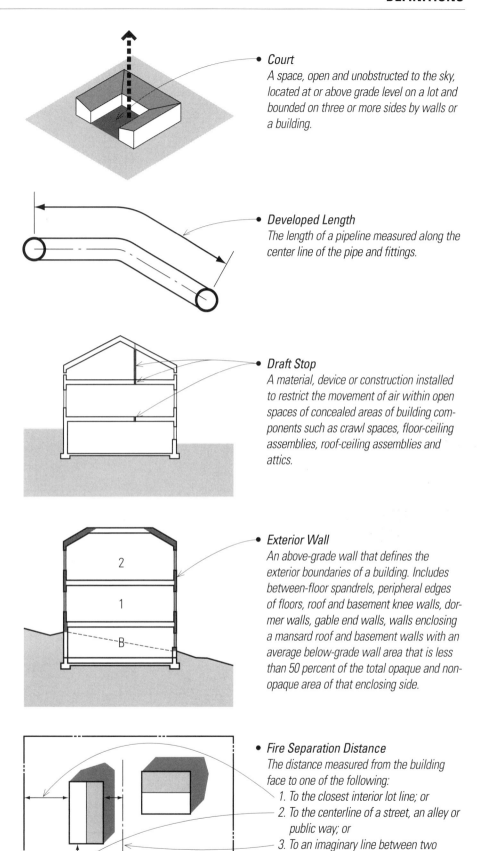

Court
A space, open and unobstructed to the sky, located at or above grade level on a lot and bounded on three or more sides by walls or a building.

Developed Length
The length of a pipeline measured along the center line of the pipe and fittings.

Draft Stop
A material, device or construction installed to restrict the movement of air within open spaces of concealed areas of building components such as crawl spaces, floor-ceiling assemblies, roof-ceiling assemblies and attics.

Exterior Wall
An above-grade wall that defines the exterior boundaries of a building. Includes between-floor spandrels, peripheral edges of floors, roof and basement knee walls, dormer walls, gable end walls, walls enclosing a mansard roof and basement walls with an average below-grade wall area that is less than 50 percent of the total opaque and non-opaque area of that enclosing side.

Fire Separation Distance
The distance measured from the building face to one of the following:
1. To the closest interior lot line; or
2. To the centerline of a street, an alley or public way; or
3. To an imaginary line between two buildings on the lot.

The distance shall be measured at a right angle from the face of the wall.

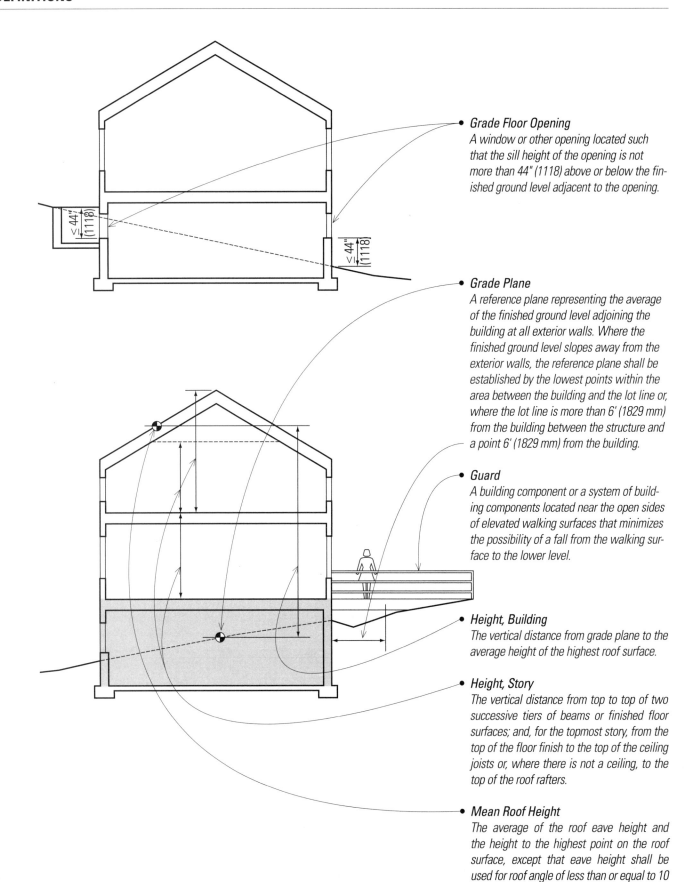

Grade Floor Opening
A window or other opening located such that the sill height of the opening is not more than 44" (1118) above or below the finished ground level adjacent to the opening.

Grade Plane
A reference plane representing the average of the finished ground level adjoining the building at all exterior walls. Where the finished ground level slopes away from the exterior walls, the reference plane shall be established by the lowest points within the area between the building and the lot line or, where the lot line is more than 6' (1829 mm) from the building between the structure and a point 6' (1829 mm) from the building.

Guard
A building component or a system of building components located near the open sides of elevated walking surfaces that minimizes the possibility of a fall from the walking surface to the lower level.

Height, Building
The vertical distance from grade plane to the average height of the highest roof surface.

Height, Story
The vertical distance from top to top of two successive tiers of beams or finished floor surfaces; and, for the topmost story, from the top of the floor finish to the top of the ceiling joists or, where there is not a ceiling, to the top of the roof rafters.

Mean Roof Height
The average of the roof eave height and the height to the highest point on the roof surface, except that eave height shall be used for roof angle of less than or equal to 10 degrees (0.18 rad).

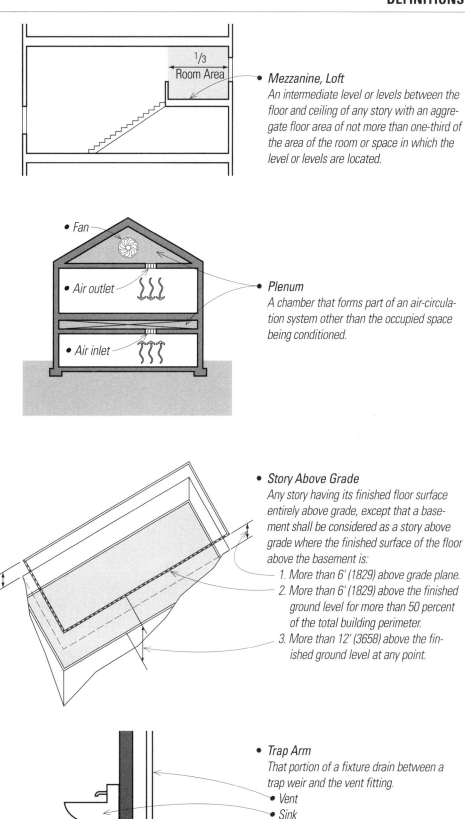

- *Mezzanine, Loft*
  An intermediate level or levels between the floor and ceiling of any story with an aggregate floor area of not more than one-third of the area of the room or space in which the level or levels are located.

- *Plenum*
  A chamber that forms part of an air-circulation system other than the occupied space being conditioned.

- *Story Above Grade*
  Any story having its finished floor surface entirely above grade, except that a basement shall be considered as a story above grade where the finished surface of the floor above the basement is:
  1. More than 6' (1829) above grade plane.
  2. More than 6' (1829) above the finished ground level for more than 50 percent of the total building perimeter.
  3. More than 12' (3658) above the finished ground level at any point.

- *Trap Arm*
  That portion of a fixture drain between a trap weir and the vent fitting.
  - *Vent*
  - *Sink*
  - *Trap fitting*
  - *Trap arm*
  - *Trap*

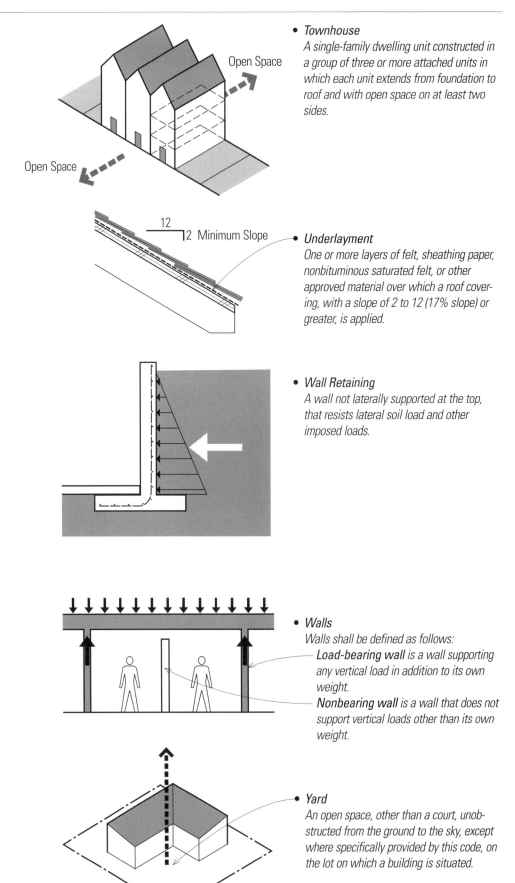

• *Townhouse*
  A single-family dwelling unit constructed in a group of three or more attached units in which each unit extends from foundation to roof and with open space on at least two sides.

• *Underlayment*
  One or more layers of felt, sheathing paper, nonbituminous saturated felt, or other approved material over which a roof covering, with a slope of 2 to 12 (17% slope) or greater, is applied.

• *Wall Retaining*
  A wall not laterally supported at the top, that resists lateral soil load and other imposed loads.

• *Walls*
  Walls shall be defined as follows:
    Load-bearing wall is a wall supporting any vertical load in addition to its own weight.
    Nonbearing wall is a wall that does not support vertical loads other than its own weight.

• *Yard*
  An open space, other than a court, unobstructed from the ground to the sky, except where specifically provided by this code, on the lot on which a building is situated.

3
Building Planning

Chapter 3 sets out the basic design criteria for the dwellings covered by the IRC. The chapter begins with general design criteria based on geographic location. Expected conditions outside the dwellings such as wind loads, snow loads or seismic activity are to be based on the building location. The proposed location of the project must be determined so that site-specific design standards can be applied. After these broad location-based design criteria are established then the code sets out minimum standards for the safety and utility of the dwelling. Subsequent chapters deal with how specific systems, such as foundations, walls, floors and roofs are to be designed.

The IRC is a "cookbook"-style code, when the stated prescriptive standards are combined in the specified way a code-compliant structure is the result. The code organization for building elements moves from a broad view of requirements to a series of more specific ones. The first broadly applicable criteria are regional in scope. The second set of criteria is general requirements to be used as the minimum design standards for all dwellings. The more detailed requirements contained in subsequent code chapters are for specific construction systems based on various construction materials and configurations.

Organization of the Chapter

Due to the arrangement of the figures and tables in this chapter breaking up the text, the language can be hard to follow. The section numbering can give you a clue about what parts go with each other. For example, §R301 is the Design Criteria section. §R301.2 is the climatic and geographic design criteria section under which wind and seismic criteria are located. If you get confused by what the language is referring to, look at the sequence of the section number and refer back upward in the code until you locate the code section where the series of the subsection you are looking at begins. Thus §R301.2.**1** contains wind limitations, §R301.2.**2** contains seismic provisions and §R301.2.**3** states snow loads. It does not help the clarity of the code that the description of design criteria for major conditions occurs within subsections. A chart of the subsections and their hierarchy in §R301, without the intervening figures and tables, looks like the chart to the right. Key elements of the differences in the hierarchy of criteria are noted in **bold** type.

R301: **DESIGN CRITERIA**
R301.1 **Application**

    R301.1.1 **Alternative provisions**
    R301.1.2 **Construction systems**
    R301.1.3 **Engineered design**

R301.2 **Climatic and geographic design criteria**

    R301.2.1 Wind limitations
        R301.2.1.1 Design criteria
        R301.2.1.2 Protection of openings
        R301.2.1.3 Wind speed conversion
        R301.2.1.4 Exposure category
        R301.2.1.5 Topographic wind effects
            R301.2.1.5.1 Simplified topographic wind speed-up method

    R301.2.2 Seismic provisions
        R301.2.2.1 Determination of seismic design category
            R301.2.2.1.1 Alternate determination of seismic design category
            R301.2.2.1.2 Alternative determination of Seismic Design Category E

        R301.2.2.2 Seismic Design Category C
            R301.2.2.2.1 Weights of materials
            R301.2.2.2.2 Stone and masonry veneer
            R301.2.2.2.3 Masonry construction
            R301.2.2.2.4 Concrete construction
            R301.2.2.2.5 Irregular buildings

        R301.2.2.3 Seismic Design Categories D_0, D_1 and D_2
            R301.2.2.3.1 Height limitations
            R301.2.2.3.2 Stone and masonry veneer
            R301.2.2.3.3 Masonry construction
            R301.2.2.3.4 Concrete construction
            R301.2.2.3.5 Cold-formed steel framing in Seismic Design Categories D_0, D_1 and D_2
            R301.2.2.3.6 Masonry chimneys
            R301.2.2.3.7 Anchorage of water heaters

    R301.2.3 Snow loads

    R301.2.4 Floodplain construction

R301.3 **Story height**
R301.4 **Dead load**
R301.5 **Live load**
R301.6 **Roof load**
R301.7 **Deflection**
R301.8 **Nominal sizes**

Structural Design Criteria

The first sets of design criteria are structural in nature. The basic application and criteria for success of the IRC is succinctly and simply set forth in §R301.1. Buildings are to safely support all anticipated forces that can influence the dwelling, whether imposed on the structure from inside or outside of the building. These loads include: dead loads, live loads, roof loads, flood loads, snow loads, wind loads and seismic loads. The code relies on the concept of a "load path," where a force applied to one part of a structure has a way of getting from the structural elements resisting that force along a discernable path through the building structural system to the building foundation where the force is resolved into the ground supporting the building. Per §R301.1, buildings constructed per the code are deemed to comply with requirements of this section.

The code allows alternative design provisions to be used. The design standards noted for wood are the *Wood Frame Construction Manual,* developed by the American Forest and Paper Products Association. The design standards noted for steel framing are the *Standard for Cold-Formed Steel Framing,* developed by the American Iron and Steel Institute. There are also design standards for log homes: ICC 400 *Standard on the Design and Construction of Log Homes.*

Wind load forces create deflections in wall and roof members. These forces are transferred through the structure and must be resisted by the strength of the members, or transferred to the foundations for resolution.

Wind is to be assumed to come from any horizontal direction and wind pressures are to be assumed to act "normal" [perpendiculatr to the surface considered].

Building foundation system must resist the wind load force by providing an equal but opposing force.

Scope, Purpose, and Permits

The code design criteria assume a method of construction for residential buildings. These are described in code vernacular as being of "conventional construction." The idea is that the residential code is based on common knowledge and accepted best practices for the construction of these very common types of buildings. This method is described in §R301.1.2 as "platform and balloon-frame construction" for light-frame [wood and metal stud] buildings. Concrete and masonry requirements assume a balloon frame building. The overall criteria for any framing system are the same, as noted above, which is to ensure that forces applied to the structure are transferred in a continuous path to the foundation with acceptable and comparable deformations of the framing members between various structural systems. When there are elements of residential design that exceed the standardized criteria contained in the IRC, the structure shall be designed in accordance with accepted engineering practice, using the International Building Code (IBC).

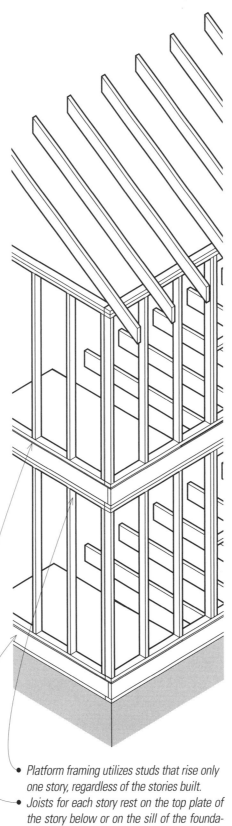

- *Platform framing utilizes studs that rise only one story, regardless of the stories built.*
- *Joists for each story rest on the top plate of the story below or on the sill of the foundation wall.*

- *Balloon framing utilizes studs that rise the full height of the frame from the sill plate to the roof plate.*
- *First-floor joists bear on a continuous foundation sill plate.*
- *Second-floor joists lap the continuous wall studs.*

Climatic and Geographic Design Criteria

The broad, regional criteria for design are related to where the building is to be located. The code provides guidance for design based on location and anticipated external influences on the building. The IRC also provides a format, in Table R301.2.(1) which allows local jurisdictions to establish additional specific design criteria for factors that can impact building design. What are the anticipated wind loads, based on historical data about the proposed location? Is the region subject to snow and, if so, what are the anticipated snow loads? Is the building located in an area subject to seismic activity? If so, what is the anticipated magnitude of an earthquake that the building is to be designed to resist? Is the building subject to frost, termites, floods, freezing soil or ice building up on the structure?

For the purposes of examining the impact of design criteria on residential construction we will assume a site location in Kansas City, Missouri. This is near the geographic center of the 48 contiguous United States. The city has adopted the International Residential Code as the code for one- and two-family dwellings. It also has a sufficient number of specific site characteristics to allow us to illustrate the use of the design criteria in the IRC.

The values for the set of criteria for Kansas City contained in the suggested format of Table R301.2(1) are:

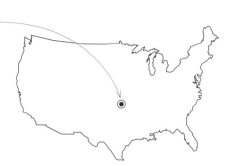

Table R301.2 (1)
CLIMATIC AND GEOGRAPHIC DESIGN CRITERIA
[Kansas City, MO for this example]
(Some footnotes omitted for this example)

Ground Snow Load	WIND SPEED (mph)	Seismic Design Category	Subject to Damage From			Winter Design Temp	Ice Barrier Under-Layment Required	Flood Hazards	Air Freezing Index	Mean Annual Temp
			Weathering	Frost Line Depth	Termite					
20 psf	90	A	Severe	36"	Moderate To Heavy	60°F	No	See Chapter 28 of KC Code	1000°F-Days	53°F

d The jurisdiction shall fill in this part of the table with the wind speed from the basic wind speed map [Figure R301.2(4)]. **Wind exposure category shall be determined on a site-specific basis in accordance with §R301.2.1.4.**

Wind Design Criteria

One of the primary design criteria related to the building's site location are the historical and anticipated wind conditions. The IRC contains several sets of charts for determining design criteria for various exterior elements exposed to wind loads; such as walls, roof coverings, windows, skylights and doors. The determination of these loads requires cross referencing between several tables. There is a lot of jumping back and forth necessary between wind tables and figures to determine what precise wind design criteria will apply to your project.

The first determination to make is the wind speed to be used for design. This uses the maps of the United States from Figure R301.2(4) which are spread over several pages. Figure R301.2(4), is for determining the basic wind speed that is expected to recur at a given site over a 50-year interval. The basic wind speed is defined as Three-second gust speed at 33' (10058) above the ground in Exposure "C."

To determine the Basic Wind Speed for Kansas City, Missouri, locate the appropriate map showing the city's location, which is on the figure located on page 34 of the 2009 IRC. For this entire area of the Midwest the wind speed is noted as 90 mph (40 m/s). Note that this is the figure entered into the example local table from Kansas City, MO in R301.2(1) shown on the previous page. Once the basic wind speed is determined, you should refer to §R301.2.1.1 to determine if the wind speeds from Figure R301.2(4) equal or exceed 100 mph (45 m/s) in hurricane-prone regions or 110 miles per hour (49 m/s) elsewhere; then the designer is to use design criteria from outside the IRC for wood and cold-formed steel structures. Concrete for buildings regulated by the IRC is to be designed per this code.

Wind Load Adjustments for Height and Exposure

The impact of wind on a structure is influenced by the height at which the wind pressure is applied, the shape of the building, and what part of the building is being considered. Table R301.2(2) gives wind pressures at various locations on the building exterior surfaces, based on anticipated wind speeds. These values are to be applied to the building zones described in Figure R301.2(7). The zones are determined by various elements of the building: by element, such as a roof or a wall; by configuration, such as roof slope; and by the zone of the building, listed in the "ZONE" column of Table R301.2(2).

Per Footnote d to Table 301.2(1), shown in bold on page 29, wind exposure categories are based on a site-specific evaluation of the location of the proposed building in relation to terrain and surrounding buildings. Per §R301.2.1.4 the exposure is based on the exposure conditions on the upwind side of the side of the building under consideration. If the building is in a zone that is a transitional zone between exposures the exposure that will generate the highest wind forces is to be selected. The basic descriptions and illustrations for the four exposure classifications are shown here. Examine the detailed text of §R301.2.1.4 for further specific details regarding exposure categories.

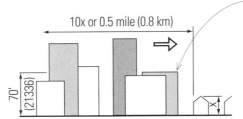

1. Exposure A. Large city centers with at least 50 percent of the buildings having a height in excess of 70' (21336). Use of this exposure category shall be limited to those areas for which terrain representative of Exposure A prevails in the upwind direction for a distance of at least 0.5 mile (0.8 km) or 10 times the height of the building or other structure, whichever is greater.

2. Exposure B. Urban and suburban areas, wooded areas, or other terrain with numerous closely spaced obstructions having the size of single-family dwellings or larger. Exposure B shall be assumed unless the site meets the definition of another type of exposure.

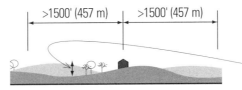

3. Exposure C. Open terrain with scattered obstructions, including surface undulations or other irregularities, having heights generally less than 30' (9144) extending more than 1,500' (457 m) from the building site in any quadrant. This category includes flat open country, grasslands and shorelines in hurricane-prone regions.

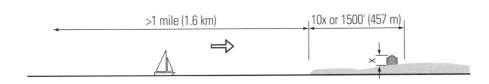

4. Exposure D. Flat, unobstructed areas exposed to wind flowing over open water (excluding shorelines in hurricane-prone regions) for a distance of at least 1 mile (1.61 km). This exposure shall apply only to those buildings and other structures exposed to the wind coming from over the water. Exposure D extends inland from the shoreline a distance of 1,500' (457 m) or 10 times the height of the building or structure, whichever is greater.

DESIGN CRITERIA

Some of the reference documents used to supplement or replace the design criteria of the IRC make use of the "fastest mile wind speed." When those documents are used, the basic wind speeds given in Figure R301.2(4) are to be adjusted per §R301.2.1.3 based on factors for the roof height and exposure categories described in Table R301.2 (3).

Example

Assume a two-story-tall dwelling, with a gable roof of 25 degree slope and a mean roof height of 25' (7620), effective roof area for Roof Zone 2 of 50 square feet (4.65 m²) on each side of the gable and effective wall area for Wall Zone 4 of 100 square feet (9.29 m²). The building is located in flat, open country near Kansas City. The following design criteria would be used for the elements noted. Places where the data are located is noted also:

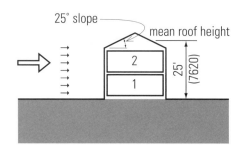

Basic Wind Speed:	90 mph (40 m/s)	Local KC, MO Table R301.2(1) & Table R301.2(4)
Exposure Category:	C, Open terrain	§R301.2.1.4.3
Roof, Zone 2, psf loads for component/cladding	10.0/–22.1	Table R301.2(2) for Roof slope of 10–30 degrees and 50 sf effective area
Wall, Zone 4, loads for component/cladding	12.4/–13.6	Table R301.2(2) for wall with **psf** 100 sf (9.29 m²) effective area
Adjustment for Exposure C and 25' (7620) mean roof height	1.35 times	Table R301.2.(3) Table R301.2.(2) values
Adjustment for wind speeds if using external references that use "fastest wind speeds"	76 mph (122.3 km/h) based on 90 mph (144.8 km/h) basic wind speed	Table R301.2.1.3

In areas subject to windborne debris, such as where hurricanes may occur, §R301.2.1.2 has provisions for application of temporary plywood window coverings. Note that Table R301.2.1.2 Footnote a. states that the fastening requirements of window coverings are based on a wind speed of 130 mph (14.5 m/s) and a mean roof height of 33' (10058). Verify with the local AHJ whether your project is subject to these provisions and what the design criteria should be for fastening of the window coverings.

Seismic Design Criteria

The seismic design criteria are contained in §R301.2.2. This section appears to start in the middle of another section so it may be confusing to find these criteria. Per §R301.2.2 the IRC seismic design provisions apply to buildings in Seismic Design Categories C, D_0, D_1 and D_2. As with the prescriptive wind provisions, a building must meet the conditions described in order to be able to use the IRC. If they do not meet these criteria the building will likely require engineering design, and the *International Building Code* is to be used. Buildings in Seismic Design Category E are to be designed per the *International Building Code* (IBC) by default unless they can be reclassified as Seismic Design Category. Note that per the Exception to §R301.2.2 detached one- and two-family dwellings located in Seismic Design Category C are exempt from the seismic design provisions of this code. Read another way, this means that townhouses in Seismic Design Category C are required to comply with the seismic design provisions of the IRC.

The broad, regional criteria for seismic design are related to where the building is to be located. In order to apply the seismic design requirements of the IRC the designer needs to know several basic items. These are based on the actual site location of the project. It is possible to reclassify buildings from Seismic Design Category E to Seismic Design Category D_2, which is a category from the IRC not contained in the IBC. This reclassification is very site specific and is beyond the scope of this book, but it is important to remember that there are limits to the use of the IRC based on which design criteria apply to the location of the building and, as discussed below, the shape and size of the proposed building. The prescriptive standards are based on assumed building configurations, which the proposed building must match.

The seismic design criteria are subdivided into two parts—one for Seismic Design Category C and one for Seismic Design Categories C, D_0, D_1 and D_2. The seismic design criteria for Category C are in §R301.2.2.2. Those for the D categories are in §R301.2.2.3.

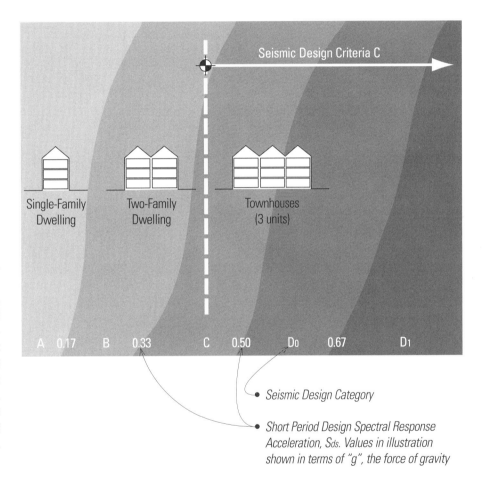

Single-Family Dwelling

Two-Family Dwelling

Townhouses (3 units)

Seismic Design Criteria C

A 0.17   B 0.33   C 0.50 D_0 0.67 D_1

● *Seismic Design Category*

● *Short Period Design Spectral Response Acceleration, S_{ds}. Values in illustration shown in terms of "g", the force of gravity*

DESIGN CRITERIA

Determination of Seismic Design Categories

The determination of the building's seismic design category is based on its location. Note also that the Seismic Design Categories are based on the soil conditions of the site being comparable to "Site Class D" soils. These conditions are described in *International Building Code* §1613.5.2. The soil is described in IBC Table 1613.5.2 as a "Stiff Soil Profile" in the top 100 feet of the site with values:

- Soil Shear Wave Velocity, v_s (ft/s) of $600 \leq v_s \leq 1,200$;
- Standard Penetration Resistance, N of $15 \leq N \leq 50$; and
- Soil Undrained Shear Strength, s_u, of $1,000 \leq s_u, \leq 2,000$.

If different soil conditions are found than those classified as Site Class D then the Short Period Design Spectral Response Acceleration SDS from the IBC is to be used to determine the Seismic Design Category based on the values in Table R301.2.2.1.1.

See the graphic depiction of the anticipated lateral force, expressed in terms of a percent of "g" for gravity against the 1g gravity we all experience every day.

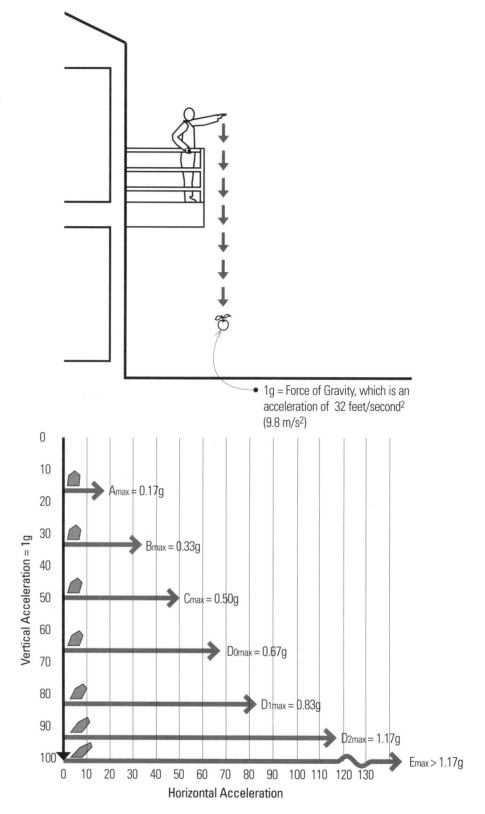

- 1g = Force of Gravity, which is an acceleration of 32 feet/second² (9.8 m/s²)

$A_{max} = 0.17g$

$B_{max} = 0.33g$

$C_{max} = 0.50g$

$D_{0max} = 0.67g$

$D_{1max} = 0.83g$

$D_{2max} = 1.17g$

$E_{max} > 1.17g$

Vertical Acceleration = 1g

Horizontal Acceleration

Determination of Seismic Design Categories

Maps showing the various seismic design categories in the United States are contained in Figure R301.2(2) in Chapter 3. Our Table 301.2(1) example for Kansas City, Missouri, discussed above in this chapter, shows our house in that location is in seismic Design Category A; therefore, it need not meet the seismic design requirements of the IRC. For an example of how to use Figure R301.2(2), we will choose a location in Las Vegas, Nevada. As illustrated, the Seismic Design Category for a building in Las Vegas on soil of Site Class D is 0.50 g. Graphically the value appears to be Category D_0. This can further be confirmed by examining the value of the seismic zones on the illustration. Las Vegas is located in the region noted as "50." This corresponds to the value of D_0 in Table R301.2.2.1.1. Also, per our recommendation to know the local codes at your site, if you go to the Internet and locate the Las Vegas Building Department Web site you will find Table R301.2.(1) filled in for that city. It indicates that Las Vegas is indeed located in the area assigned to Seismic Design Category D_0. [Note, at the time of the publication of this book, the City of Las Vegas is using the *2006 International Building Code*. Another reason to check and be certain which code you are working with in a particular jurisdiction.]

• *The model building is assumed to be in Kansas City, Missouri. This location is near the geographic center of the 48 contiguous United States and represents most, if not all, conceptual conditions that designers will encounter in any locale. This area was also selected because it has weather with wide variations through all four seasons. It also falls into the middle range of design criteria such as degree-days of heating and cooling, climate zones and susceptibility to termite infestation. Kansas City is in Seismic Design Category A.*

• *Las Vegas, Nevada located in Seismic Design Category D_0.*

Seismic Limitations

In order for the prescriptive design criteria to be appropriate for use, they must make assumptions about the materials of construction and about the configuration of buildings.

Weights of Materials

There are limitations on the weights of materials, which if exceeded dictate that the building use engineering design principles instead of the prescriptive design standards in the IRC. These limitations apply to all of the Seismic Design Categories regulated by the IRC: C, D_0, D_1 and D_2. Note that the seismic design criteria do not need to be applied in Categories A and B, and that unless modifications per §R301.2.2.1.2 apply, buildings in Seismic Design Category E are to be designed in accordance with the IBC.

See the accompanying illustration on page 37 that graphically represents the allowable dead loads of materials. Dead loads are considered to be the weight of all materials, finishes and fixed equipment that are a permanent part of the building. Added movable loads, such as people, furniture or loose equipment are considered live loads. Other loads such as wind, seismic or snow loads are superimposed environmental loads and are to be considered separately from both dead and live loads.

While weights of materials appear in §R301.2.2.2.1 under Seismic Design Category C, these weights also apply to Seismic Design Categories D_0, D_1, and D_2 since, per §R301.2.2.3, these categories are to conform to the requirements for Category C as well as additional requirements for the D categories.

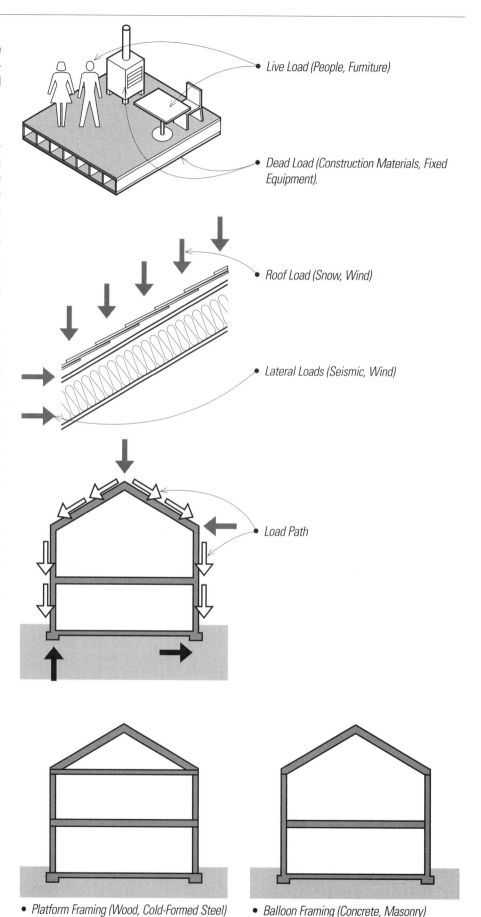

• Live Load (People, Furniture)

• Dead Load (Construction Materials, Fixed Equipment).

• Roof Load (Snow, Wind)

• Lateral Loads (Seismic, Wind)

• Load Path

• Platform Framing (Wood, Cold-Formed Steel)

• Balloon Framing (Concrete, Masonry)

Weights of Materials

Horizontal assemblies are treated differently than vertical assemblies. The average dead loads for combined roof and ceiling assemblies are to be 15 psf (0.72 kPa) measured on a horizontal projection which thus accounts for roof slopes. Per exception 1 to R301.2.2.2.1, roof and ceiling dead loads may be increased to 25 psf (1.19 kPa) if the wall bracing amounts required in Chapter 6 are increased per Table R301.2.2.2.1. Note that for dead loads between 15 psf and 25 psf (0.72–1.19 kPa), linear interpolation is permitted. Floors are to be no more than 10 pounds per square foot (0.48 kPa) average dead loads. Dead loads for walls above grade are as shown in the illustration below.

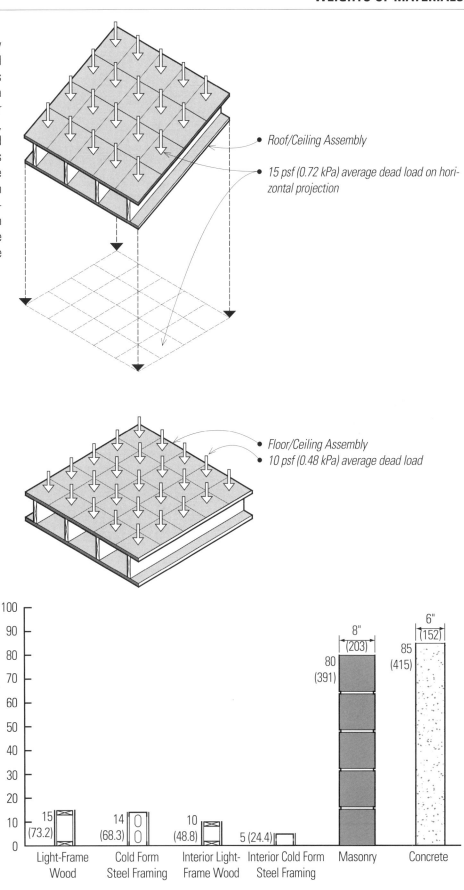

- Roof/Ceiling Assembly
- 15 psf (0.72 kPa) average dead load on horizontal projection

- Floor/Ceiling Assembly
- 10 psf (0.48 kPa) average dead load

Wall Dead Loads

Seismic Design Category C §R301.2.2.2

There are material references for Seismic Design Category C contained in §R301.2.2.2. These requirements also apply to Seismic Design Categories D0, D1 and D2 per §R301.2.2.3. Stone and masonry veneer are to comply with the requirements of §R702.1 and §R703. Masonry construction is to comply with §R606.11.2. Concrete construction is to comply with §R611, PCA 100 or ACI 318. Townhouses with above-grade exterior concrete walls are to comply with PCA 100 or ACI 318.

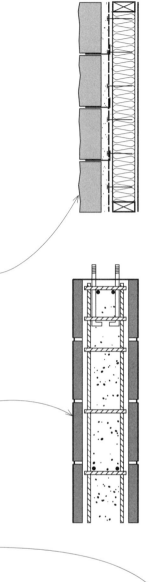

Category C

1. Stone and masonry veneers are to conform to the requirements of §R702.1 [for interior stone and masonry veneers] and §R703 [for exterior stone and masonry veneers]. Note that in each of these sections there are specific requirements dictated by the seismic design category.

2. Masonry construction is to conform to the requirements of §R606.11.2 [correct reference is to Figure R606.11(2) which depicts the requirements for grouted masonry construction in Seismic Zone C].

3. Concrete construction is to comply with §R611, or with the external references noted in §R301.2.2.2.4. Note that townhouses with above-grade concrete walls must use the external references PCA 100 or ACI 318.

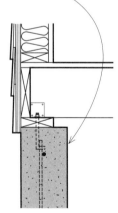

Irregular Buildings

The prescriptive standards are based on modeling structural performance for such loads as wind, seismic or snow loads. The standards rely on actual buildings bearing a determined amount of resemblance to the configurations tested and modeled in calculations. For seismic design, one of the criteria is whether the building or portions of a building, are deemed to be "irregular" as described in §R301.2.2.2.5. The simplest concept of a regular house is a square shape in plan with a gable roof and no projecting bays or notches in plan. Irregular buildings are not to use the prescriptive design standards. Irregular portions of buildings are to be designed using accepted engineering practice. If the forces in the irregular portion can be resolved, then the regular portion of the building may use the prescriptive standards. The conditions that determine if a building is irregular are illustrated here.

Note that most of the "irregular" conditions described in the code are ones where vertical discontinuities exist.

Note also that while contained in the code section pertaining to Seismic Design Category C per §R301.2.2.2.5, the provisions regarding irregular buildings also apply to Seismic Design Categories D_0, D_1 and D_2.

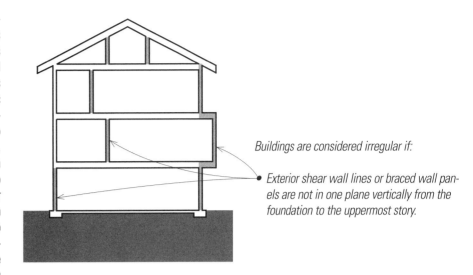

Buildings are considered irregular if:

- *Exterior shear wall lines or braced wall panels are not in one plane vertically from the foundation to the uppermost story.*

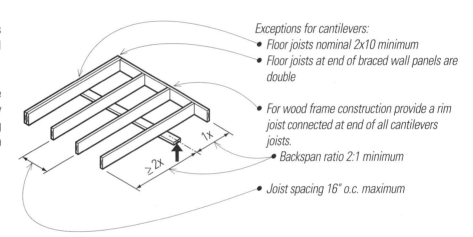

Exceptions for cantilevers:
- *Floor joists nominal 2x10 minimum*
- *Floor joists at end of braced wall panels are double*

- *For wood frame construction provide a rim joist connected at end of all cantilevers joists.*
  - *Backspan ratio 2:1 minimum*
- *Joist spacing 16" o.c. maximum*

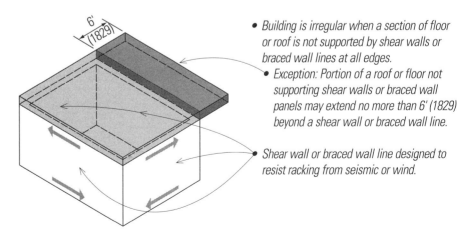

6'
(1829)

- *Building is irregular when a section of floor or roof is not supported by shear walls or braced wall lines at all edges.*
  - *Exception: Portion of a roof or floor not supporting shear walls or braced wall panels may extend no more than 6' (1829) beyond a shear wall or braced wall line.*

- *Shear wall or braced wall line designed to resist racking from seismic or wind.*

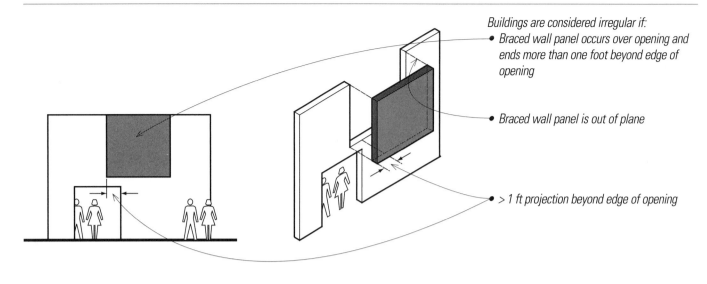

Buildings are considered irregular if:
- Braced wall panel occurs over opening and ends more than one foot beyond edge of opening

- Braced wall panel is out of plane

- > 1 ft projection beyond edge of opening

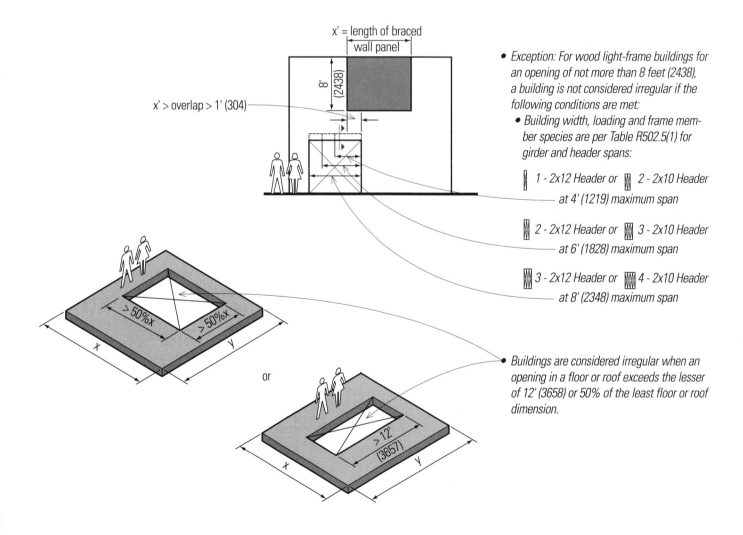

x' = length of braced wall panel

8' (2438)

x' > overlap > 1' (304)

- Exception: For wood light-frame buildings for an opening of not more than 8 feet (2438), a building is not considered irregular if the following conditions are met:
  - Building width, loading and frame member species are per Table R502.5(1) for girder and header spans:

    1 - 2x12 Header or 2 - 2x10 Header at 4' (1219) maximum span

    2 - 2x12 Header or 3 - 2x10 Header at 6' (1828) maximum span

    3 - 2x12 Header or 4 - 2x10 Header at 8' (2348) maximum span

> 50%x   50%x

x

y

or

> 12' (3657)

x

y

- Buildings are considered irregular when an opening in a floor or roof exceeds the lesser of 12' (3658) or 50% of the least floor or roof dimension.

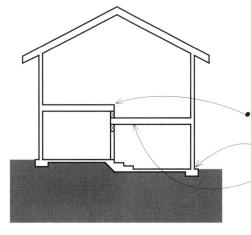

- Building is irregular if floor levels are offset vertically except:
  - If framing is supported directly by continuous perimeter foundation
  - For light-frame construction the floor framing is lapped or tied together per §R506.2.1. [minimum 3" lap with 3-10d nails or wood or metal splice]

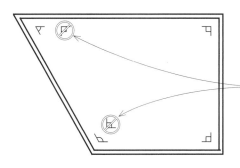

- Building is irregular when shear walls and braced wall lines do not occur in two perpendicular directions
  - Braced walls not at 90° to each other in plan.

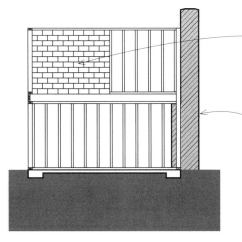

- A building is irregular if there is inclusion of masonry or concrete construction in stories above grade that are braced by wood construction [per §R602] or steel construction [per §R603]
- Exceptions are made for fireplaces, chimneys and masonry veneer as permitted by the IRC.
- When this condition occurs the entire story is to be designed in accordance with accepted engineering practice. We interpret this requirement to apply to at least the lower story, since the building must provide a load path to get forces from the upper levels to the foundation.

Categories D₀, D₁ and D₂, §R301.2.2.3

In addition to the requirements above for Seismic Design Category C, the D categories impose further restrictions, based on the increased severity of anticipated ground motion in these zones as compared to those in categories A, B or C.

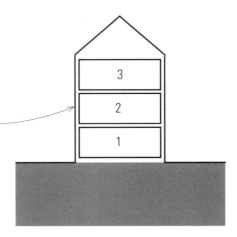

1. Wood-framed buildings are limited to three stories in height. Note that this is consistent with the overall limitations for using the IRC contained in §R101.2. Note also that the definition of story can be impacted by bracing requirements for such things as cripple walls. See further discussion in Chapter 6. Cold-formed steel buildings are limited to two stories in height for category D buildings. Note also that mezzanines, as defined in Chapter 2, do not count as stories.

2. Stone and masonry veneers are to conform to the requirements of §R702.1 [for interior stone and masonry veneers] and §R703 [for exterior stone and masonry veneers]. Note that in each of these sections there are specific requirements dictated by the seismic design category.

3. Masonry construction is to conform to the requirements of "§R606.11.3" per §R301.2.2.3.3 [correct reference is to **Figure** R606.11(3), which depicts the requirements for grouted masonry construction in Seismic Design Categories D₀, D₁ and D₂].

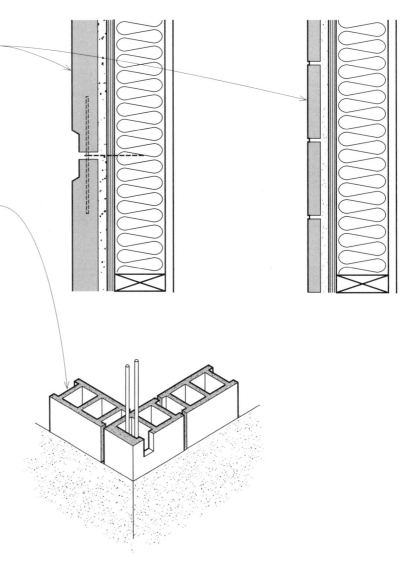

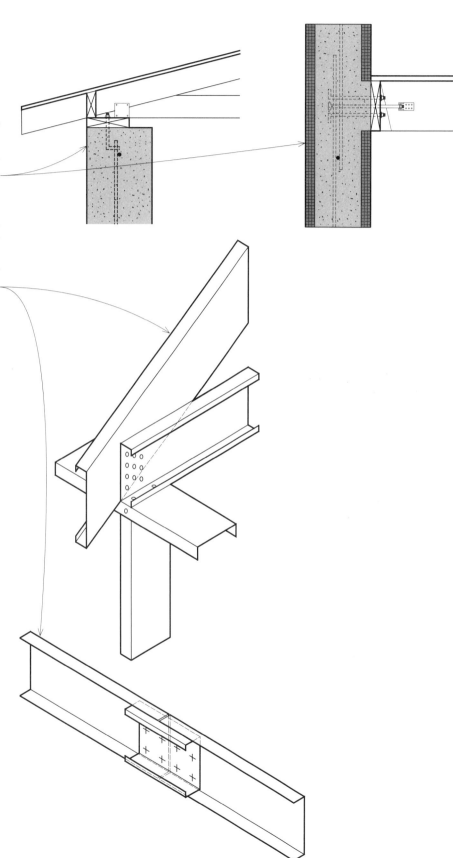

4. Concrete construction is to conform to the specific requirements of §R611, PCA 100 or ACI 318 for category D0, D1 and D2 buildings, or be designed according to accepted engineering practice [in other words, engineered design and not prescriptive design].

5. Cold-formed steel construction in Seismic Design Categories D0, D1 and D2 must comply not only with the IRC but with additional requirements contained in the Standard for Cold-Formed Steel Framing—Prescriptive Method for One- and Two-Family Dwellings (COFS/PM).

Snow Load Design Criteria

Where the snow load is 70 psf (3.35 kPa) or less, buildings may be designed using the design standards in IRC Chapters 5, 6 and 8 for all types of construction: wood frame, cold-formed steel, masonry, concrete and structural insulated panel construction.

Where the snow load exceeds that value the buildings are to be designed in accordance with accepted engineering practice.

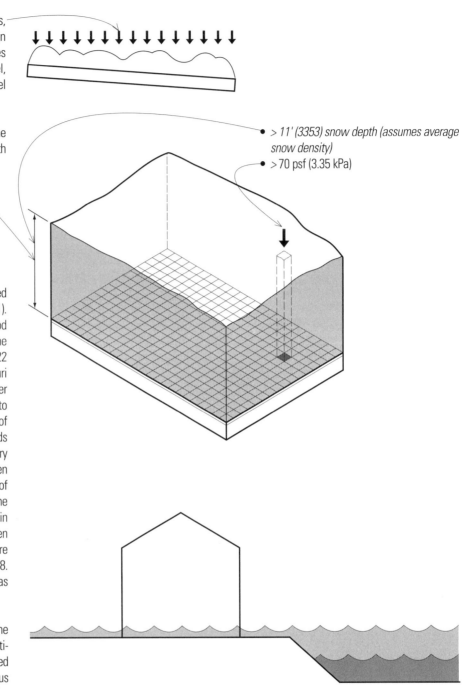

• > 11' (3353) snow depth (assumes average snow density)
• > 70 psf (3.35 kPa)

Floodplain Construction Design Criteria

Flood hazards are described in the customized local information contained in Table R301.2(1). For buildings completely or even partly in flood hazard areas including "A" or "V" zones the flood-resistant construction standards of §R322 are to be used. For our Kansas City, Missouri example, the flood hazard refers to "Chapter 28." For this jurisdiction this corresponds to Chapter 28 of the City of Kansas City "Code of Ordinances," which sets out the local standards for "Floodplain Management." This is a very good example of the research that is often necessary to determine the precise nature of the applicable local codes for your projects. The local flood-resistant design criteria for work in Kansas City are not in the IRC, but to be taken from the IRC. The precise set of criteria are found in the applicable parts of Chapter 28. They are to be found in Chapter 28 of Kansas City's ordinances.

Note also that when buildings are shown in the local version of Table R301.2(1) to be in identified floodways the buildings are to be designed in accordance with ASCE 24 and are thus outside the scope of the IRC requirements. The IRC cannot be used in such high flood-hazard areas. For our Kansas City, Missouri example, this is the kind of data that needs to be gleaned from study of the local requirements and then compared to the IRC requirements.

The detailed prescriptive requirements for flood-resistant construction are described and illustrated later in this chapter in the discussion of the requirements of §R322.

Story Heights

Per §R301.3, use of the IRC for prescriptive design is based on limitations to story heights, based on the construction materials. Story heights are defined in IRC Chapter 2 as being measured from the top surfaces of a floor to the floor or roof above, as shown in the illustrations on this page and page 46 for each of the limits for various materials. Note that the floor framing assembly is assumed to have a depth of 16" (406), but may vary for all of the story heights. This is added to the stud length measured from the floor surface of the story where the measurements start.

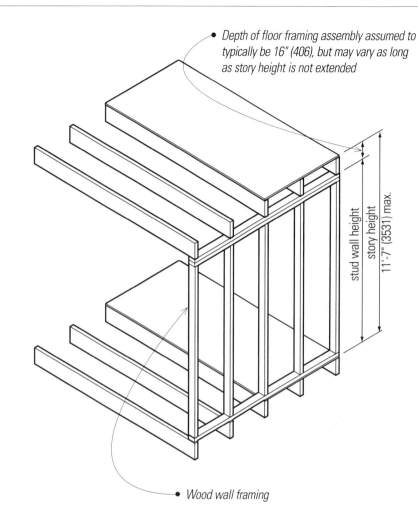

Depth of floor framing assembly assumed to typically be 16" (406), but may vary as long as story height is not extended

stud wall height

story height

11'-7" (3531) max.

Wood wall framing

When bracing per Table R602.10.1.2(1) and Table R602.10.1.2(2) is provided, the wall stud height may be increased to 12' (3658) provided that the length of bracing required by Table R602.10.1.2(1) is increased by multiplying by a factor of 1.10 and the length of bracing required by Table R602.10.1.2(2) is increased by multiplying by a factor of 1.20. Wall studs are still subject to the requirements of this section.

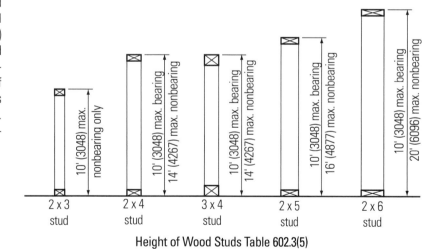

| 2 x 3 stud | 2 x 4 stud | 3 x 4 stud | 2 x 5 stud | 2 x 6 stud |

10' (3048) max. nonbearing only

10' (3048) max. bearing / 14' (4267) max. nonbearing

10' (3048) max. bearing / 14' (4267) max. nonbearing

10' (3048) max. bearing / 16' (4877) max. nonbearing

10' (3048) max. bearing / 20' (6096) max. nonbearing

Height of Wood Studs Table 602.3(5)

Story Heights

Per §R301.3.2, steel wall stud heights are limited to 10' (3048) with the floor framing allowed to be no more than 16" (406) deep as is assumed for wood floor framing in §R301.3.1 as shown.

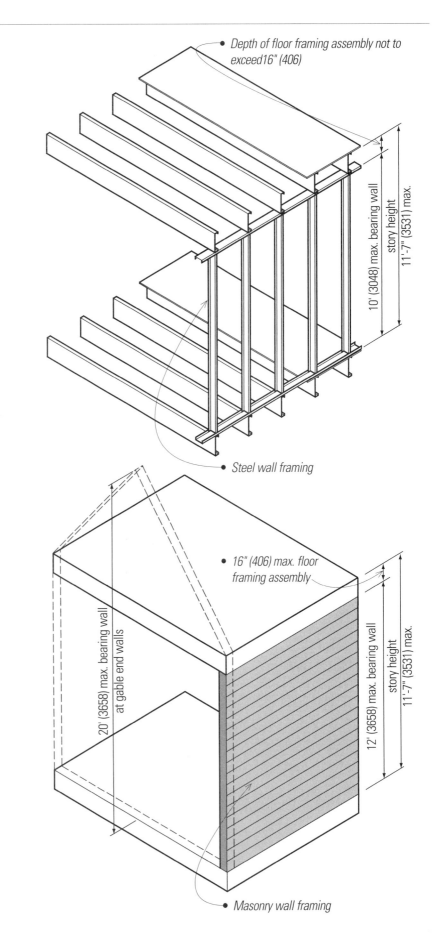

• Depth of floor framing assembly not to exceed 16" (406)

10' (3048) max. bearing wall

story height 11'-7" (3531) max.

• Steel wall framing

• 16" (406) max. floor framing assembly

20' (3658) max. bearing wall at gable end walls

12' (3658) max. bearing wall

story height 11'-7" (3531) max.

• Masonry wall framing

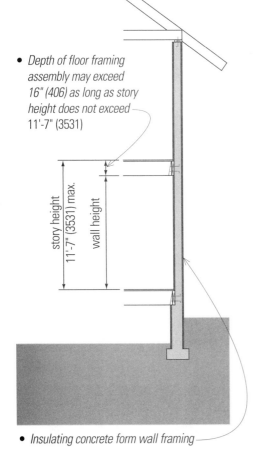

• Depth of floor framing assembly may exceed 16" (406) as long as story height does not exceed 11'-7" (3531)

story height 11'-7" (3531) max.

wall height

• Insulating concrete form wall framing

Dead Loads

Per §R301.4, dead loads are to take into account the weights of materials and all of the fixed service equipment that is permanently attached to the building, such as ductwork, furnaces, plumbing fixtures, plaster and tile. The loading criteria for structural design are based on dead loads. It is important to accurately determine the dead loads of actual materials and systems to be used in the proposed building to be sure the correct dead load factors are applied. Be sure and include the dead loads from permanent partitions in the building, whether they are load bearing or non-load bearing as both wall types contribute to the dead loads.

Live Loads

Per §R301.5, live loads are to be accounted for according to Table R301.5. Live loads are movable, and are to be assumed to be applied at any point in the area under consideration for loading. The live load factors are thus assumed to be uniformly applied over the whole area under consideration. Live loads are of course assumed for all the habitable areas of the house and take into account having the occupants moving around in the spaces, but they also assume furniture and non-fixed equipment such as refrigerators. The live load to a sleeping room is somewhat lower than that for other rooms in the house based on the anticipated load of beds being less than the type of furniture and number of occupants found in a living room or a dining room. Live loads are also to be provided for in areas such as attics, where workers may need to go in for maintenance or in the types of attic configurations where some storage is assumed to be likely. Where a stair provides access to an attic it is presumed possible that it will be a sleeping room and the attic is to be designed to accommodate the live load for a sleeping room. Live loads are thought of as being applied either in a vertical or horizontal direction. Vertical loads are assumed to be for gravity loads for things such as people or furniture. Lateral loads are assumed for people leaning or falling on guard rails or grasping stair railings. Items such as stairs, where people are moving and not standing still are to consider 300-pound (136.2 kg) concentrated loads, as from a footfall, along with an evenly distributed live load of 40 pounds per square foot (195.3 kg) and be designed to accommodate whichever load produces the greatest stress on the stair components.

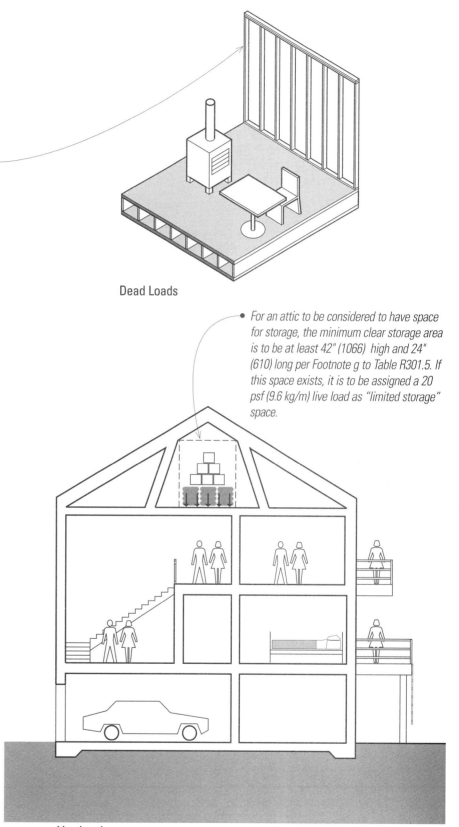

Dead Loads

For an attic to be considered to have space for storage, the minimum clear storage area is to be at least 42" (1066) high and 24" (610) long per Footnote g to Table R301.5. If this space exists, it is to be assigned a 20 psf (9.6 kg/m) live load as "limited storage" space.

Live Loads

Roof Load

Roof live loads are to be applied per the requirements of Table R301.6 or the snow load requirements of Table R301.2(1), whichever is greater. The roof live loads from Table R301.6 are based on the roof slope. The basic live load of 20 psf (0.96 kPa) assumes concentrated loads from maintenance workers moving around at any location on the roof. These loads are reduced as the slope increases based on the assumption that there is less likelihood of live loads being applied to steep roofs since access is more difficult. The loads are also reduced as the tributary area on the structural members increases since the live load will be distributed over a larger area. The criteria recognize that the likelihood of a large live load over the entire roof is very low and makes allowances in the criteria to account for how the roof will be loaded in reality.

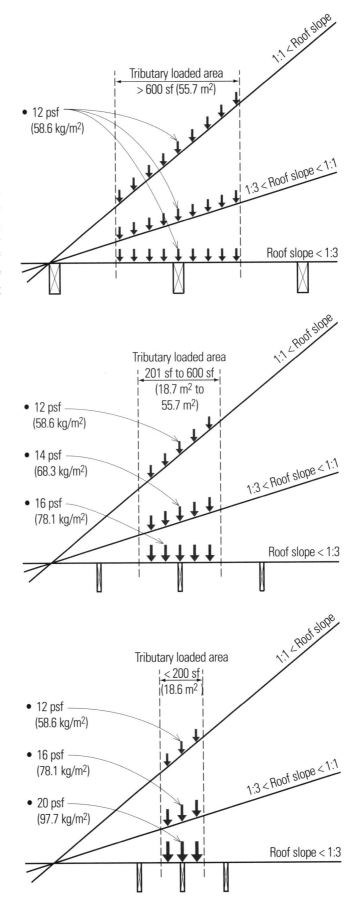

Deflections

When loaded according to the live loads on floors per Table R301.5 and roofs per Table 301.6, structural members will move under the load, whether it is live loading, wind or snow. The movement they may undergo is relative to the depth of the members, their spacing and their materials. This movement is in addition to the dead load deflection the member will undergo based on its own dead weight. The members may not deflect more than the allowable values in Table R301.7. The table lists deflections for both vertical and horizontal components. The deflections are expressed in terms of offsets versus the length of the span of the structural member. The deflection limits also take into account the flexibility of finish materials, so plaster ceilings and plastered walls have a lower deflection limit to reduce cracking in brittle materials. The prescriptive design tables in the IRC are set up to take these deflection limits into account, so unless a member is to be engineered the deflections need not be calculated. However, engineered designs must comply with the stated deflection limits in Table R301.7. Be sure to remember to convert feet spans into inches to express the deflections in inches rather than fractions of feet since the dimensions are relatively small. For example, for a 20' (6096) ceiling span with a plaster ceiling and an allowable deflection of L/360:

$$20'/360 = 0.0556' \ (6096/360 = 16.93)$$
which is hard to conceive of
vs.
$$20' \times 12''/360 = .6667''$$
[Approximately 5/8" (15.9)]

Note that since cantilevers are unsupported at the end, the length of the span is assumed by the formula to be 2 times the length of the cantilever, effectively increasing the deflection by 2 times and requiring a larger structural member to meet the deflection criteria.

Nominal Lumber Sizes

§R301.8 states that lumber dimensions are assumed to be "nominal" dimensions unless specifically stated otherwise. The prescriptive design tables take the size reductions due to milling into account and further reductions need not be applied by the designer when using the prescriptive standards.

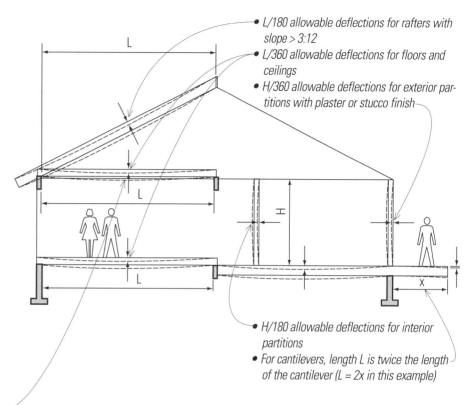

- *L/180 allowable deflections for rafters with slope > 3:12*
- *L/360 allowable deflections for floors and ceilings*
- *H/360 allowable deflections for exterior partitions with plaster or stucco finish*

- *H/180 allowable deflections for interior partitions*
- *For cantilevers, length L is twice the length of the cantilever (L = 2x in this example)*

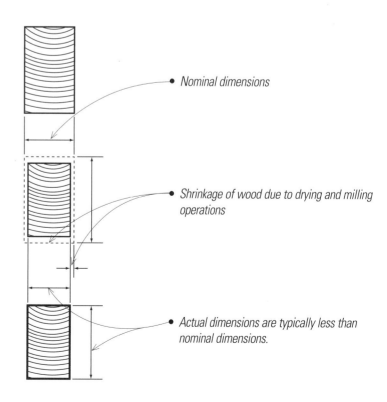

- *Nominal dimensions*

- *Shrinkage of wood due to drying and milling operations*

- *Actual dimensions are typically less than nominal dimensions.*

FIRE-RESISTANT CONSTRUCTION

Fire Protection Based on Exterior Wall Location

Per §R302.1, residential walls that are more or less parallel to a property line must be located a prescribed distance from adjacent buildings, property lines or streets, or be provided with fire-resistance rated construction. The distance is defined as "fire separation distance" and illustrated in Chapter 2. Note that by definition the fire separation distance is measured at right angles to the face of the wall, not in relation to the property line. The requirements are spelled out in Table R302.1. These criteria apply to wall fire-resistance, the length and fire-resistance of projections, the amount and fire resistance of openings and requirements for foundation vents and penetrations. Per the text of the code section the requirements of Table R302.1 are modified by the exceptions.

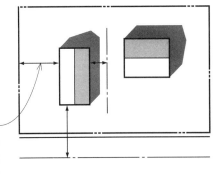

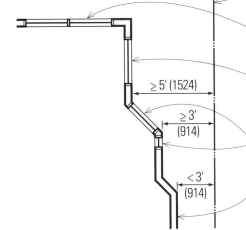

- Fire separation distance from lot line
- No limit to opening size and no fire-resistance rating required if perpendicular to fire-resistance rating lot line
- Unlimited area opening if fire separation distance is ≥ 5' (1524)
- Unprotected openings if total opening area is < 25% of wall area in 3'–5' (914–1524) distance range
- No openings if fire separation distance is < 3' (914)

≥ 5' (1524)

≥ 3' (914)

< 3' (914)

1. Structures such as playhouses or sheds, for which a permit is not required, may be placed anywhere on the lot, without wall or opening protection, but none of the structure, including any projections, may extend over the lot line.

2. Detached garages within 2' (610) of the lot line may have projections of up to 4" (102). This does not remove the fire-resistance rating requirements for fire separation distances contained in the table but applies to projections only. The other requirements for wall and projection fire-resistance contained in the table would still apply in this situation.

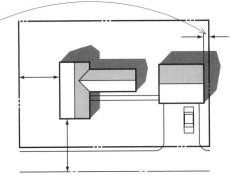

3. Foundation vents that are in compliance with the code may occur where openings would otherwise be prohibited. See the discussion of §R408 for the requirements for under-floor space ventilation.

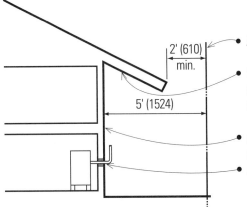

2' (610) min.

5' (1524)

- Fire separation distance from lot line
- 1-hour protection at underside of projection if < 5' (1524) and ≥ 2' (610) fire separation distance
- No fire-resistance rating required if ≥ 5' (1524)
- Penetrations to be per §R302.4

Townhouse Unit Separation

Townhouses are considered to be separate buildings by §R302.2 of the IRC and are to be treated as if each wall between two townhouses is an exterior wall per §R302.1. Each wall between townhouses immediately adjacent to each other has zero fire separation distance per Table R302.1 and each unit is to have a separate wall with a minimum 1-hour fire-resistance rating. Per the Exception to §R302.2, the wall may be a common 1-hour fire-resistance rated wall, but there cannot be any plumbing or mechanical ducts or vents in the cavity of the common wall. Electrical conduit and boxes may be installed in the common wall, but they must be installed per the general electrical requirements of IRC Chapters 34 through 43 and be treated for fire-resistance of penetrations per §R302.4 as described below. §R302.2.1 requires the fire-resistance-rated wall or assembly separating townhouses to be continuous from the foundation to the underside of the roof sheathing, deck or slab. The intent is that regardless of how the buildings are constructed each townhouse is to be separate from the other townhouses.

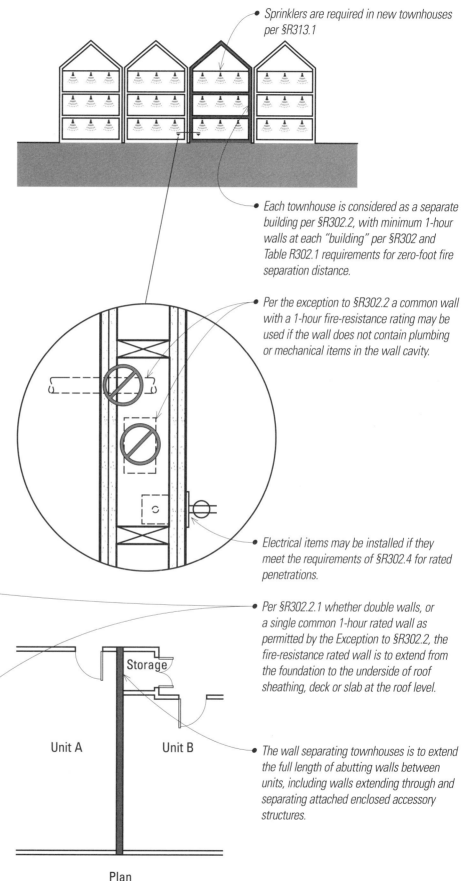

Sprinklers are required in new townhouses per §R313.1

Each townhouse is considered as a separate building per §R302.2, with minimum 1-hour walls at each "building" per §R302 and Table R302.1 requirements for zero-foot fire separation distance.

Per the exception to §R302.2 a common wall with a 1-hour fire-resistance rating may be used if the wall does not contain plumbing or mechanical items in the wall cavity.

Electrical items may be installed if they meet the requirements of §R302.4 for rated penetrations.

Per §R302.2.1 whether double walls, or a single common 1-hour rated wall as permitted by the Exception to §R302.2, the fire-resistance rated wall is to extend from the foundation to the underside of roof sheathing, deck or slab at the roof level.

The wall separating townhouses is to extend the full length of abutting walls between units, including walls extending through and separating attached enclosed accessory structures.

Unit A   Unit B

Storage

Unit A   Unit B

Section

Plan

Townhouse Unit Separation

Townhouses are to have parapets between units constructed per §R302.2.3. The requirements for parapets vary based on the relationship of each townhouse to the others, as illustrated. The parapet requirements apply only to townhouses and only to the walls between units, not to other exterior walls.

Since townhouses are considered separate buildings, each townhouse is to be structurally independent of each other. However, the code considers typical construction practices and the exceptions to §R302.2.4 recognizes that most townhouses will be constructed with the common wall allowed by the Exception to §R302.2. See the Exceptions to §R302.2.4 for the requirements for when structural independence need not be provided. These conditions are mainly related to shared foundations, or fastening finishes to walls shared by both units, except for Exception 5, which is the 1-hour fire-resistance rated common wall.

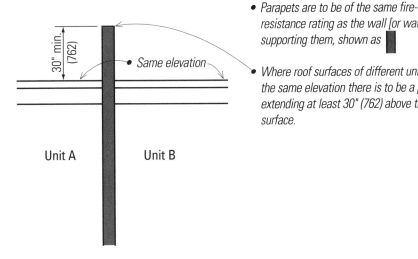

- Parapets are to be of the same fire-resistance rating as the wall [or walls] supporting them, shown as

- Where roof surfaces of different units are at the same elevation there is to be a parapet extending at least 30" (762) above the roof surface.

- Where the elevations of adjacent unit roof surfaces are less than 30" (762) apart, the parapet is to extend at least 30" (762) above the lower roof elevation.

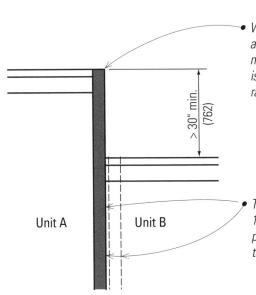

- Where the elevation of roof surfaces at adjacent units is more than 30" (762) apart, no parapet is required. The projected wall is to be not less than 1-hour fire-resistance rated.

- The walls separating units are either two 1-hour walls or one 1-hour wall with no penetrations per §R302.2 or the exception to that section.

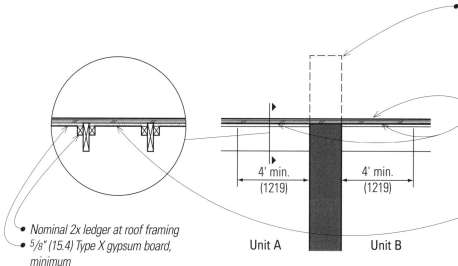

- Per the Exception to Part 2 of §R302.2.2, parapets may be eliminated for the conditions where roofs at adjacent units are at the same elevation or stepped less than 30" (762) when the following conditions occur:
- Provide a minimum Class C roof covering
- Roof decking or sheathing is noncombustible or of approved fire retardant-treated wood for a distance of 4' (1219) minimum on each side of the wall

or

- Provide a ⅝" (15.4) Type X gypsum board minimum directly under the roof sheathing supported on nominal 2" (51) ledgers attached to the sides of the roof framing for a minimum of 4' (1219) on each side of wall [or walls].
  [Note that it is not stated, but a Class C roof should be provided with this detail to meet the intent of the code]

- Nominal 2x ledger at roof framing
- ⅝" (15.4) Type X gypsum board, minimum

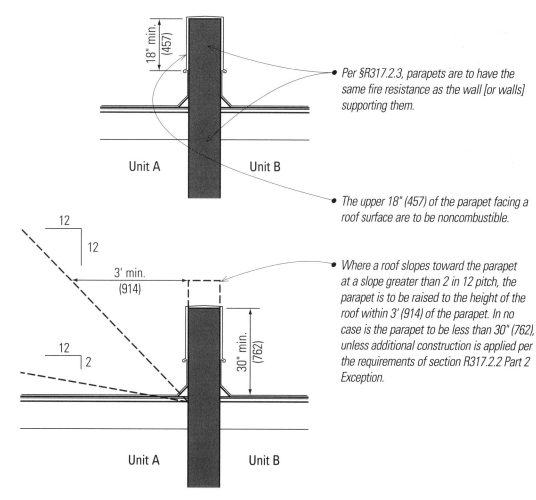

- Per §R317.2.3, parapets are to have the same fire resistance as the wall [or walls] supporting them.

- The upper 18" (457) of the parapet facing a roof surface are to be noncombustible.

- Where a roof slopes toward the parapet at a slope greater than 2 in 12 pitch, the parapet is to be raised to the height of the roof within 3' (914) of the parapet. In no case is the parapet to be less than 30" (762), unless additional construction is applied per the requirements of section R317.2.2 Part 2 Exception.

Dwelling Unit Separation

§R302.3 contains requirements for separations between dwelling units in two-family dwellings and townhouses. For two-family dwellings each dwelling unit—whether beside or above the other units—is to be separated by wall and floor assemblies having at least a 1-hour fire-resistance rating. The assemblies are to provide a continuous fire barrier by extending tightly to the exterior wall and to the underside of the roof sheathing. Providing sprinklers allows reduction of the fire-resistance ratings to $1/2$-hour assemblies. Note that sprinklers will be required in these buildings, as well as in single family residences, after January 1, 2011 per §R313.2. Wall assemblies are not required to extend through attic spaces between dwelling units per §R302.3 Exception 2 when the ceiling is constructed of $5/8$" Type X gypsum board and a draft stop per §R302.12.1 is constructed above the wall between the units. The structure, as illustrated, supporting the ceiling, which is basically the walls below the ceiling, is also to be fire protected with minimum $1/2$" gypsum board or other equivalent fire protection materials. There is also a similar requirement to support floor/ceiling fire-resistive assemblies between units per §R302.3.1. Note that the two dwelling units in two-family dwelling units, while providing fire separations between them, are not considered by the code to be separate buildings as are townhouses.

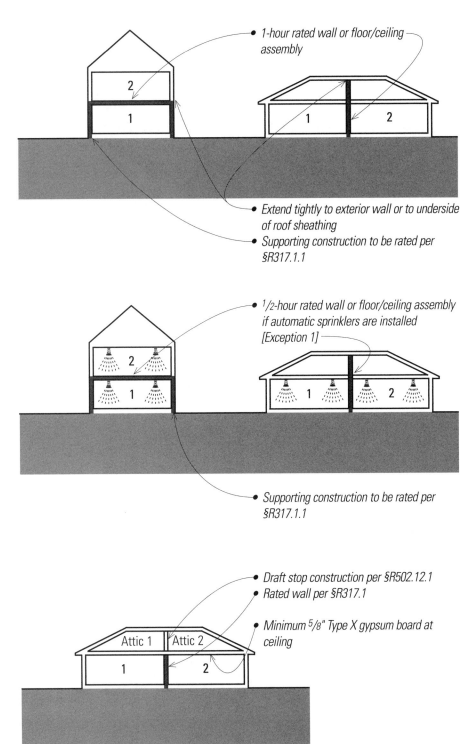

1-hour rated wall or floor/ceiling assembly

Extend tightly to exterior wall or to underside of roof sheathing

Supporting construction to be rated per §R317.1.1

$1/2$-hour rated wall or floor/ceiling assembly if automatic sprinklers are installed [Exception 1]

Supporting construction to be rated per §R317.1.1

Draft stop construction per §R502.12.1

Rated wall per §R317.1

Minimum $5/8$" Type X gypsum board at ceiling

Dwelling Unit Separation

Fire-resistance ratings for wall and floor/ceiling assembly penetrations are discussed in §R302.4. These requirements apply to both two-family dwellings and townhouses. The requirements are in two categories. One category is "through penetrations," which occur where an element such as a pipe or duct goes through both sides of a wall or floor/ceiling assembly. The other type of penetration is a "membrane penetration" where an element such as an electrical box or a recessed light fixture pierces only one of the fire-resistance elements, such as a sheet of gypsum board, of a wall or floor/ceiling assembly. Both penetrations are to be sealed to prevent the passage of flame and hot gases into or through the walls, floors, or ceilings. There are some exceptions that are based on the size of the penetrating element being of a limited dimension. See the accompanying illustrations.

The general requirements for through penetrations are contained in §R302.4.1. The first exception to this section deals with generally accepted practices for grouting penetrations of concrete or masonry wall and floor assemblies by pipes of limited sizes. The second exception specifies the performance of materials that fill the annular spaces around penetrations. Note that while the exception is generic it does have specific test criteria related to the ASTM E119 time temperature curve and requirements for a pressure differential. It is to have an "F" rating equal to the wall penetrated.

The requirements for membrane penetrations refer back to the requirements for through penetrations in §R302.4.2. There are some exceptions to membrane protection requirements based on the size of the penetrating element being of a limited dimension. The verification process for most membrane penetrations with the AHJ will be the same as for through penetrations and will involve provision of data to the AHJ verifying compliance with the rating requirements for the proposed applications. See the accompanying illustrations.

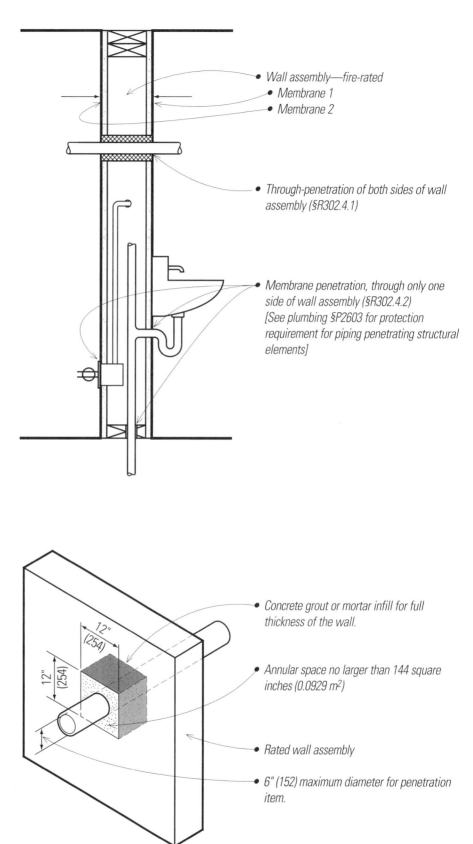

- Wall assembly—fire-rated
- Membrane 1
- Membrane 2

- Through-penetration of both sides of wall assembly (§R302.4.1)

- Membrane penetration, through only one side of wall assembly (§R302.4.2) [See plumbing §P2603 for protection requirement for piping penetrating structural elements]

12" (254)

12" (254)

- Concrete grout or mortar infill for full thickness of the wall.

- Annular space no larger than 144 square inches (0.0929 m²)

- Rated wall assembly

- 6" (152) maximum diameter for penetration item.

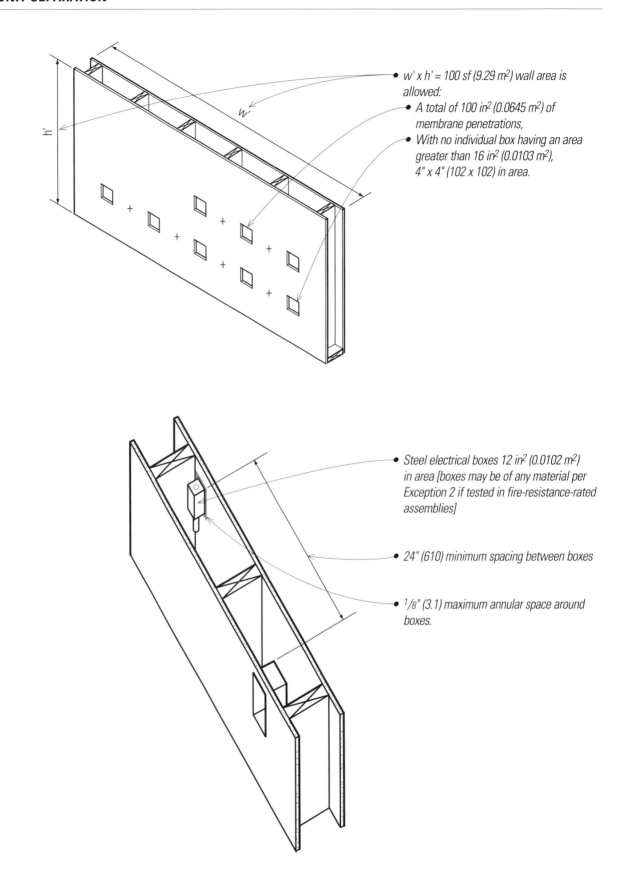

$w' \times h' = 100$ sf (9.29 m²) wall area is allowed:
- A total of 100 in² (0.0645 m²) of membrane penetrations,
- With no individual box having an area greater than 16 in² (0.0103 m²), 4" x 4" (102 x 102) in area.

Steel electrical boxes 12 in² (0.0102 m²) in area [boxes may be of any material per Exception 2 if tested in fire-resistance-rated assemblies]

24" (610) minimum spacing between boxes

1/8" (3.1) maximum annular space around boxes.

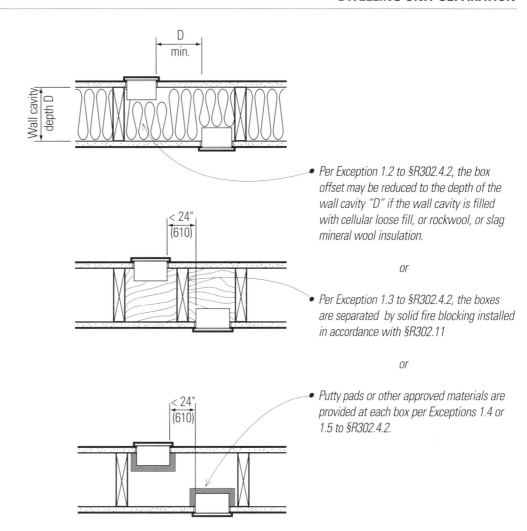

• Per Exception 1.2 to §R302.4.2, the box offset may be reduced to the depth of the wall cavity "D" if the wall cavity is filled with cellular loose fill, or rockwool, or slag mineral wool insulation.

or

• Per Exception 1.3 to §R302.4.2, the boxes are separated by solid fire blocking installed in accordance with §R302.11

or

• Putty pads or other approved materials are provided at each box per Exceptions 1.4 or 1.5 to §R302.4.2.

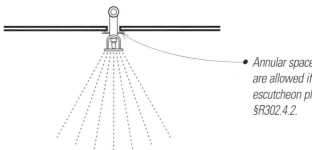

• Annular spaces at fire sprinkler penetrations are allowed if covered with a metal escutcheon plate per Exception 3 to §R302.4.2.

Dwelling/Garages Opening and Penetration Protection

§R302.5 regulates fire resistance requirements between dwellings and garages. Garages are not to open to sleeping rooms. Doors between garages and dwellings are to have solid wood, or solid or honeycomb steel doors not less than 1³/₈" (35) in thickness. Any door with a 20-minute fire-resistance rating is permitted.

Heating and air conditioning units are often located in garages. Ducts in the garage and ducts that penetrate the walls or ceilings separating the garage from the dwelling are to be constructed of minimum 26-gage (0.48) sheet metal or other approved materials and are to have no openings into the garage.

Per Table R302.6, the garage is to be separated from the residence and its attic area by not less than ¹/₂" (12.7) gypsum board applied to the garage side. Where the garage is located beneath habitable rooms the garage is to be separated from the rooms above by not less than ⁵/₈" (15.9) Type X gypsum board or equivalent. Where the separation is a floor ceiling assembly, as is likely, the separation is also to be protected by not less than ¹/₂" (12.7) gypsum board or equivalent. Also, walls supporting a floor ceiling assembly that is providing the separation are required to be protected by not less than ¹/₂" (12.7) gypsum board or equivalent. The same protection is required if the garage is located less than 3' (914) from a dwelling unit at the interior side of the garage exterior walls. Openings are to have doors as specified in §R302.5.1 as noted above. This provision does not apply to garage walls that are perpendicular to the adjacent dwelling unit wall.

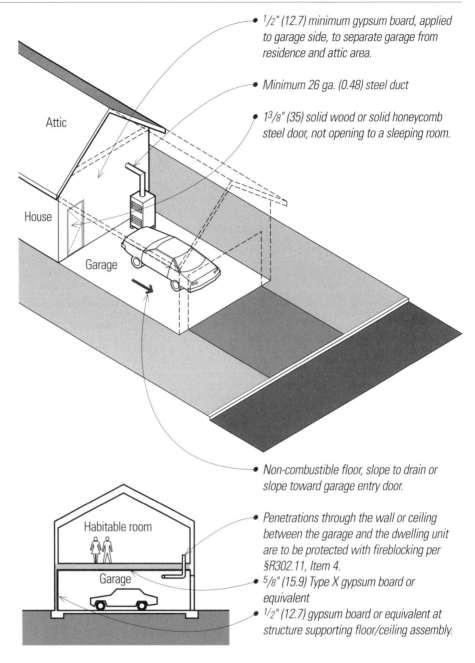

- ¹/₂" (12.7) minimum gypsum board, applied to garage side, to separate garage from residence and attic area.

- Minimum 26 ga. (0.48) steel duct

- 1³/₈" (35) solid wood or solid honeycomb steel door, not opening to a sleeping room.

- Non-combustible floor, slope to drain or slope toward garage entry door.

- Penetrations through the wall or ceiling between the garage and the dwelling unit are to be protected with fireblocking per §R302.11, Item 4.
- ⁵/₈" (15.9) Type X gypsum board or equivalent
- ¹/₂" (12.7) gypsum board or equivalent at structure supporting floor/ceiling assembly.

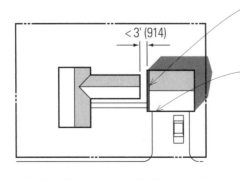

- ¹/₂" (12.7) gypsum board minimum at interior side of exterior garage wall where distance between dwelling and garage is less than 3' (914)
- Fire-resistant protection not required at perpendicular walls.

Flame Spread and Smoke Density Requirements

§R302.9 contains the standards for flame spread and smoke density for wall and ceiling finishes. Note that these standards do not apply to floor finishes, only walls and ceilings. As clarified in the exception, the intent of the code is to regulate finishes that are applied to walls in thicknesses greater than wall paper and over areas larger than what would be considered "trim," such as baseboards, chair rails or handrails. Windows and doors and their frames are also exempted from the flame spread and smoke density requirements. This section can be considered to apply to items such as paneling and decorations larger than those pieces listed in the exception. Note that if foam trim is used then the limitations of §R316.5.9 and §R316.5.10 will apply.

The goal of the requirements in this section is to limit the spread of fire and limit the amount of dense smoke released by burning building materials. The tests to be applied are designed to measure how fast flames move across the surface of walls or ceilings and the density, but not the toxicity of the smoke generated. The tests do not look at the fuel load contributions of the materials, but rather at how the burning of the materials will impact the ability of occupants to safely leave a space during a fire. The code specifies ASTM E84 as the primary test criteria and allows the use of NFPA 286 as an alternate test method. Each of the methods is equally acceptable to verify the performance of materials against the specified criteria. The tests are quite different and it should be verified which test is used when materials are specified. The results are expressed in different metric terms and indicate different performance characteristics.

ASTM E84 is commonly called the "Steiner Tunnel Test." It measures the flame spread and smoke generation performance of materials applied to the wall or ceiling of the tunnel when exposed to a controlled heat source in relation to various materials. For flame-spread, Asbestos-cement board is assigned a value of zero. Red oak, a common wood, with a known density and moisture content, is assigned a flame-spread value of 100 to calibrate the furnace. Acceptable materials are not to exceed a flame-spread value of 200, which would mean that the flame front would move across the

surface of the tested material twice as fast as across the red oak specimen. Similar relative criteria are applied to measure smoke density in terms of obscuration which would impede occupants' ability to see escape routes in an emergency.

NFPA 286 is commonly known as the "room corner test." Here a fire of a specified size and type of material, using a crib of wood members, or a specified amount of propane or other flammable gas is set in the corner of a room of specified size. The performance of the materials, which are placed on the walls of the test furnace, is to be observed at two points as the fire grows in size and heat output. The first point is when the fire energy output is 40 kilowatts, which is to be observed for 5 minutes. The second test point is when the fire energy output is 160 kilowatts, which is to be observed for 10 minutes.

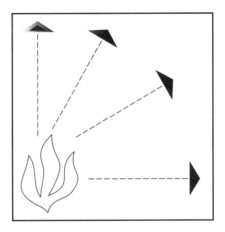

Flame Spread Index and Smoke Developed Index

§R302.10 contains the flame spread and smoke generation requirements for insulation materials other than foam plastics. The test criteria are ASTM E84 or UL 723. Where insulation materials, including membranes and faced insulation have a face that may be exposed to fire, the flame spread index of the material is not to exceed 25. The smoke-developed index is not to exceed 450. Where these materials are installed in concealed spaces, such as on top of ceiling finishes in attics, and the facing materials are thus in close contact on the unexposed side with materials such as gypsum board that form the ceiling, then the flame spread and smoke-developed criteria do not apply. The principal here is that the potentially flammable facings of the insulation are protected by the ceiling materials on one side and the insulation itself on the other.

Loose insulation, which may be spray applied or blown in as loose fill, has different criteria than batt or membrane insulations. If the material is not cellulose and cannot be attached to the top of the ASTM E84 tunnel then §R302.10.2 applies and the test methods are per federal standards from the Consumer Products Safety Commission.

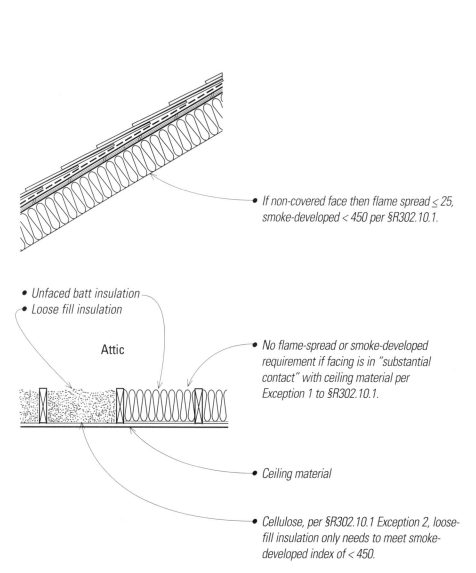

If non-covered face then flame spread $\leq$ 25, smoke-developed < 450 per §R302.10.1.

• *Unfaced batt insulation*
• *Loose fill insulation*

Attic

• *No flame-spread or smoke-developed requirement if facing is in "substantial contact" with ceiling material per Exception 1 to §R302.10.1.*

• *Ceiling material*

• *Cellulose, per §R302.10.1 Exception 2, loose-fill insulation only needs to meet smoke-developed index of < 450.*

Fireblocking

The requirements for fireblocking in combustible construction are listed in §R302.11. For code users familiar with the previous editions of the IRC, these provisions used to be contained in §R602.8 of the 2006 IRC. They were moved to Chapter 3 to be more generally applicable to all combustible construction, not just walls.

Fireblocking is defined as an approved material used to resist the free passage of flame through concealed spaces. Materials may be themselves of combustible construction of sufficient thickness to limit the passage of hot gases and flames from concealed spaces that would otherwise be interconnected, like where floor joist cavities intersect wall stud cavities. Fireblocking is to form an effective fire barrier between stories in a multi-story building. The words "fireblocking," "draftstops," and "firestops" are often used interchangeably in the construction industry. The International Residential Code does not define "Firestop" but refers to "through penetration firestops" to describe assemblies that resist the passage of heat or flame around such items as pipes penetrating wall membranes or fireblocking itself. "Draft Stop" is defined as an assembly used to prevent the movement of air within open spaces such as crawl spaces or attics. Draft stops are assemblies, that divide large concealed areas, such as attics into separate areas to prevent the spread of fire through these concealed spaces. We have tried to describe fireblocking consistently in our illustrations, but be aware that these assemblies may be referred to as "firestops" or "draft stops" in the field. Keep the word "blocking" in mind when visualizing the use of these assemblies. The purpose of fireblocking is to "block" the passage of fire and hot gases in concealed spaces, such as stud cavities.

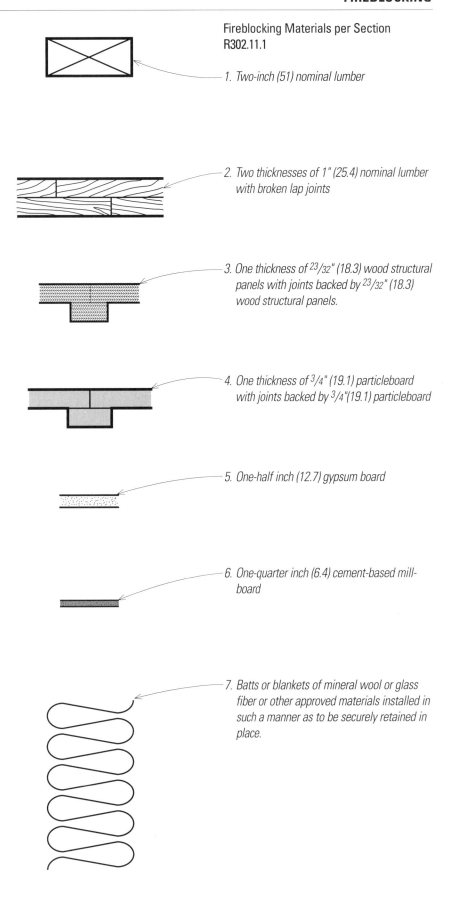

Fireblocking Materials per Section R302.11.1

1. Two-inch (51) nominal lumber

2. Two thicknesses of 1" (25.4) nominal lumber with broken lap joints

3. One thickness of $^{23}/_{32}$" (18.3) wood structural panels with joints backed by $^{23}/_{32}$ (18.3) wood structural panels.

4. One thickness of $^3/_4$" (19.1) particleboard with joints backed by $^3/_4$"(19.1) particleboard

5. One-half inch (12.7) gypsum board

6. One-quarter inch (6.4) cement-based millboard

7. Batts or blankets of mineral wool or glass fiber or other approved materials installed in such a manner as to be securely retained in place.

Fireblocking Locations

Fireblocking is to be installed in the locations illustrated at a typical platform-framed building. Similar requirements would apply to balloon-framed buildings.

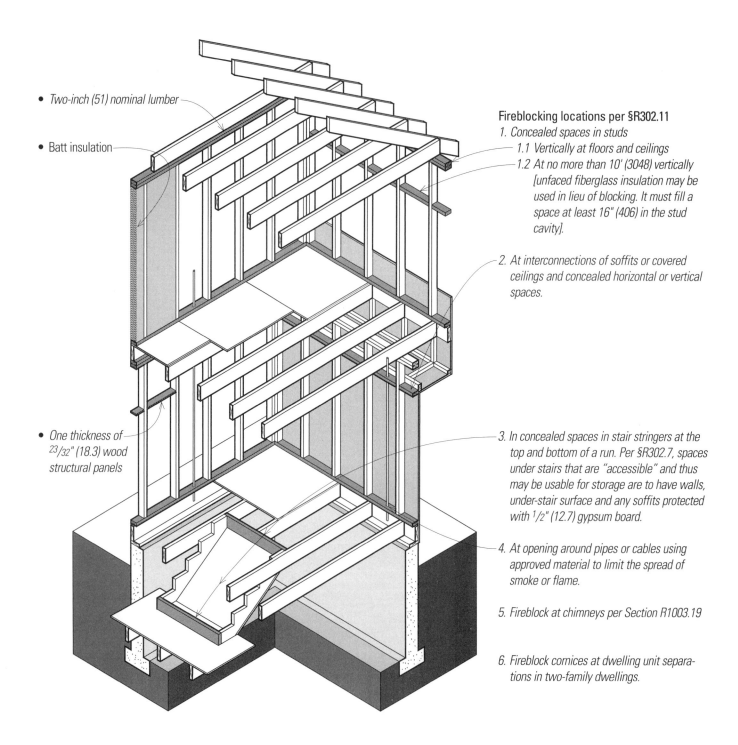

- *Two-inch (51) nominal lumber*
- Batt insulation
- *One thickness of 23/32" (18.3) wood structural panels*

Fireblocking locations per §R302.11

1. *Concealed spaces in studs*
   1.1 *Vertically at floors and ceilings*
   1.2 *At no more than 10' (3048) vertically [unfaced fiberglass insulation may be used in lieu of blocking. It must fill a space at least 16" (406) in the stud cavity].*

2. *At interconnections of soffits or covered ceilings and concealed horizontal or vertical spaces.*

3. *In concealed spaces in stair stringers at the top and bottom of a run. Per §R302.7, spaces under stairs that are "accessible" and thus may be usable for storage are to have walls, under-stair surface and any soffits protected with 1/2" (12.7) gypsum board.*

4. *At opening around pipes or cables using approved material to limit the spread of smoke or flame.*

5. *Fireblock at chimneys per Section R1003.19*

6. *Fireblock cornices at dwelling unit separations in two-family dwellings.*

Lighting, Ventilation and Heating Requirements

The requirements for glazing for natural light, ventilation for spaces and heating of occupied spaces are contained in §R303. The arrangements of rooms in relation to the exterior walls and in relationship to each other are specified. Ventilation requirements for operable windows may be replaced with mechanical ventilation systems.

Habitable Rooms, Adjoining Rooms and Bathroom Light and Ventilation

§R303.1 requires all habitable rooms—whether for sleeping or for any other uses—to have an aggregate glazing area of at least 8 percent of the floor area. Natural ventilation equal to one-half of that area (4 percent) is to be provided by operable windows, doors, louvers or approved openings. Typically the easiest way to meet these requirements is with windows with one half of their areas operable. Per Exception 1 to this section mechanical ventilation producing 0.35 air changes per hour in the room may be installed. A whole-house fan capable of supplying 15 cfm (78 L/s) per occupant, with two occupants for the first (master) bedroom and one occupant for each additional bedroom, may also be used. Per Exception 2, where mechanical ventilation is provided, artificial light may be used to provide light in lieu of glazing. Note that where emergency escape and rescue openings are required by §R310, mechanical ventilation cannot be substituted for the required operable rescue openings. See the discussion of §R310 for illustrations of those requirements. Sunroom additions and patio covers as defined in §R202 which cover openings into the rest of the dwelling can be used for natural ventilation if at least 40 percent of the exterior walls are open or are enclosed only by insect screening.

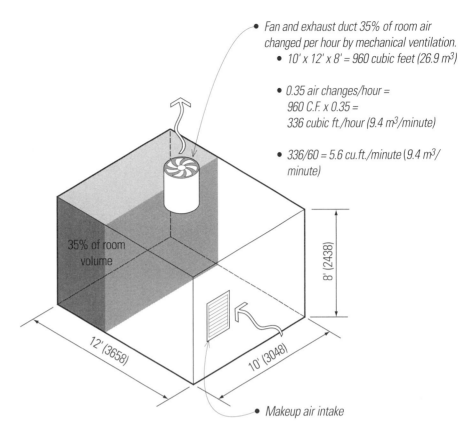

- Fan and exhaust duct 35% of room air changed per hour by mechanical ventilation.
  - 10' x 12' x 8' = 960 cubic feet (26.9 m³)
  - 0.35 air changes/hour = 960 C.F. x 0.35 = 336 cubic ft./hour (9.4 m³/minute)
  - 336/60 = 5.6 cu.ft./minute (9.4 m³/minute)

35% of room volume

8' (2438)

12' (3658)   10' (3048)

- Makeup air intake

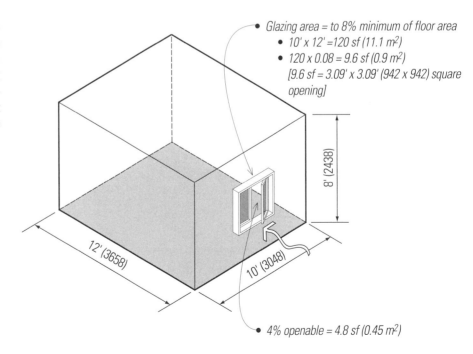

- Glazing area = to 8% minimum of floor area
  - 10' x 12' = 120 sf (11.1 m²)
  - 120 x 0.08 = 9.6 sf (0.9 m²) [9.6 sf = 3.09' x 3.09' (942 x 942) square opening]

8' (2438)

12' (3658)   10' (3048)

- 4% openable = 4.8 sf (0.45 m²)

Adjoining Rooms and Bathroom Light and Ventilation

Adjoining rooms are considered by §R303.2 to be those where at least one half of the area of the common wall between the two rooms is open and unobstructed, the opening is not less than 10 percent of the floor area of the interior room "borrowing" light and ventilation and the opening is not smaller than 25 sf (2.3 m²). Rooms adjoining sunrooms, which are usually added on to the exterior of a dwelling and are thus thermally isolated from the interior, are required to have openings of not less than 10 percent of the floor area of the interior room, but the opening need only be a minimum of 20 sf (2 m²) in area. There may be several rooms attached to the sunroom so the requirements for ventilations openings to the outdoors are to be based on the total floor area being ventilated.

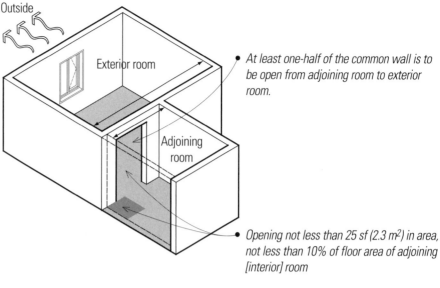

Outside

Exterior room

Adjoining room

- At least one-half of the common wall is to be open from adjoining room to exterior room.

- Opening not less than 25 sf (2.3 m²) in area, not less than 10% of floor area of adjoining [interior] room

Room 2

Room 1

- Opening in each room to be not less than 10% of floor area of the interior room and minimum 20 sf (2.0 m²) in area.
- Ventilation openings in sunroom to be based on total floor area being ventilated.

Per §R303.3 bathrooms and water closet compartments are to have glazing of at least 3 sf (0.3 m²) of which at least one-half must be openable. Per the Exception to this section, artificial ventilation and artificial light may be substituted for operable glazing if specified ventilation rates are met. Note that while the code specifies the level of artificial light in other rooms no light level is specified for bathrooms.

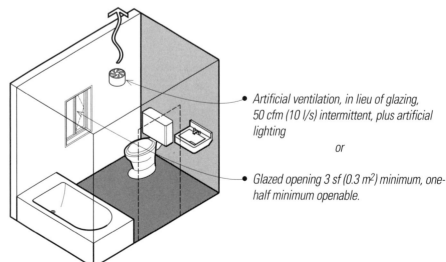

- Artificial ventilation, in lieu of glazing, 50 cfm (10 l/s) intermittent, plus artificial lighting

or

- Glazed opening 3 sf (0.3 m²) minimum, one-half minimum openable.

Location of Ventilation Openings

Openings for taking outside air into the dwelling or for exhausting interior air are to be located per §R303.4.1 and §R303.4.2. The requirements cover all openings that can bring air into the dwelling, whether by natural or mechanical means.

These requirements apply to such elements as doors, windows, soffit vents, combustion air inlets, or intakes for heating or cooling systems. The requirements are designed to maintain indoor air quality in the dwelling while recognizing the need to bring in outside air for combustion, makeup air, tempering conditioned air and natural ventilation. Contaminant sources are to be at least 10' (3048) away from air intakes. The code also recognizes that air contaminants are likely lighter than air so the code allows placement of air intakes 2' (610) below contaminant sources if the air intake must be located closer than 10' (3048) to a contaminant source. Exhaust air from kitchens, bathrooms and toilet rooms are not considered by the code to be hazardous or noxious. However, the code requires that exhaust openings be located to not create a nuisance. It requires that exhaust air not be directed at walkways, which could create discomfort to people on the walkway. The designer should also be aware of the proximity of other structures and prevailing wind conditions when locating both air exhausts and intakes.

Per §R303.5, openings that terminate outside are to be protected by the use of screens or small openings. This is primarily to protect against vermin getting into the building. These openings in the exterior wall are also to be protected against weather intrusion and are to meet the same opening protection criteria for fire-separation distance as for any other opening covered by §R302.1.

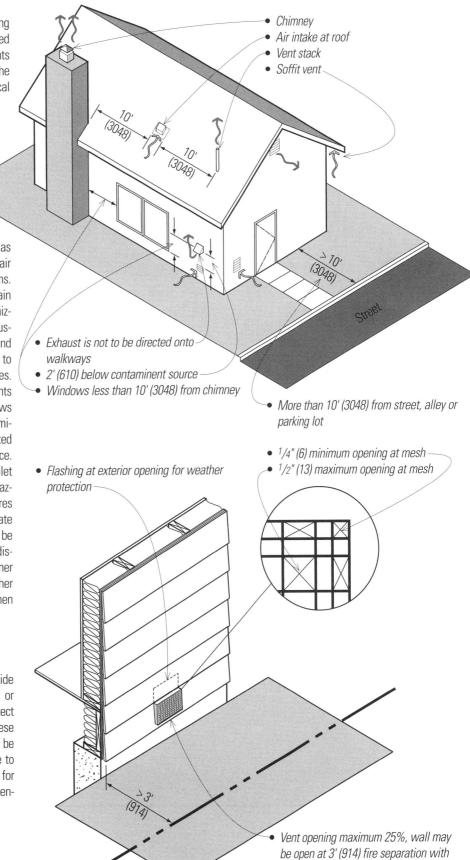

- Chimney
- Air intake at roof
- Vent stack
- Soffit vent

10' (3048)

10' (3048)

> 10' (3048)

Street

- Exhaust is not to be directed onto walkways
- 2' (610) below contaminent source
- Windows less than 10' (3048) from chimney
- More than 10' (3048) from street, alley or parking lot

- Flashing at exterior opening for weather protection

- 1/4" (6) minimum opening at mesh
- 1/2" (13) maximum opening at mesh

> 3' (914)

- Vent opening maximum 25%, wall may be open at 3' (914) fire separation with unprotected openings [per Table R302.1].

Stairway Lighting

Per §R303.6, stairs are to be illuminated with artificial illumination to allow safe movement on the stairs by residents at all times of the day or night. The illumination at interior stairs should provide a minimum of 1 foot-candle (11 lux) on the center of all of the treads and landings. For stairs with six or more risers, light switches are to be located at each end of the stairs per §R304.6.1. Exterior stairs must have an artificial light source near the top landing of the stairway. Per §R303.6.1, the lights for exterior stairs are to be controlled from inside the unit to illuminate the stair for people either leaving or to light up the entry stairs for people coming into the dwelling from outside. Exterior stairs that lead to basements from exterior grade level are to have illumination located in the immediate vicinity of the bottom landing of the stairway. We interpret this to be illumination in addition to that provided at the top landing of these stairs as is required for all exterior stairs. Per the Exception to R303.6.1, where lights are on continuously or where automatic controls are provided, the switch locations are not relevant as either interior or exterior stairs will be illuminated when in use in either of those conditions.

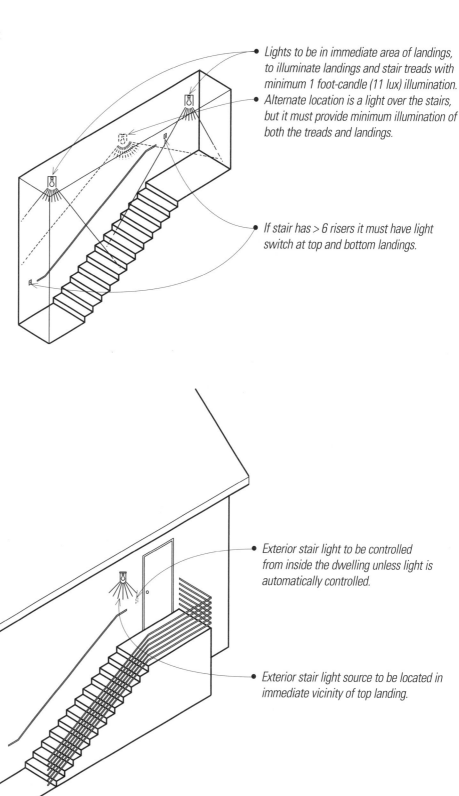

Lights to be in immediate area of landings, to illuminate landings and stair treads with minimum 1 foot-candle (11 lux) illumination.

Alternate location is a light over the stairs, but it must provide minimum illumination of both the treads and landings.

If stair has > 6 risers it must have light switch at top and bottom landings.

Exterior stair light to be controlled from inside the dwelling unless light is automatically controlled.

Exterior stair light source to be located in immediate vicinity of top landing.

Locations for Required Glazing Openings

Glazed openings required by the code for light or ventilation are to open directly onto a public way or to a yard or court as those are defined per §R303.7. However, these openings may open to roofed porches per §R303.7.1 if the porch abuts these exterior elements and also if the longest side of the porch is at least 65 percent open and the porch ceiling height is not less than 7' (2134). Sunrooms may also be used under similar conditions per §R303.7.2 if they abut the specified exterior elements, have at least 40 percent of all of the sunroom walls open or enclosed only by insect screening. The sunroom is also to be a minimum of 7' (2134) high.

- *Sunroom: 7' (2134) min. height*
- *All walls > 40% open or insect screening only*
- *Roofed porch: 7' (2134) min. roof height*
- *Longest side > 65% open*

Street

- *Fronting street, court or yard*

Required Heating

When the site-specific requirements contained in the locally adopted version of Table R301.2(1) specify a winter design temperature of less than 60°F (16°C), §R303.8 requires that heating be provided. These must be capable of maintaining a minimum room temperature of 68°F (20°C) at a point located 3' (914) above the floor and within 2' (610) of exterior walls when measured in all habitable rooms when exterior conditions are at the specified winter design temperature. While the type of permanent heating is not specified, the intent of the code is that the heating facilities be permanent, since the code forbids the use of portable space heaters to meet the requirements of this section.

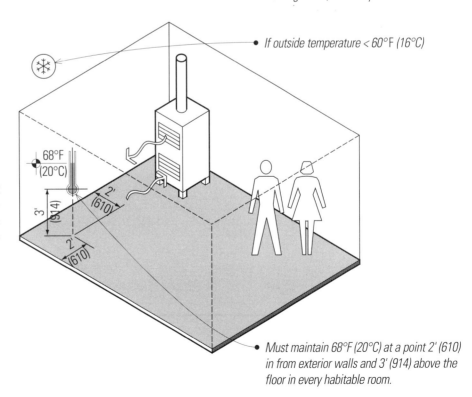

- *If outside temperature < 60°F (16°C)*

68°F (20°C)

2' (610)

3' (914)

2' (610)

- *Must maintain 68°F (20°C) at a point 2' (610) in from exterior walls and 3' (914) above the floor in every habitable room.*

Minimum Room Areas and Ceiling Heights

§R304 specifies minimum plan dimensions for habitable rooms. §R305 specifies the minimum ceiling heights for habitable rooms. The height requirements recognize sloping ceilings and specify different requirements depending on the use of the room, such as for kitchens or bathrooms. There is also a relationship between the height and area requirements for rooms with sloped ceilings that are below the minimum allowable height. Rooms may thus have sloping areas below the minimum heights, but those areas may not be counted as meeting the minimum area requirements for habitable space.

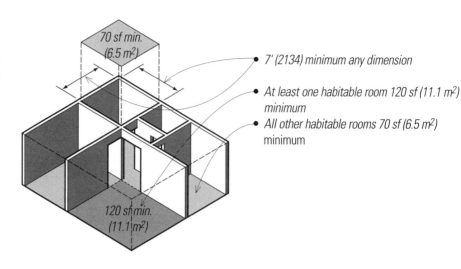

- *7' (2134) minimum any dimension*
- *At least one habitable room 120 sf (11.1 m²) minimum*
- *All other habitable rooms 70 sf (6.5 m²) minimum*

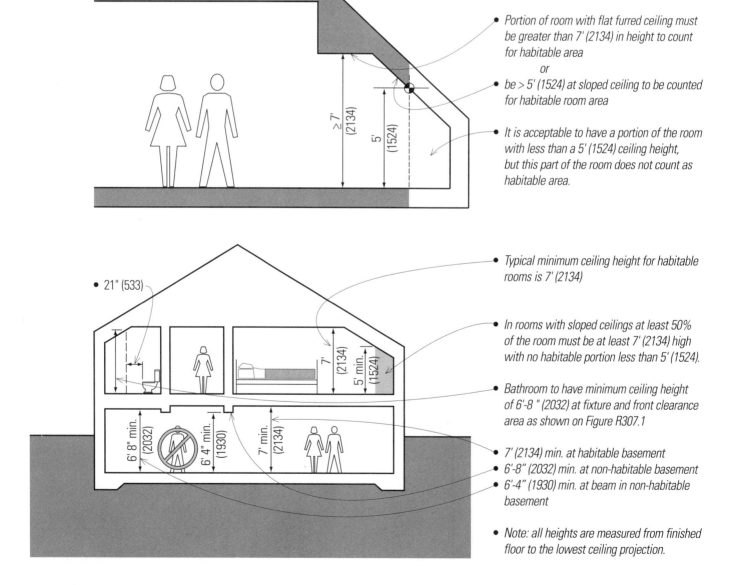

- *Portion of room with flat furred ceiling must be greater than 7' (2134) in height to count for habitable area*
  or
- *be > 5' (1524) at sloped ceiling to be counted for habitable room area*

- *It is acceptable to have a portion of the room with less than a 5' (1524) ceiling height, but this part of the room does not count as habitable area.*

- *Typical minimum ceiling height for habitable rooms is 7' (2134)*

- *In rooms with sloped ceilings at least 50% of the room must be at least 7' (2134) high with no habitable portion less than 5' (1524).*

- *Bathroom to have minimum ceiling height of 6'-8 " (2032) at fixture and front clearance area as shown on Figure R307.1*

- *7' (2134) min. at habitable basement*
- *6'-8" (2032) min. at non-habitable basement*
- *6'-4" (1930) min. at beam in non-habitable basement*

- *Note: all heights are measured from finished floor to the lowest ceiling projection.*

Kitchens, Baths and other Sanitary Facilities

Per §R306.1 every dwelling unit, which per the intent of the definition in §R202, provides independent living facilities for one or more persons, is to have its own bathroom facilities, cooking facilities, sewage disposal and water supply with hot water, as indicated in the illustration. The plumbing fixtures are to be provided with space around them to allow safe use as shown in Figure R307.1, as illustrated on page 70.

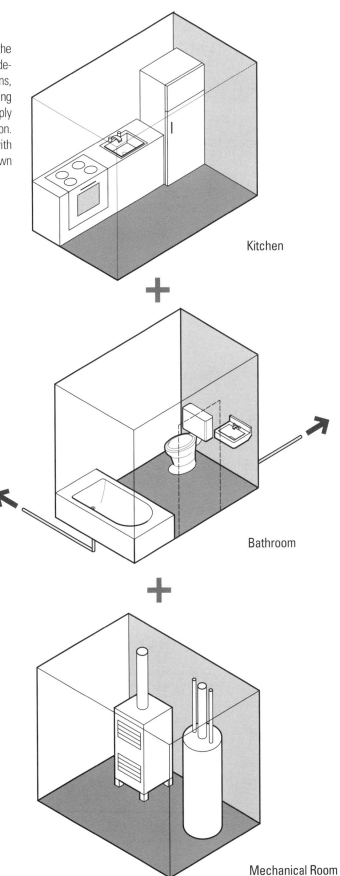

Kitchen

Bathroom

Mechanical Room

Kitchens, Baths and other Sanitary Facilities

The plumbing fixtures are to be provided with space around them to allow safe use as shown in Figure R307.1, which is illustrated here. Note that the requirements for having non-absorbent surfaces for bathroom floors with tubs or showers are contained in §R307.2 where they may not be readily found by designers. The requirements of this section are shown on the illustration as well.

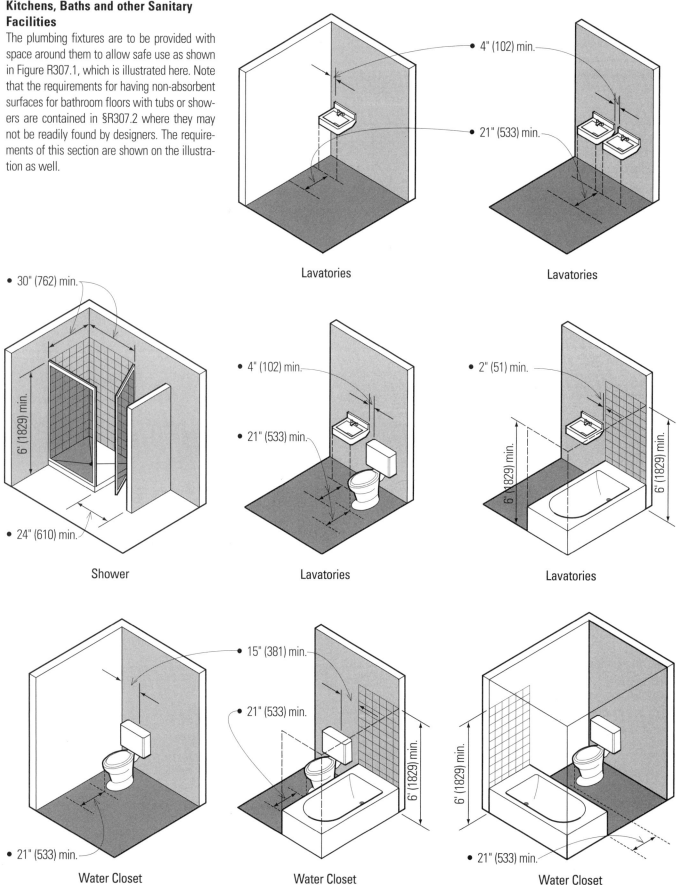

Lavatories

Lavatories

Shower

Lavatories

Lavatories

Water Closet

Water Closet

Water Closet

Glazing in Hazardous Locations

In areas where glazing may be subject to human impact §R308 requires the use of safety glazing to protect against injuries if someone walks or falls against the glazing materials. Safety glazing is to meet the standards for human impact contained in the Consumer Product Safety Commission standards published as CPSC 16 CFR (Code of Federal Regulations), Part 1201, or ANSI Z97.1. There are two sets of criteria in the CPSC Standard, designated as "Category I" and "Category II." Per the standards, the distinction between these two categories is determined primarily by pane size. Installations with pane sizes of 9 sf (0.836 m²) or less in size are generally Category I and those with pane sizes in excess of 9 sf (0.836 m²) are in Category II. See Table R308.3.1(1) for the code categories for the CPSC and Table R308.3.1(2) for ANSI Z97.1.

There are many types of safety glazing. Per the CPSC Standard, "glazing" in this context basically means glass in various forms. It does not include plastics, although plastics may be acceptable to the AHJ in some of the hazardous locations noted below. Examples of safety glazing include:

Tempered glass, which is glass that is heat or chemically treated after fabrication to make it resistant to breaking, Tempered glass cannot be cut after tempering, this will cause it to shatter. When tempered glass is shattered it breaks into small nuggets of glass, which while they may have sharp edges do not form shards of glass that are like knives. The breakage pattern of tempered glass can be noted when the side window of an automobile breaks into popcorn-size pieces of glass.

Laminated glass is made up of two layers of glass that are bonded to a plastic inner layer. When laminated glass breaks the inner layer keeps the broken pieces of glass together, creating a distinctive "spider-web" pattern often seen in broken automobile windshields, which are made of laminated glass.

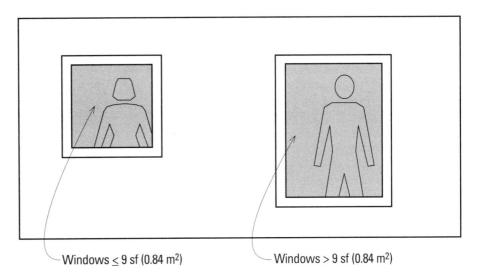

Windows ≤ 9 sf (0.84 m²)   Windows > 9 sf (0.84 m²)

Glazing Classification Categories

CPSC 16 CFR 1201	ANSI Z97.1		CPSC 16 CFR 1201	ANSI Z97.1
Storm doors-I	–		Storm doors-II	–
Doors-I	–		Doors-II	–
Item 7, R308.4-NR	NR		Item 7, R308.4-II	A
Item 6, R308.4-I	B		Item 6, R308.4-II	A
Item 5, R308.4-II	A		Item 5, R308.4-II	A
Sliding doors-II	–		Sliding doors-II	–

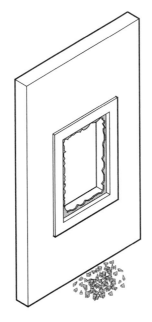

Tempered glass
breakage pattern

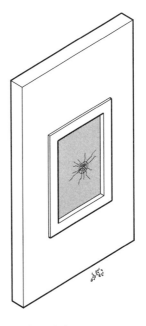

Laminated glass
breakage pattern

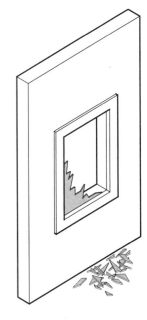

Annealed glass
breakage pattern

Glazing in Hazardous Locations

Glazing located in hazardous locations as defined in §R308.4 is to have designations applied by the manufacturer to allow identification of these special glazing materials during field inspections. These designations are typically applied by the manufacturer in such a way that they are a permanent part of the glazing, such as by laser etching, embossing or sandblasting. Removable labels are acceptable, as long as they cannot be removed without destroying them. This is to prevent transferring the designations to glass that does not meet the standards. For other than tempered glass, affidavits may be acceptable to the building official per Exception 1 to §R308.1. Multipane assemblies with glazing lites of less than 1 sf (0.09 m^2) in size may be marked in one panel, but all panes must be marked with at least a "16 CFR 1201" designation.

Louvered windows or jalousies have unsupported edges. §R308.2 requires individual panes in this type of window to be at least 3/16" (5) in thickness and have a span no longer than 48" (1210). Also, §R308.2.1 forbids the use of wire glass in such windows as there is no trim to protect against the rough edge of the wire glass.

Hazardous Locations

Table R308.3 lists the required glazing classifications based on their locations. The table subdivides the conditions based on the exposed surface area of the face of each glazing lite. Thus the standard should be applied to conditions either on the inside or outside of the glazing. A walkway alongside a dwelling may make the glazing susceptible to human impact, as could interior conditions. The table subdivides the exposed surface requirements between lite sized of 9 sf (0.836 m^2) or less and more than 9 sf (0.836 m^2) in face surface area. This is because smaller lites will be somewhat less hazardous to a person who might break the lite by running into it than would a larger pane of glazing.

§R308.4 lists eleven specific conditions that are considered to be hazardous locations for glazing purposes. See the illustrations on pages 72–74 for details.

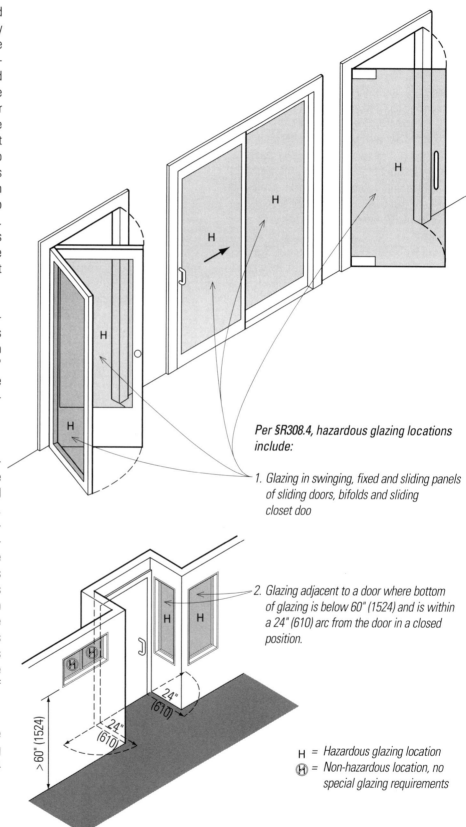

Per §R308.4, hazardous glazing locations include:

1. Glazing in swinging, fixed and sliding panels of sliding doors, bifolds and sliding closet doo

2. Glazing adjacent to a door where bottom of glazing is below 60" (1524) and is within a 24" (610) arc from the door in a closed position.

H = Hazardous glazing location
Ⓗ = Non-hazardous location, no special glazing requirements

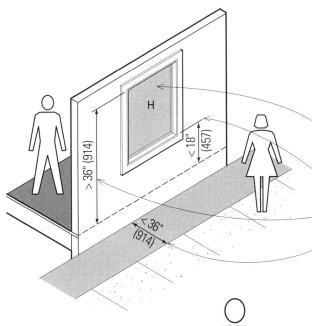

Hazardous glazing locations include:

Individual fixed <u>or</u> operable glazing panel
3. Hazardous glazing location occurs if <u>all</u> of the conditions in 3.1–3.4 are met

3.1 Exposed area of individual pane is > 9 sf (0.84 m²).

3.2 Bottom edge of pane is < 18" (457) above floor

3.3 Top edge of pane is > 36" (914) above floor.

3.4 One or more interior or exterior walking surfaces is < 36" (914) from glazing.

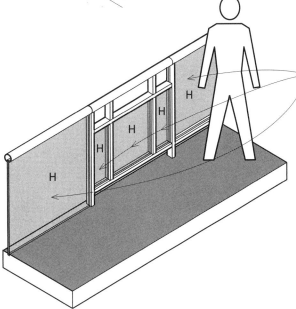

4. All glazing in railings regardless of area or height above walking surface, including structural balustrades and infill panels.

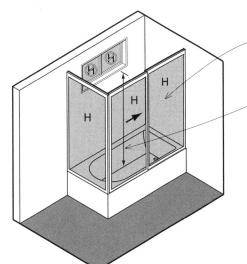

5. Glazing at bathing facilities such as bathtubs, showers, hot tubs, sauna, etc.

• Dimension to standing surface in the tub > 60" (1524),

H = Hazardous glazing location
Ⓗ = Non-hazardous location, no special glazing requirements

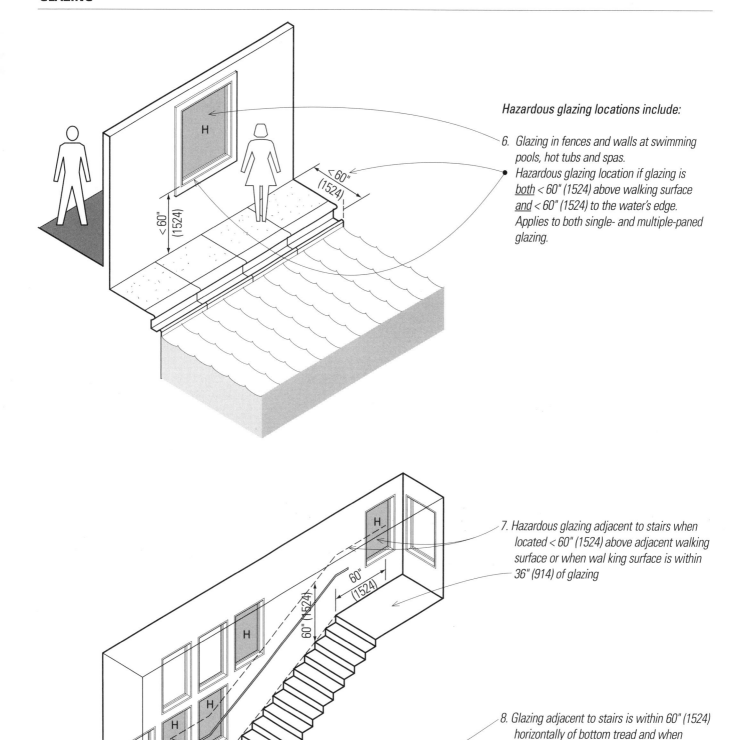

Hazardous glazing locations include:

6. Glazing in fences and walls at swimming pools, hot tubs and spas.
    Hazardous glazing location if glazing is <u>both</u> < 60" (1524) above walking surface <u>and</u> < 60" (1524) to the water's edge. Applies to both single- and multiple-paned glazing.

7. Hazardous glazing adjacent to stairs when located < 60" (1524) above adjacent walking surface or when wal king surface is within 36" (914) of glazing

8. Glazing adjacent to stairs is within 60" (1524) horizontally of bottom tread and when exposed surface of glazing is less than 60" (1524) above nose of the tread.

H = *Hazardous glazing location*
Ⓗ = *Non-hazardous location, no special glazing requirements*

Hazardous Glazing Exceptions

There are numerous exceptions to the requirements contained in §R308.4. Some of the exceptions are related to protection of the glazing from human impact. Some are related to the use of decorative glazing, which is exempted from the CPSC standards. Most decorative glazing is not clear and is thus readily visible. It is also often assembled in small pieces, such as stained glass or "dale" glazing, which is made up of glass embedded in a mortar matrix. Exceptions are also included for very small glazing panels and for louvered and jalousie windows. See the illustration for details.

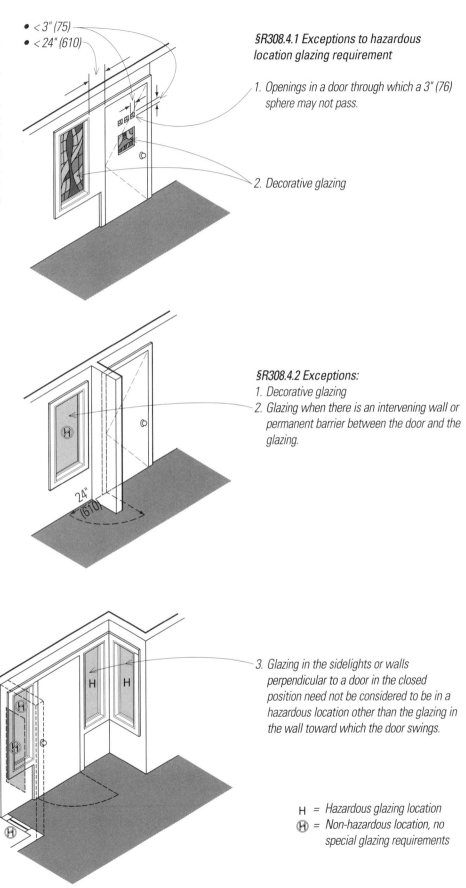

- < 3" (75)
- < 24" (610)

§R308.4.1 Exceptions to hazardous location glazing requirement

1. *Openings in a door through which a 3" (76) sphere may not pass.*

2. *Decorative glazing*

§R308.4.2 Exceptions:
1. *Decorative glazing*
2. *Glazing when there is an intervening wall or permanent barrier between the door and the glazing.*

24" (610)

3. *Glazing in the sidelights or walls perpendicular to a door in the closed position need not be considered to be in a hazardous location other than the glazing in the wall toward which the door swings.*

H = *Hazardous glazing location*
Ⓗ = *Non-hazardous location, no special glazing requirements*

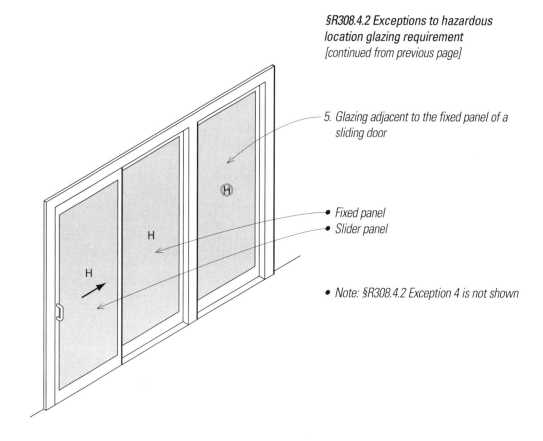

§R308.4.2 Exceptions to hazardous location glazing requirement
[continued from previous page]

5. Glazing adjacent to the fixed panel of a sliding door

• Fixed panel
• Slider panel

• Note: §R308.4.2 Exception 4 is not shown

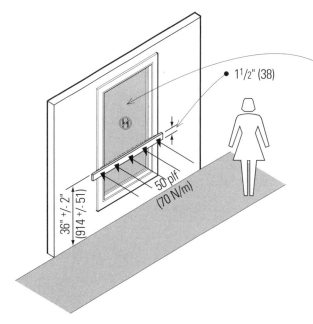

§R308.4.3 Exceptions to hazardous location glazing requirement

2. Glazing meeting all criteria of §R308.4.7 and §R308.4.10 are not considered as hazardous locations when a bar not less than $1^1/_2$" (38) in height is located on the accessible side 36" +/- 2" (914 +/- 51) above the floor. The bar is to be capable of withstanding a horizontal load of 50 pounds per linear foot (70 N/m) without deflecting enough to contact the glazing.

• Note: §R308.4.3 Exceptions 1 and 3 are not shown

H = Hazardous glazing location
Ⓗ = Non-hazardous location, no special glazing requirements

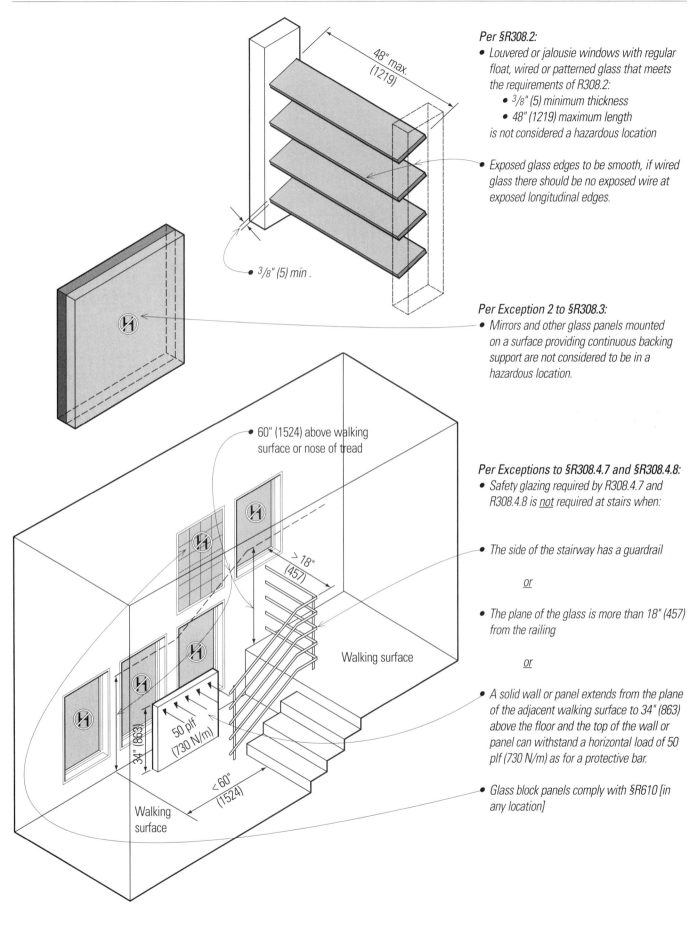

Per §R308.2:

- *Louvered or jalousie windows with regular float, wired or patterned glass that meets the requirements of R308.2:*
  - *3/8" (5) minimum thickness*
  - *48" (1219) maximum length*
  is not considered a hazardous location

- *Exposed glass edges to be smooth, if wired glass there should be no exposed wire at exposed longitudinal edges.*

48" max. (1219)

3/8" (5) min.

Per Exception 2 to §R308.3:

- *Mirrors and other glass panels mounted on a surface providing continuous backing support are not considered to be in a hazardous location.*

60" (1524) above walking surface or nose of tread

> 18" (457)

Walking surface

50 plf (730 N/m)

34" (863)

< 60" (1524)

Walking surface

Per Exceptions to §R308.4.7 and §R308.4.8:

- *Safety glazing required by R308.4.7 and R308.4.8 is not required at stairs when:*

- *The side of the stairway has a guardrail*

  or

- *The plane of the glass is more than 18" (457) from the railing*

  or

- *A solid wall or panel extends from the plane of the adjacent walking surface to 34" (863) above the floor and the top of the wall or panel can withstand a horizontal load of 50 plf (730 N/m) as for a protective bar.*

- *Glass block panels comply with §R610 [in any location]*

Skylights and Sloped Glazing

Skylights and sloped glazing are defined as glazing installed at an angle of more than 15 degrees (0.26 rad) from vertical. Because sloped glazing could endanger people below if it breaks, raining shards of material down on them, the code specifies measures to mitigate the effects if the glazing shatters. The code either requires the glazing to remain in place if broken, be caught by screens under the glazing or that the glazing areas of each pane of material be limited. Screens and their fasteners are to be designed to hold up to twice the weight of the glazing and be of a mesh size not larger than 1" by 1" (25 x 25). Screens are not often used in practice. Most skylights and sloped glazing either use materials that do not require screens or subdivide the glazing panels into code-compliant areas. See the illustration for details. Per §R308.6.7, glazing materials for greenhouses may be any installed without screens if the greenhouse ridge is lower than 20 ' (6096) above grade.

Skylights that are installed in roofs with a pitch less than 3 in 12 (25 percent slope) are to be mounted on curbs that place the skylight at least 4" (102) above the surface of the roof. The curb may be lower if the manufacturer's installation instructions specifically allow a lower curb.

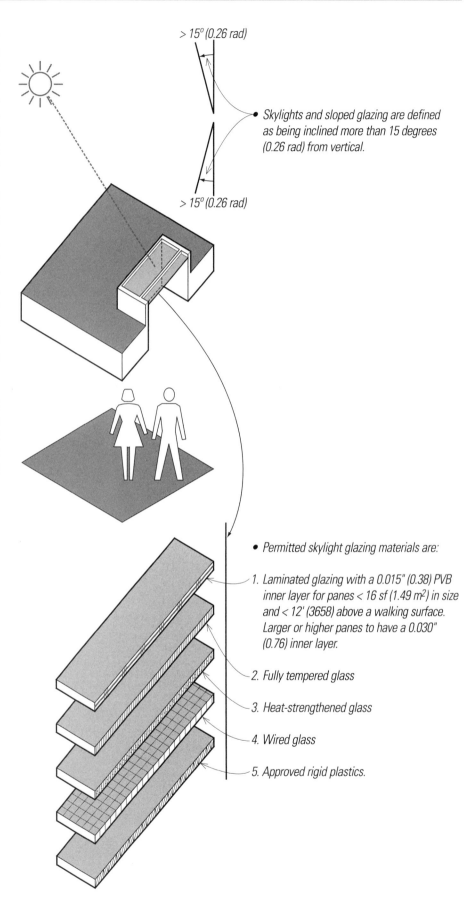

> 15° (0.26 rad)

> 15° (0.26 rad)

• Skylights and sloped glazing are defined as being inclined more than 15 degrees (0.26 rad) from vertical.

• Permitted skylight glazing materials are:

1. Laminated glazing with a 0.015" (0.38) PVB inner layer for panes < 16 sf (1.49 m²) in size and < 12' (3658) above a walking surface. Larger or higher panes to have a 0.030" (0.76) inner layer.

2. Fully tempered glass

3. Heat-strengthened glass

4. Wired glass

5. Approved rigid plastics.

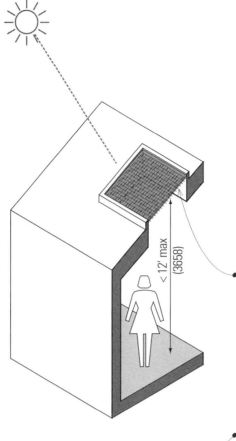

• 1" x 1" (25 x 25) screen required unless fully tempered glass is used in the inner pane of multiple glazing or in single glazing and glazing area is < 16 sf (1.49 m^2) and the highest point of glazing is < 12' (3658) above a walking surface—glazing $3/16$" (4.8) thickness

or

• Glass area may be > 16 sf (1.49 m^2) if glazing slope is < 30° (0.52 rad) from vertical and the highest point of glazing is < 10' (3048) above the walking surface.

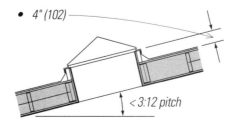

• Unit skylights in roofs with less than 3:12 pitch are to have curb at least 4" (102) above the plane of the roof.

GARAGES AND CARPORTS

Per §R309, garage floors are to be of noncombustible materials. They are to be sloped to facilitate drainage of liquids to a drain, or out the main vehicle entry door. Carports are to be open on at least two sides. Carport flooring material requirements are the same as for garages, including those for drainage slopes. Asphalt flooring surfaces are permitted for carports, but not for garages. If they do not meet the requirements for carports the structure is to be treated as a garage.

Garages located in flood hazard areas are to be elevated above the design flood plain elevation established for the project site in Table R301.2(1) or they may be located below the design flood plain elevation if they are at site grade, used solely for parking, building access or storage and meet the requirements of §R322 for flood-resistant construction. See the discussion about both dwelling and garage requirements later in this chapter.

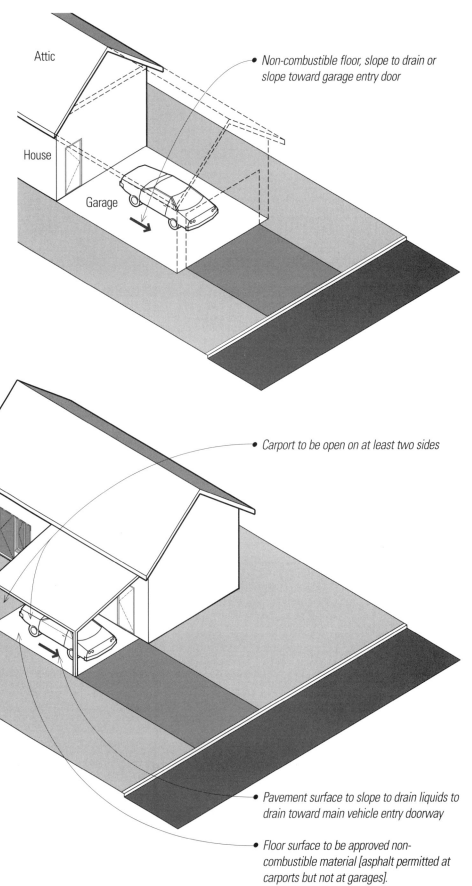

Attic

House

Garage

• *Non-combustible floor, slope to drain or slope toward garage entry door*

• *Carport to be open on at least two sides*

• *Pavement surface to slope to drain liquids to drain toward main vehicle entry doorway*

• *Floor surface to be approved non-combustible material [asphalt permitted at carports but not at garages].*

Emergency Escape and Rescue Openings

Basement rooms and every sleeping room on any level are to have a least one operable emergency and rescue window. These windows are to open directly to a public street, public alley, yard, or court. If there are sleeping rooms in the basement the emergency escape and rescue openings are to be in those sleeping rooms. Additional openings are not required in other rooms in the basement. See the illustration for the dimensions of rescue openings and window wells.

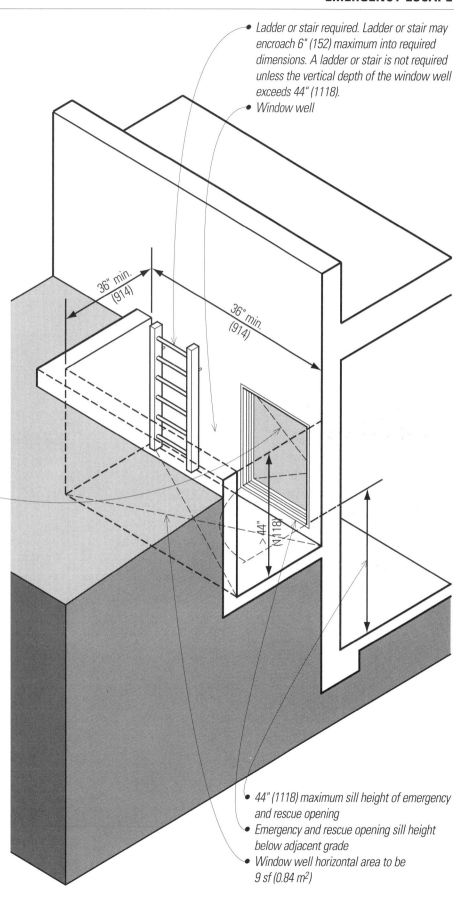

- Ladder or stair required. Ladder or stair may encroach 6" (152) maximum into required dimensions. A ladder or stair is not required unless the vertical depth of the window well exceeds 44" (1118).
- Window well

36" min. (914)

36" min. (914)

> 44" (1118)

- Window well must be of sufficient size to allow emergency and rescue openings to fully open.

- 44" (1118) maximum sill height of emergency and rescue opening
- Emergency and rescue opening sill height below adjacent grade
- Window well horizontal area to be 9 sf (0.84 m²)

Emergency Escape and Rescue Openings

Bars, grilles, covers and screens may be placed over rescue windows as long as they are releasable or removable from the inside without the use of a key, tool, special knowledge or force. When open, the bars are to provide the minimum clearances required in §R310.1.1 and §R310.1.3 for minimum areas and opening dimensions. These rescue windows may be installed under decks and porches, provided the location of the deck in relation to the opening allows the window to be fully opened and provide a path not less than 36" (914) in height to a yard or court.

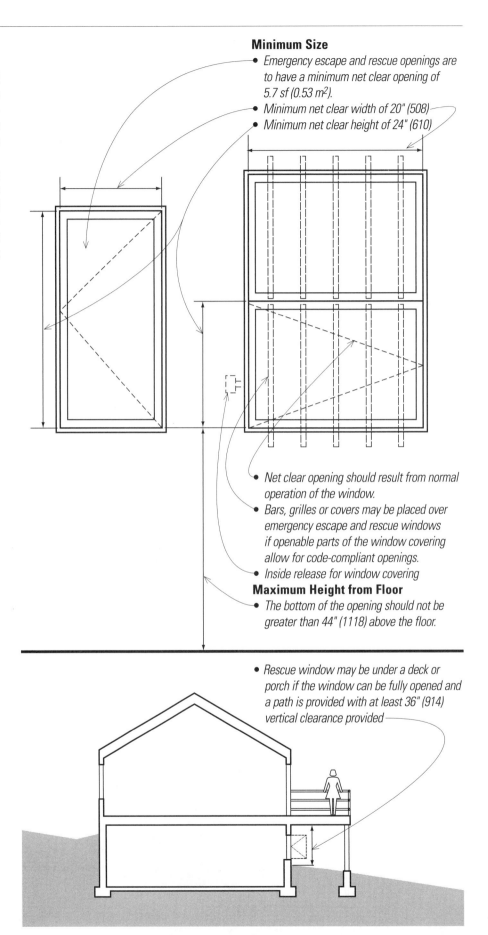

Minimum Size
- Emergency escape and rescue openings are to have a minimum net clear opening of 5.7 sf (0.53 m²).
- Minimum net clear width of 20" (508)
- Minimum net clear height of 24" (610)

- Net clear opening should result from normal operation of the window.
- Bars, grilles or covers may be placed over emergency escape and rescue windows if openable parts of the window covering allow for code-compliant openings.
- Inside release for window covering

Maximum Height from Floor
- The bottom of the opening should not be greater than 44" (1118) above the floor.

- Rescue window may be under a deck or porch if the window can be fully opened and a path is provided with at least 36" (914) vertical clearance provided

Means of Egress

The provisions of §R311 for means of egress apply to all parts of the means of egress: stairways, ramps, exterior egress balconies, hallways and doors. Enclosed space under stairs which is accessible is to be protected with 1/2" (13) gypsum board.

The minimum width of hallways is to be at least 3' (914). At least one side-hinged exit door with a minimum clear width of 32" (813) and 6'-8" (2032) in height is to be provided for each dwelling unit. The path of egress from this door is not to travel through a garage. Other doors in the dwelling are not required to comply with the dimensional requirements for egress doors. There is to be a floor or landing on each side of each exterior door. The floor or landing is to not be more than 1 1/2" (38) lower than the top of the door threshold. The landing is permitted to have a slope not to exceed 1/4" per foot (2%) horizontal slope. See the illustrations for door conditions and exceptions to those requirements.

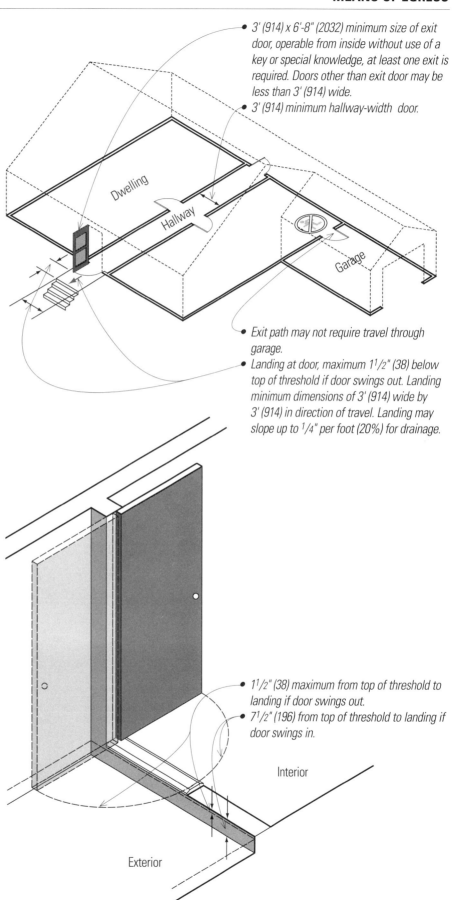

- 3' (914) x 6'-8" (2032) minimum size of exit door, operable from inside without use of a key or special knowledge, at least one exit is required. Doors other than exit door may be less than 3' (914) wide.
- 3' (914) minimum hallway-width door.

Dwelling

Hallway

Garage

- Exit path may not require travel through garage.
- Landing at door, maximum 1 1/2" (38) below top of threshold if door swings out. Landing minimum dimensions of 3' (914) wide by 3' (914) in direction of travel. Landing may slope up to 1/4" per foot (20%) for drainage.

- 1 1/2" (38) maximum from top of threshold to landing if door swings out.
- 7 1/2" (196) from top of threshold to landing if door swings in.

Interior

Exterior

Means of Egress

Stairways are to be at least 36" (914) in width at all points above the handrail height. Handrails may not project more than 4$\frac{1}{2}$" (114) on either side of the stairway into the required stair width. Stairs are to have a minimum clear height of 6'-8" (2036) measured vertically from a sloped plane adjoining the tread nosing or above the flat surfaces at landings. Stair risers are to no more than 7$\frac{3}{4}$" (196). Stair treads are to be 10" (254) minimum depth. See the illustrations for how the measurements are to be taken and for stair tread profiles.

There is to be a floor or landing at the top and bottom of each stairway. Treads and risers are not to vary too much in a flight of stairs and may vary in length or height no more than $\frac{3}{8}$" from the maximum height or length in a flight of stairs.

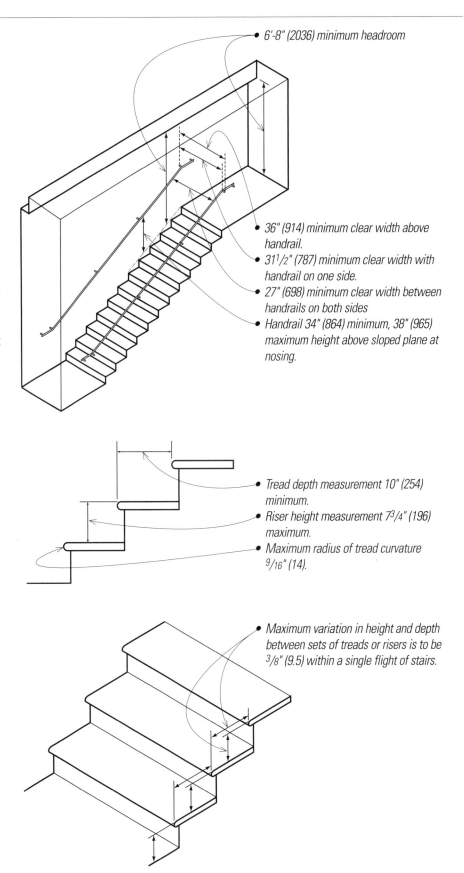

- *6'-8" (2036) minimum headroom*

- *36" (914) minimum clear width above handrail.*
- *31$\frac{1}{2}$" (787) minimum clear width with handrail on one side.*
- *27" (698) minimum clear width between handrails on both sides*
- *Handrail 34" (864) minimum, 38" (965) maximum height above sloped plane at nosing.*

- *Tread depth measurement 10" (254) minimum.*
- *Riser height measurement 7$\frac{3}{4}$" (196) maximum.*
- *Maximum radius of tread curvature $\frac{9}{16}$" (14).*

- *Maximum variation in height and depth between sets of treads or risers is to be $\frac{3}{8}$" (9.5) within a single flight of stairs.*

Means of Egress

Winder treads are to have dimensions as illustrated. Stair nosings are to be as illustrated. Open risers are allowed, but there must be material closing the area between risers so that a foot or a child will not get caught in them. Thus the materials in this area must not allow passage of a 4" (102) diameter sphere. This is the same spacing requirement as for guards. However there is an exception to §R312.2 that allows spacing of guard elements located along the side of a stair to be $4^3/_8$" (107). This may be useful in coordinating vertical picket spacing with tread and riser proportions.

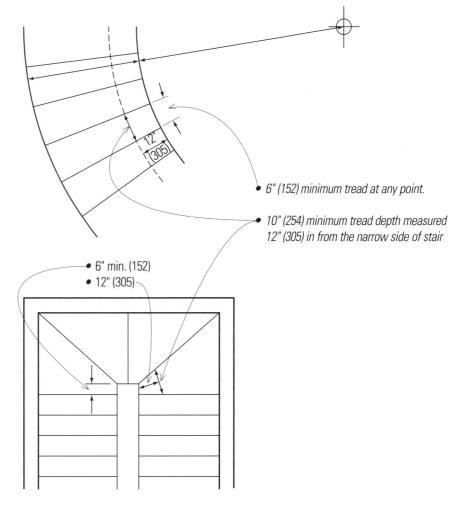

6" (152) minimum tread at any point.

10" (254) minimum tread depth measured 12" (305) in from the narrow side of stair

6" min. (152)
12" (305)

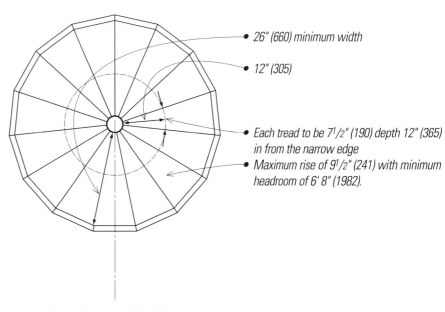

26" (660) minimum width

12" (305)

Each tread to be $7^1/_2$" (190) depth 12" (365) in from the narrow edge
Maximum rise of $9^1/_2$" (241) with minimum headroom of 6' 8" (1982).

Spiral Stairway, §R311.7.9.1

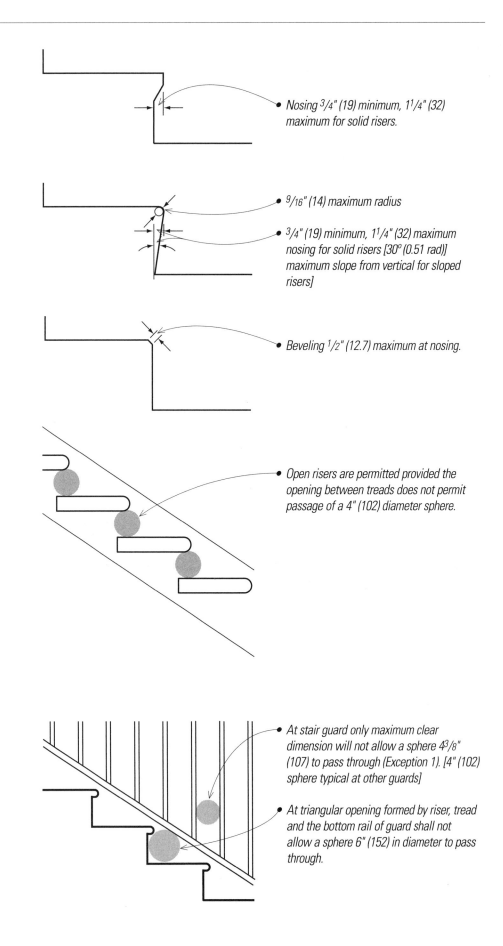

- Nosing ³/4" (19) minimum, 1¹/4" (32) maximum for solid risers.

- ⁹/16" (14) maximum radius

- ³/4" (19) minimum, 1¹/4" (32) maximum nosing for solid risers [30° (0.51 rad)] maximum slope from vertical for sloped risers]

- Beveling ¹/2" (12.7) maximum at nosing.

- Open risers are permitted provided the opening between treads does not permit passage of a 4" (102) diameter sphere.

- At stair guard only maximum clear dimension will not allow a sphere 4³/8" (107) to pass through (Exception 1). [4" (102) sphere typical at other guards]

- At triangular opening formed by riser, tread and the bottom rail of guard shall not allow a sphere 6" (152) in diameter to pass through.

Means of Egress

A floor or landing is not required at the top of an interior flight of stairs provided a door does not swing over the stairs. A flight of stairs must have an intermediate landing for a vertical rise of more than 12" (3658). The width of a landing is not to be less than the width of the stair served. Thus stair landings are to be square in plan as a minimum dimension. Landings may not have a slope in excess of $1/4$" per foot (2%).

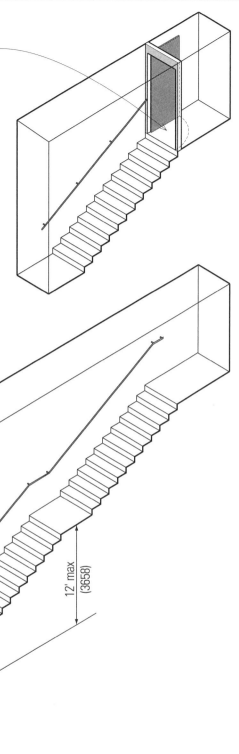

12' max (3658)

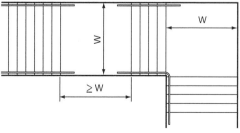

W

W

≥ W

Means of Egress

Handrails at stairs are to be provided on at least one side of any stair with four or more risers. The handrail for stairs or ramps is to be not less than 34" (864) or more than 38" (965) measured vertically from a plane adjoining the stair tread nosings or the ramp surface. Stair handrails are to be continuous for the full length of each flight of stairs. They are to extend from at least a point directly above the top riser in the flight and a point directly above the lowest riser in the flight. The rails are to be returned to the wall or terminate in newel posts or in safety terminals to protect stair users from impacting the unprotected ends of the rail. A newel post may be used at the turn in a stair that switches back and a decorative element such as a volute, turnout, or starting easing may be used at the lowest tread in a flight of stairs.

The rail is to have a handgrip clearance of 1¹/₂" (38) between adjacent walls and the handrail. Stair handrails are a safety feature for stairs, allowing occupants to maintain stability in using them. Therefore the handrails are to be graspable. Various configurations are allowed, divided into regular-shaped Type I rails, and irregular-shaped Type II rails.

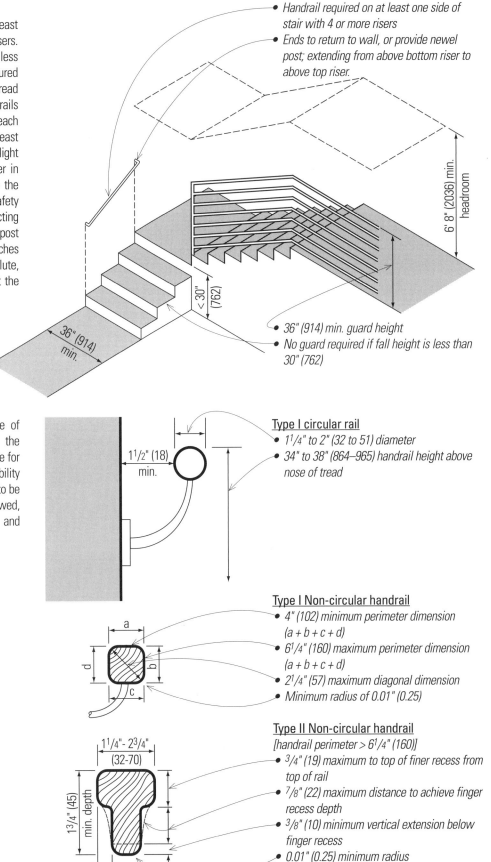

- Handrail required on at least one side of stair with 4 or more risers
- Ends to return to wall, or provide newel post; extending from above bottom riser to above top riser.

6' 8" (2036) min. headroom

< 30" (762)

36" (914) min.

- 36" (914) min. guard height
- No guard required if fall height is less than 30" (762)

1¹/₂" (18) min.

Type I circular rail
- 1¹/₄" to 2" (32 to 51) diameter
- 34" to 38" (864–965) handrail height above nose of tread

Type I Non-circular handrail
- 4" (102) minimum perimeter dimension (a + b + c + d)
- 6¹/₄" (160) maximum perimeter dimension (a + b + c + d)
- 2¹/₄" (57) maximum diagonal dimension
- Minimum radius of 0.01" (0.25)

Type II Non-circular handrail
[handrail perimeter > 6¹/₄" (160)]
- ³/₄" (19) maximum to top of finer recess from top of rail
- ⁷/₈" (22) maximum distance to achieve finger recess depth
- ³/₈" (10) minimum vertical extension below finger recess
- 0.01" (0.25) minimum radius
- ⁵/₁₆" (8) graspable finger recess [both sides]

1¹/₄" - 2³/₄" (32-70)

1³/₄" (45) min. depth

Means of Egress

The code makes allowances for special stairways. Spiral stairs are permitted if they meet the minimum width and provide the necessary tread depth at the specified locations. The spiral is to be constructed so as to allow a minimum of 6'-6" (1981) headroom while on the stairs.

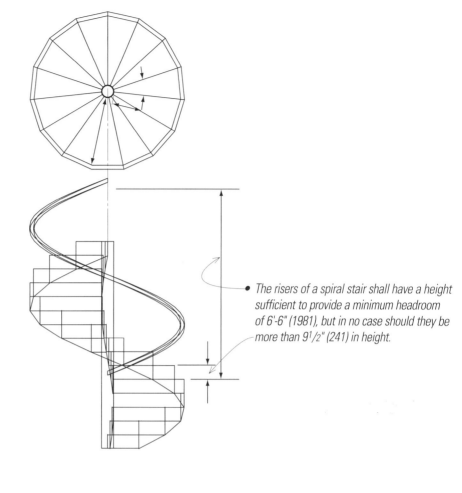

- The risers of a spiral stair shall have a height sufficient to provide a minimum headroom of 6'-6" (1981), but in no case should they be more than 9$^1/_2$" (241) in height.

The code also permits the use of "bulkhead enclosure stairs," as illustrated, to allow access into a basement from the building exterior. These stairs are not to be considered part of the means of egress. Even if the basement is of habitable dimensions, other means of egress for the basement would be required. The stair is to have a bulkhead enclosure with hinged doors or other approved coverings to protect against persons falling into the stairwell inadvertently.

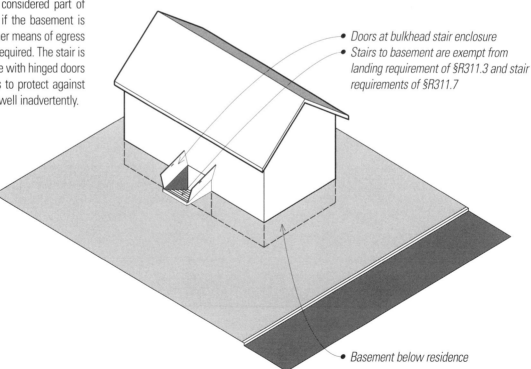

- Doors at bulkhead stair enclosure
- Stairs to basement are exempt from landing requirement of §R311.3 and stair requirements of §R311.7

- Basement below residence

Means of Egress

Ramps are to have a maximum slope of one unit vertical in twelve units horizontal (8.33% slope) except that if site constraints make such slope technically infeasible, a slope of 1:8 (12.5%) may be used. Ramps are to have 3' x 3' (914 x 914) landings at the top and bottom of the ramp, at changes in direction or at any point where a door opens onto the ramp. The door landing is required no matter which way the door swings. We recommend that the door not swing over the ramp whenever possible. Ramps are to have at least one handrail, with configurations, continuity and height requirements the same as for stairs as described above.

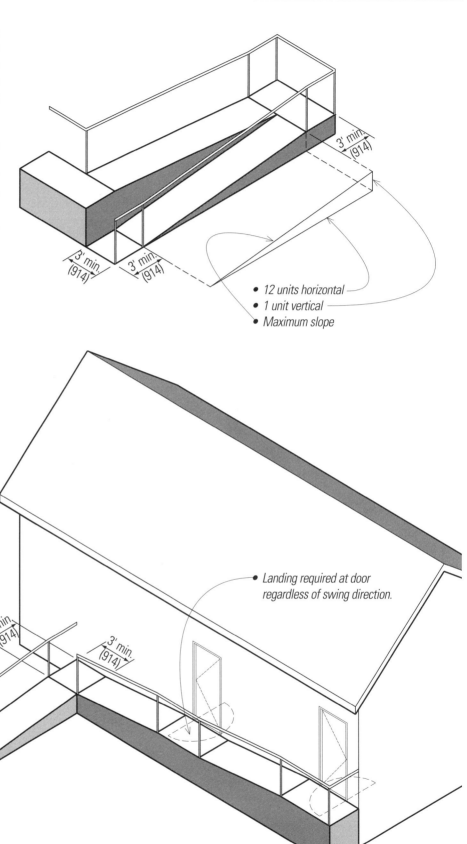

- 12 units horizontal
- 1 unit vertical
- Maximum slope

3' min. (914)

- Landing required at door regardless of swing direction.

Guards

Areas where people may fall more than 30" (762) below the location where they are standing are required to have guards. This includes porches, balconies, ramps, or raised floor surfaces. The guards are to be at least 36" (914) in height. Porches or decks enclosed with screens are also to have guards if they meet the 30" (762) criteria for height above grade. The open sides of stairs with a rise of more than 30" (762) are to have guards located at least 34" (864) above the same plane used to determine handrail heights. Guards are to have a pattern of material which does not allow passage of a sphere 4" (102) or more in diameter. See the illustrations on pages 86 and 88 for exceptions related to the requirements for guards at stairs.

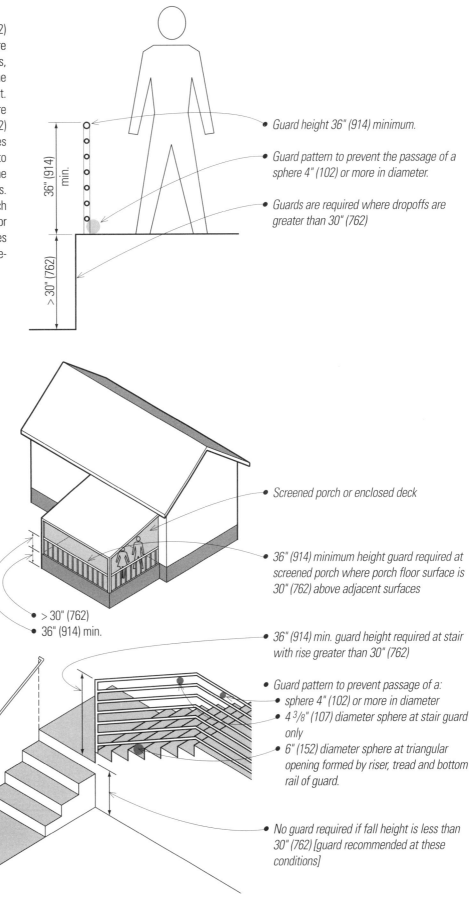

- Guard height 36" (914) minimum.

- Guard pattern to prevent the passage of a sphere 4" (102) or more in diameter.

- Guards are required where dropoffs are greater than 30" (762)

- Screened porch or enclosed deck

- 36" (914) minimum height guard required at screened porch where porch floor surface is 30" (762) above adjacent surfaces

- > 30" (762)
- 36" (914) min.

- 36" (914) min. guard height required at stair with rise greater than 30" (762)

- Guard pattern to prevent passage of a:
  - sphere 4" (102) or more in diameter
  - 4 3/8" (107) diameter sphere at stair guard only
  - 6" (152) diameter sphere at triangular opening formed by riser, tread and bottom rail of guard.

- No guard required if fall height is less than 30" (762) [guard recommended at these conditions]

AUTOMATIC FIRE SPRINKLER SYSTEMS

Per §R313, automatic fire sprinkler systems are to be installed in townhouses, and one- and two-family dwellings. This requirement is effective immediately for new townhouses and goes into effect on January 1, 2011 for one- and two-family dwellings. Automatic residential fire sprinkler systems are to be designed and installed in accordance with §P2904. Sprinklers are not required for additions or alterations to buildings not already provided with such systems. See the illustration for the locations where sprinkler heads may be omitted per §P2904.

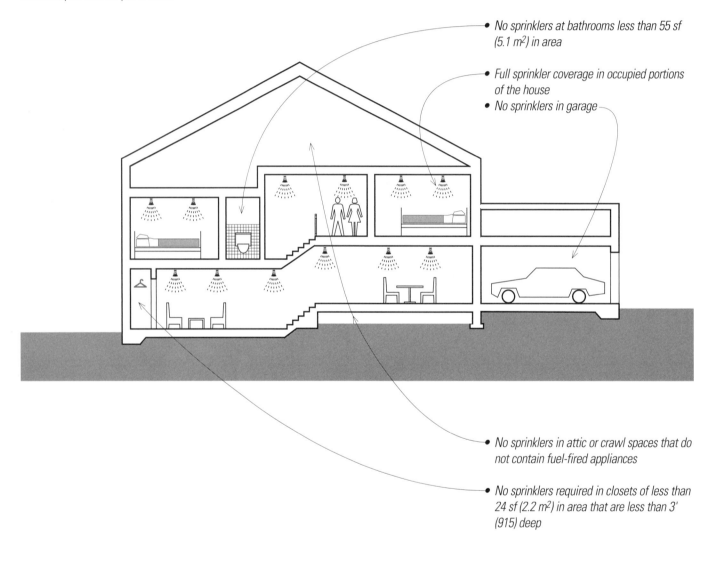

- No sprinklers at bathrooms less than 55 sf (5.1 m²) in area

- Full sprinkler coverage in occupied portions of the house
- No sprinklers in garage

- No sprinklers in attic or crawl spaces that do not contain fuel-fired appliances

- No sprinklers required in closets of less than 24 sf (2.2 m²) in area that are less than 3' (915) deep

§R314 Smoke Alarms

Smoke alarms are an important part of residential fire safety. Their purpose is to alert residents in the event of a fire to allow them to get out of the dwelling. They are designed to function as an early warning device, detecting smoke and other products of combustion when a fire is just beginning and is generating smoke before a fire is really going. The alarms are loud enough to alert sleeping residents to a dangerous condition and allow them escape before being overcome by smoke. These alarms are a life-saving technology that is well proven in reducing deaths and injuries in residential fires. Their installation has been mandatory for many years. The latest code requires them to be located in every sleeping room, also in the immediate vicinity of the bedrooms and in each level of the building, including basements, but not including crawl spaces or uninhabitable attics. For split-level houses in which portions of the house are offset vertically by less than a full story, the smoke detectors required for each floor are to be installed at the upper of the two levels. Note that if sleeping rooms are located at the lower level they would also need smoke alarms. Also, if there are doors between the split-levels that would prevent smoke movement between levels, then smoke alarms are required on both sides of the door. The alarms are to be listed per UL 217. Smoke alarms in new residences are to be hard wired with battery backup. The smoke alarms are to be interconnected so that the activation of any alarm will active all of the smoke alarms. The code sees such great value in smoke alarms that it requires their installation in interior alteration, repairs and additions. The location requirements are the same for this work as for new dwellings. It is the intent of the code that any interior renovations will trigger installation of smoke alarms throughout the dwelling. Where the scope of the work does not require removal of wall or ceiling finishes, the code allows the use of battery-powered alarms without interconnection.

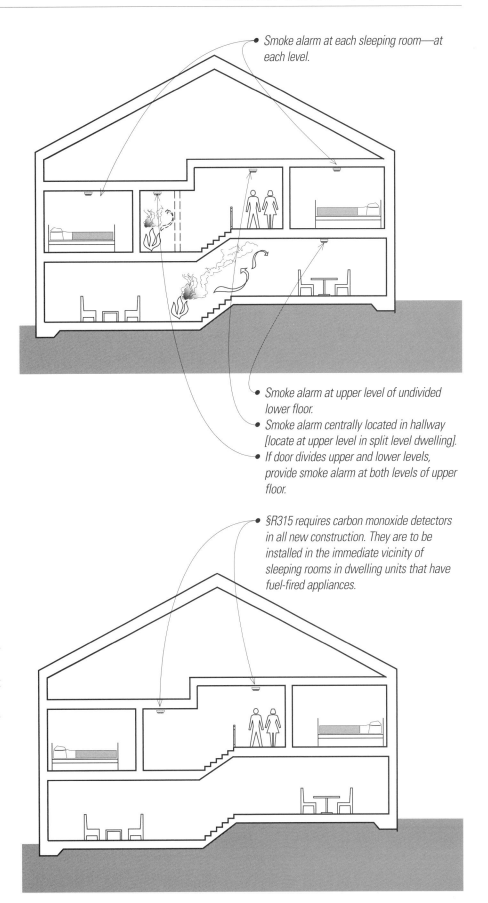

Smoke alarm at each sleeping room—at each level.

Smoke alarm at upper level of undivided lower floor.

Smoke alarm centrally located in hallway [locate at upper level in split level dwelling].

If door divides upper and lower levels, provide smoke alarm at both levels of upper floor.

§R315 requires carbon monoxide detectors in all new construction. They are to be installed in the immediate vicinity of sleeping rooms in dwelling units that have fuel-fired appliances.

Foam Plastic

§R316 governs the design and use of foam plastic materials. Foam plastics have a wide range of uses in modern dwellings, for foam plastic insulation, thermal barriers, sheathing, and fill for doors, backer boards, interior trim and substrates for exterior finishes. Note that additional requirements for Exterior Insulation and Finish Systems (EIFS) are contained in §R703.9. Those requirements are discussed in the Wall Covering section of this book.

Foam plastics are combustible materials, and the code regulates their use based on two sets of criteria. The first set of criteria regards the combustibility of the materials themselves, based on flame spread and smoke generation. Materials used on site are to bear labels of an approval agency to allow those working on the site and those inspecting the work to determine that the foam plastic materials are code compliant. The second set of criteria involves separating the foam plastic materials from the interior of the dwelling to mitigate any flame or smoke propagation inside occupied spaces.

The requirements for foam plastics regulated both materials manufactured off-site such as boards or panels and foam that are manufactured on-site through the combination of approved chemical components to create foam in place. Per IRC §R316.3 foam plastics are to have a flame-spread index of not more than 75 and a smoke-developed index of not more than 450 when tested in assemblies up to 4" (102) in thickness when installed in accordance with the specific approvals listed in §R316.6. Per the definition in §R202, "foam plastic insulation" has a density of less than 20 pounds per cubic foot (320 kg/m^3) unless it is used for interior trim. The use of such foam as interior trim is discussed in §R316.5.9 as illustrated.

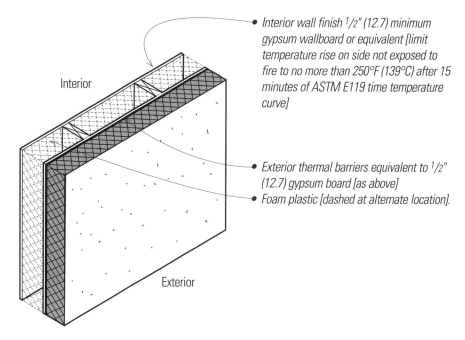

Interior

Exterior

• Interior wall finish $1/2$" (12.7) minimum gypsum wallboard or equivalent [limit temperature rise on side not exposed to fire to no more than 250°F (139°C) after 15 minutes of ASTM E119 time temperature curve]

• Exterior thermal barriers equivalent to $1/2$" (12.7) gypsum board [as above]
• Foam plastic [dashed at alternate location].

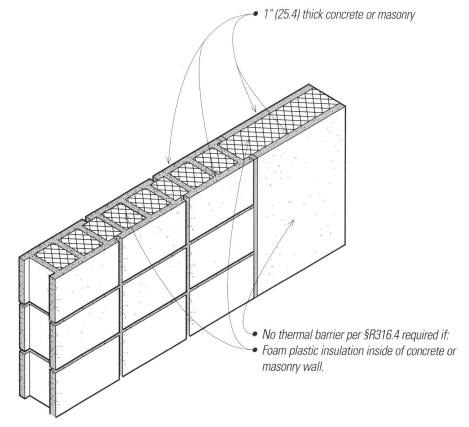

• 1" (25.4) thick concrete or masonry

• No thermal barrier per §R316.4 required if:
• Foam plastic insulation inside of concrete or masonry wall.

Foam Plastic

See the illustrations for details of the treatments required by §R316.4 for thermal barriers. It is unclear from the text whether the thermal barrier separating the foam plastic insulation is to be completely outside of the structure of the building or if it can be the interior layer of finish materials. The local interpretation of this section should be confirmed with the AHJ prior to completion of detailing the dwelling. §R316.5 lists alternates to thermal barriers for various installed conditions. These specific requirements are also illustrated.

§R316.6 says that for installations not meeting the criteria of §R316.3, or the thermal barrier requirements of §R316.4 or installed per the assemblies noted in §R316.5, the installation must meet the approval criteria listed in §R316.6. These criteria are to be applied to the actual end use configuration and material thickness proposed for the actual building. Test criteria cannot simply be extrapolated but must be based on the actual thickness and assembly configurations proposed. Verification of compliance can be shown by providing test data to the AHJ or by obtaining an ICC Evaluation Service "ES" Evaluation Report that applies to the proposed end use application.

The use of foam plastics is limited in areas where "very heavy" termite infestation is probable. See the discussion of §R318.4 regarding the use of foam plastics in these situations.

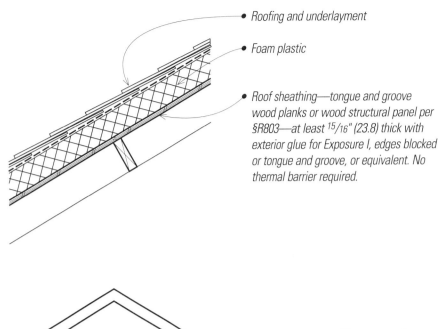

- Roofing and underlayment

- Foam plastic

- Roof sheathing—tongue and groove wood planks or wood structural panel per §R803—at least $^{15}/_{16}$" (23.8) thick with exterior glue for Exposure I, edges blocked or tongue and groove, or equivalent. No thermal barrier required.

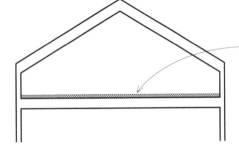

- Thermal barrier per §R316.4 at attics, not required where access is required per §R807.1

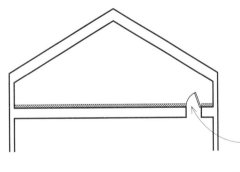

- For attics with access protect foam plastic with ignition barrier materials:
  1. 1.5" (38) mineral fiber insulation
  2. 0.25" (6.4) wood structural panels
  3. 0.375" (9.5) particleboard
  4. 0.25" (6.4) hardboard
  5. 0.375" (9.5) gypsum board
  6. 0.016" (0.408) corrosion-resistant steel
     or
- Foam plastic tested per §R316.6

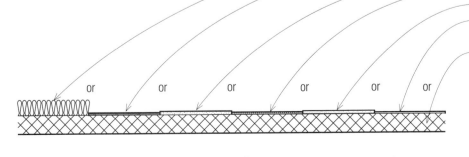

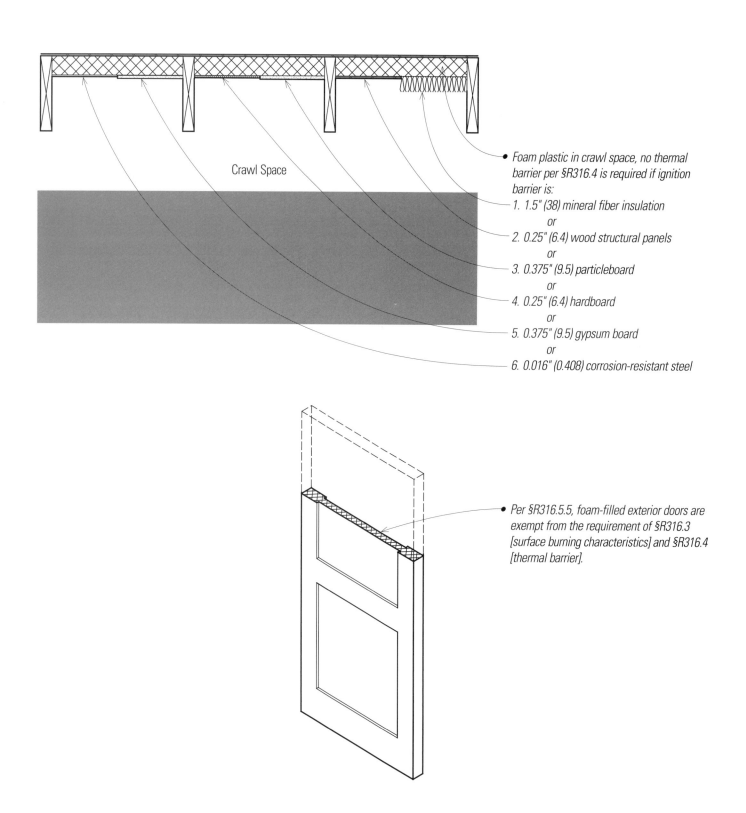

Crawl Space

- Foam plastic in crawl space, no thermal barrier per §R316.4 is required if ignition barrier is:
  1. 1.5" (38) mineral fiber insulation
     or
  2. 0.25" (6.4) wood structural panels
     or
  3. 0.375" (9.5) particleboard
     or
  4. 0.25" (6.4) hardboard
     or
  5. 0.375" (9.5) gypsum board
     or
  6. 0.016" (0.408) corrosion-resistant steel

- Per §R316.5.5, foam-filled exterior doors are exempt from the requirement of §R316.3 [surface burning characteristics] and §R316.4 [thermal barrier].

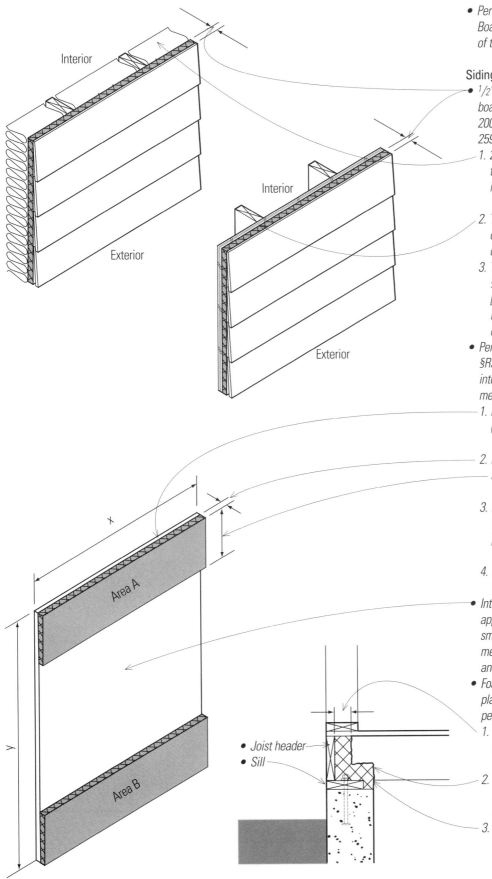

- Per the definition in §R202 "Foam Backer Board" is foam plastic used as a component of the siding.

Siding Material
- 1/2" (12.7) maximum thickness foam backer board with a potential heat of less than 2000 btu/sf (22,720 kj/m²) tested per NFPA 259 and:
  1. 2" (51) mineral fiber insulation separates the foam plastic insulation from the interior of the building
     or
  2. The foam plastic insulation is installed over existing exterior wall finish
     or
  3. The foam plastic insulation is tested per §R316.6
     [No thermal barrier required for this installation or per §R316.5 for re-siding over existing wall finish]
- Per §R316.5.9, no thermal barrier per §R316.4 is required for exposed foam plastic interior trim provided all of the following are met:
  1. Maximum density of foam is 20 pcf (320 kg/m³)
     and
  2. Maximum thickness of trim is 1/2" (12.7) and maximum width is 8" (204)
     and
  3. Interior trim is less than 10% of aggregate wall and ceiling area
     [Area A + Area B < 0.10 (x × y)]
     and
  4. Flame spread index < 75 per ASTM E84 testing.
- Interior finish may be foam plastics when approved per §R316.6, flame spread and smoke generation < 200 and < 450 when meeting the approval criteria of §R302.9.1 and §R302.9.2.
- Foam plastic may be spray applied to a sill plate and header without a thermal barrier per §R316.4 if all of the following are met:
  1. The maximum thickness of the foam plastic is 3 1/4" (83)
     and
  2. The density of the foam plastic is in the range of 1.5 –2.0 pcf (24–32 kg/m³)
     and
  3. The foam plastic has a flame spread index of ≤ 25 and smoke developed index of ≤ 450 when tested per ASTM E84.

- Joist header
- Sill

Protection Against Decay

§R317 is based on the assumption that most dwellings under the IRC contain wood construction materials. These materials are subject to decay. The basic mechanism of decay of wood comes from direct contact with moist soil or concrete or from exposure to moisture-laden air in such areas as unventilated crawl spaces or attics. The code provides several alternative methods that can provide decay resistance or decay prevention. The code recognizes the efficacy of preservative treatments for wood and that some wood species have natural decay-resistant properties. The requirements of §R317 use a combination of material resistance, physical barriers between wood and moisture, provision for air movement to provide ventilation to prevent accumulation of moisture, and provisions of specified separation distances between wood products and soil or concrete. The detailed requirements are as follows, and when the minimum separation distances are not met require the use of naturally durable wood, defined in §R202 as being of "decay-resistant redwood, cedars, black locust and black walnut." Alternatively, preservative-treated wood per Section 4 of the American Wood Protection Association (AWPA) Standard "U1" may be used. Provision of an impervious moisture barrier is required under conditions where wood touches concrete that in turn rests on the ground. These requirements assume that underfloor spaces are adequately ventilated, per the requirements of §R408. The requirements, as illustrated on pages 98–100, are:

1. Wood joists or the bottom of a wood structural floor when closer than 18" (457) or wood girders when closer than 12" (305) to the exposed ground in crawl spaces or unexcavated area located within the periphery of the building foundation.

2. All wood framing members that rest on concrete or masonry exterior foundation walls and are less than 8" (203) from the exposed ground.

3. Sills and sleepers on a concrete or masonry slab that is in direct contact with the ground unless separated from such slab by an impervious moisture barrier.

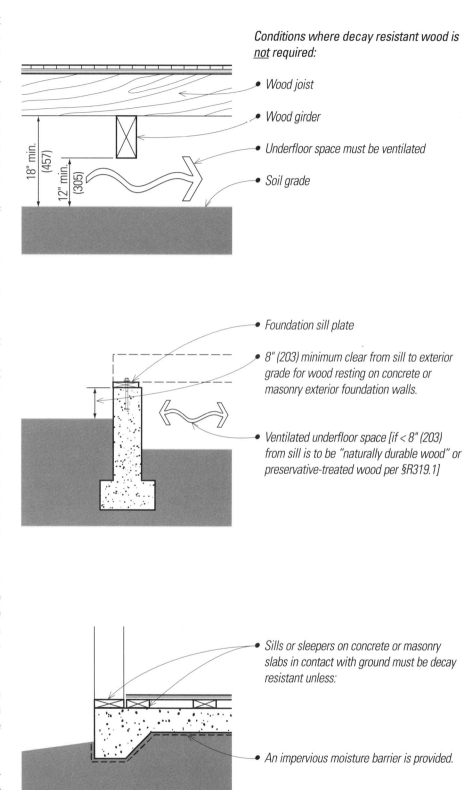

Conditions where decay resistant wood is not required:

- *Wood joist*
- *Wood girder*
- *Underfloor space must be ventilated*
- *Soil grade*

18" min. (457)

12" min. (305)

- *Foundation sill plate*
- *8" (203) minimum clear from sill to exterior grade for wood resting on concrete or masonry exterior foundation walls.*
- *Ventilated underfloor space [if < 8" (203) from sill is to be "naturally durable wood" or preservative-treated wood per §R319.1]*

- *Sills or sleepers on concrete or masonry slabs in contact with ground must be decay resistant unless:*
- *An impervious moisture barrier is provided.*

4. The ends of wood girders entering exterior masonry or concrete walls having clearances of less than 1/2" (12.7) on tops, sides and ends.

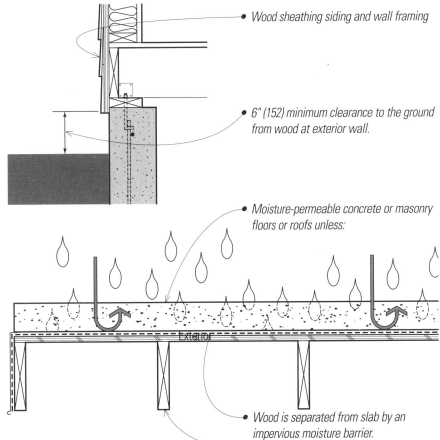

Conditions where decay resistant wood is not required:

- Concrete or masonry wall
- 1/2" (12.7) minimum clearance at top, sides and end from wood member to wall material

- Wood girder or beam

- Wood sheathing siding and wall framing

5. Wood siding, sheathing and wall framing on the exterior of a building having a clearance of less than 6" (152) from the ground.

- 6" (152) minimum clearance to the ground from wood at exterior wall.

- Moisture-permeable concrete or masonry floors or roofs unless:

6. Wood structural members supporting moisture-permeable floors or roofs that are exposed to the weather, such as concrete or masonry slabs, unless separated from such floors or roofs by an impervious moisture barrier.

- Wood is separated from slab by an impervious moisture barrier.
- Wood structural members supporting slab

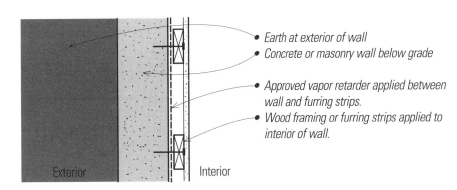

7. Wood furring strips or other wood framing members attached directly to the interior of exterior masonry walls or concrete walls below grade except where an approved vapor retarder is applied between the wall and the furring strips or framing members.

- Earth at exterior of wall
- Concrete or masonry wall below grade

- Approved vapor retarder applied between wall and furring strips.
- Wood framing or furring strips applied to interior of wall.

§R317.1.3 allows local jurisdictions to require the use of naturally durable wood or pressure-preservative-treated wood when there has been experience that dictates added requirements. These requirements are typically applied to locations where members are exposed to weather without added protection from roofs or overhangs.

Per §R317.1.4 wood columns are to be of approved wood of natural decay resistance or pressure-preservative-treated unless they meet the requirements of the exceptions to this section. Exception 1 allows the use of common framing lumber if the column is raised at least 1" (25.4) above a concrete floor or 6" (152) above exposed earth and the earth is covered by an approved moisture barrier. Exception 2 allows the use of common wood if a pier 8" (203) is provided under the column base and the earth is covered by an impervious moisture barrier. See the illustrations.

Where glued-laminated lumber are part of the building's structural frame, the parts of those members that may be exposed to weather are to be made of naturally durable or preservative-treated wood. It was common practice to cover the tops and ends of exposed beam ends or the bases or arches with sheet metal flashing. Experience has shown that such details do not provide adequate long-term protection, thus the added requirement in §R317.1.5 for decay-resistant materials in the portions of the glued-laminated structural members that will be exposed to the weather.

Per §R317.2, members that are required to be pressure-preservative-treated are to have markings indicating that the wood used in the building meets the necessary code criteria. §R317.2.1 lists the contents of the required quality marks that each such treated member is to bear. This allows the home builder, the AHJ and the homeowner to verify code compliance. Labels may vary, but per the standards of the American Lumber Standard Committee the label should contain the illustrated information as a minimum.

Pressure-preservative and fire-retardant-treated wood may cause corrosion of fasteners over the life of buildings. Therefore §R317.3 of the code requires that fasteners for such treated materials be corrosion resistant. This is accomplished

by requiring the fasteners to be hot-dipped zinc-coated galvanized steel, stainless steel, silicon bronze or copper. Interior steel bolts 1/2" (12.7) and larger need not meet these material requirements. Fasteners other than nails and timber rivets may be of mechanically deposited zinc-coated steel if they meet the requirements of ASTM B695, Class 55 at a minimum. This exception as written thus requires that nails be hot-dipped zinc galvanized.

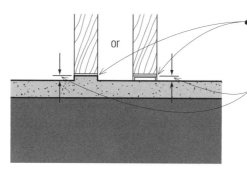

- Per §R317.1.4 columns exposed to weather or located in basements may be untreated wood if they are supported by concrete or metal pedestals a minimum of 1" (25.4) above a concrete floor

or

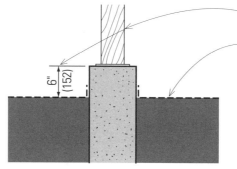

- If supported at least 6" (152) above exposed earth when the earth is covered by an
- Approved imperious moisture barrier.

- If column is located in a crawl space or unexcavated area within the periphery of the building, the height of the pier is to be a minimum of 8" (203) above exposed earth. The earth is to have an approved impervious moisture barrier at this condition as well.

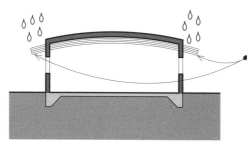

- Portions of glue-laminated timbers that are part of the structural support of the building exposed to weather and not protected by roof, eave or similar covering must be made of naturally durable or preservative-treated wood or shall be pressure treated with preservative.

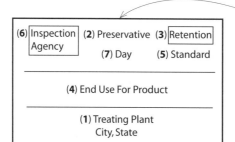

- The label contents per §R317.2.1 for pressure-treated wood are:
  1. Treating plant identification
  2. Type of preservative
  3. Minimum preservative retention
  4. End use of treated product
  5. Standard to which product was rated
  6. Identity of Approval Inspection Agency
  7. "Dry" designation, if applicable

Protection Against Subterranean Termites

Where Figure R301.2.(6) indicates a probability of termite infestation §R318 sets forth the requirements for termite protection. The code does not specify the cut off regarding termite protection is required. There is a very limited part of the United States where the probability is considered to be "none to slight" per Figure R301.2(6). The local requirements for termite protections should be verified with the local AHJ early in the design process for any residential project.

The code provides several alternative methods for providing termite protection. The methods are as follows:

1. Chemical treatment with termiticides applied per §R318.2.

2. Use of termite-baiting systems installed and maintained per their labeling.

3. Use of pressure-preservative-treated wood. The wood is to meet the quality standards of AWPA per §R317.1 and bear a quality mark per §R318.1.1. Note also that per §R318.1.2, end cuts, notches and drilled holes in pressure treated members must be retreated per AWPA M4. This is to maintain the termite-resistant qualities of the members if their surface treatments are breached.

4. Physical termite barriers may be used, but they must be applied per §R318.3. Note that when such barriers are placed on top of exterior foundation walls, then another method of protection must also be provided.

§R318.4 restricts the use of foam plastic insulation where the probability of termite infestation is "very heavy" per Figure R301.2(6). The foam is not to be in contact with earth, and it is to be separated from the earth by at least 6" (152). The exceptions to this section allow use of the foam in structures of entirely non-combustible construction or of pressure-preservative-treated wood (thus not attractive to termites). Protected foam may be used if it is in conjunction with the added termite protection requirements of §R320.1. Foam plastic insulation may also be used on the inside face of basement walls.

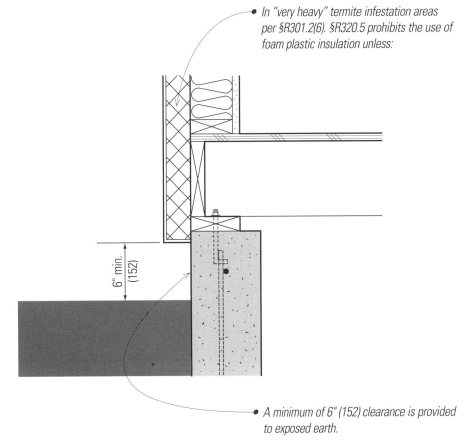

In "very heavy" termite infestation areas per §R301.2(6). §R320.5 prohibits the use of foam plastic insulation unless:

6" min. (152)

A minimum of 6" (152) clearance is provided to exposed earth.

Site Address

Per §R319, every new building is required to have an address visible and legible from the street or road facing the property. This is to facilitate emergency responders such as fire, medical or police services being able to readily locate the property. Note that this requirement is tied to the visibility and legibility from the street and thus may not always be located on the building itself. The proposed location for site address information should be confirmed with the AHJ during plan review.

Accessibility

One- and two-family dwellings are not required by the IRC to be accessible for persons with disabilities. Note that since townhouses are under the purview of the IRC, where there are four or more townhouses in a single structure they are under the accessibility provisions of Chapter 11 of the International Building Code per §R320. Also, note that many jurisdictions make extensive local amendments to accessibility regulations. Locally applicable accessibility regulations should be confirmed with the AHJ.

Elevators and Platform Lifts

Where elevators or platform lifts are provided for convenience or for accessibility, §R321 lists the various national standards to be used for elevators and platform lifts.

Flood-resistant Construction

Where flood-prone areas are designated by the local AHJ in Table R301.2(1), per the requirements of the Federal Emergency Management Agency National Flood Insurance Program, §R322 is to be used. Note that per the Exception to §R322, buildings located in "floodways" per the locally adopted version of Table R301.2(1) are to use ASCE 24 for design criteria, not the IRC.

The requirements of §R322 only apply to buildings located in the flood hazard areas shown diagrammatically in the illustration taken from the ICC/FEMA publication *Reducing Flood Losses Through the International Code Series: Meeting the Requirements of the National Flood Insurance Program.*

Construction elements and systems must be designed to resist flood-induced forces such as flotation, lateral pressures, moving water and debris damage anticipated in designated flood-prone areas. Also, systems such as mechanical and electrical systems are to be located above the "design flood elevation" or to be designed to be essentially waterproof under flood conditions. This elevation is defined in §R322.1.4 as the peak of a 100-year flood, including wave heights. This may be set by the Flood Insurance Rate Map (FIRM) or by Table R301.2(1). This height may be specified in the locally adopted version of Table R301.2(1). If not, the local AHJ has the authority per §R322.1.4.1 to require the applicant for a permit find other sources or perform an engineering analysis to set the design flood elevation.

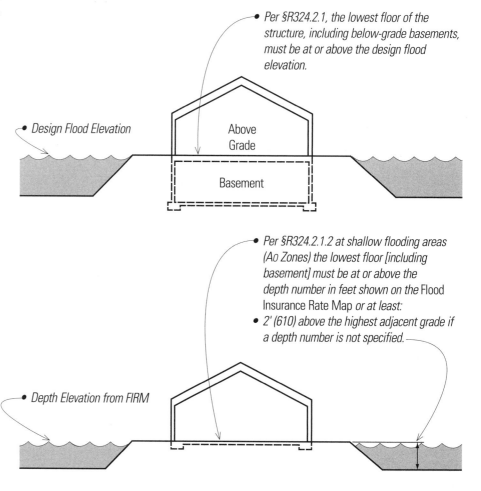

Per §R324.2.1, the lowest floor of the structure, including below-grade basements, must be at or above the design flood elevation.

Design Flood Elevation

Above Grade

Basement

Per §R324.2.1.2 at shallow flooding areas (Ao Zones) the lowest floor [including basement] must be at or above the depth number in feet shown on the Flood Insurance Rate Map or at least:

2' (610) above the highest adjacent grade if a depth number is not specified.

Depth Elevation from FIRM

The lowest floor, per §R322.1.5, is defined as the lowest enclosed area and includes basements. The definition of basement for these flood requirements differs from that in Chapter 2 in that it assumes basements are below grade on all sides, as described in §R322.2.1. Where buildings are elevated to avoid flooding, the National Flood Insurance Program recognizes that the buildings must touch grade at some point in the potential flood area to allow access to the building. In this section the code allows parking of vehicles, building access or limited storage to occur in what would otherwise be considered to be the lowest enclosed area by the code. §R322.2 defines flood hazard areas as those areas prone to flooding but not subject to high-velocity wave action, including "A" Zones. §R322.2 describes the requirements for enclosed areas, including crawl spaces or basements, located below the design flood elevation that is in the "A" zones, located below the design flood elevation. These requirements are illustrated. §R322.3 describes the requirements for "V" zones, which are coastal high-hazard areas subject to wave heights in excess of 3' (914), high-velocity wave action, or wave-induced erosion, as illustrated.

Note that, even for the dwellings constructed under the IRC, documentation of the setting of elevations related to flooding must be prepared and sealed by a registered design professional. This is a more stringent standard for buildings in flood-prone areas than for those not located in such areas. Note also that in addition to this requirement, §R322.3.6 requires a registered design professional to meet the criteria of §R322.3 related to design for coastal high-hazard areas.

- Enclosed areas below flood elevation in flood hazard areas:
1. Area be used solely for parking, building access or storage.

2.1 Flood openings provided on at least two different sides.

2.2 Net area of opening at least 1 in^2/sf (645 mm^2/0.093 m^2) of enclosed area or designed to equalize in opposite pressure.
2.3 Bottom of opening maximum of 1' (305) above adjacent ground.
2.4 Openings at least 3" (76) in diameter.
2.5 Louvers or screens allow floodwater flow.
2.6 Solid doors or windows do not count toward opening requirement.

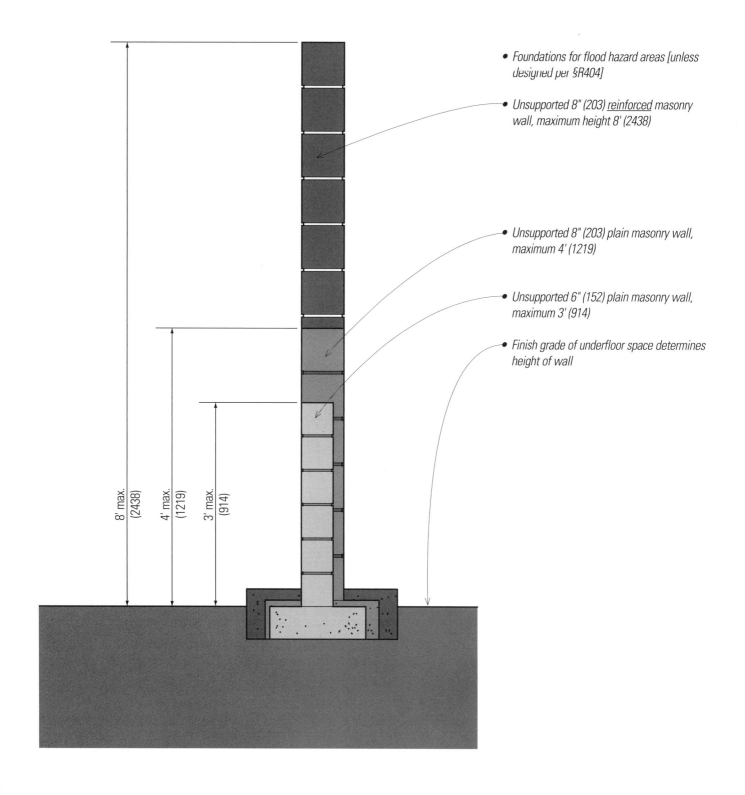

- Foundations for flood hazard areas [unless designed per §R404]

- Unsupported 8" (203) <u>reinforced</u> masonry wall, maximum height 8' (2438)

- Unsupported 8" (203) plain masonry wall, maximum 4' (1219)

- Unsupported 6" (152) plain masonry wall, maximum 3' (914)

- Finish grade of underfloor space determines height of wall

8' max. (2438)

4' max. (1219)

3' max. (914)

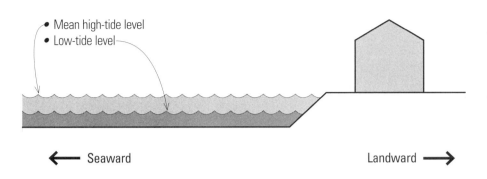

- *Mean high-tide level*
- *Low-tide level*

← Seaward

Landward →

- *Buildings in coastal high hazard areas [including V zones] shall be located landward of the reach of mean high tide and:*

- *The lowest portion of structural members supporting the lowest floor is above the design flood elevation.*

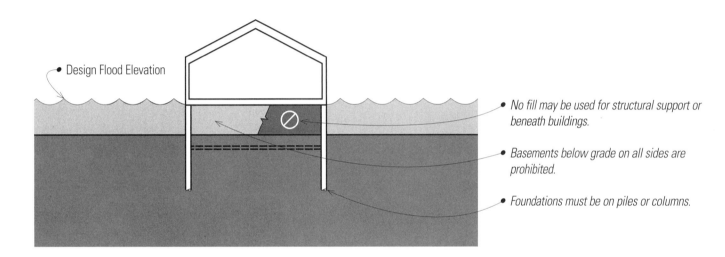

- Design Flood Elevation

- *No fill may be used for structural support or beneath buildings.*

- *Basements below grade on all sides are prohibited.*

- *Foundations must be on piles or columns.*

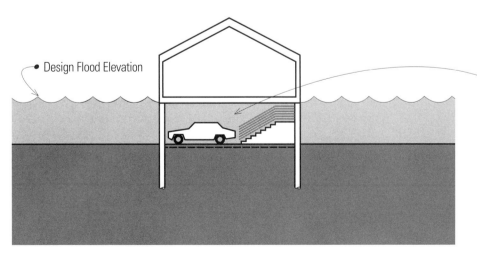

- Design Flood Elevation

- *Enclosed areas below the design flood elevation are allowed if they meet the break-away requirements of §R322.2.2 and are used only for parking, building access or storage.*

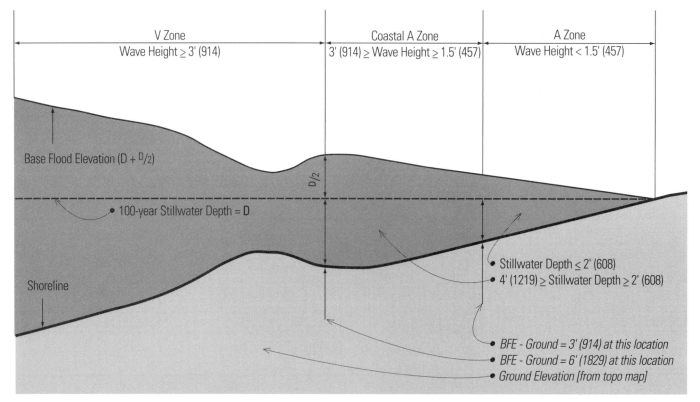

V Zone
Wave Height ≥ 3' (914)

Coastal A Zone
3' (914) ≥ Wave Height ≥ 1.5' (457)

A Zone
Wave Height < 1.5' (457)

Base Flood Elevation (D + $D/2$)

$D/2$

• 100-year Stillwater Depth = **D**

Shoreline

• Stillwater Depth ≤ 2' (608)
• 4' (1219) ≥ Stillwater Depth ≥ 2' (608)

• *BFE - Ground = 3' (914) at this location*
• *BFE - Ground = 6' (1829) at this location*
• *Ground Elevation [from topo map]*

Diagram of Flood Hazard Zones in Coastal Areas Under the National Flood Insurance Program
From *Reducing Flood Losses Through the International Codes*© 2008, by ICC in cooperation with FEMA

4

Foundations

Chapter 4 of the International Residential Code establishes requirements for the design and construction of foundations for buildings. It also establishes requirements for materials, footings, retaining wall drainage, waterproofing and dampproofing.

General Scope of the Chapter

§R401.1 provides the information necessary for the design and construction of foundations for the buildings included in the scope of the IRC. The type of foundation must be selected to accommodate the proposed building size and geometry, but it also must respond to the site location, site subsurface soil conditions and site drainage. Note that in areas prone to flooding, the requirements of §R322 are also to be met. While most foundations will likely be constructed of concrete or masonry, the code recognizes the efficacy of permanent wood foundations. These wood foundations are to be constructed according to the recognized standards contained in the reference document noted in §401.1 AF&PA Technical Report 7 (available from the American Wood Council as the 2007 Permanent Wood Foundation Standard). The IRC allows the use of these foundations for buildings that are relatively lightly loaded and located in areas of low to moderate seismic activity. Wood foundations may be used for buildings with no more than two occupied stories and the walls must be braced with internal basement or foundation walls at maximum intervals of 50' (15240). The wood foundation system is described in more detail below in the section-by-section discussions of other foundation systems such as concrete and masonry.

The essential requirements for foundations are contained in §401.2. The foundation is to accommodate the loads specified in §R301 and transmit them from the structure above into the soil supporting the foundation. This "load path" must be complete and the components of the path must accommodate the forces moving through it. These forces may be from dead loads of materials; live loads of occupants; loads from weather conditions such as wind, snow or water; and lateral or vertical loads imposed by seismic activity. The foundation is the link between the structure above and the material below the foundation. The capacity of the materials supporting the foundation, be it native soil, earth fill or materials such as sand or gravel, must be designed and maintained in a condition to transmit the loads from the structure into the supporting materials. The requirements for drainage in §401.3 recognize the important role played in long-term foundation success

in keeping water away from foundations and underfloor areas. Soils are to be tested to determine their bearing capacity so that the necessary foundation sizes may be determined so as to not over-stress the bearing capacity of the soils. The AHJ may waive tests if they feel confident that the capacity of the soil can be determined based on common practices in the area of the project. If no tests are required or provided, the bearing capacities of Table R401.4.1 are to be used. The AHJ may require that soils prone to compression or shifting be removed and replaced to a depth they determine to be sufficient to assure stability.

All the requirements for foundations and soil capacities are subject to the AHJ interpretation of "accepted engineering practice." The definition of "common practice" in any jurisdiction will be subject to local interpretation, and if there is any doubt as to whether proposed means and methods of foundation design meet these criteria, this should be discussed with the AHJ early in the design process.

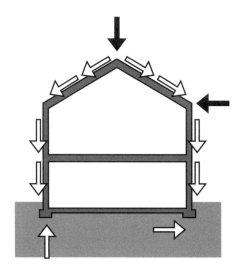

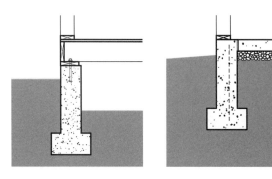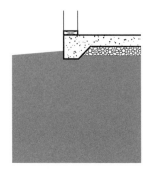

Site Drainage

There are two tasks that must be accomplished by the design of site drainage for individual building lots. The first task is to meet the specific conditions contained in §R401.3. The second is to direct and contain drainage on the site to minimize drainage impacts on adjacent structures not on the lot. We will focus in this discussion on the specific requirements related to foundation drainage from §R401.3. The illustrations show only the minimum code requirements in a general manner, they are not intended to describe how to grade a site for proper drainage.

Drainage is to be directed away from the building foundation on all sides, which means that swales or surface drainage must be provided on the upslope and sideslope portions of sloping lots to direct water around the structure. The specified minimum slope is 6" (152) within the first 10' (3048) as one moves away from the foundation. This translates into a 1-foot fall in 20' (6056), or a 5% minimum slope. Swales must be sloped at least 2% if they must be located within 10' (3048) of the structure due to site constraints such as property lines or physical barriers. The illustration shows a structure situated on a site with a moderate slope from the back of the site to a roadway at the front of the site.

Slope away at minimum fall of 6" (152) in 10' (3048) [5% slope] at all four sides of structure.

Street

Swale

2% minimum slope along swale

Soil Load-Bearing Capacities

Table R401.4.1 shows the assumed bearing capacities for various types of subsurface materials under foundations. These are the values to be used if no soils tests are performed. The illustration shows the relative sizes of a footing with an assumed loading of 20,000 pounds (9080 kg). Per footnote "b" to the table where in-place soils are determined by the AHJ to have a bearing capacity of less than 1500 psf (71.85 kPa) then a geotechnical soils investigation will be required. Where soils are compressible or shifting, a soils report may not need to be prepared where the questionable soil is removed from the site to a depth sufficient to assure stability per §R401.4.2.

20,000 pound (9080 k) vertical load on foundation from structure above

1.67 sf (0.16 m^2) foundation on crystalline bedrock at 12,000 psf (574.8 kN/m^2) bearing pressure = 1.29' x 1.29' (393 x 393) square footing

5.0 sf (0.46 m^2) foundation on sedimentary or floated rock at 4,000 psf (191.6 kN/m^2) bearing pressure = 2.23' x 2.23' (678 x 678) square footing

6.67 sf (0.62 m^2) foundation on sandy gravel or gravel at 3,000 psf (143.7 kN/m^2) bearing pressure = 2.58' x 2.58' (786 x 786) square footing

10.0 sf (0.93 m^2) foundation on sandy, silt sand, etc. at 2,000 psf (95.8 kN/m^2) bearing pressure = 3.16' x 3.16' (963 x 963) square footing

13.3 sf (1.24 m^2) foundation on clay, sandy clay, etc. at 1,500 sf (71.9 kN/m^2) bearing pressure = 3.65' x 3.65' (1113 x 1113) square footing

Foundation Materials

Foundations are to meet the materials criteria contained in §R402. Two of the subsections of §402 address the materials that are expected to be found in almost every building constructed using the §R402.1 addresses wood foundations and §R402.2 addresses concrete. §R402.3 addresses precast concrete as a manufactured item.

Concrete compressive strength requirements, described in Table R402.2, are based on several factors. One is the concrete weathering potential at the building's geographical location, as determined per Figure 301.2(3) and entered by the AHJ into the locally adopted version of Table 301.2(1). The compressive strength requirements also depend on where the foundation concrete is located in the building as listed in Table R402.2. Where the concrete is in "moderate" or "severe" weathering areas, in certain locations in the building air is to be entrained per the requirements of Footnote "d" to Table R402.2. The air entrained is to be between 5% and 7% of the total volume of concrete, except for special conditions for high-strength concrete in steel-trowel finished slabs per Footnote "f". The concrete admixture criteria in this section refer the user to an outside reference, ACI 318, based on the location of the foundation concrete. Note that per the table, concrete compressive strength is to be at least 2,500 psi (17250 kPa) for all location conditions. Since concrete gets stronger as it cures, the required strength is to be achieved at a standardized testing age, which is 28 days after concrete placement.

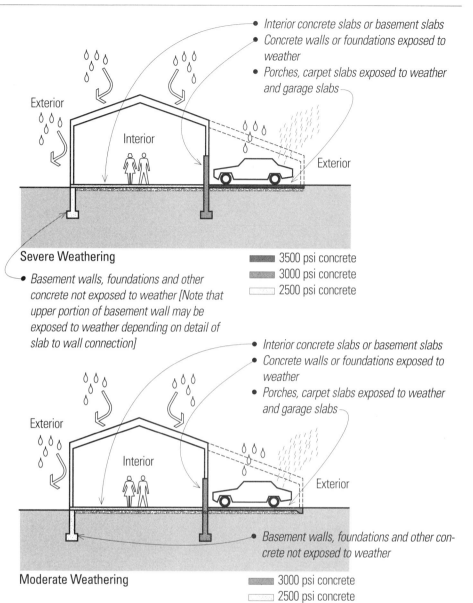

Severe Weathering

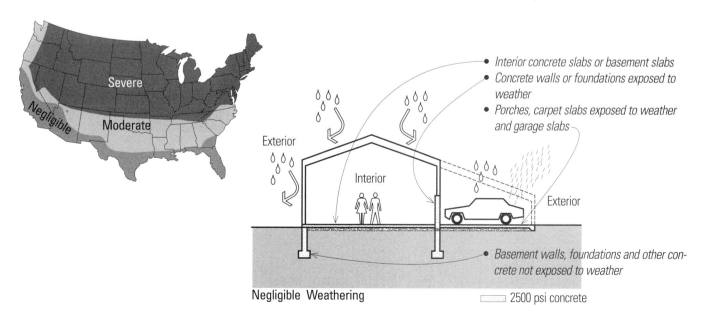

Negligible Weathering

Footings

Solid or continuously grouted footings are to be provided under all exterior walls. They are to rest on undisturbed natural soil or on engineered fill. Minimum footing dimensions are established in two places in the code. The first is Table R403.1, where the widths of the footings are related to the height of the dwelling in stories and to the bearing capacity of the soil under the footing. Footing configurations for concrete footings are illustrated in Figure R403.1(1). The value for "W" in that figure is derived from Table R403.1. Per §R403.1.1, the footings are to be at least 6" (152) thick and are to project a minimum of 2" (51) past the edge of the wall they are supporting. Note that wide walls configurations, such as doubled-up super insulated bearing walls could require that the footing be wider than the minimum widths from Table R403.1. Note also that while §R403.1 states that footing requirements apply to "all exterior walls," Figure R403.1 contains an illustration of interior bearing wall footings where the "W" requirement is specified. Per Figure R403.1(1), concrete slabs on-grade are to be a minimum of $3^{1}/_{2}$" (89) thick whether they are monolithic or placed independently of the foundations and footings.

23" (584)
17" (432)
12" (305)
6" min. (152)
3-story

15" (381)
12" (305)
6" min. (152)
2-story

12" min. (305)
6" min. (152)
1-story

500 psf
24 kN/m²

2000 psf
95.8 kN/m²

3000 psf
143.7 kN/m²

4000 psf
191.6 kN/m²

Soil Load Bearing Capacity

500 psf (24 kN/m²)
1000 psf (48 kN/m²)
1500 psf (71.8 kN/m²)
2000 psf (95.8 kN/m²)
2500 psf (119.8 kN/m²)
3000 psf (143.7 kN/m²)
3500 psf (167.7 kN/m²)
4000 psf (191.6 kN/m²)
> 4000 psf (191.6 kN/m²)

Table R403.1 Minimum Width of Concrete or Masonry Footings
Conventional Light-frame Construction

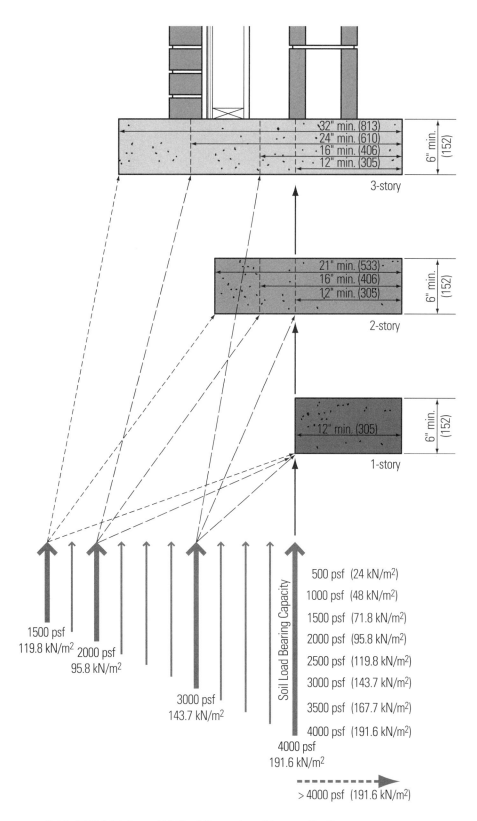

32" min. (813)
24" min. (610)
16" min. (406)
12" min. (305)
6" min. (152)
3-story

21" min. (533)
16" min. (406)
12" min. (305)
6" min. (152)
2-story

12" min. (305)
6" min. (152)
1-story

Soil Load Bearing Capacity

500 psf (24 kN/m²)
1000 psf (48 kN/m²)
1500 psf (71.8 kN/m²)
2000 psf (95.8 kN/m²)
2500 psf (119.8 kN/m²)
3000 psf (143.7 kN/m²)
3500 psf (167.7 kN/m²)
4000 psf (191.6 kN/m²)

1500 psf
119.8 kN/m²   2000 psf
95.8 kN/m²

3000 psf
143.7 kN/m²

4000 psf
191.6 kN/m²

> 4000 psf (191.6 kN/m²)

Table R403.1 Minimum Width of Concrete or Masonry Footings
4-inch Brick Veneer over Light-frame Construction or 8-inch Hollow Concrete Masonry

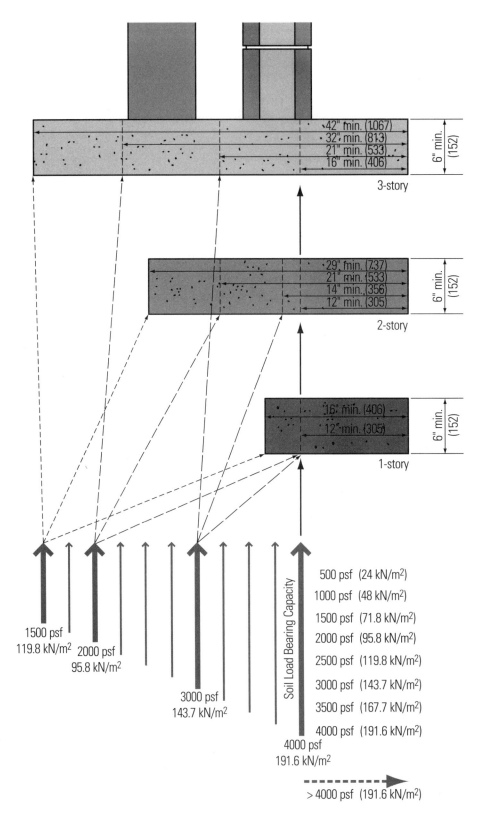

42" min. (1.067)
32" min. (813)
21" min. (533)
16" min. (406)

6" min. (152)

3-story

29" min. (737)
21" min. (533)
14" min. (356)
12" min. (305)

6" min. (152)

2-story

16" min. (406)
12" min. (305)

6" min. (152)

1-story

500 psf (24 kN/m²)

1000 psf (48 kN/m²)

1500 psf (71.8 kN/m²)

2000 psf (95.8 kN/m²)

2500 psf (119.8 kN/m²)

3000 psf (143.7 kN/m²)

3500 psf (167.7 kN/m²)

4000 psf (191.6 kN/m²)

Soil Load Bearing Capacity

1500 psf
119.8 kN/m²

2000 psf
95.8 kN/m²

3000 psf
143.7 kN/m²

4000 psf
191.6 kN/m²

> 4000 psf (191.6 kN/m²)

Table R403.1 Minimum Width of Concrete or Masonry Footings
8-inch Solid or Fully Grouted Masonry

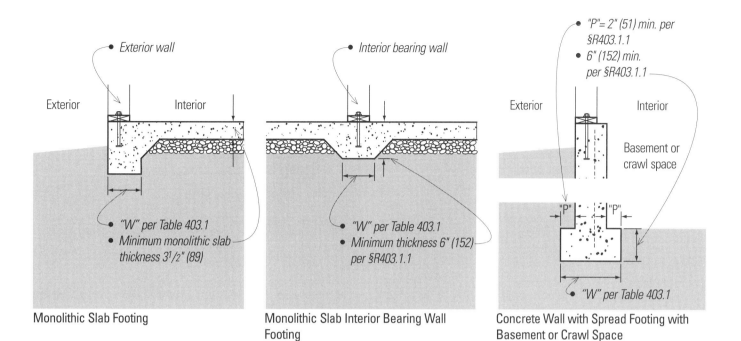

Monolithic Slab Footing

- *"W" per Table 403.1*
- *Minimum monolithic slab thickness 3^1/$_2$" (89)*

Monolithic Slab Interior Bearing Wall Footing

- *"W" per Table 403.1*
- *Minimum thickness 6" (152) per §R403.1.1*

Concrete Wall with Spread Footing with Basement or Crawl Space

- *"P"= 2" (51) min. per §R403.1.1*
- *6" (152) min. per §R403.1.1*
- *"W" per Table 403.1*

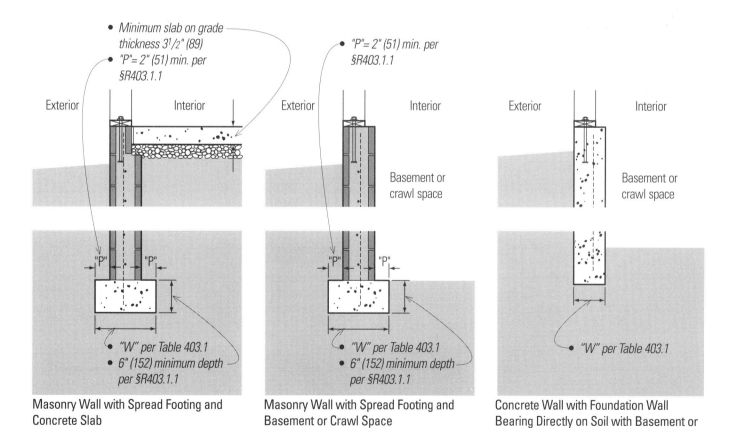

Masonry Wall with Spread Footing and Concrete Slab

- *Minimum slab on grade thickness 3^1/$_2$" (89)*
- *"P"= 2" (51) min. per §R403.1.1*
- *"W" per Table 403.1*
- *6" (152) minimum depth per §R403.1.1*

Masonry Wall with Spread Footing and Basement or Crawl Space

- *"P"= 2" (51) min. per §R403.1.1*
- *"W" per Table 403.1*
- *6" (152) minimum depth per §R403.1.1*

Concrete Wall with Foundation Wall Bearing Directly on Soil with Basement or Crawl Space

- *"W" per Table 403.1*

Footings

Per §R403.1.3, continuous footings are required under braced wall panels resisting seismic forces in zones of high seismic design categories, D_0, D_1 and D_2. Such footings are also to be reinforced in those Seismic Design Categories. See the illustrations for the requirements. Per the exception to this section there are no reinforcement requirements for detached single-family dwellings with wood stud bearing walls if such dwellings are less than three stories in height. Where stem wall foundations are used, however, §R403.1.3.1 requires #4 bars at the top and bottom of such footings, as illustrated. Where turned-down footings are cast in two phases there is to be a vertical bar with hooks at each end at top and bottom bars per §R403.1.3.2. This is illustrated at Figure R403.1.3.2 in the IRC. See the illustration for the requirements and for the bar placement options offered in the exception to this section.

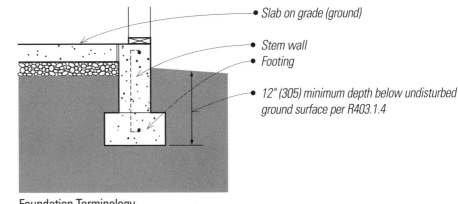

- Slab on grade (ground)
- Stem wall
- Footing
- 12" (305) minimum depth below undisturbed ground surface per R403.1.4

Foundation Terminology

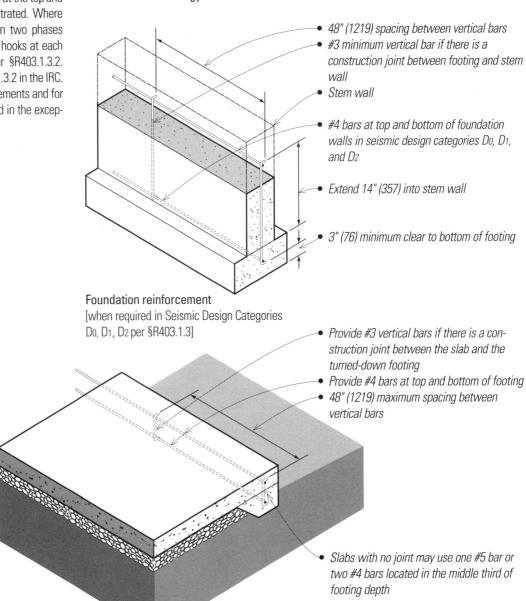

- 48" (1219) spacing between vertical bars
- #3 minimum vertical bar if there is a construction joint between footing and stem wall
- Stem wall
- #4 bars at top and bottom of foundation walls in seismic design categories D_0, D_1, and D_2
- Extend 14" (357) into stem wall
- 3" (76) minimum clear to bottom of footing

Foundation reinforcement
[when required in Seismic Design Categories D_0, D_1, D_2 per §R403.1.3]

- Provide #3 vertical bars if there is a construction joint between the slab and the turned-down footing
- Provide #4 bars at top and bottom of footing
- 48" (1219) maximum spacing between vertical bars

- Slabs with no joint may use one #5 bar or two #4 bars located in the middle third of footing depth

Foundation Reinforcement at
Slab-on-grade with Turned-down Footing
[at Seismic Design Categories D_0, D_1, D_2]

See the illustrations for the requirements for footing depth and for the relationship of the footing depth to the frost line in the locale of the dwelling. Note that §R403.1.4.1 offers several alternatives (not exceptions) one of which must be met. They are: extending footings below the frost line, insulating the footings per §R403.3, meeting the requirements of ASCE 32 (which offers design guidance regarding frost-protected shallow foundations) or if the footings rest on solid rock. For foundation freeze protection see the illustrations later in this chapter where §R403.3 is discussed.

Per §R403.1.5 the tops of footings are to be level so that the vertical load imposed on them by the building above will not induce them to move laterally. For the same reasons the bottoms of footings are to be nearly level, with no slope exceeding 1:10 at the bottom of the footing. Foundations on steep sites need to be stepped when wall heights shift or when footing depths must be offset to keep the foundations underground. See the illustration for an example of how footing steps are related to site slopes.

Walls resting on continuous foundations are to be anchored to the foundations per §R403.1.6. Minimum requirements are that these anchors are $1/2$" (12.7) diameter anchor bolts extending at least 7" (178) into the concrete or grouted cells of concrete masonry units of the foundation below. There are to be at least two anchor bolts for each length of sill and they are to be no more than 6' (1829) on center. The bolts are to have washers and tightened nuts. The bolts are to be no more than 12" (305) or seven bolt diameters from the ends of the sill plates, whichever is less.

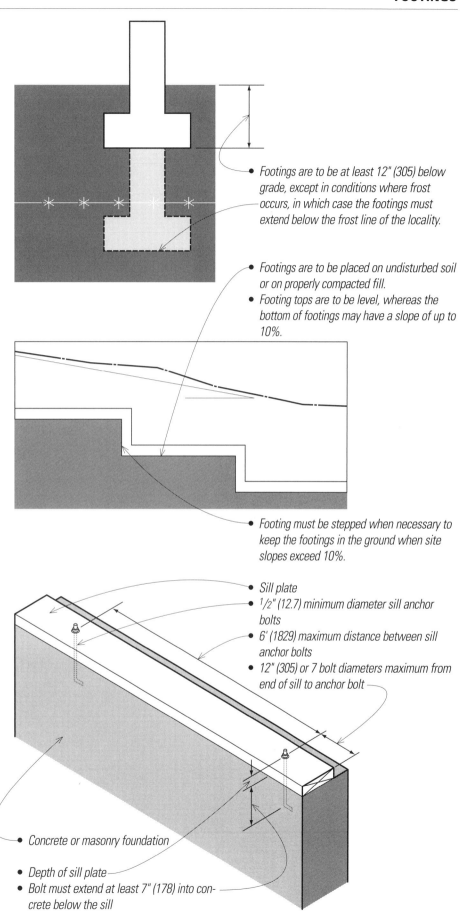

- Footings are to be at least 12" (305) below grade, except in conditions where frost occurs, in which case the footings must extend below the frost line of the locality.

- Footings are to be placed on undisturbed soil or on properly compacted fill.
- Footing tops are to be level, whereas the bottom of footings may have a slope of up to 10%.

- Footing must be stepped when necessary to keep the footings in the ground when site slopes exceed 10%.

- Sill plate
- $1/2$" (12.7) minimum diameter sill anchor bolts
- 6' (1829) maximum distance between sill anchor bolts
- 12" (305) or 7 bolt diameters maximum from end of sill to anchor bolt

- Concrete or masonry foundation

- Depth of sill plate
- Bolt must extend at least 7" (178) into concrete below the sill

FOOTINGS

Buildings whose sites slope more than 1:3 (33.3% slope) must meet the setback criteria in §R403.1.7 and illustrated in Figure R403.1.7.1. These clearance requirements are to ensure that there is room for provision of site drainage, for erosion protection and prevention of shallow failures near foundations when the soil shifts away from them.

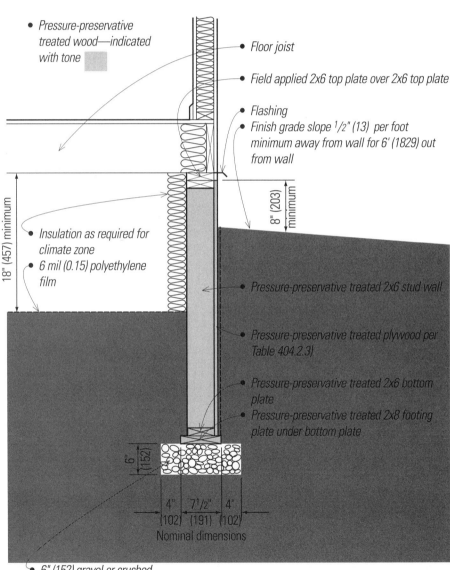

- H = top of slope to toe of slope
- H/3 from face of footing to daylight at slope but need not exceed 40' (12192)
- H/2 from face of structure to toe of slope, but need not exceed 15' (4572)
- Top of slope
- Toe of slope

Figure R403.1.7.1

Footings for Wood Foundations

Per §R403.1 foundations and footings may be made of pressure-preservative treated wood. Wood foundation systems are illustrated in Figures R403.1(2) and R403.1(3). Wood foundations are to rest on washed and well-graded gravel, sand or crushed rock per §R403.2. The gravel size can not exceed 3/4" (19.1). Sand may be used, but must be coarse with no grains smaller than 1/16" (1.6). Crushed stone may also be used, but it may not be any larger than 1/2" (12.7) in size. See the illustrations for a depiction of the components of wood foundation systems.

- Pressure-preservative treated wood—indicated with tone
- Floor joist
- Field applied 2x6 top plate over 2x6 top plate
- Flashing
- Finish grade slope 1/2" (13) per foot minimum away from wall for 6' (1829) out from wall
- Insulation as required for climate zone
- 6 mil (0.15) polyethylene film
- Pressure-preservative treated 2x6 stud wall
- Pressure-preservative treated plywood per Table 404.2.3)
- Pressure-preservative treated 2x6 bottom plate
- Pressure-preservative treated 2x8 footing plate under bottom plate
- 6" (152) gravel or crushed stone per §R403.2

18" (457) minimum

8" (203) minimum

6" (152)

4" (102) 7 1/2" (191) 4" (102)

Nominal dimensions

Figure R403.1(3) Section at Permanent Wood Foundation with Crawl Space

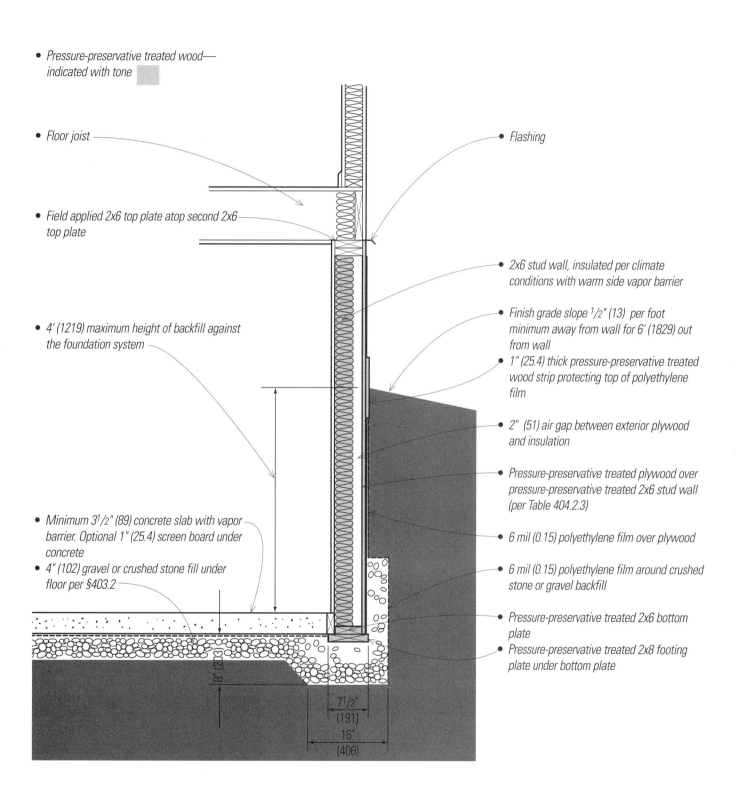

- Pressure-preservative treated wood— indicated with tone

- Floor joist

- Field applied 2x6 top plate atop second 2x6 top plate

- 4' (1219) maximum height of backfill against the foundation system

- Minimum 3¹/₂" (89) concrete slab with vapor barrier. Optional 1" (25.4) screen board under concrete
- 4" (102) gravel or crushed stone fill under floor per §403.2

- Flashing

- 2x6 stud wall, insulated per climate conditions with warm side vapor barrier

- Finish grade slope ¹/₂" (13) per foot minimum away from wall for 6' (1829) out from wall
- 1" (25.4) thick pressure-preservative treated wood strip protecting top of polyethylene film

- 2" (51) air gap between exterior plywood and insulation

- Pressure-preservative treated plywood over pressure-preservative treated 2x6 stud wall (per Table 404.2.3)

- 6 mil (0.15) polyethylene film over plywood

- 6 mil (0.15) polyethylene film around crushed stone or gravel backfill

- Pressure-preservative treated 2x6 bottom plate
- Pressure-preservative treated 2x8 footing plate under bottom plate

8" (203)

7¹/₂" (191)

16" (406)

Figure R403.1(2) Basement Wall Section at Permanent Wood Foundation

FOOTINGS

Frost Protected Shallow Foundations

Where the monthly mean temperature of the building is maintained at a minimum of 64°F (18°C), per §R403.3, footings are not required to extend below the frost line when protected from frost by insulation in accordance with Figure R403.3(1) and Table R403.3(1). Such foundations are not to be used for unheated spaces such as porches or carports or any other space where the temperature will not be maintained to the specified warmth. See Figure R403.3(1) for frost protection measures to be installed in heated buildings.

The requirements for insulation are balanced with the depth of the footing in relation to the frost line. The foundation depth requirements in relation to the frost line are determined by examining Table R301.2(1) for the location of the project. The local jurisdiction will note the required foundation depth in this table. This is then to be compared with the requirements of §R403.1.4 to determine what the foundation frost protection treatments will be, determined by footing depth, foundation insulation, use of ASCE 32 or foundation bearing on solid rock. The determination of which foundation frost protection treatment can then be determined based on the most logical and economical criteria applicable the to the project at hand. The requirements of Table R301.2(1) are to be read in concert with those of Table R403.3(1) along with Figure R403.3 (2) and Table R403.3(2) to determine footing depths versus insulation extent based on the geographic location of the project site.

Where unheated buildings or portions of buildings abut heated buildings with insulation for frost protection, the conditions shown in Figure 403.3(1) are to be used. See Figure R403.3 (3) for further information.

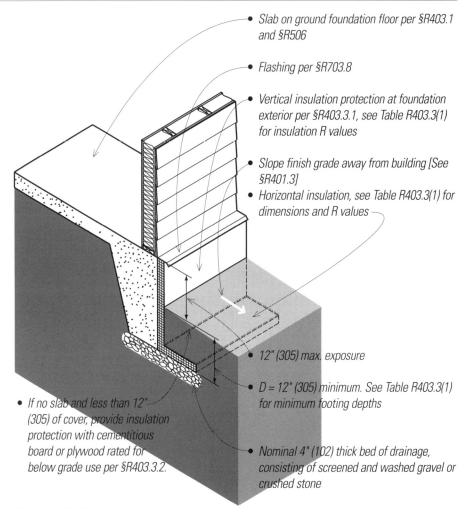

- Slab on ground foundation floor per §R403.1 and §R506
- Flashing per §R703.8
- Vertical insulation protection at foundation exterior per §R403.3.1, see Table R403.3(1) for insulation R values
- Slope finish grade away from building [See §R401.3]
- Horizontal insulation, see Table R403.3(1) for dimensions and R values
- If no slab and less than 12" (305) of cover, provide insulation protection with cementitious board or plywood rated for below grade use per §R403.3.2.
- 12" (305) max. exposure
- D = 12" (305) minimum. See Table R403.3(1) for minimum footing depths
- Nominal 4" (102) thick bed of drainage, consisting of screened and washed gravel or crushed stone

Figure R403.3(1) Insulation at Frost Protected Footings in Heated Buildings

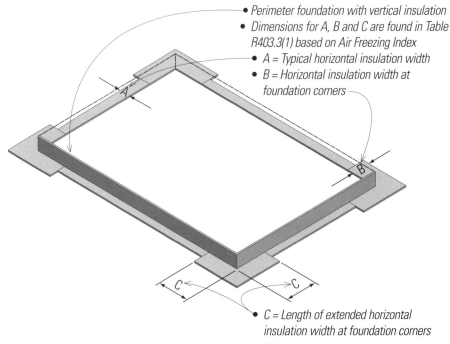

- Perimeter foundation with vertical insulation
- Dimensions for A, B and C are found in Table R403.3(1) based on Air Freezing Index
- A = Typical horizontal insulation width
- B = Horizontal insulation width at foundation corners
- C = Length of extended horizontal insulation width at foundation corners

Figure R403.3(1) Horizontal Insulation Layout and Width

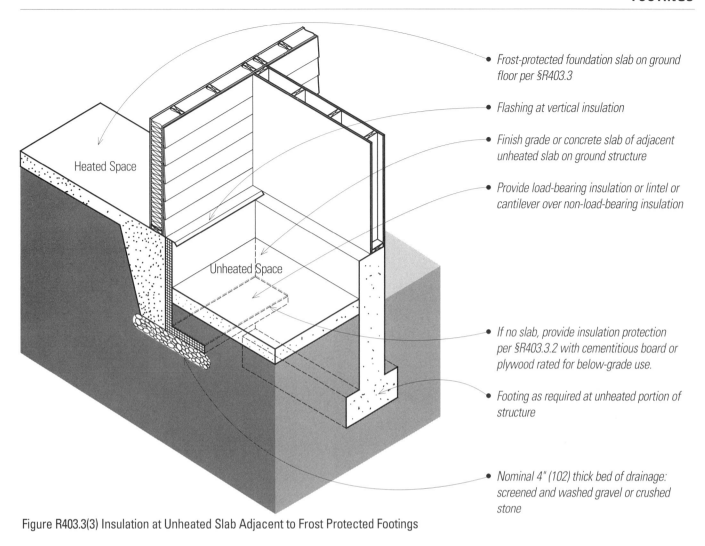

• Frost-protected foundation slab on ground floor per §R403.3

• Flashing at vertical insulation

• Finish grade or concrete slab of adjacent unheated slab on ground structure

• Provide load-bearing insulation or lintel or cantilever over non-load-bearing insulation

• If no slab, provide insulation protection per §R403.3.2 with cementitious board or plywood rated for below-grade use.

• Footing as required at unheated portion of structure

• Nominal 4" (102) thick bed of drainage: screened and washed gravel or crushed stone

Figure R403.3(3) Insulation at Unheated Slab Adjacent to Frost Protected Footings

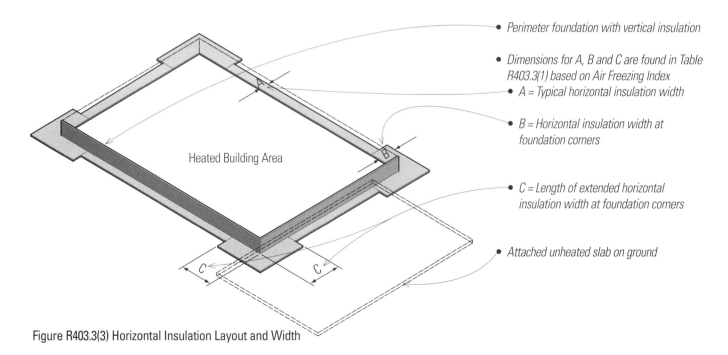

• Perimeter foundation with vertical insulation

• Dimensions for A, B and C are found in Table R403.3(1) based on Air Freezing Index

• A = Typical horizontal insulation width

• B = Horizontal insulation width at foundation corners

• C = Length of extended horizontal insulation width at foundation corners

• Attached unheated slab on ground

Figure R403.3(3) Horizontal Insulation Layout and Width

FOOTINGS

Frost-Protected Shallow Foundations

Portions of heated buildings with insulated foundations may abut other portions of heated buildings that comply with §R403.1, §R403.2 or §R403.3. Where connection of two heated structures occurs, horizontal insulation and vertical wall insulation shall not be required between the frost-protected shallow foundation and the adjoining structure. The insulation may be stopped where this occurs as shown on Figure R403.3 (4).

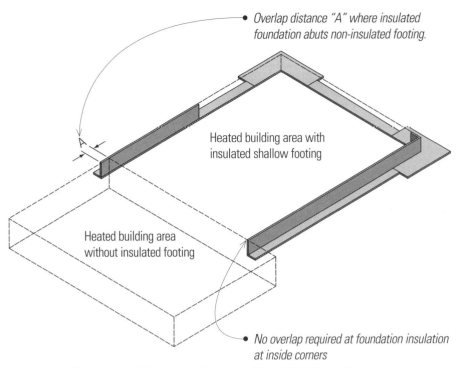

• Overlap distance "A" where insulated foundation abuts non-insulated footing.

Heated building area with insulated shallow footing

Heated building area without insulated footing

• No overlap required at foundation insulation at inside corners

Figure R403.3(4) Insulation Placement where Two Heated Buildings Abut

Footings for Precast Concrete Foundations

Footings for precast concrete foundations are to be per §R403.4.1. This section requires that the precast foundation base section be installed on clean crushed stone footings or concrete spread footings. The depth and width of the stone base are determined per Table R403.4—the width of the foundation wall, the site's soil load-bearing capacity and by the height and construction materials in the building to be supported. Crushed stone footings may be used in Seismic Design Categories A, B and C. Installation of crushed stone footings is shown in Figure R403.4 (1). Concrete spread footings may also be used under precast concrete foundations. These footings are to be per §R403.1 and Figure R403.4 (2).

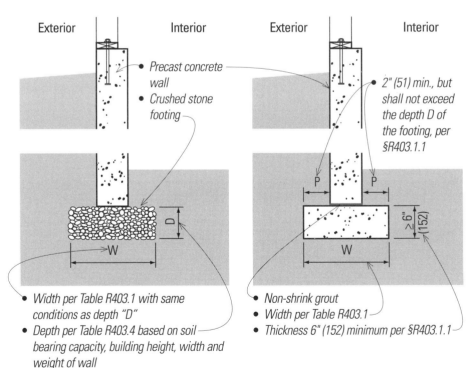

Exterior   Interior   Exterior   Interior

• Precast concrete wall
• Crushed stone footing

• 2" (51) min., but shall not exceed the depth D of the footing, per §R403.1.1

P   P

≥ 6" (152)

W   W

• Width per Table R403.1 with same conditions as depth "D"
• Depth per Table R403.4 based on soil bearing capacity, building height, width and weight of wall

• Non-shrink grout
• Width per Table R403.1
• Thickness 6" (152) minimum per §R403.1.1

Figure 403.4 Footings at Precast Concrete Foundations

§R404, Foundations and Retaining Walls

Foundation walls that sit atop the footings are to be designed per §R404. Foundation walls are typically constructed of cast-in-place concrete, precast concrete or masonry. Under limited conditions outside of Seismic Zones D0, D1 and D2, rubble stone masonry may be used for foundations, but we will focus on concrete and masonry walls, as they are the most typical construction materials used for foundation and retaining walls. Masonry walls are to be designed and constructed per the provisions of §R404.1.1. Concrete walls are to be designed and constructed per §R404.1.2.

Masonry Foundation Walls

Masonry foundation walls may be designed using criteria from §R404.1.1 of the IRC or, alternative design provisions promulgated by the American Concrete Institute or National Concrete Masonry Association may be used. The applicable provisions are ACI530/ASCE 5/ TMS 402 or NCMA TR68-A. When the IRC or listed alternate design provisions are used for masonry foundation wall design the signature of a licensed design professional such as an architect or engineer is not required unless it is required by the state law of the jurisdiction having authority over the project.

Masonry foundation walls using the IRC are to be constructed per the provisions of the tables in §R404.1.1. The tables specify allowable heights, wall thicknesses for walls that are unreinforced "Plain Masonry" [Table R401.1.1(1)], 8" (203) thick masonry with reinforcing [Table R401.1.1(2)], 10" (254) thick masonry with reinforcing [Table R401.1.1(3)], or 12" (305) thick masonry with reinforcing [Table R401.1.1(4)]. The requirements of the tables must be read in concert with §R404.1.4.1 when buildings are located in Seismic Zones C, D0, D1 and D2. Masonry foundation walls are also to comply with the applicable masonry wall construction requirements in Chapter 6 of the IRC.

The requirements for wall thickness and for reinforcing are determined by several factors. The factors include the soil bearing-capacity, the overall height of the wall, the placement of reinforcing (if present) and the relationship of the height of soil outside the wall to the soil height inside the wall. Walls that are retaining earth need to be thickened, reinforced or supported at the top of the wall to resist movement

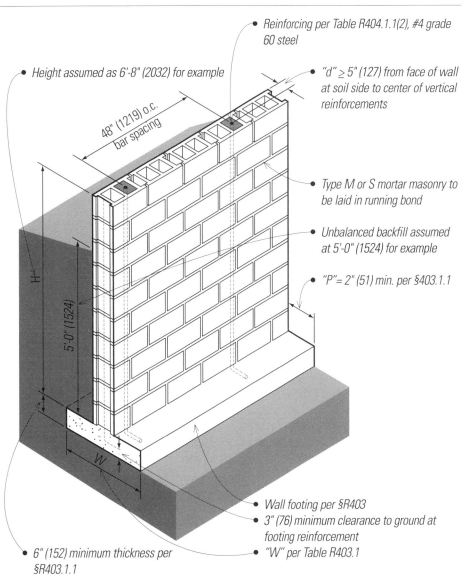

- Reinforcing per Table R404.1.1(2), #4 grade 60 steel
- Height assumed as 6'-8" (2032) for example
- 48" (1219) o.c. bar spacing
- "d" ≥ 5" (127) from face of wall at soil side to center of vertical reinforcements
- Type M or S mortar masonry to be laid in running bond
- Unbalanced backfill assumed at 5'-0" (1524) for example
- "P"= 2" (51) min. per §403.1.1
- H
- 5'-0" (1524)
- W
- Wall footing per §R403
- 3" (76) minimum clearance to ground at footing reinforcement
- "W" per Table R403.1
- 6" (152) minimum thickness per §R403.1.1

Example: 8" (203) Reinforced Masonry Foundation Wall per Table R404.1.1(2), 6'-8" (2032) Tall Wall Height, 5'-0" (1524) Unbalanced Backfill, All Soil Classes and Loads

imposed by the pressure of the soil against the wall. The height of the soil is described by the term "unbalanced backfill." Unbalanced backfill height is defined as the difference in height between the exterior finish ground level and the lower elevation of either the top of the concrete footing that supports the foundation wall or the finish ground level at the interior of the foundation wall. Where an interior concrete slab-on-grade is provided and is in contact with the interior surface of the foundation wall, measurement of the unbalanced backfill height from the exterior finish-ground level to the top of the interior concrete slab is permitted. We will illustrate an example 8" (203)

thick reinforced concrete masonry wall using the criteria from Table R404.1.1(2) to show how these various elements interact. Note that horizontal reinforcement is not required in masonry walls unless they are in Seismic Zones D0, D1 and D2 where the reinforcing is to be per §R404.1.4, which is discussed later in this chapter. Horizontal reinforcement may also be required per Chapter 6, depending on how the masonry units are laid up and what lateral forces, such as wind, may act on the structure. See Chapter 6 regarding masonry wall construction for additional information.

Concrete Foundation Walls

Per §R404.1.2, the basic designs for concrete foundation walls are to be done using either the IRC or the standards from ACI 318, ACI 332 or PCA 100. These standards are meant to be used for foundation walls supporting light-frame construction or concrete construction that falls within the limits of applicability for size and anticipated lateral forces that are spelled out in §R611.2. Concrete foundation walls are to be flat cast-in-place walls or walls using grid- or waffle-forming systems that conform to the profiles described in Table R611.3. Per §R404.1.2.1 if a wall-forming system does not comply with these criteria it is to be designed per ACI 318.

§R404.1.2.2 calls for concrete foundation walls to be laterally supported at the top and bottom. This is read in this case to mean that reinforcing steel is required in concrete foundation walls. This is supported by the tables for reinforcing where wall heights are called out as "unsupported" heights. Note however that per §R404.1.3 Item 2 that walls supporting unbalanced backfill must be designed if they support earth more than 48" (1219) deep if they do not have permanent lateral support at the top and bottom of the wall. Horizontal reinforcing is to be provided at these walls per Table R404.1.2 (1) based on the maximum unsupported height of the "basement wall." See the illustrations for example conditions of flat cast-in-place concrete foundation walls in relationship to their footings and the structure above them showing how the tables are to be used.

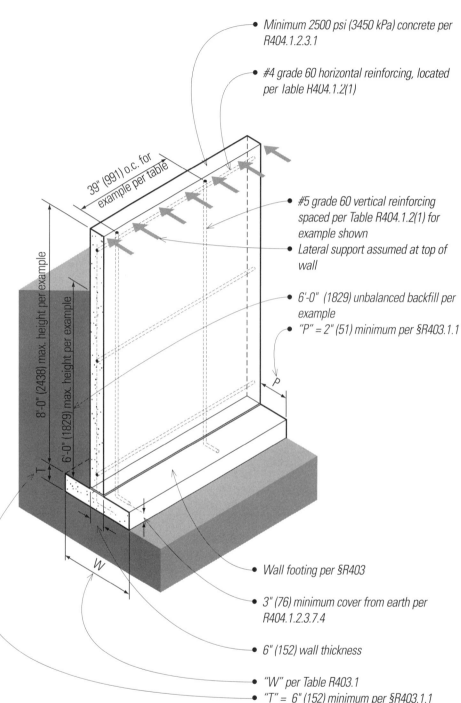

- Minimum 2500 psi (3450 kPa) concrete per R404.1.2.3.1
- #4 grade 60 horizontal reinforcing, located per Table R404.1.2(1)
- #5 grade 60 vertical reinforcing spaced per Table R404.1.2(1) for example shown
- Lateral support assumed at top of wall
- 6'-0" (1829) unbalanced backfill per example
- "P" = 2" (51) minimum per §R403.1.1
- Wall footing per §R403
- 3" (76) minimum cover from earth per R404.1.2.3.7.4
- 6" (152) wall thickness
- "W" per Table R403.1
- "T" = 6" (152) minimum per §R403.1.1

39" (991) o.c. for example per table

8'-0" (2438) max. height per example

6'-0" (1829) max. height per example

Example: 6" (152) Flat Concrete Basement Wall per Table R404.1.2(2), 8'-0" (2438) Tall Wall Height, 6'-0" (1829) unbalanced Backfill Height Soil Classes assumed as G_w, G_p, S_w, S_p with 30 psf (146 kg/m²) design lateral load

Concrete Materials, Reinforcing and Placing

§R404.1.2.3 contains various criteria for the materials that make up concrete foundation walls and how to put them in place. These criteria are basic standards and may be modified by custom concrete mix designs as approved by the Authorities Having Jurisdiction. Per §R404.1.2.3.1 concrete for foundation walls is to have a minimum compressive strength of 2,500 psi (17.2 MPa) at the standard strength measurement time of 28 days after placement. The compressive strength is to be 3,000 psi (20.5 MPa) in Seismic Zones D_0, D_1 and D_2. Maximum aggregate sizes are specified in §R404.1.2.3.3 and are related to the width of the walls and the ability of placement of the concrete without having voids in the concrete where movement of the concrete into the forms is impeded by reinforcing or aggregate sizes. Basic concrete slump is not to exceed 6" (152) unless the mix is designed to resist segregation of concrete elements. Concrete is to be consolidated as it is placed so that it will fill all of the formwork without voids.

Forms are to be stable while concrete is placed and form ties are to be used to keep the forms from deflecting. Forms may be removable or designed to remain in place. Some forming systems are made of foam that may be finished when they remain or left in place to provide thermal insulation.

Concrete reinforcement is to be steel at least Grade 40, with a yield strength of at least 40,000 psi (276 MPa). In Seismic Zones D_0, D_1 and D_2 the steel is to be Grade 60, with yield strength of at least 60,000 psi (414 MPa). Reinforcing tables in §R404.1.2.2 are based on the use of Grade 60 steel, but lower-strength steel may be used if placed at closer spacing per Table R404.1.2.(9). Reinforcement is to be located essentially in the center of the wall or as required by various tables, as illustrated. The reinforcing is not to vary from its vertical location more than 10 percent of the thickness of the wall. Steel, in thinner concrete basement walls where there is dirt present on the outside of the wall, is to be placed near the inside face of the wall, with a maximum cover of $1^{1}/4$" (32) to be sure that the steel is not too close to the damp exterior face of the concrete wall and thus subject to corrosion. Reinforcing in concrete cast against earth is to have 3" (75) minimum concrete cover. Openings in walls that interrupt vertical reinforcement are to have additional vertical reinforcing adjacent to the opening, as illustrated. Reinforcing is to be the longest possible lengths, and where the steel is interrupted the reinforcing steel is to be lapped per §R611.5.4.3 and Figure R611.5.4(1). Where the code refers to a "standard hook" for rebar termination it is to be as illustrated, per Figure R611.5.4.(3) see Chapter 6 for illustrations. Construction joints in concrete foundation walls are to be as shown in the illustration.

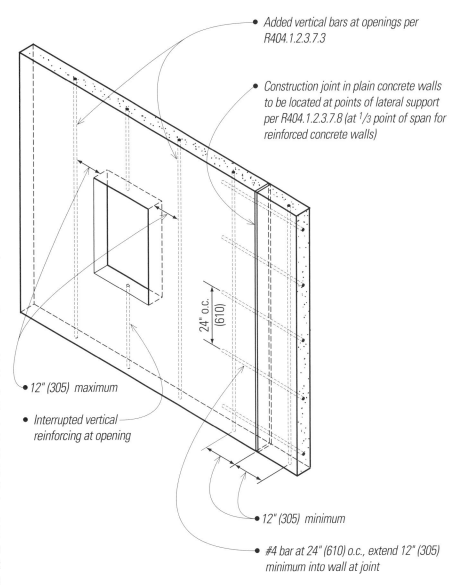

- *Added vertical bars at openings per R404.1.2.3.7.3*

- *Construction joint in plain concrete walls to be located at points of lateral support per R404.1.2.3.7.8 (at $^1/_3$ point of span for reinforced concrete walls)*

24" o.c. (610)

- *12" (305) maximum*

- *Interrupted vertical reinforcing at opening*

- *12" (305) minimum*

- *#4 bar at 24" (610) o.c., extend 12" (305) minimum into wall at joint*

Openings and Construction Joints at Foundation Walls

Requirements for Seismic Design of Foundation Walls

Per §R404.1.4 when the building is located in Seismic Design Categories D0, D1 and D2 per Table R301.2 (1) additional criteria are set forth for both masonry foundation walls and concrete foundation walls.

Plain masonry foundation walls are to be designed per Table 404.1.1(1); in addition in Seismic Design Categories D0, D1 and D2 the walls must meet the following additional conditions from §R404.1.4.1:

1. The walls may not exceed 8' (2438) in height.
2. There may not be unbalanced backfill in excess of 4' (1219) in height.
3. The wall must be at least 8" (203) in nominal thickness.
4. Masonry stem walls must have minimum vertical reinforcing of #3 bars at a maximum of 4' (1219) on center in grouted cells. The vertical reinforcement is to be tied to the horizontal reinforcement in the footings.

When masonry walls located in these seismic zones support more than 4' (1219) of unbalanced fill or exceed 8' (2438) in height they are to be designed as reinforced masonry walls per Tables R404.1.1 (2), R404.1.1 (3) or R404.1.1 (4). These walls are also to have at least two #4 horizontal reinforcing bars located in the upper 12" (305) of the wall.

Concrete foundation walls located in Seismic Design Categories D0, D1 and D2 are to be designed per the provisions of §404.1.4.2. For light-frame buildings, horizontal reinforcing is to be per Table R404.1.2 (1). Plain concrete may be used for walls less than 8' (2438) high, supporting less than 4' (1219) of unbalanced backfill and at least 6" (152) for a height of up to 4'-6" (1372) and 7 1/2" (191) up to a height of 8' (2438). Basic reinforcing is required, the exact size and spacing of the reinforcing is to be determined by reading Tables 404.1.2(1–8). But in no case, per §404.1.4.2, should concrete walls in Seismic Design Categories D0, D1 and D2 have less vertical steel reinforcing than #4 bars at 48" (1219) on center and horizontal steel reinforcing than per Table R404.1.2 (1) which requires a #4 bar at the top of the wall and at mid-height for walls less than 8' (2438) high and at third points

for walls taller than 8' (2438). Foundation walls supporting concrete or masonry walls, that is, other than light-framing, are to be per ACI 318, ACI 332 or PCA 100 per §R404.1.2. See the illustration.

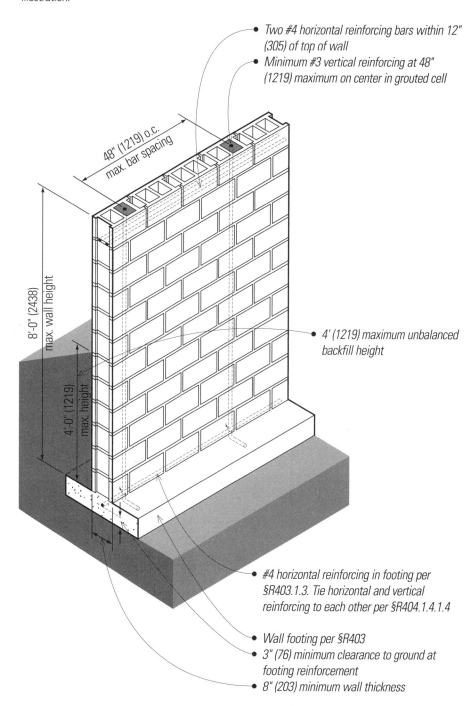

- Two #4 horizontal reinforcing bars within 12" (305) of top of wall
- Minimum #3 vertical reinforcing at 48" (1219) maximum on center in grouted cell

48" (1219) o.c. max. bar spacing

8'-0" (2438) max. wall height

4'-0" (1219) max. height

- 4' (1219) maximum unbalanced backfill height

- #4 horizontal reinforcing in footing per §R403.1.3. Tie horizontal and vertical reinforcing to each other per §R404.1.4.1.4

- Wall footing per §R403
- 3" (76) minimum clearance to ground at footing reinforcement
- 8" (203) minimum wall thickness

Plain Masonry Foundation Wall in Seismic Design Categories D0, D1, or D2 per §R404.1.4.1

Foundation Wall Thickness Based on the Wall Supported

§404.1.5 deals with the thickness of foundation walls in relation to the thickness and the materials of the walls supported on top of the foundation walls. §404.1.5.1 addresses requirements for masonry foundation walls and §404.1.5.2 addresses requirements for concrete foundation walls. See the illustrations for examples for both types of walls.

Pier and Curtain Wall Foundations

"Curtain wall" foundations are not defined in the IRC, but they may be presumed to be relatively thin non-bearing foundation walls that enclose the interior space at the foundation level with vertical loads being taken primarily by spaced piers that occur in the walls. There are a number of conditions imposed on such foundations. See the illustrations on page 129 for details.

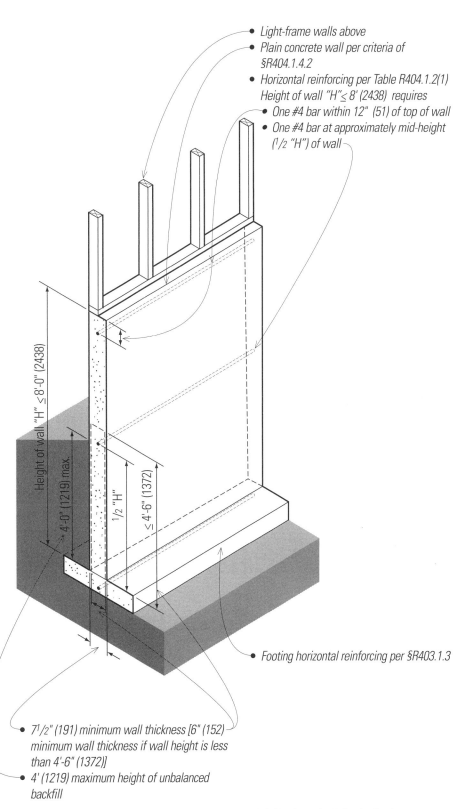

- Light-frame walls above
- Plain concrete wall per criteria of §R404.1.4.2
- Horizontal reinforcing per Table R404.1.2(1) Height of wall "H" ≤ 8' (2438) requires
  - One #4 bar within 12" (51) of top of wall
  - One #4 bar at approximately mid-height ($\frac{1}{2}$ "H") of wall

Height of wall "H" ≤ 8'-0" (2438)

4'-0" (1219) max.

$\frac{1}{2}$ "H"

≤ 4'-6" (1372)

- Footing horizontal reinforcing per §R403.1.3

- 7$\frac{1}{2}$" (191) minimum wall thickness [6" (152) minimum wall thickness if wall height is less than 4'-6" (1372)]
- 4' (1219) maximum height of unbalanced backfill

Plain Concrete Foundation Wall with Light-frame Walls above in Seismic Design Categories D0, D1, or D2 per §R404.1.4.2

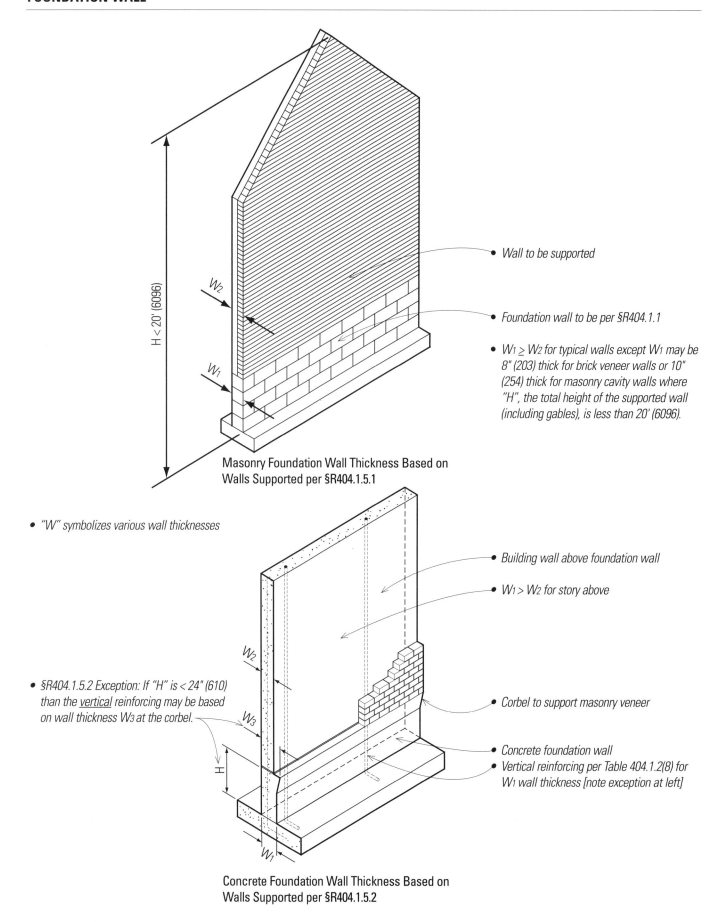

- Wall to be supported

- Foundation wall to be per §R404.1.1

- $W_1 \geq W_2$ for typical walls except W_1 may be 8" (203) thick for brick veneer walls or 10" (254) thick for masonry cavity walls where "H", the total height of the supported wall (including gables), is less than 20' (6096).

$H < 20' (6096)$

W_2

W_1

Masonry Foundation Wall Thickness Based on Walls Supported per §R404.1.5.1

- "W" symbolizes various wall thicknesses

- §R404.1.5.2 Exception: If "H" is < 24" (610) than the <u>vertical</u> reinforcing may be based on wall thickness W_3 at the corbel.

W_2

W_3

H

W_1

- Building wall above foundation wall
- $W_1 > W_2$ for story above

- Corbel to support masonry veneer

- Concrete foundation wall
- Vertical reinforcing per Table 404.1.2(8) for W_1 wall thickness [note exception at left]

Concrete Foundation Wall Thickness Based on Walls Supported per §R404.1.5.2

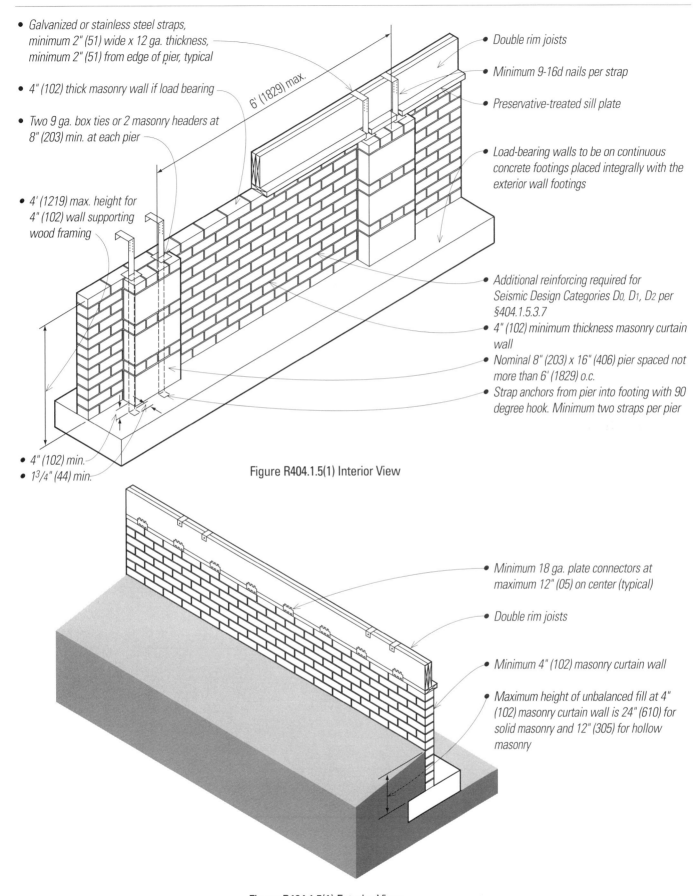

- Galvanized or stainless steel straps, minimum 2" (51) wide x 12 ga. thickness, minimum 2" (51) from edge of pier, typical

- 4" (102) thick masonry wall if load bearing

- Two 9 ga. box ties or 2 masonry headers at 8" (203) min. at each pier

- 4' (1219) max. height for 4" (102) wall supporting wood framing

- 4" (102) min.
- 1³/4" (44) min.

6' (1829) max.

- Double rim joists

- Minimum 9-16d nails per strap

- Preservative-treated sill plate

- Load-bearing walls to be on continuous concrete footings placed integrally with the exterior wall footings

- Additional reinforcing required for Seismic Design Categories D_0, D_1, D_2 per §404.1.5.3.7
- 4" (102) minimum thickness masonry curtain wall
- Nominal 8" (203) x 16" (406) pier spaced not more than 6' (1829) o.c.
- Strap anchors from pier into footing with 90 degree hook. Minimum two straps per pier

Figure R404.1.5(1) Interior View

- Minimum 18 ga. plate connectors at maximum 12" (05) on center (typical)

- Double rim joists

- Minimum 4" (102) masonry curtain wall

- Maximum height of unbalanced fill at 4" (102) masonry curtain wall is 24" (610) for solid masonry and 12" (305) for hollow masonry

Figure R404.1.5(1) Exterior View

Height of Foundation Walls Above Grade and Backfill Placement

§R404.1.6 governs minimum height above grade for various types of finish materials, as illustrated. §R404.1.7 says that backfill at foundations should not be placed until the walls have achieved sufficient strength to resist the pressure of the backfill. The section also notes that the top of walls must be braced to resist backfill pressure, either by temporary bracing or installation of the floor framing at the top of the wall. Note that §R404.4 requires that retaining walls that support more than 24" (610) are not laterally supported at the top are to be designed to ensure stability against overturning, sliding, excessive foundation pressure and water uplift. Retaining walls shall be designed for a safety factor of 1.5 against lateral sliding and overturning.

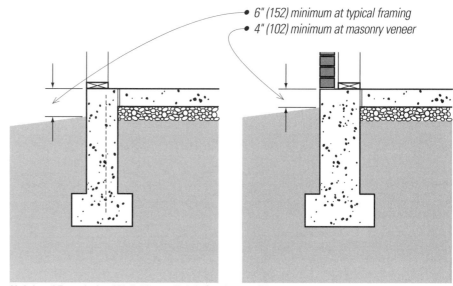

- 6" (152) minimum at typical framing
- 4" (102) minimum at masonry veneer

Height of Foundation Wall Above Finish Grade per §R404.1.6

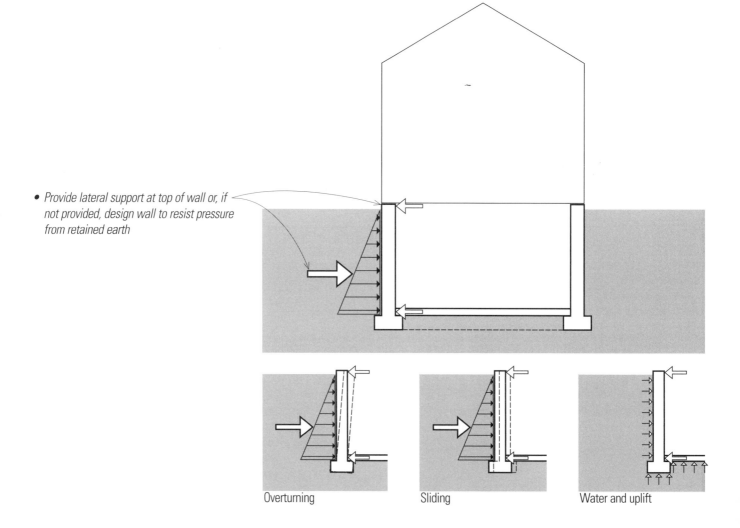

- Provide lateral support at top of wall or, if not provided, design wall to resist pressure from retained earth

Overturning

Sliding

Water and uplift

Other Foundation Wall Materials

Rubble stone foundation walls are to be installed per §R404.1.8.

Wood foundations are to be as shown in the illustrations for §403 of Chapter 4. Wood foundation wall plywood is described in Table R404.2.3 with the plywood thickness and stud spacing dependent upon the height of fill adjacent to the wood foundation wall. See the illustrations in §403 of Chapter 4 in this book. Note also that per Table R404.2.3 the maximum height of earth that may be retained by a wood foundation is 4' (1219). Precast concrete foundation walls are to be designed in accordance with accepted engineering practice. §R404.5.2 lists the criteria for what a submittal for approval of a precast foundation design is to contain to allow the building official to approve the design.

§R405, Foundation Drainage and Soil Classification

Per §R405 foundations that retain earth and enclose usable or habitable space below grade are to have a foundation drainage system to keep liquid water from entering the building or accumulating against foundation materials that may be damaged by prolonged exposure to moisture. There are varying requirements for different foundation wall materials as shown in the illustrations. For wood foundations see Figures R403.1(2) and R403.1(3). We have called out the drainage pipes as 4" (102) in diameter per the plumbing requirements for subsoil drains in §P3302.1.

Note that per the Exception to §R405.1 foundation drainage is not required when the foundation is considered to be "well-drained ground" for Group I soils as classified by the Uniform Soil Classification System described in Table R405.1. Note that the soil classification per this system is also the basis for reinforcing steel size and spacing per the foundation wall tables in R404.1.2. We have provided a graphic illustration of the characteristics of each soil type described in Table R405.1 on page 132.

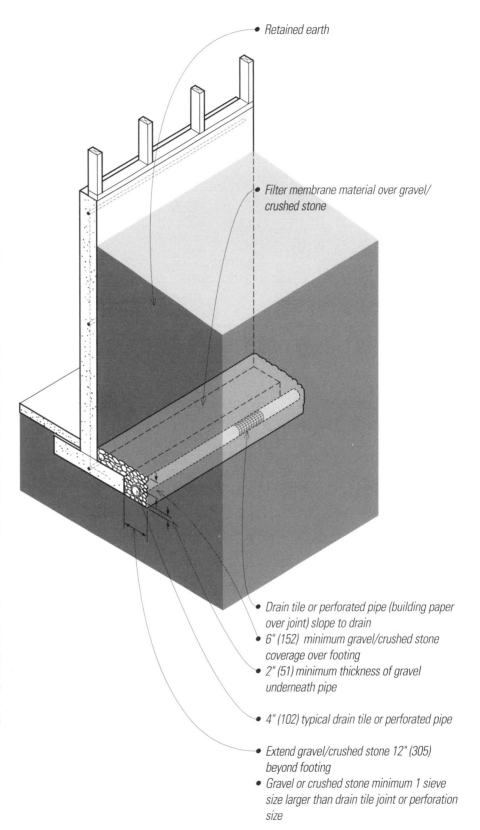

• Retained earth

• Filter membrane material over gravel/ crushed stone

• Drain tile or perforated pipe (building paper over joint) slope to drain
• 6" (152) minimum gravel/crushed stone coverage over footing
• 2" (51) minimum thickness of gravel underneath pipe
• 4" (102) typical drain tile or perforated pipe
• Extend gravel/crushed stone 12" (305) beyond footing
• Gravel or crushed stone minimum 1 sieve size larger than drain tile joint or perforation size

Foundation Drainage at Concrete or Masonry Foundation per §R405.1

SOIL CLASSIFICATION

Illustrated Uniform Soil Classification System from Table R405.1

Soil Group	Unified Soil Classification System Designation	Soil Description	Typical Report Symbol	Drainage Characteristics	Frost Heave Potential	Volume Change Potential
Group I, No Drain per Exception to §305.1	GW	Well-graded gravels, gravel sand mixtures, little or no fines.		Good	Low	Low
	GP	Poorly graded gravels or gravel sand mixtures, little or no fines		Good	Low	Low
	SW	Well-graded sands, gravelly sands, little or no fines		Good	Low	Low
	SP	Poorly graded sands or gravelly sands, little or no fines		Good	Low	Low
	GM	Silty gravels, gravel-sand-silt mixtures		Good	Medium	Low
	SM	Silty sand, sand-silt mixtures		Good	Medium	Low
Group II	GC	Clayey gravels, gravel-sand-clay mixtures		Medium	Medium	Low
	SC	Clayey sands, sand-clay mixture		Medium	Medium	Low
	ML	Inorganic silts and very fine sands, rock flour, silty or clayey fine sands or clayey silts with slight plasticity		Medium	High	Low
	CL	Inorganic clays of low-to-medium plasticity, graveley clays, sandy clays, silty clays, lean clays		Medium	Medium	Medium
Group III	CH	Inorganic clays of high plasticity, fat clays		Poor	Medium	High
	MH	Inorganic silts, micaceous or diatomaceous fine sandy or silty soils, elastic silts		Poor	High	High
Group IV	OL	Organic silts and organic silty clays of low plasticity		Poor	Medium	Medium
	OH	Organic clays of medium-to-high plasticity, organic silts		Unsatisfactory	Medium	High
	PT	Peat and other highly organic soils		Unsatisfactory	Medium	High

Symbols Key

	Drainage		Frost Heave		Volume Change
	Good		Low		Low
	Medium		Medium		Medium
	Low		High		High
	Poor				
	Unsatisfactory				

§R406, Foundation Waterproofing and Dampproofing

Where foundation walls retain earth and enclose interior spaces below grade they are to be dampproofed or waterproofed depending on the surrounding soil conditions. All foundation walls that meet these criteria are to have at least dampproofing measures applied from the top of the footing to the finished grade. Where there is a known high water-table, or other severe water-soil conditions are known to exist, then waterproofing is to be applied per §R406.2. Since waterproofing measures are more extensive and water-resistant than dampproofing measures, when waterproofing is applied the code considers those measures sufficient for dampproofing as well. Once it has been determined from consultation with the AHJ which measures are required for a specific project, either dampproofing or waterproofing measures are to be applied to foundation walls enclosing occupiable interior spaces below grade. See the illustrations for descriptions of the measures to be taken for dampproofing and waterproofing at concrete and masonry foundation walls.

Note that §R406.3 contains dampproofing requirements for wood foundations. There are no waterproofing requirements for wood foundations. Dampproofing for wood foundations is not illustrated here.

§R406.4 refers back to dampproofing requirements for precast concrete foundations enclosing habitable space to those requirements for concrete and masonry foundations in §R406.1. Where precast foundations are to be waterproofed they are to be treated with one of the concrete or masonry waterproofing methods specified in §R406.1.

- Masonry foundation wall requires $3/8$" (9.5) portland cement parging at exterior of wall from grade to top of footing*
  *parging is not required at masonry walls where a dampproofing material is approved for direct application to masonry.

- Parging is dampproofing with one of the following:
  1. Bituminous coating, or:
  2. Three lbs/sf (1.63 kg/m²) of acrylic modified cement, or
  3. $1/8$" (3.2) coat of surface bonding cement per ASTM C887, or
  4. Any waterproofing material per §R406.2, or
  5. Other approved methods

- Concrete walls may be dampproofed with any of the methods described above or with waterproofing materials per §R406.2

- Below-grade interior space

Dampproofing at Masonry or Concrete Foundation Walls per §R406.1

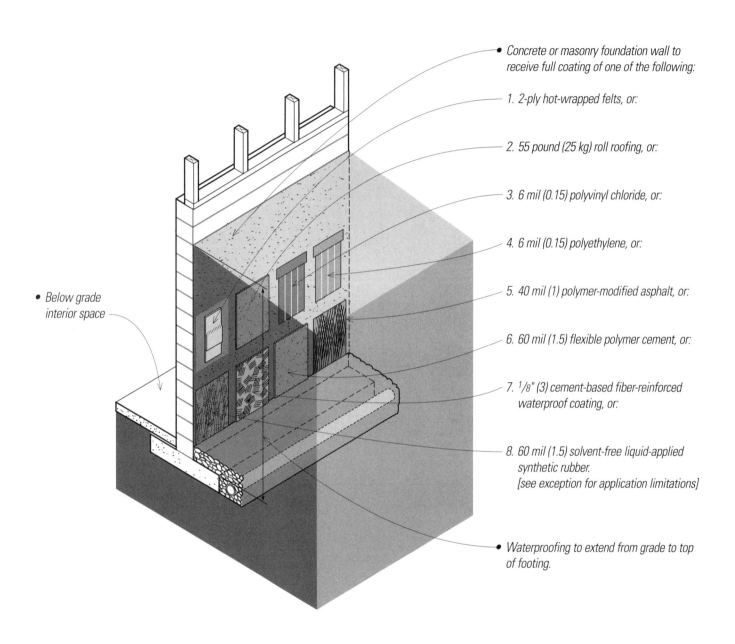

Concrete or masonry foundation wall to receive full coating of one of the following:

1. 2-ply hot-wrapped felts, or:

2. 55 pound (25 kg) roll roofing, or:

3. 6 mil (0.15) polyvinyl chloride, or:

4. 6 mil (0.15) polyethylene, or:

5. 40 mil (1) polymer-modified asphalt, or:

6. 60 mil (1.5) flexible polymer cement, or:

7. ¹/₈" (3) cement-based fiber-reinforced waterproof coating, or:

8. 60 mil (1.5) solvent-free liquid-applied synthetic rubber.
[see exception for application limitations]

Waterproofing to extend from grade to top of footing.

Below grade interior space

Waterproofing at Masonry or Concrete Foundation Walls per §R406.2

Columns

Per §R407 wood columns are to be protected against decay per the provisions of §R317 regarding protection of wood against decay. See the illustrations for that section regarding how wood columns are to be separated from earth. Steel columns are to be coated on all inside and outside surfaces with rust-inhibitive paint or be treated with other corrosion-resistant materials.

The minimum sizes of columns are specified for wood and steel in §R407.3. See the illustrations for examples. Note that except for short columns of 48" (1219) or less under specific conditions and located in Seismic Design Categories A, B and C, columns are to be restrained at their bottom ends to prevent lateral displacement. The methods for prevention of lateral displacement are not specified in the code.

Underfloor Space

§R408 addresses requirements for treatment of what is commonly called "crawl space," or unoccupied areas under floors. This section is meant to apply to unoccupiable spaces; requirements for occupied basements occur elsewhere. This section specifies requirements for such things as ventilation of these spaces to prevent moisture damage to structures as well as the requirements for access to these areas for maintenance.

Ventilation

Per §R408.1 through §R408.3 the underfloor space is to be passively or actively ventilated or provided with vapor retarders to prevent moisture or vapor intrusion. There are many alternative methods provided, as illustrated. These spaces need not be provided with passive ventilation when vapor retarders or mechanical ventilation is provided, or if the space acts as a plenum in an air handling system.

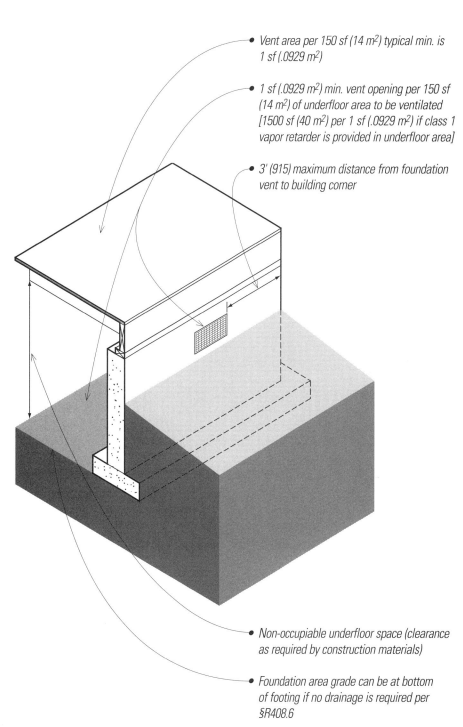

- Vent area per 150 sf (14 m²) typical min. is 1 sf (.0929 m²)

- 1 sf (.0929 m²) min. vent opening per 150 sf (14 m²) of underfloor area to be ventilated [1500 sf (40 m²) per 1 sf (.0929 m²) if class 1 vapor retarder is provided in underfloor area]

- 3' (915) maximum distance from foundation vent to building corner

- Non-occupiable underfloor space (clearance as required by construction materials)

- Foundation area grade can be at bottom of footing if no drainage is required per §R408.6

Typical Underfloor Ventilation per §R408.1

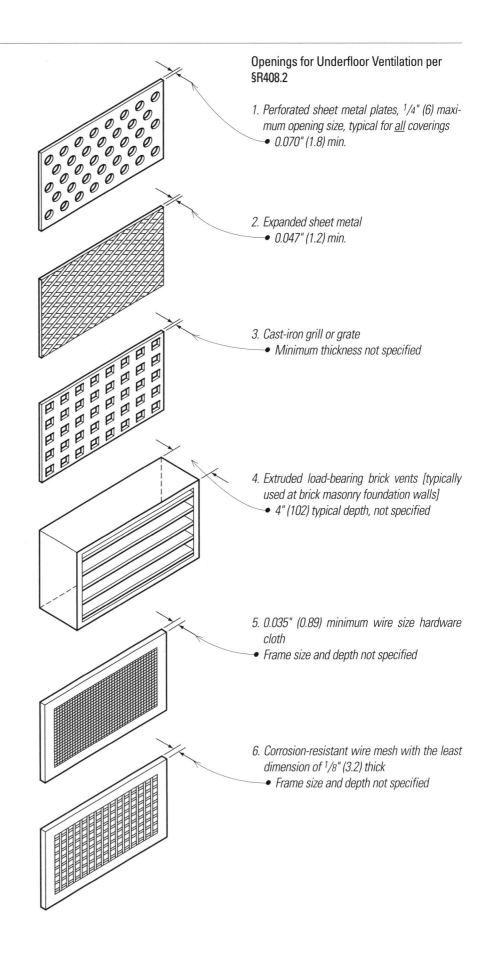

Openings for Underfloor Ventilation per §R408.2

1. Perforated sheet metal plates, 1/4" (6) maximum opening size, typical for _all_ coverings
   • 0.070" (1.8) min.

2. Expanded sheet metal
   • 0.047" (1.2) min.

3. Cast-iron grill or grate
   • Minimum thickness not specified

4. Extruded load-bearing brick vents [typically used at brick masonry foundation walls]
   • 4" (102) typical depth, not specified

5. 0.035" (0.89) minimum wire size hardware cloth
   • Frame size and depth not specified

6. Corrosion-resistant wire mesh with the least dimension of 1/8" (3.2) thick
   • Frame size and depth not specified

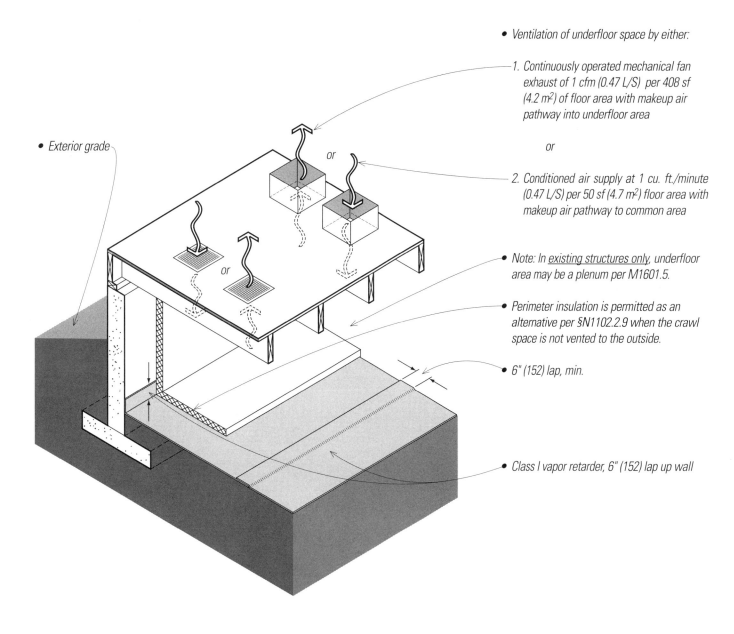

- Ventilation of underfloor space by either:

1. Continuously operated mechanical fan exhaust of 1 cfm (0.47 L/S) per 408 sf (4.2 m²) of floor area with makeup air pathway into underfloor area

or

2. Conditioned air supply at 1 cu. ft./minute (0.47 L/S) per 50 sf (4.7 m²) floor area with makeup air pathway to common area

- Exterior grade

- Note: In _existing structures only_, underfloor area may be a plenum per M1601.5.

- Perimeter insulation is permitted as an alternative per §N1102.2.9 when the crawl space is not vented to the outside.

- 6" (152) lap, min.

- Class I vapor retarder, 6" (152) lap up wall

Unventilated Crawl Space per §R408.3

Access and Debris Cleanup

Per §R408.4 underfloor spaces are to be provided with access hatches of a size to allow a person to get into the spaces to work on items in them, as illustrated. The access may be inside the dwelling or may be provided through the perimeter foundation. Where exterior access is provided and it is below grade, an area way is to be provided to allow a person to readily use the access opening. Note that access openings that go through a wall are not to be located under a door into the residence. This is to prevent accidents where people could fall into the area way at the door. There are additional requirements for access to underfloor mechanical equipment contained in §M1305.1.4. The requirements for the size of such equipment openings are based on the smallest size of the mechanical units to be accessed, to allow service and replacement if necessary. See the illustrations accompanying §M1305.1.4 for further information.

§R408.5 states the requirement that underfloor spaces are to be free of vegetation and all organic matter. The space is to be cleared of any construction debris. Wood forms are to be removed from concrete. The intent of this section is that the underfloor area not have any materials in it that could be conducive to decay, moisture damage or vermin infestation.

Finished Grade at Underfloor Areas

The grade level in underfloor areas may be set at the bottom of the footings, which makes excavation easier. However, where there is an expectation that the groundwater level may rise to within 6" (152) of the finished floor, or that surface water at the site will not drain well, then the underfloor area must be filled to be level with the surrounding grade, or a drainage system provided. Note that when the interior is filled, then the house floor level may have to be raised, or framing materials altered in wood-framed buildings to provide necessary clearances between earth and wood framing members as required by §R317.

In flood-prone areas, as called out in the locally adopted version of Table 301.2(1), §R408.7 specifies flood-resistance requirements. See the requirements spelled out in §R322.2.2 for flood openings. An exception notes that crawl space designs meeting the requirements of FEMA Flood Insurance Program Technical Bulletin 11-1 for crawlspace design in special flood hazard areas are acceptable. Note that the requirements in TB 11-1 are similar to those in the IRC.

5
Floors

Moving upward in the building from foundations, the next set of elements to be addressed in the IRC are floors. These are the components that rest on the foundations and upon which the other parts of the structure will be built in turn.

Floor systems addressed fall into one of four categories: wood-framed floors made up of multiple framing elements with wood sheathing; wood floors resting on the ground; steel-framed floors, which are similar in configuration to wood-framed floors, but with steel framing elements and sheathing; and concrete floor slabs.

Floors

In two-family dwellings where they are separated by the floor system, the floor is to be a minimum 1-hour fire-resistance-rated assembly per §R302.3. Floor depth and the spacing of elements are based on assumed loads. Size and spacing of elements are facilitated by the use of the allowable-span tables included in this chapter. Floor assemblies will also act as diaphragms for resistance to lateral forces imposed by wind or seismic loading. The transfer of lateral forces into foundations or to the ground via the floor systems designed per Chapter 5 is included in the assumptions built into this chapter and Chapter 6 governing wall construction. The intent of this section is that it covers all interior horizontal surfaces that may have superimposed loads. Thus §R501.1 says that this chapter also includes the design of attic spaces used to house mechanical or plumbing equipment.

For the examples illustrated in this chapter, we have assumed the following floor spans and loadings for all materials so that we can illustrate the use of the span tables. The assumptions are based on single spans where that affects member sizes. The assumptions are:

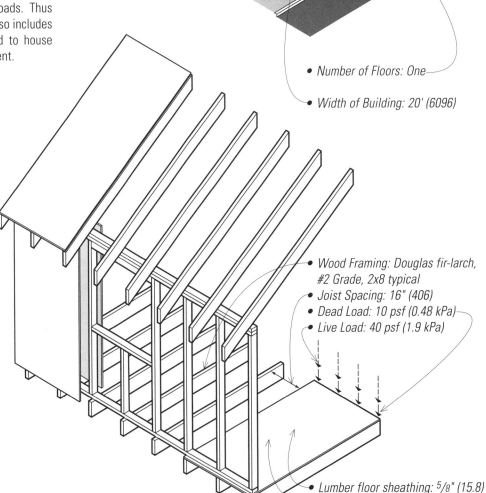

- *Number of Floors: One*
- *Width of Building: 20' (6096)*

- *Wood Framing: Douglas fir-larch, #2 Grade, 2x8 typical*
- *Joist Spacing: 16" (406)*
- *Dead Load: 10 psf (0.48 kPa)*
- *Live Load: 40 psf (1.9 kPa)*

- *Lumber floor sheathing: 5/8" (15.8)*
- *Wood Panel Floor Sheathing: Span Rating: 32/16 Thickness: 1/2" (12.7)*
- *Steel Framing: 10" (254) web depth, designation-thickness/strength: 1000S162-43/33 ksi*

§R502 Wood Floor Framing

Wood used in floor framing is to be identified in such a way that inspectors may determine its level of quality during plan review or field inspections. Load-bearing dimensional lumber members are to be graded and bear a grade mark. Where preservative-treated wood is to be used it is to comply with the requirements of §R317.1. Blocking is to be minimum utility grade, while subflooring materials are to be minimum utility grade or No. 4 common grade boards. Specifications for other wood and wood-like materials, such as end-jointed wood and prefabricated wood I-joists and wood/plastic composite deck boards are spelled out in §R502.1.

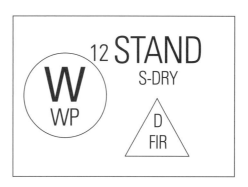

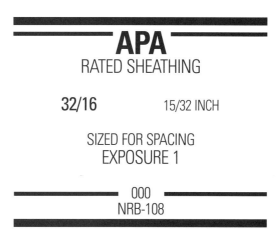

Wood Floor Framing Design and Construction

Per §502.2 wood floor framing designed and constructed in accordance with Chapter 5 is to use the criteria set forth in Figure R502.2 in the code, which is in turn keyed to various sections in §502. Wood floor framing must also meet the provisions of §R317 for decay resistance and §R318 for termite resistance. Per this section AF&PA/NDS standards may also be used, but a discussion of those standards is outside the purview of this book.

A load path for vertical and lateral forces as specified in §R602.10.6 is to be provided from braced walls into the foundations, per §R502.2.1.

The IRC discusses deck attachment to buildings before it describes wood floor framing. We will follow the order of the IRC in our discussion. Accordingly, the Figure R502.2 occurs after that for Figure R502.2.2.3.

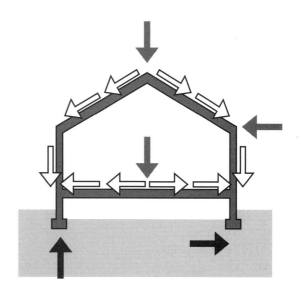

Decks

Deck is not a defined term, but it may be considered as an extension of usable floor area beyond the exterior wall of the building. Decks are assumed to be either supported on at least two sides, usually by the building on one side and by posts or piers on the other side, or to be cantilevered. Per §R502.2.2 decks are to be positively anchored to the primary structure and designed for both vertical and lateral loads. Decks with cantilevered framing members, connections to exterior walls or other framing members are to be designed and constructed to resist uplift resulting from the full live load of 40 pounds per square foot (1.9 kPa) specified in Table R301.5 acting on the cantilevered portion of the deck. Decks attached to the building are to be designed for vertical loads as noted and are also to be designed to resist lateral loads. An acceptable method of providing lateral support is illustrated in Figure 502.2.2.3. See the illustration, which describes attachment of a supported deck to the building and the lateral support described in Figure 502.2.2.3.

- $^{15}/_{32}$" (12) exterior sheathing

- Flashing

- 50 psf (244 kg/m^2) deck loading (dead load plus live load)

- Decking dashed for clarity

- Deck joist

- 2" (51)

- 6" (152) max.

- Nail joist with hold down at 6" (152) o.c. max.

- 2" (51) nominal band joist

- Tip of lag screw to extend fully beyond inside back of band joist

- $^1/_2$" (13) gap between deck ledger and exterior sheathing

- $^1/_2$" (12.7) lag screws 2" (51) in from top and bottom of deck ledger, staggered space per Table 502.2.2.1

- Deck lateral load attachment per Figure 502.2.2.3 located at each end of deck, minimum

- Deck ledger minimum 2x8 pressure preservative-treated #2 grade or approved equal

Deck Ledger Attachment per §R502.2.2.1

Floor Framing

As noted, Figure R502.2 illustrates where detailed requirements are found in the code text for various elements of floor framing. We will use portions of this figure repeatedly to illustrate and call out these detailed code requirements.

- At girders, lap joist or splice per §R502.6.1

- 2" (510) minimum clearance to combustible framing at fireplace per §R1001.11

- Header at fireplace, double if more than 4' (1219) use hangers if span more than 6' (1829)

- Fireplace (where occurs)
- Double joists under bearing partitions per §R502.4

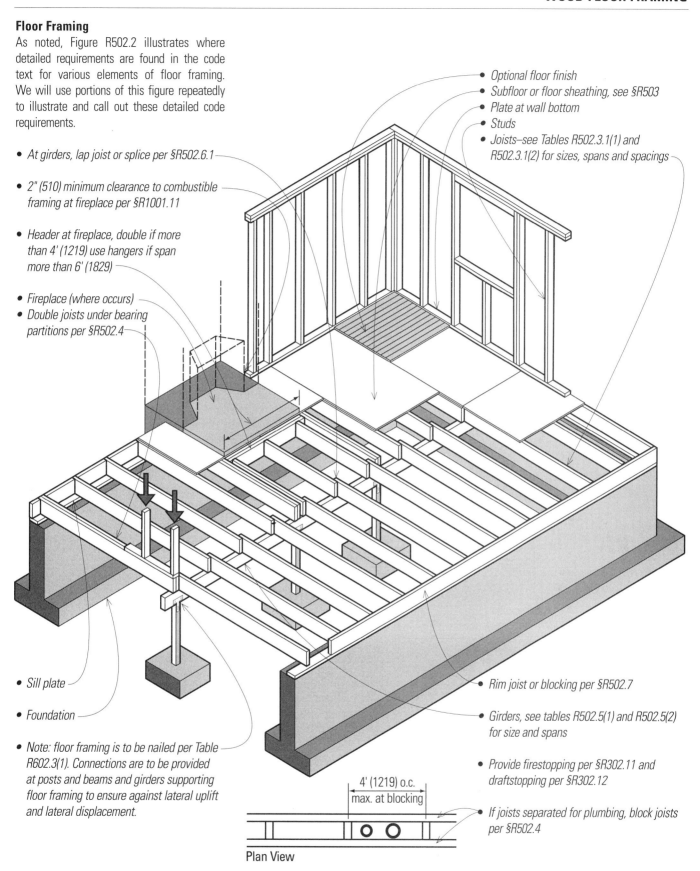

- Optional floor finish
- Subfloor or floor sheathing, see §R503
- Plate at wall bottom
- Studs
- Joists–see Tables R502.3.1(1) and R502.3.1(2) for sizes, spans and spacings

- Sill plate

- Foundation

- Note: floor framing is to be nailed per Table R602.3(1). Connections are to be provided at posts and beams and girders supporting floor framing to ensure against lateral uplift and lateral displacement.

4' (1219) o.c. max. at blocking

Plan View

- Rim joist or blocking per §R502.7

- Girders, see tables R502.5(1) and R502.5(2) for size and spans

- Provide firestopping per §R302.11 and draftstopping per §R302.12

- If joists separated for plumbing, block joists per §R502.4

Key to Wood Floor Construction per §R502.2 and Figure 502.2

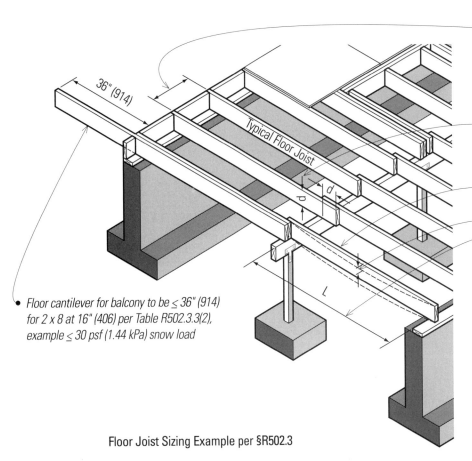

Example 16" (406) joist spacing

Floor joist cantilever span not to exceed joist depth d per §R502.3.3

Example: 2x8 douglas fir-larch #2 grade floor joist
- Deflection = L/360
- L = 12'-7" (3845) maximum per Table R502.3.1(2) with 10 psf (0.48 kPa) dead load and 40 psf (1.92 kPa) live load

Note that for sleeping areas Table R502.3.1(1) may be used. Sleeping areas are assumed to have live loads of 30 psf (1.44 kPa) and other areas 40 psf (1.92 kPa) per §R502.3.1 and §R502.3.2.

Floor cantilever for balcony to be ≤ 36" (914) for 2 x 8 at 16" (406) per Table R502.3.3(2), example ≤ 30 psf (1.44 kPa) snow load

Typical Floor Joist

Floor Joist Sizing Example per §R502.3

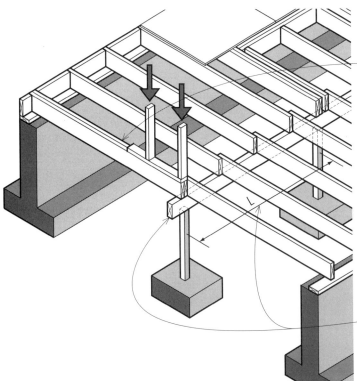

Example: one floor only, 20' (6096) building width

Two jack studs required at bearing wall headers

Typical floor girder two 2x10 douglas fir-larch girder for example span "L" = 7'-0" (2134)

Floor Girder Sizing Example per §R502.5 and Table R502.5(2)

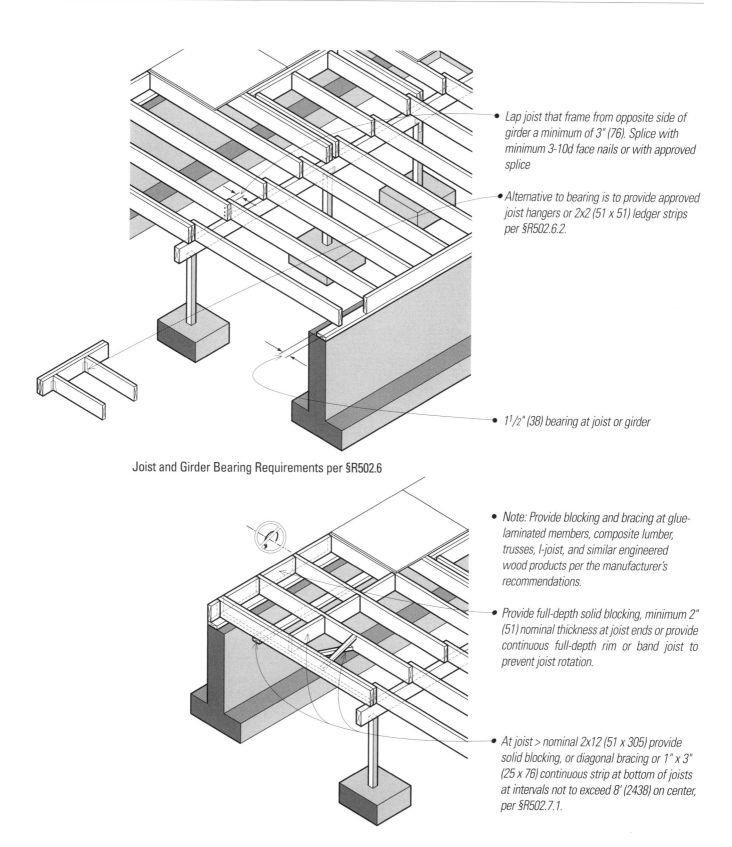

Lap joist that frame from opposite side of girder a minimum of 3" (76). Splice with minimum 3-10d face nails or with approved splice

Alternative to bearing is to provide approved joist hangers or 2x2 (51 x 51) ledger strips per §R502.6.2.

$1^1/_2$" (38) bearing at joist or girder

Joist and Girder Bearing Requirements per §R502.6

Note: Provide blocking and bracing at glue-laminated members, composite lumber, trusses, I-joist, and similar engineered wood products per the manufacturer's recommendations.

Provide full-depth solid blocking, minimum 2" (51) nominal thickness at joist ends or provide continuous full-depth rim or band joist to prevent joist rotation.

At joist > nominal 2x12 (51 x 305) provide solid blocking, or diagonal bracing or 1" x 3" (25 x 76) continuous strip at bottom of joists at intervals not to exceed 8' (2438) on center, per §R502.7.1.

Lateral Restraint at Supports for Wood Floors per §R502.7

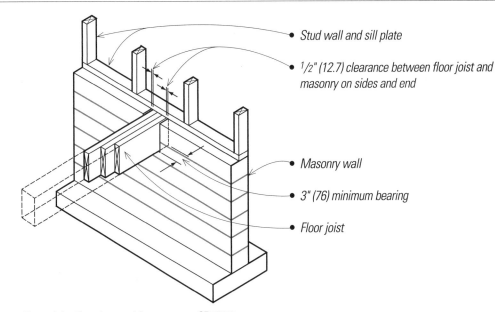

- Stud wall and sill plate
- ¹/₂" (12.7) clearance between floor joist and masonry on sides and end
- Masonry wall
- 3" (76) minimum bearing
- Floor joist

Floor Joist Bearing on Masonry per §R502.6

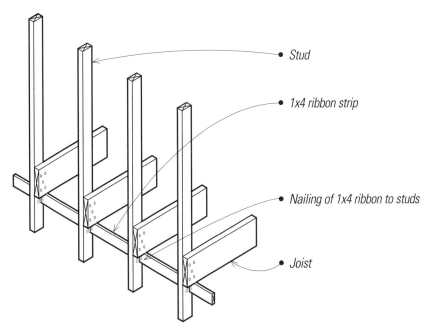

- Stud
- 1x4 ribbon strip
- Nailing of 1x4 ribbon to studs
- Joist

Floor Joist Bearing on Ribbon Strip per §R502.6

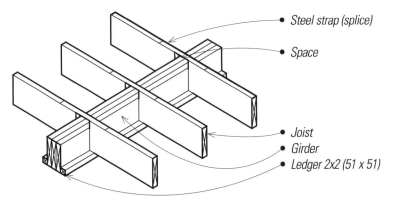

- Steel strap (splice)
- Space
- Joist
- Girder
- Ledger 2x2 (51 x 51)

Alternate Joist Bearing at Girders per §R502.6

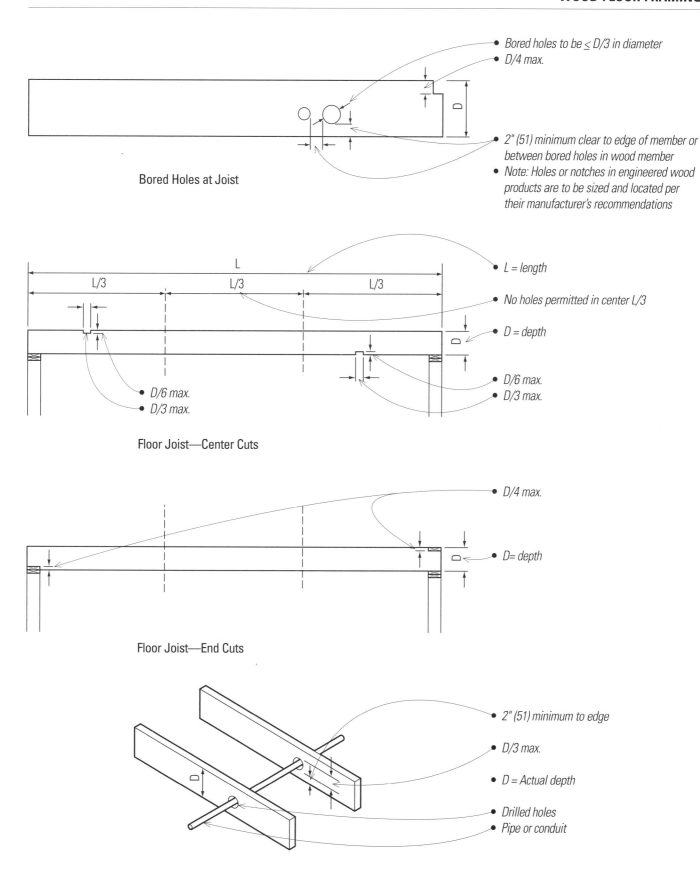

Bored Holes at Joist

- Bored holes to be ≤ D/3 in diameter
- D/4 max.
- 2" (51) minimum clear to edge of member or between bored holes in wood member
- Note: Holes or notches in engineered wood products are to be sized and located per their manufacturer's recommendations

Floor Joist—Center Cuts

- L = length
- No holes permitted in center L/3
- D = depth
- D/6 max.
- D/3 max.
- D/6 max.
- D/3 max.

L

L/3   L/3   L/3

Floor Joist—End Cuts

- D/4 max.
- D= depth

Drilling and Notching at Wood Floors per §R502.8

- 2" (51) minimum to edge
- D/3 max.
- D = Actual depth
- Drilled holes
- Pipe or conduit

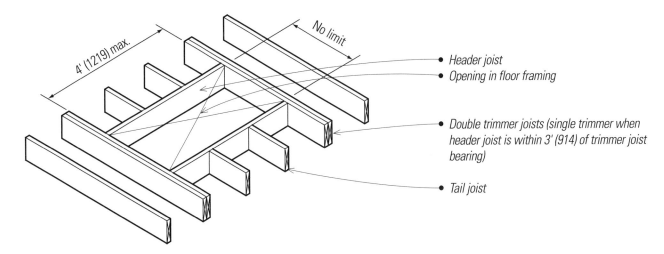

4' (1219) max.

No limit

- Header joist
- Opening in floor framing

- Double trimmer joists (single trimmer when header joist is within 3' (914) of trimmer joist bearing)

- Tail joist

Floor Framing for Openings up to 4 feet (1219) per §R502.10

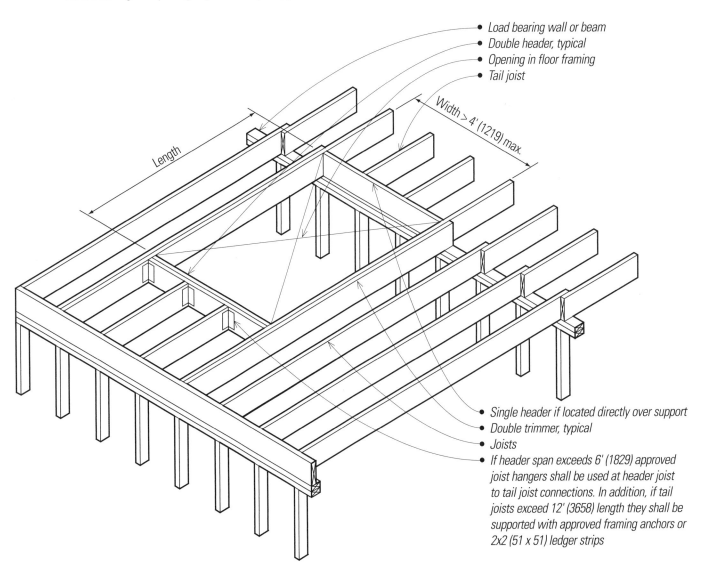

- Load bearing wall or beam
- Double header, typical
- Opening in floor framing
- Tail joist

Length

Width > 4' (1219) max.

- Single header if located directly over support
- Double trimmer, typical
- Joists
- If header span exceeds 6' (1829) approved joist hangers shall be used at header joist to tail joist connections. In addition, if tail joists exceed 12' (3658) length they shall be supported with approved framing anchors or 2x2 (51 x 51) ledger strips

Floor Framing for Openings Greater than 4 feet (1219) per §R502.10

Wood Trusses

Wood trusses, such as metal plate connected wood trusses, are required to meet the requirements of §R502.11. Trusses are designed products and the code requires that the trusses be designed by whichever category of registered design professional is applicable in the jurisdiction where the project is to be constructed. See §R502.11.4 for the detailed list of what is required for truss design drawings.

Because trusses are relatively deep in relationship to their width they are to be braced to prevent them from toppling over and to provide lateral restraint for them. Also, since trusses are a designed product they cannot be treated in the field the same as solid wood members. Trusses are not to be cut, notched, altered, or have their loads increased unless the alteration or additional loading is reviewed and approved by a registered design professional. Ideally, this review and approval should be made by a registered design professional working for the truss manufacturer, or who is familiar with the design of such trusses.

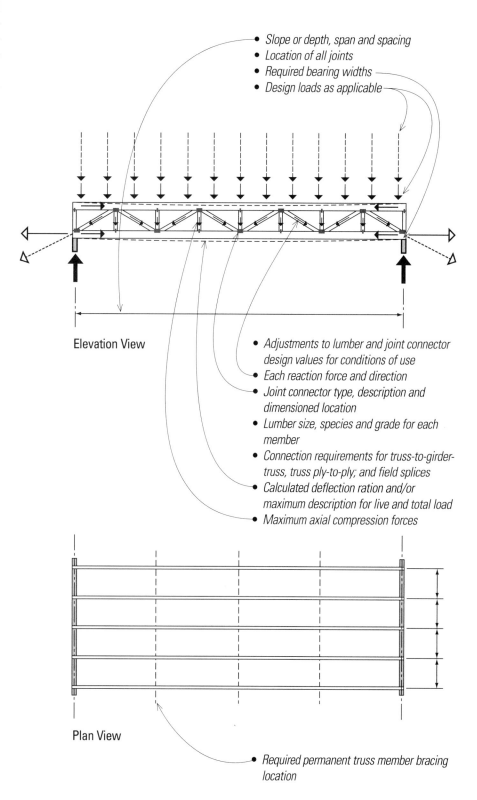

- *Slope or depth, span and spacing*
- *Location of all joints*
- *Required bearing widths*
- *Design loads as applicable*

Elevation View

- *Adjustments to lumber and joint connector design values for conditions of use*
- *Each reaction force and direction*
- *Joint connector type, description and dimensioned location*
- *Lumber size, species and grade for each member*
- *Connection requirements for truss-to-girder-truss, truss ply-to-ply; and field splices*
- *Calculated deflection ration and/or maximum description for live and total load*
- *Maximum axial compression forces*

Plan View

- *Required permanent truss member bracing location*

§R503 Floor Sheathing

Flooring can consist of three parts, some of which may serve the same function in the floor. The subfloor is the structural material spanning between the joists that provides strength to rest materials upon and ties the floor plane together horizontally for lateral force resistance. Atop that subfloor is an underlayment material that provides backing for the finish flooring material, which is the possible third layer of flooring materials, such as wood-strip flooring, carpet or sheet vinyl. Sheathing can be either lumber, wood panels or a combination of the two when a subfloor/underlayment combination is used. For our purposes there are really two types of subfloor: lumber sheathing and wood structural panel sheathing. We will discuss and illustrate them separately. Note that the floor sheathing described in §R503 can be used with either.

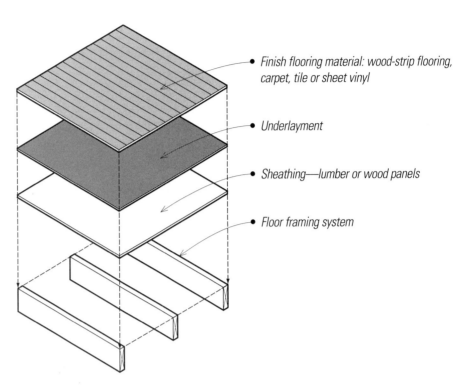

- Finish flooring material: wood-strip flooring, carpet, tile or sheet vinyl

- Underlayment

- Sheathing—lumber or wood panels

- Floor framing system

Lumber Sheathing

Lumber floor sheathing is to be per the requirements of §R503.1 and the spans called out in Table R503.1. See the illustrations for the relationship of the direction of the sheathing, thickness and whether the materials are of tongue-and-groove configuration in the field, the same as solid wood members.

Lumber Sheathing Example:
- *16" (406) joist spacing*
- *Minimum lumber sheathing thickness:*
  - *Perpendicular to joist: 5/8" (15.9)*
  - *Diagonal to joist: 5/8" (15.9)*
  - *Tongue and groove floor: 1/2" (12.7) max. span up to 60" (1524) between joists depending on F_b and E values, tongue and groove must be perpendicular to joist, per Table R503.1*

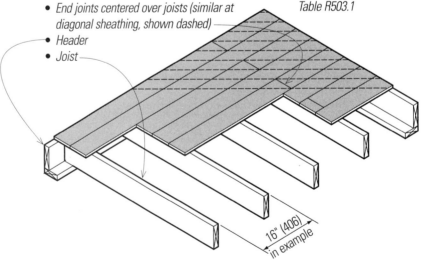

- *End joints centered over joists (similar at diagonal sheathing, shown dashed)*
- *Header*
- *Joist*

16" (406) in example

Lumber Sheathing at Joists per §R503.1 and Table R503.1

Wood Structural Panel Sheathing

Wood structural panels are engineered wood products such as plywood, oriented strand board or composite panels. These structural panels are rated for loads based on their orientation in relation to the floor framing, the spacing of the joists supporting the panels, and whether the panels span over multiple floor joists. Table R503.2.1.1(1) is used for plywood structural panels that are typically unsanded and meant to be covered with other materials. The tables are based on the information contained in grade stamp markings that are placed on structural panels that describe the span rating, exposure rating and thickness for these panels. See the illustration for an explanation of the information on structural grade marks and how to use the table for unsanded plywood. Sanded plywood panels used as combination subfloor and underlayment are to conform to Table R503.2.1.1(2). See the illustrations for an example of a sanded plywood grade mark and how to use the sanded plywood table.

Note that the floor sheathing panels described in §R503.2 can be used with either wood or steel floor framing systems. Structural panels are to be fastened to wood floor framing per the requirements of Table R602.3(1) and to steel framing per the requirements of Table R505.3.1(2).

Particleboard may be used in floor assemblies, but only for underlayment. Particleboard used for underlayment is to be at least $1/4$" (6.4) thickness and meet the grading requirements of §R503.3.

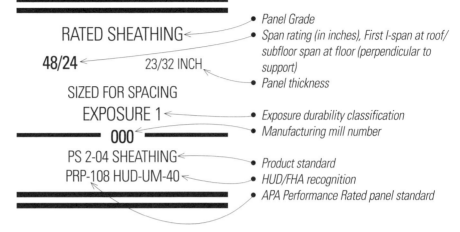

Example of Floor Sheathing Grade Stamp for Unsanded Sheathing per §R503.2.1 and Table R503.2.1.1(1)

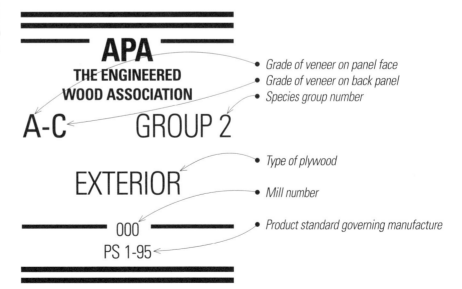

Example of Floor Sheathing Grade Stamp for Sanded Plywood per Table R503.2.1.1(2)

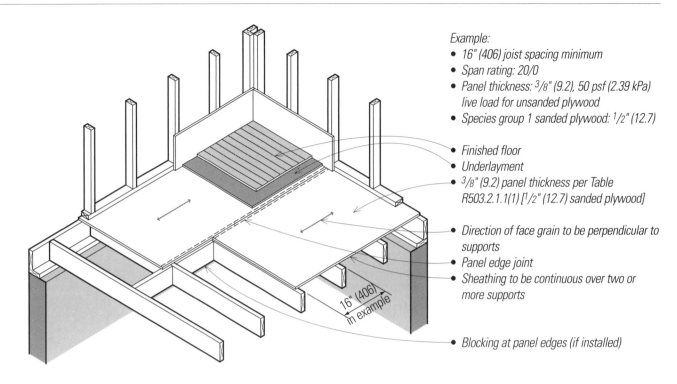

Example:
- *16" (406) joist spacing minimum*
- *Span rating: 20/0*
- *Panel thickness: 3/8" (9.2), 50 psf (2.39 kPa) live load for unsanded plywood*
- *Species group 1 sanded plywood: 1/2" (12.7)*

- *Finished floor*
- *Underlayment*
- *3/8" (9.2) panel thickness per Table R503.2.1.1(1) [1/2" (12.7) sanded plywood]*

- *Direction of face grain to be perpendicular to supports*
- *Panel edge joint*
- *Sheathing to be continuous over two or more supports*

- *Blocking at panel edges (if installed)*

16" (406) in example

Subfloor and Underlayments per §R503.2, Tables R503.2.1.1(1) and R503.2.1.1(2)

Pressure-Preservative Treated Wood Floors on Ground

Wood foundations are described and illustrated in §R403.1 of Chapter 4. The provisions of §R504 provide for pressure-preservative treated wood floors as an accompaniment to wood foundation systems.

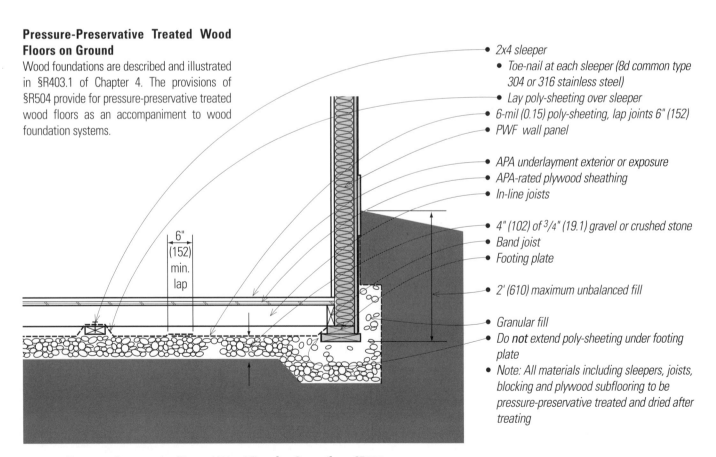

- *2x4 sleeper*
  - *Toe-nail at each sleeper (8d common type 304 or 316 stainless steel)*
  - *Lay poly-sheeting over sleeper*
- *6-mil (0.15) poly-sheeting, lap joints 6" (152)*
- *PWF wall panel*

- *APA underlayment exterior or exposure*
- *APA-rated plywood sheathing*
- *In-line joists*

- *4" (102) of 3/4" (19.1) gravel or crushed stone*
- *Band joist*
- *Footing plate*

- *2' (610) maximum unbalanced fill*

- *Granular fill*
- *Do **not** extend poly-sheeting under footing plate*
- *Note: All materials including sleepers, joists, blocking and plywood subflooring to be pressure-preservative treated and dried after treating*

6" (152) min. lap

Pressure-Preservative Treated Wood Floor [on Ground] per §R504

Steel Floor Framing

§R505 sets out the requirements for cold-formed steel floor framing for buildings of specified dimensions and heights. The length parallel to the floor framing may not exceed 60' (18288) in length; the width perpendicular to the floor framing may not exceed 40' (12192) in width parallel to the joist span and less than or equal to three stories in height. When using the provisions of this section the sites must be located where wind speed is less than 110 mph (40 m/s) in Exposures B or C. Snow loads may not exceed 70 psf (3.35 kPa). See the illustration for a graphic description of the limitations.

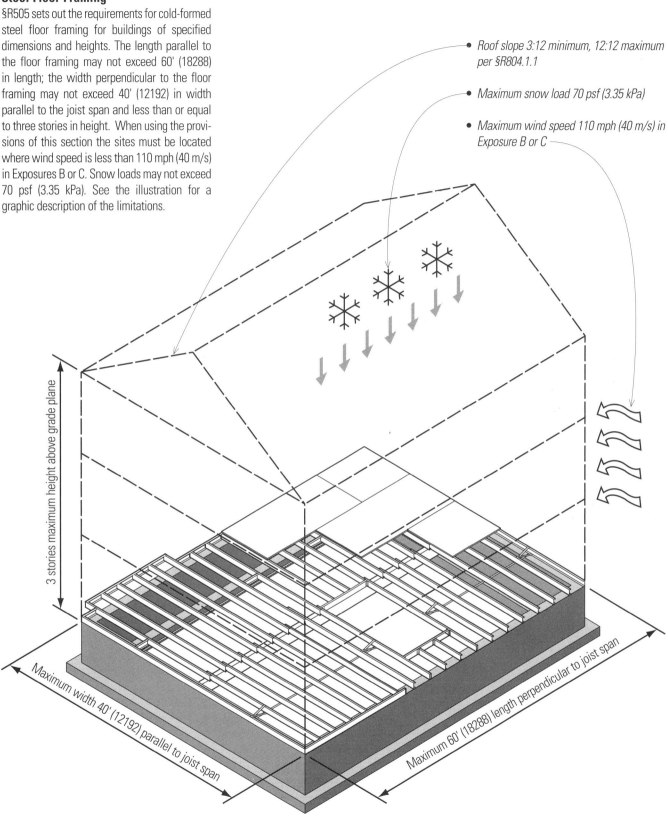

- *Roof slope 3:12 minimum, 12:12 maximum per §R804.1.1*

- *Maximum snow load 70 psf (3.35 kPa)*

- *Maximum wind speed 110 mph (40 m/s) in Exposure B or C*

3 stories maximum height above grade plane

Maximum width 40' (12192) parallel to joist span

Maximum 60' (18288) length perpendicular to joist span

Limits on Cold-formed Steel Floor Framing per §R505.1

Steel Floor Framing

Horizontal floor framing members resting on walls framed per §R603 must be essentially in-line with load bearing studs below, per §R505.1.2. See the illustration showing the limitations on offsets for different framing conditions. Note the presences of "bearing stiffeners" in the illustration. These stiffeners are shown in Figure R505.1.2 and should be provided as shown here and in the code illustration. Note that putting the bearing stiffener inside or beside the horizontal framing member determines which set of dimensional criteria are to be used.

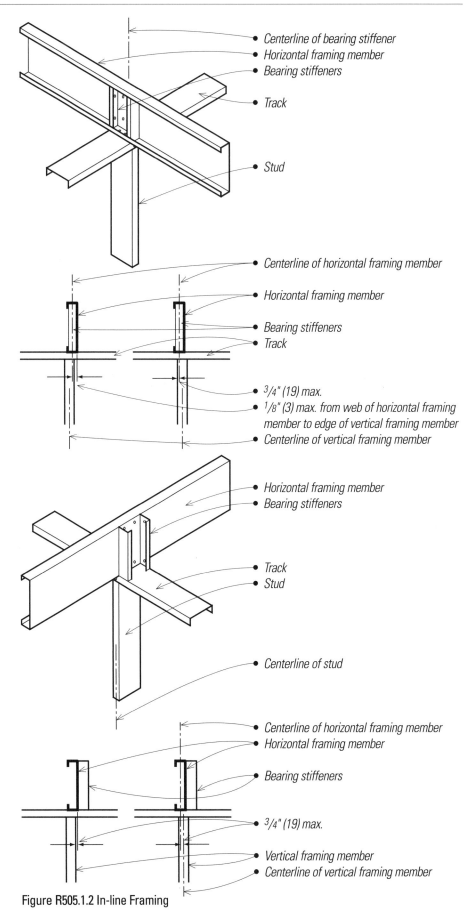

- Centerline of bearing stiffener
- Horizontal framing member
- Bearing stiffeners
- Track
- Stud

- Centerline of horizontal framing member
- Horizontal framing member
- Bearing stiffeners
- Track
- 3/4" (19) max.
- 1/8" (3) max. from web of horizontal framing member to edge of vertical framing member
- Centerline of vertical framing member

- Horizontal framing member
- Bearing stiffeners
- Track
- Stud
- Centerline of stud

- Centerline of horizontal framing member
- Horizontal framing member
- Bearing stiffeners
- 3/4" (19) max.
- Vertical framing member
- Centerline of vertical framing member

Figure R505.1.2 In-line Framing

Steel Floor Framing

Trusses using cold-formed steel members may be used, but they must be designed and installed per AISI S100. As with pre-engineered trusses made from other materials such as wood, steel trusses are not to be cut, notched or altered in the field unless such work is in accordance with the approved design. These types of multiple-piece members rely on having their installed conditions match their design conditions and they must maintain the integrity on which their design is based.

Cold-formed steel floor framing members are to be of sizes specified in §R505.2 and as illustrated. Members are divided into two broad categories—load-bearing "C" shaped members with a return lip on the side of the web, and tracks in which members nest and thus do not have a return leg on the web. Members are to be identified per the requirements of §R505.2.2 with at minimum:

1. The manufacturer's identification
2. The minimum steel base coat (before corrosion protection is applied) in inches (mm)
3. Information about the corrosion coating
4. Minimum steel yield strength in kips per square inch (MPa)

The members are to have a metallic anti-corrosion coating, such as galvanizing, per the requirements of §R505.2.3. Minimum material thicknesses are to be per the requirements of Table 505.2(2) where the materials thicknesses are expressed in both sets of terms that may be found in the field: "designation thickness," listed in mils, and the corresponding minimum base steel thickness (prior to corrosion coating), expressed in inches.

Member designations, per Table 505.2(1), are defined in the table as: xxxxSyyy-t where xxxx is the web depth in 0.10 inch increments, "S" indicates the member may be used as a stud or joist, "yyyy" is the width of the flange in 0.10 in increments and "t" is the minimum thickness of the base metal in mils. Thus an 8 inch (203) deep floor joist with a 1.625 inch (41) flange and base metal thickness of 0.0428" (1.08) [43 mils] would be designated as "800S162-43."

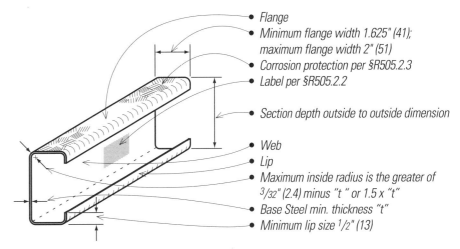

- Flange
- Minimum flange width 1.625" (41); maximum flange width 2" (51)
- Corrosion protection per §R505.2.3
- Label per §R505.2.2

- Section depth outside to outside dimension

- Web
- Lip
- Maximum inside radius is the greater of $^3/_{32}$" (2.4) minus "t" or 1.5 x "t"
- Base Steel min. thickness "t"
- Minimum lip size $^1/_2$" (13)

Typical C-Shaped Section at Load-bearing Cold-Formed Steel Floor Framing per §R505.2 and Figure R505.2(1)

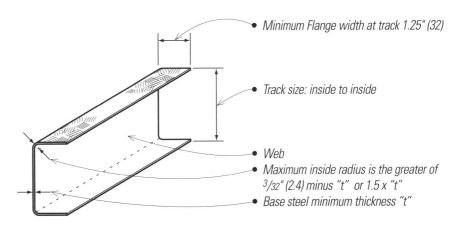

- Minimum Flange width at track 1.25" (32)

- Track size: inside to inside

- Web
- Maximum inside radius is the greater of $^3/_{32}$" (2.4) minus "t" or 1.5 x "t"
- Base steel minimum thickness "t"

Typical Track Section at Cold-Formed Steel Floor Framing per §R505.2 and Figure R505.2(2)

Steel Floor Framing Fasteners

Fastening requirements for floor framing members are specified in §R505.2.4. See the illustrations for depictions of edge spacing and fastener spacing. The requirements for member to member, floor sheathing and ceiling gypsum wallboard attachments are described in this section. The fastener requirements are based on the assumption of using #8 screw sizes. See the illustration related to Table R505.2.4 for a depiction of the proportional reduction in the number of fasteners required when the thickness of the framing member base metal is increased. There is also a proportional decrease in the number of fasteners required per this table when the size of the fasteners is decreased. Note that the spacing requirements of §R505.2.4 apply to all sizes of fasteners.

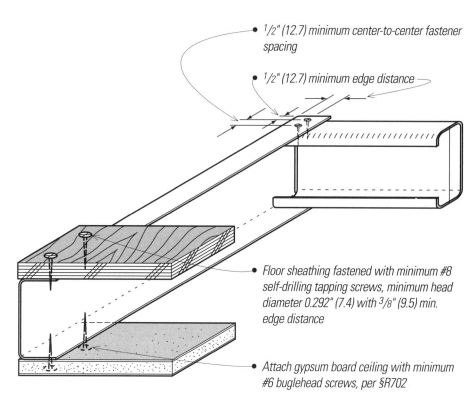

- $1/2"$ (12.7) minimum center-to-center fastener spacing

- $1/2"$ (12.7) minimum edge distance

- Floor sheathing fastened with minimum #8 self-drilling tapping screws, minimum head diameter 0.292" (7.4) with $3/8"$ (9.5) min. edge distance

- Attach gypsum board ceiling with minimum #6 buglehead screws, per §R702

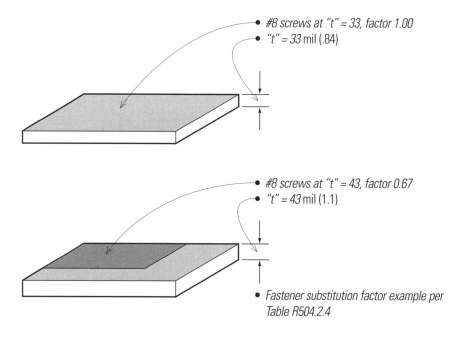

- #8 screws at "t" = 33, factor 1.00
- "t" = 33 mil (.84)

- #8 screws at "t" = 43, factor 0.67
- "t" = 43 mil (1.1)

- Fastener substitution factor example per Table R504.2.4

Fastening Requirements at Cold-Formed Steel Floor Framing per §R505.2.4

Joists may have holes punched in them for such things as electrical conduits or plumbing lines. The holes may only be of a certain size and must be separated by certain distances from bearing points and from each other. See the illustrations related to §R505.2.5 for information regarding holes and reinforcement. Note that holes that exceed the spacing requirements or reinforcement requirements of this section must be replaced with members whose holes comply with the requirements. As an alternative the floor member(s) with holes too large or too close together to comply with the code may be designed to comply with the stress and deflection requirements of the code using accepted engineering practices. Examples of remedies for holes that are too large include increasing the gage of the framing members, increasing the depth of the framing members, doubling up framing, decreasing joist spacing and decreasing joist spans to reduce loading on the floor framing members.

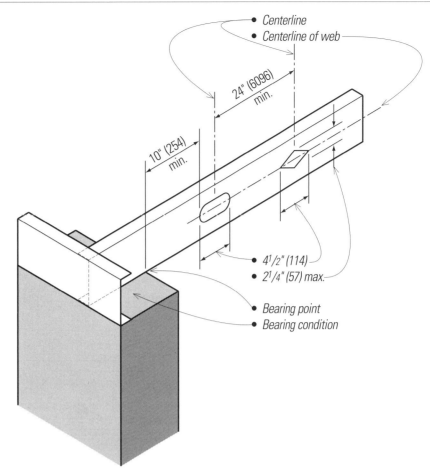

- *Centerline*
- *Centerline of web*
- *24" (6096) min.*
- *10" (254) min.*
- *4¹/₂" (114)*
- *2¹/₄" (57) max.*
- *Bearing point*
- *Bearing condition*

Cold-formed Steel Floor Joist Web Holes
per §R505.2.5.1

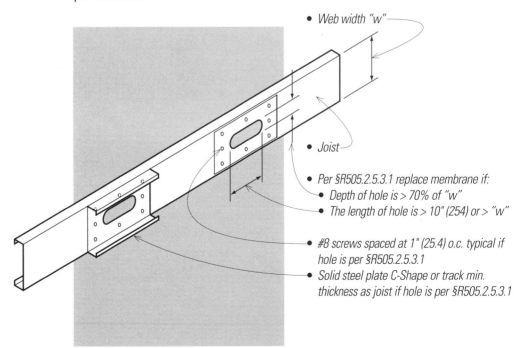

- *Web width "w"*
- *Joist*
- *Per §R505.2.5.3.1 replace membrane if:*
  - *Depth of hole is > 70% of "w"*
  - *The length of hole is > 10" (254) or > "w"*
- *#8 screws spaced at 1" (25.4) o.c. typical if hole is per §R505.2.5.3.1*
- *Solid steel plate C-Shape or track min. thickness as joist if hole is per §R505.2.5.3.1*

Web Hole Patch Criteria at Cold-Formed
Steel Floor Framing per §R505.2.5.3

Floor Construction

Floor construction using cold-formed steel members are to be constructed per the requirements of §R505.3. Anchorage to concrete foundations, wood sills or metal framing below the floor level is to be in accordance with Table R505.3.1(1). Various configurations of conditions are described in the accompanying illustrations. Fastening of cold-formed steel joists is to be per §R505.2.4 and Table R505.3.1.(2). These fastening requirements are noted in the illustrations.

Floor Joist

Floor joist sizes are to be per Table R505.3.2(1) for single spans and Table R505.3.2(2) and Table R505.3.2(3) for multiple spans. Tables R505.3.2(1) and (2) are based on 33 ksi steel, while Table R505.3.2(3) is based on 50 ksi steel. The tables assumed floor loadings of either 30 psf (1.44 kPa) or 40 psf (1.92 kPa). As with any framing member the sizes are related to spans, spacing of members and loading. We have used an 8" (203) x 1.62" (41) x 43 mil joist [800S162-43] at 16" (406) o.c. as an example in the illustration. See the following figures for detailed requirements from §R505.3.

Joist Span Example per Table R505.3.2(1) and Table R505.3.2(2)

Example: 800S/62-43 joist

- *Joist with spans greater than 12' (3658) to have bottom flange blocking, either:*
  1. *Gypsum board with #6 screws installed per §R702*

  or
  2. *Blocking per Figure R505.3.3.2(1) or R505.3.3.2(2)*

- *Deflection: L/480 for live loads*
  L/240 for total loads

- *Live load = 30–40 psf (14.37–19.16 kPa) per table*
- *Dead load = 10 psf (0.479 kPa)*

- *Support at midpoint +/- 2' (610) of mid-span of multiple span*
- *Continuous 1^1/$_2$" (38) x 33 mil. (0.84) steel strap at 12" (3058) o.c. max.*

- *8" (203)*
- *16" (406) o.c.*
- *1.62" (41)*

Single span = "L"

Multiple spans

- *Track minimum 33 mil (0.84)*
- *1^1/$_2$"" (38) bearing at exterior wall 3^1/$_2$" (89) at interior wall support*

- *For 800S/62-3:*
  - *"L" = 15'-6" (4724) at 30 psf (14.37 kPa) live load*
  - *"L" = 14'-1" (4293) at 40 psf (19.15 kPa) live load*

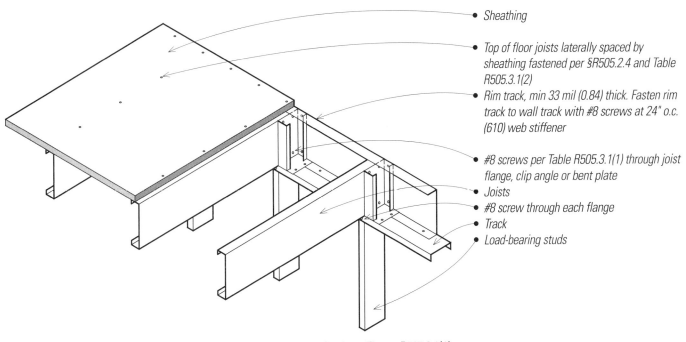

- Sheathing
- Top of floor joists laterally spaced by sheathing fastened per §R505.2.4 and Table R505.3.1(2)
- Rim track, min 33 mil (0.84) thick. Fasten rim track to wall track with #8 screws at 24" o.c. (610) web stiffener
- #8 screws per Table R505.3.1(1) through joist flange, clip angle or bent plate
- Joists
- #8 screw through each flange
- Track
- Load-bearing studs

Floor to Exterior Load-Bearing Wall Stud per Figure R505.3.1(1)

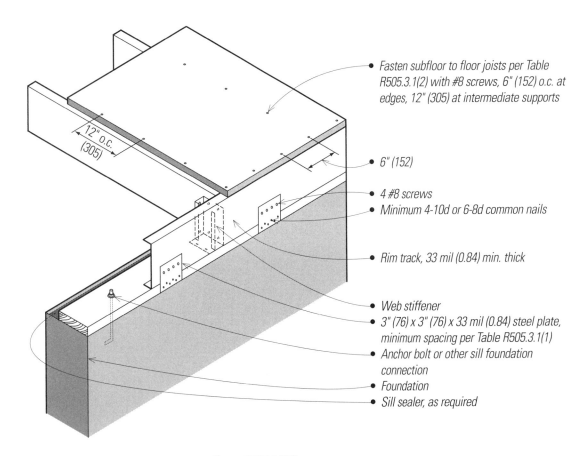

- Fasten subfloor to floor joists per Table R505.3.1(2) with #8 screws, 6" (152) o.c. at edges, 12" (305) at intermediate supports
- 6" (152)
- 4 #8 screws
- Minimum 4-10d or 6-8d common nails
- Rim track, 33 mil (0.84) min. thick
- Web stiffener
- 3" (76) x 3" (76) x 33 mil (0.84) steel plate, minimum spacing per Table R505.3.1(1)
- Anchor bolt or other sill foundation connection
- Foundation
- Sill sealer, as required

Floor to Wood Sill Connection per Figure R505.3.1(2)

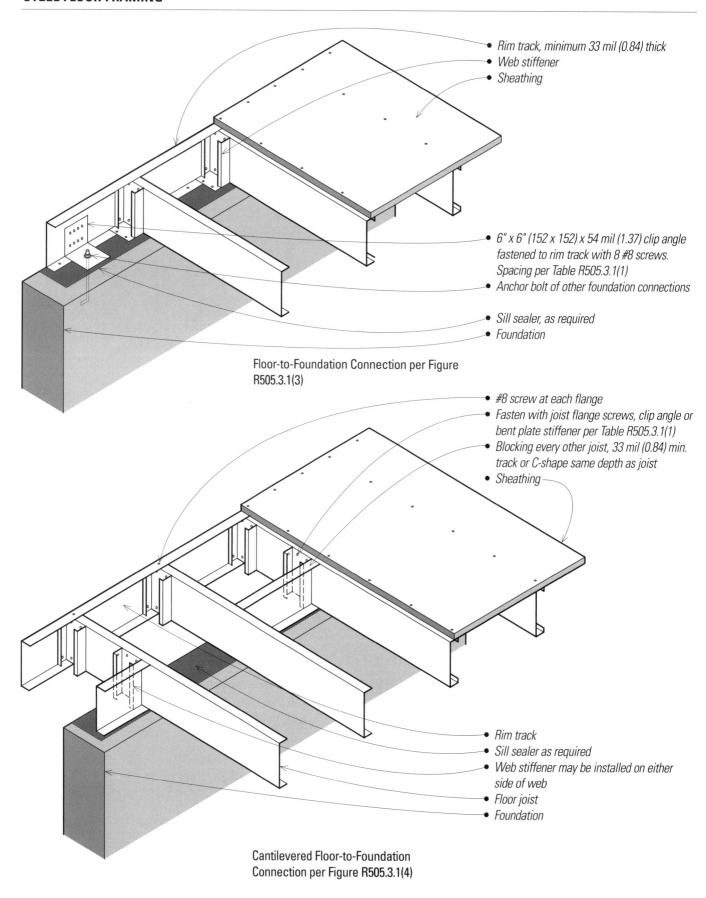

- Rim track, minimum 33 mil (0.84) thick
- Web stiffener
- Sheathing

- 6" x 6" (152 x 152) x 54 mil (1.37) clip angle fastened to rim track with 8 #8 screws. Spacing per Table R505.3.1(1)
- Anchor bolt of other foundation connections

- Sill sealer, as required
- Foundation

Floor-to-Foundation Connection per Figure R505.3.1(3)

- #8 screw at each flange
- Fasten with joist flange screws, clip angle or bent plate stiffener per Table R505.3.1(1)
- Blocking every other joist, 33 mil (0.84) min. track or C-shape same depth as joist
- Sheathing

- Rim track
- Sill sealer as required
- Web stiffener may be installed on either side of web
- Floor joist
- Foundation

Cantilevered Floor-to-Foundation Connection per Figure R505.3.1(4)

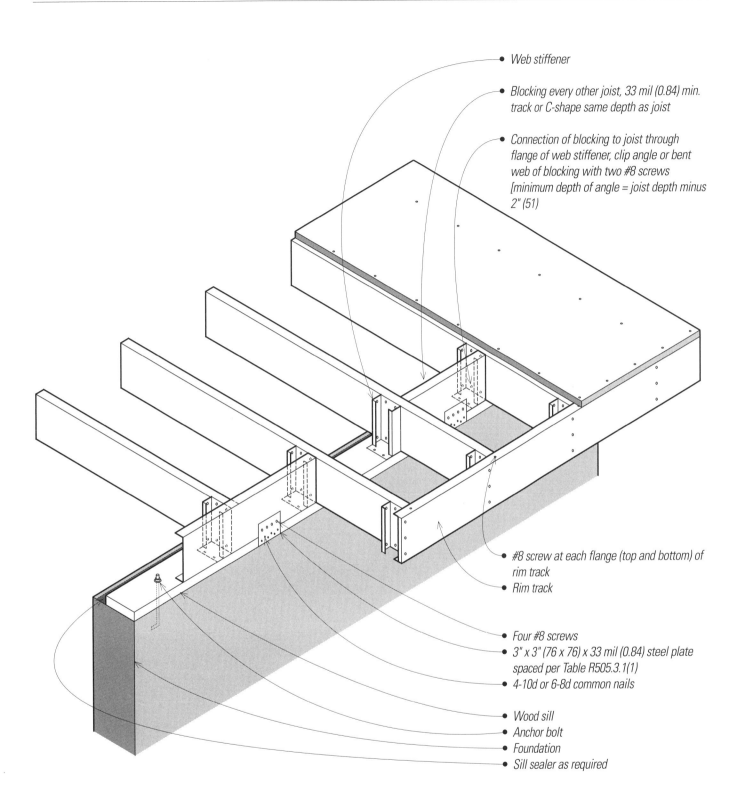

Web stiffener

Blocking every other joist, 33 mil (0.84) min. track or C-shape same depth as joist

Connection of blocking to joist through flange of web stiffener, clip angle or bent web of blocking with two #8 screws [minimum depth of angle = joist depth minus 2" (51)]

#8 screw at each flange (top and bottom) of rim track

Rim track

Four #8 screws

3" x 3" (76 x 76) x 33 mil (0.84) steel plate spaced per Table R505.3.1(1)

4-10d or 6-8d common nails

Wood sill

Anchor bolt

Foundation

Sill sealer as required

Cantilevered Floor to Wood Sill Connection per Figure R505.3.1(5)

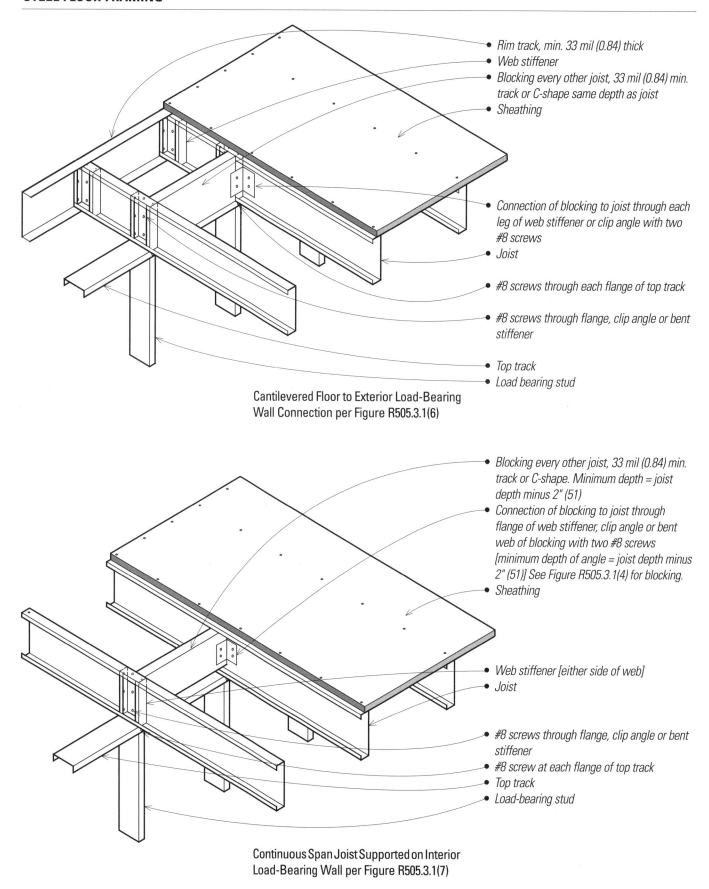

- *Rim track, min. 33 mil (0.84) thick*
- *Web stiffener*
- *Blocking every other joist, 33 mil (0.84) min. track or C-shape same depth as joist*
- *Sheathing*

- *Connection of blocking to joist through each leg of web stiffener or clip angle with two #8 screws*
- *Joist*

- *#8 screws through each flange of top track*

- *#8 screws through flange, clip angle or bent stiffener*

- *Top track*
- *Load bearing stud*

Cantilevered Floor to Exterior Load-Bearing
Wall Connection per Figure R505.3.1(6)

- *Blocking every other joist, 33 mil (0.84) min. track or C-shape. Minimum depth = joist depth minus 2" (51)*
- *Connection of blocking to joist through flange of web stiffener, clip angle or bent web of blocking with two #8 screws [minimum depth of angle = joist depth minus 2" (51)] See Figure R505.3.1(4) for blocking.*
- *Sheathing*

- *Web stiffener [either side of web]*
- *Joist*

- *#8 screws through flange, clip angle or bent stiffener*
- *#8 screw at each flange of top track*
- *Top track*
- *Load-bearing stud*

Continuous Span Joist Supported on Interior
Load-Bearing Wall per Figure R505.3.1(7)

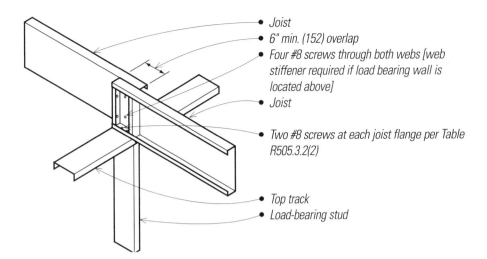

- Joist
- 6" min. (152) overlap
- Four #8 screws through both webs [web stiffener required if load bearing wall is located above]
- Joist
- Two #8 screws at each joist flange per Table R505.3.2(2)
- Top track
- Load-bearing stud

Lapped Joists Supported on Interior Load-Bearing Wall per Figure R505.3.1(8)

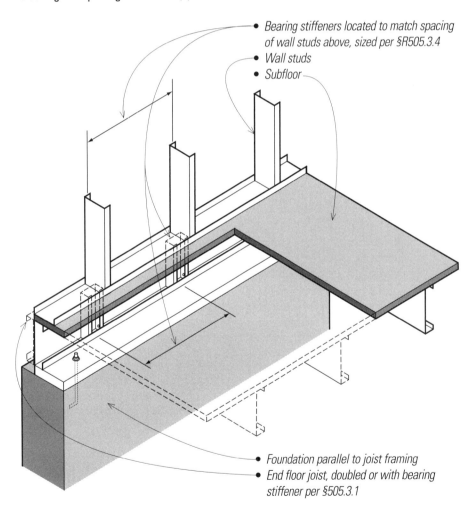

- Bearing stiffeners located to match spacing of wall studs above, sized per §R505.3.4
- Wall studs
- Subfloor
- Foundation parallel to joist framing
- End floor joist, doubled or with bearing stiffener per §505.3.1

Bearing Stiffeners for End Joist per Figure R505.3.1(9)

Floor Blocking

Blocking for the top chords of floor joists is provided by sheathing. Blocking for bottom chords is provided by gypsum sheathing or flat strapping. Blocking is also to be provided as noted in the various illustrations. Joists that are doubled up back-to-back block themselves so no added blocking is necessary per §R505.3.2. Per §R505.3.4 bearing stiffeners are to be used to reinforce joists where bearing points occur. Where floor joists occur under jamb studs there are to be two bearing stiffeners as illustrated. Figure R505.3.4(2) in the code shows various ways of fabricating and fastening bearing stiffeners. Stud and track bearing stiffeners are to be sized per the requirements of §R505.3.4.1 and §R505.3.4.2 respectively. Clip-angle bearing stiffeners are to be sized per Tables R505.3.4(1), R505.3.4(2), R505.3.4(3) or R505.3.4(4), depending on where the bearing points occur in the building, the joist size and spacing and loading.

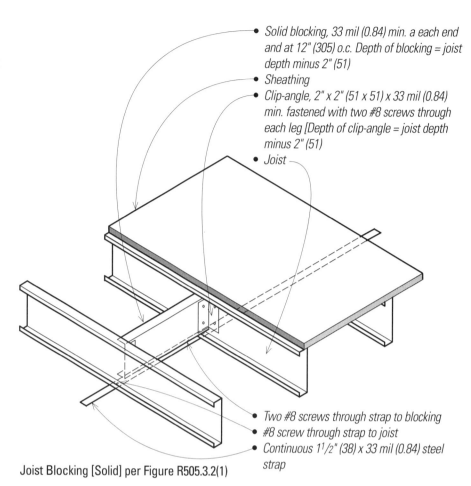

- Solid blocking, 33 mil (0.84) min. a each end and at 12" (305) o.c. Depth of blocking = joist depth minus 2" (51)
- Sheathing
- Clip-angle, 2" x 2" (51 x 51) x 33 mil (0.84) min. fastened with two #8 screws through each leg [Depth of clip-angle = joist depth minus 2" (51)
- Joist

- Two #8 screws through strap to blocking
- #8 screw through strap to joist
- Continuous 1¹/2" (38) x 33 mil (0.84) steel strap

Joist Blocking [Solid] per Figure R505.3.2(1)

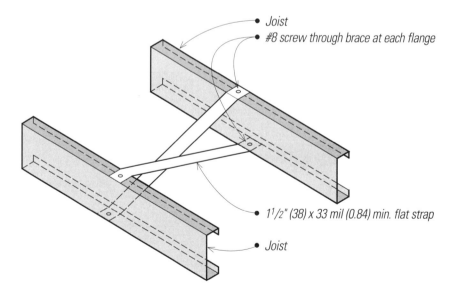

- Joist
- #8 screw through brace at each flange

- 1¹/2" (38) x 33 mil (0.84) min. flat strap
- Joist

Joist Blocking [Strap] per Figure R505.3.2(2)

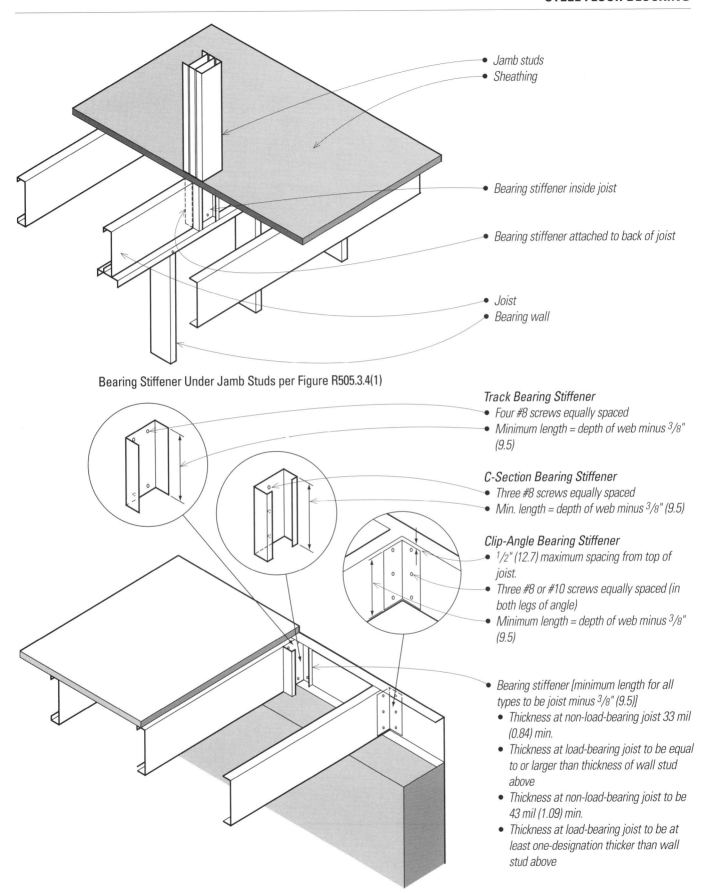

● Jamb studs
● Sheathing

● Bearing stiffener inside joist

● Bearing stiffener attached to back of joist

● Joist
● Bearing wall

Bearing Stiffener Under Jamb Studs per Figure R505.3.4(1)

Track Bearing Stiffener
● Four #8 screws equally spaced
● Minimum length = depth of web minus $^3/_8$" (9.5)

C-Section Bearing Stiffener
● Three #8 screws equally spaced
● Min. length = depth of web minus $^3/_8$" (9.5)

Clip-Angle Bearing Stiffener
● $^1/_2$" (12.7) maximum spacing from top of joist.
● Three #8 or #10 screws equally spaced (in both legs of angle)
● Minimum length = depth of web minus $^3/_8$" (9.5)

● Bearing stiffener [minimum length for all types to be joist minus $^3/_8$" (9.5)]
  ● Thickness at non-load-bearing joist 33 mil (0.84) min.
  ● Thickness at load-bearing joist to be equal to or larger than thickness of wall stud above
  ● Thickness at non-load-bearing joist to be 43 mil (1.09) min.
  ● Thickness at load-bearing joist to be at least one-designation thicker than wall stud above

Bearing Stiffener per Figure R505.3.4(2)

STEEL FLOOR CANTILEVERS

Per §R505.3.6 floor cantilevers of cold-formed metal joist systems are allowed to project 24" (610) at the upper floors of buildings, where they only support a single floor and a roof as illustrated. Where such cantilevers support two stories and a roof, they may project up to 24" (610) but in these cases the floor joists are to be doubled and the doubled joists are to extend back into the structure a minimum of 6' (1829) and be fastened as illustrated. Note that implicit in the language of this section is that such cantilevers may never support more than two stories and a roof, even though the building may be three stories in height. Joists are to be spliced as illustrated in Figure R505.3.7. Floor openings are to be framed with header and trimmer joists per §R505.3.8 as illustrated in Figures R505.3.8 (1), (2) and (3).

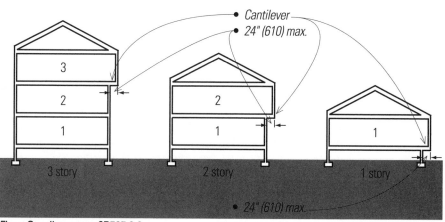

Floor Cantilever per §R505.3.6

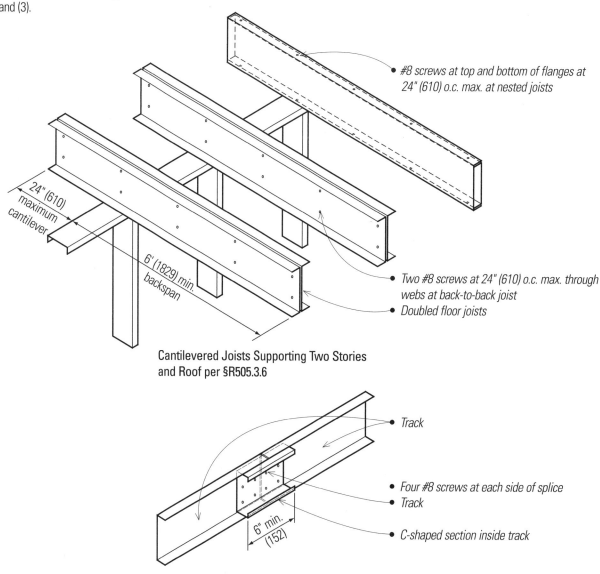

Cantilevered Joists Supporting Two Stories and Roof per §R505.3.6

Track Splice per Figure R505.3.7

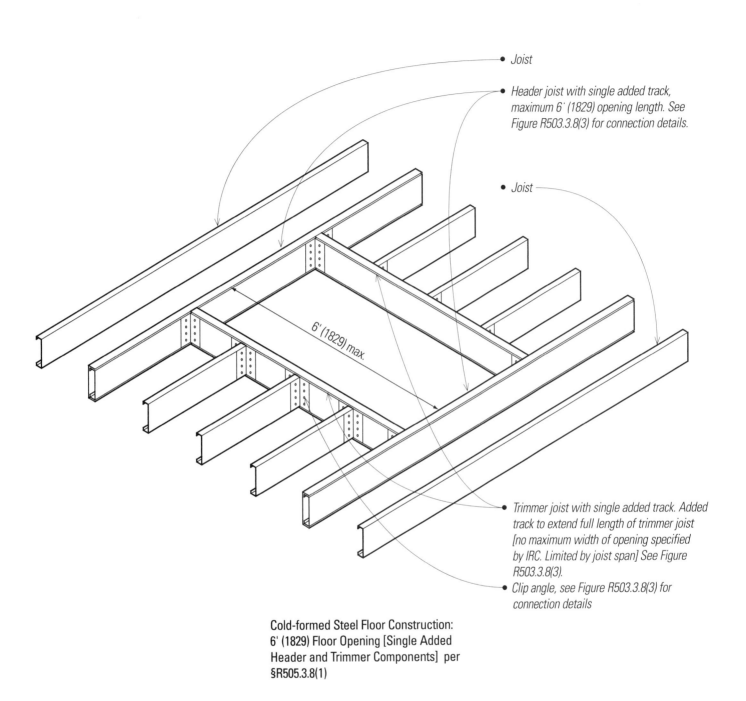

Joist

Header joist with single added track, maximum 6' (1829) opening length. See Figure R503.3.8(3) for connection details.

Joist

6' (1829) max.

Trimmer joist with single added track. Added track to extend full length of trimmer joist [no maximum width of opening specified by IRC. Limited by joist span] See Figure R503.3.8(3).

Clip angle, see Figure R503.3.8(3) for connection details

Cold-formed Steel Floor Construction: 6' (1829) Floor Opening [Single Added Header and Trimmer Components] per §R505.3.8(1)

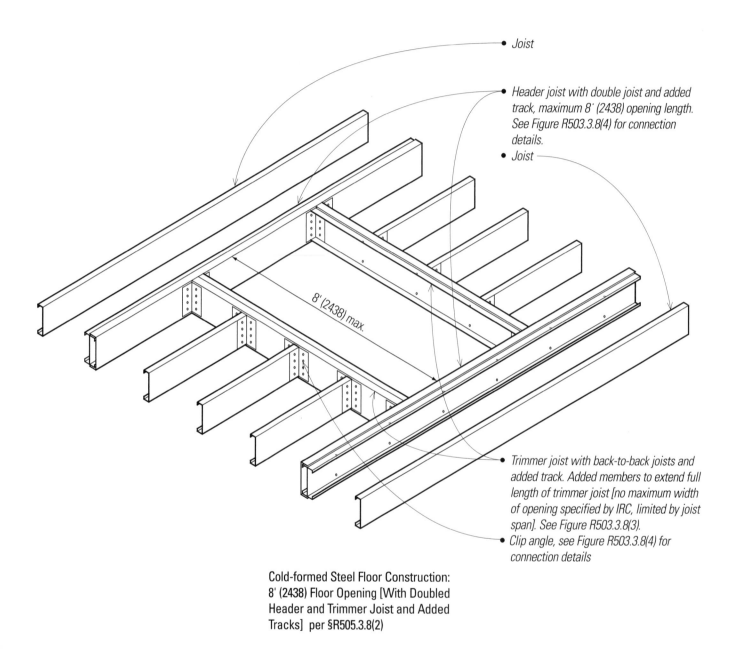

Joist

Header joist with double joist and added track, maximum 8' (2438) opening length. See Figure R503.3.8(4) for connection details.

Joist

8' (2438) max.

Trimmer joist with back-to-back joists and added track. Added members to extend full length of trimmer joist [no maximum width of opening specified by IRC, limited by joist span]. See Figure R503.3.8(3).

Clip angle, see Figure R503.3.8(4) for connection details

Cold-formed Steel Floor Construction: 8' (2438) Floor Opening [With Doubled Header and Trimmer Joist and Added Tracks] per §R505.3.8(2)

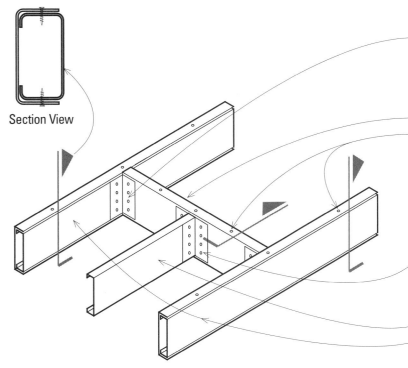

Section View

- Minimum 2" x 2" (51 x 51) clip angle with four #8 screws through each leg, both sides of connection. Thickness of clip angle to be not less than that of floor joist.

- Header joist, C-shape inside a track
- #8 screws at 24" (610) o.c. max. top and bottom flange

- Four #8 screws, evenly spaced, through each leg of clip angle [one side of connection] minimum length equals joist web depth minus 1/2" (12.7)
- Joist
- Trimmer joist C-shape inside a track

Cold-formed Steel Floor Construction:
6' (1829) Floor Opening [Single Added Components] per §R505.3.8(3)

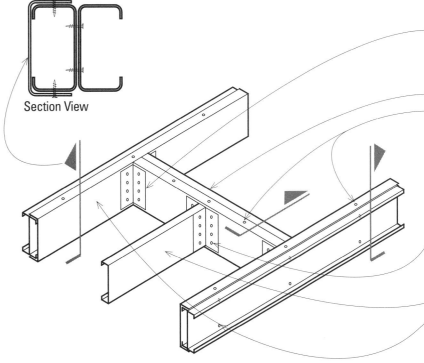

Section View

- Minimum 2" x 2" (51 x 51) clip angle with four #8 screws through each leg, both sides of connection. Thickness of clip angle to be not less than that of floor joist.
- Header joist, two C-shapes and a track
- #8 screws at 24" (610) o.c. max. top and bottom flange

- Four #8 screws, evenly spaced, through each leg of clip angle [one side of connection] minimum length equals joist web depth minus 1/2" (12.7)
- Joist
- Trimmer joist two C-shapes and a track. Two #8 screws through webs at 24" (610) o.c. max.

Cold-formed Steel Floor Construction:
8' (2438) Floor Opening [Multiple Added Components for span of 6' (1829) to 8' (2438)] per §R505.3.8(4)

Concrete Floors (In Ground)

§R506.1 sets out the requirements for concrete slabs resting on the ground. These slabs are to be a minimum of 3^1/$_2$" (89) thick. See the illustrations for a description of the basic requirements for these concrete floors.

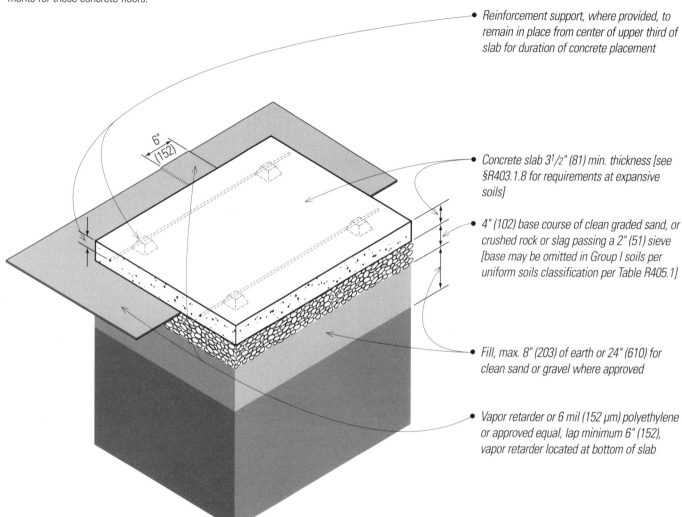

• *Reinforcement support, where provided, to remain in place from center of upper third of slab for duration of concrete placement*

6"
(152)

• *Concrete slab 3^1/$_2$" (81) min. thickness [see §R403.1.8 for requirements at expansive soils]*

• *4" (102) base course of clean graded sand, or crushed rock or slag passing a 2" (51) sieve [base may be omitted in Group I soils per uniform soils classification per Table R405.1]*

• *Fill, max. 8" (203) of earth or 24" (610) for clean sand or gravel where approved*

• *Vapor retarder or 6 mil (152 μm) polyethylene or approved equal, lap minimum 6" (152), vapor retarder located at bottom of slab*

Concrete Floors on Ground per §R506.1

6
Wall Construction

Moving up from the foundations discussed in Chapter 5, Chapter 6 addresses walls and partitions. This chapter is intended to cover all permanent walls, whether interior or exterior, and whether they are simply space dividers or bearing walls that support structure above the space.

General

The code recognizes that even non-bearing partitions may have superimposed loads. §R601.2 requires all walls to be capable of resisting imposed loads as described in §R301 and transmitting those loads to the floor or foundation supporting it. Requirements for lateral force resistance of walls related to wind or seismic loading are also addressed. This chapter provides guidance for walls constructed of various materials: wood, steel, masonry, concrete and several types of composite structural systems. It also provides performance and construction requirements for windows and doors located in exterior walls.

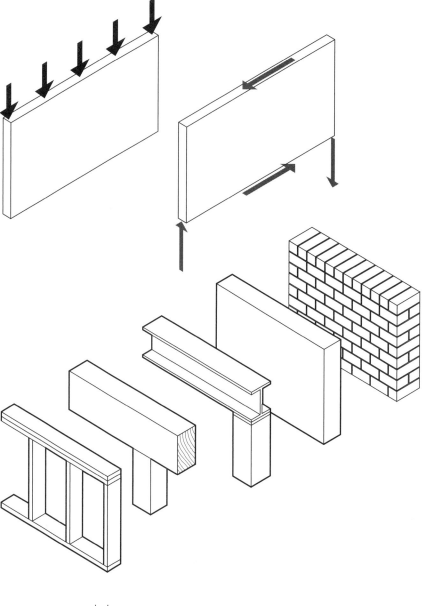

Note that the code forbids compressible flooring materials to be present under walls or partitions. This requirement would most often come into play when a renovation is being done and a partition is being installed or moved in a room with floor coverings. The requirements of §R601.2.1 should be construed to require removal of floor coverings under new walls, partitions or columns.

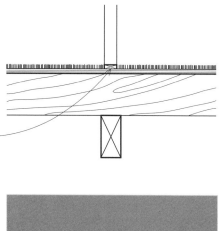

Vapor Retarders

Vapor retarders are required at the interior side of framed exterior walls in Climate Zones 5, 6, 7, 8, and Marine 4. These zones are shown in Figure N1101.2 in the Energy Efficiency Chapter of Part IV of the IRC. Climate Zones 5–8 are in the northern tier of the continental United States and in Alaska. The Marine 4 zone is located on the West Coast of the continental United States in the coastal regions of Northern California, Oregon and Washington. The vapor retarders are intended to keep out moisture from inside of the building from entering the wall cavity where they could cause mold or damage the wall construction. Vapor retarders in these zones are to be: Class I, described in §R601.3.2.

These classes are based on Perm ratings as follows:
- Class I: 0.1 Perm or less
- Class II: > 0.1 and < 1.0 Perm
- Class III: > 1.0 Perm and < 10 Perm

The following materials are deemed to comply. For Class I: sheet polyethylene, or unperforated aluminum foil; for Class II, kraft-faced fiberglass batts; for Class III, a paint film of latex or enamel paint. Class III vapor retarders are acceptable in the required climate zones where they are installed under the conditions described in Table 601.3.1. See the illustrations showing placement of the vapor barriers and their extent. For the purposes of this code, vented claddings are defined in §R601.3.3 as being vinyl lap or metal lap siding applied over a weather resistive barrier, conforming to Table R703.4. Also brick veneer conforming to §R703.7.4.2 is considered to be vented cladding. See the illustrations in Chapter 7 for further details of these systems.

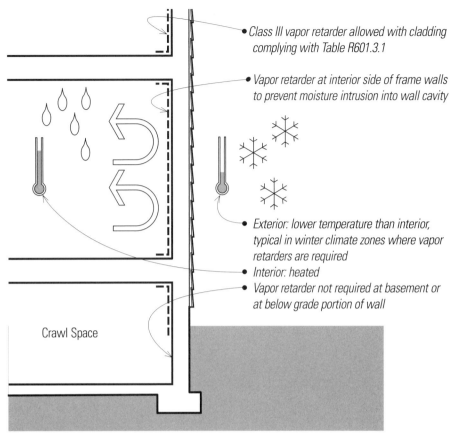

- Class III vapor retarder allowed with cladding complying with Table R601.3.1
- Vapor retarder at interior side of frame walls to prevent moisture intrusion into wall cavity
- Exterior: lower temperature than interior, typical in winter climate zones where vapor retarders are required
- Interior: heated
- Vapor retarder not required at basement or at below grade portion of wall

Crawl Space

Figure 601.3 Vapor Retarders

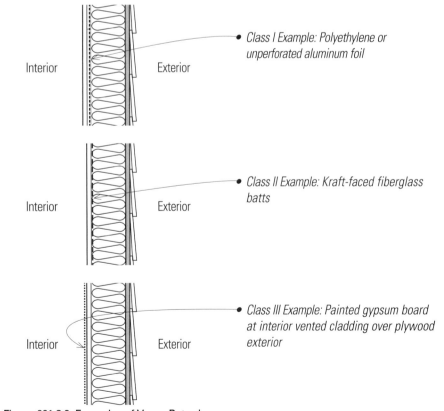

Interior   Exterior
- Class I Example: Polyethylene or unperforated aluminum foil

Interior   Exterior
- Class II Example: Kraft-faced fiberglass batts

Interior   Exterior
- Class III Example: Painted gypsum board at interior vented cladding over plywood exterior

Figure 601.3.2 Examples of Vapor Retarder Classes

Wood Wall Framing

§R602 sets forth the requirements for walls framed out of dimensional lumber, or what is known as "conventional framing" in the construction industry. Load-bearing wood is to be graded so that it meets minimum criteria for strength, stability and physical conditions such as straightness and dryness. Studs are to be minimum No. 3 Standard or Stud grade. Utility grade may be used for nonbearing partitions or partitions bearing loads other than floors if they are spaced per the requirements of Table R602.3(5). This table sets out spacing criteria based the stud height and its location in a structure.

Per §R602.3 wood framing elements for foundations, floors, walls and roofs are described in relationship to each other in Figures R602.3(1) and R602.3(2). Exterior walls are to be designed per the IRC, or in accordance with the AF&PA National Design Specifications (NDS). Exterior wall sheathing is to be fastened directly to framing members. Fastenings are to be made according to Tables R602.3(1)–(2). Walls are to be designed to resist lateral loads imposed by wind and seismic events. Sheathing materials are to conform to the requirements of Table R602.3(3), which relates panel thickness to stud spacing, nail size and spacing and design wind speeds.

Studs are to be continuous—that is, not spliced or made up of staggered pieces, from a sole plate at their base to a top plate. See the illustration for how components relate and for exceptions. Stud size, spacing and height is to be per Table R602.3(5), which relates these requirements to the size of the structure, where the studs are located in the structure and whether the partition is load bearing or not. Interior load-bearing walls are to be constructed as for exterior walls, which are presumed by the code to be load bearing. See the later illustrations regarding Table R602.3(5) stud spacing and height relationships. The code assumes that there are studs within a few inches where members bearing floor or roof loads rest on the top plate, especially when both sets of framing members are spaced as the conventional dimension of 16" (406)

on center. When the framing members resting on the plate are spaced more than 16" (406) o.c. and the wall studs are spaced at 24" (610) o.c., then the horizontal framing members are to be spaced such that they bear within 5" (127) of the studs below, or other accommodations are to be made as illustrated. Interior load-bearing walls are to be constructed, framed and fireblocked in the same manner as exterior walls. Interior non-bearing walls may be constructed of

lighter members with greater spacing, using 2x3 (51 x 76) studs at 24" (610) o.c. If not part of a braced wall line [discussed later in this chapter] the walls may use 2x4 (51 x 102) studs turned "flat" so that their long face is parallel to the face of the wall. Nonbearing stud walls may have a single top plate, but they must still be fireblocked per §R602.8. Fireblocking requirements are further described in Chapter 3 in §R302.11.

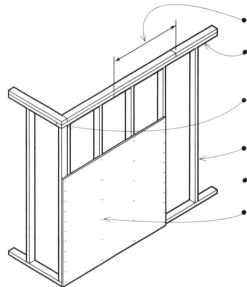

- Joints in top plates to be offset 24" (510) min.
- Double top plate typical, 2" (51) min. thickness, same width as joists below

- Overlap plates at corners and at intersection of bearing walls

- Studs to be continuous from sole plate to top plate
- Stud size spacing and height to be per Table R602.3(5)
- Structural sheathing to be fastened directly to wall framing, field nailing may vary from edge nailing

Figure 602 Typical Wood Stud Wall Framing Criteria

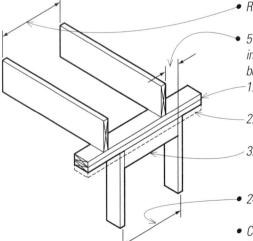

- Roof/Floor framing > 16" (406) o.c.

- 5" (127) max. offset between roof/floor framing and stud below, except: the offset may be > 5" (127) per exception to §R602.3.3 if:
  1. Double top plates are two 2x6 (38 x 140)
     or
  2. A third top plate is installed
     or
  3. Solid blocking from inside the stud is installed under each bearing to reinforce the double plate
- 24" (610) o.c. stud spacing

- Condition where roof/floor framing > 16" (406) o.c. _and_ wall studs at 24" (610) o.c.

Figure 602.3.3 Bearing Studs at Roof/Floor Framing

Wood Wall Fasteners

Table R602.3(1) describes fastening requirements for walls, but it also includes requirements for floors, roofs and panels as well. See the illustrations for examples of the types and configurations of the various types of fasteners. Table R602.3.(2) provides guidance for alternative methods of attachment from those described in Table R602.3(1). The fasteners in the second table are primarily mechanical fasteners that are installed with air or electric-powered equipment such as staple guns or nail guns.

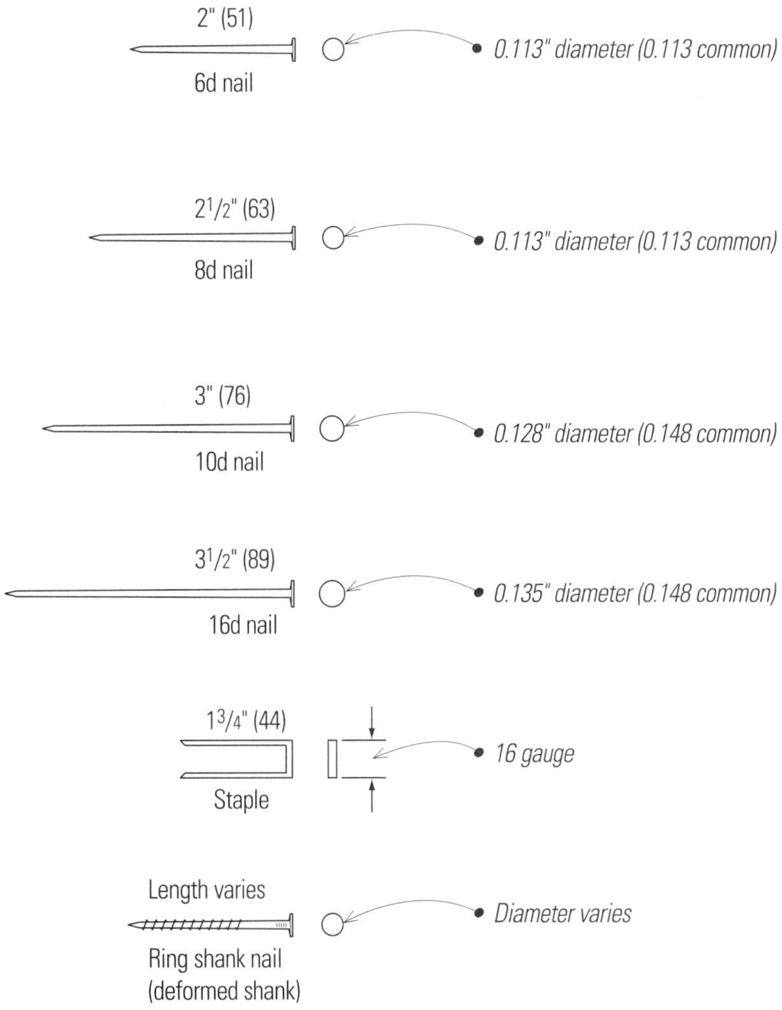

2" (51)
6d nail
● *0.113" diameter (0.113 common)*

2¹/₂" (63)
8d nail
● *0.113" diameter (0.113 common)*

3" (76)
10d nail
● *0.128" diameter (0.148 common)*

3¹/₂" (89)
16d nail
● *0.135" diameter (0.148 common)*

1³/₄" (44)
Staple
● *16 gauge*

Length varies
Ring shank nail
(deformed shank)
● *Diameter varies*

Typical Wood Fasteners from
Tables R602.3.(1) and R602.3(2)

Wood Wall Components

Wall components are to be assembled per the directions of the code sections illustrated in Figures R602.3(1) and R602.3(2).

From Table R602.3(1)

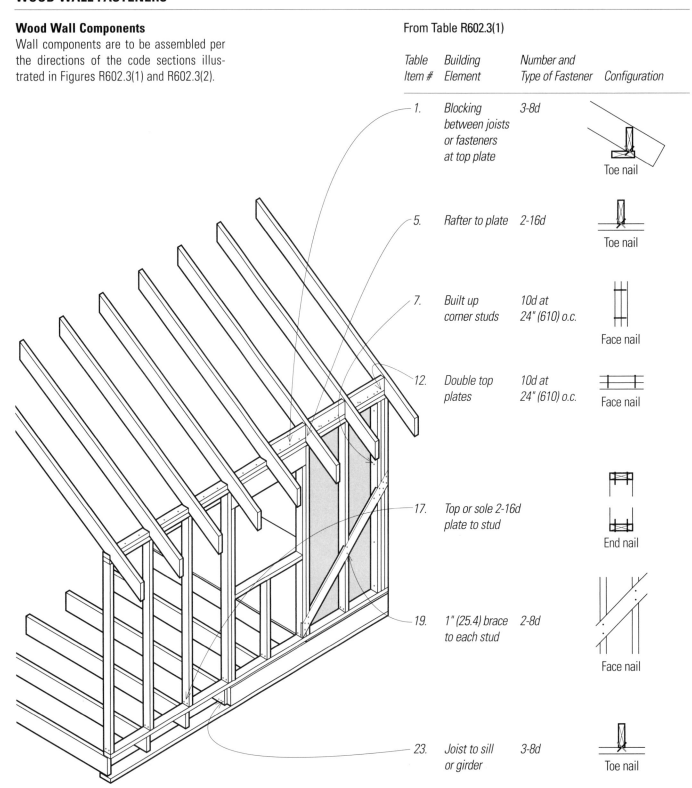

Table Item #	Building Element	Number and Type of Fastener	Configuration
1.	Blocking between joists or fasteners at top plate	3-8d	Toe nail
5.	Rafter to plate	2-16d	Toe nail
7.	Built up corner studs	10d at 24" (610) o.c.	Face nail
12.	Double top plates	10d at 24" (610) o.c.	Face nail
17.	Top or sole plate to stud	2-16d	End nail
19.	1" (25.4) brace to each stud	2-8d	Face nail
23.	Joist to sill or girder	3-8d	Toe nail

Figure R602.3.(1) Fasteners at Wood Structural Members

From Table R602.3(1)

Table Item #	Sheathing Building Element	Fastener	Spacing Edge	Spacing Intermediate (Field)
30.	$^3/_8"–^1/_2"$ (9.5–12.7) Roofing	8d	6" (152)	12" (205)
30.	$^3/_8"–^1/_2"$ (9.5–12.7) Subfloor, walls	8d	6" (152)	12" (205)
32.	$^9/_{32}"–1"$ (7.1–25.4) Roofing, walls, flooring	8d	6" (152)	12" (205)
33.	$1^1/_8"–1^1/_4"$ (28.6–31.8) Roofing, walls, flooring	10d (common) (8d deformed)	6" (152)	12" (205)

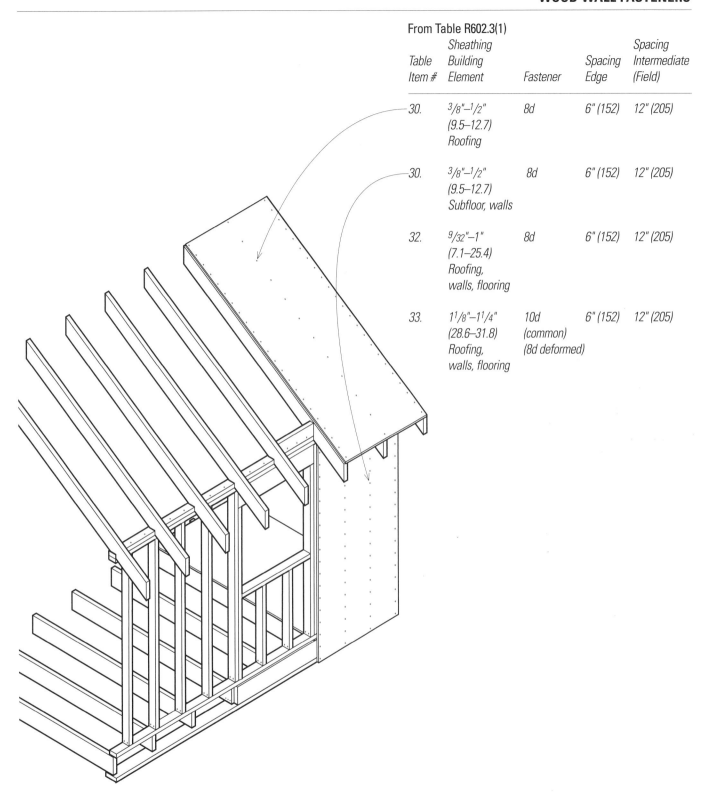

Figure R602.3.(1) Part 2 Fasteners at Wood Structural Members

Wood Wall Fasteners

Wall sheathing fastening and support requirements as noted above are contained in Table R602.3(3) for wood structural sheathing panels. Particleboard spans over studs in relation to panel thickness is to be per Table R602.3(4). See the illustrations for examples of how to apply these tables. Table R602.3(5) show the interrelated requirements for stud size, height, spacing and location in the structure. Note that for this table the unsupported length of studs is assumed to be 10' (3048) and the stud spacing varies, depending on how many floors the stud is supporting. See the illustrations for examples of how to use this table.

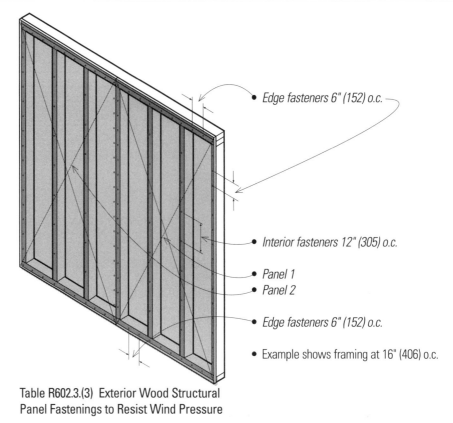

- *Edge fasteners 6" (152) o.c.*

- *Interior fasteners 12" (305) o.c.*

- *Panel 1*
- *Panel 2*

- *Edge fasteners 6" (152) o.c.*

- Example shows framing at 16" (406) o.c.

Table R602.3.(3) Exterior Wood Structural Panel Fastenings to Resist Wind Pressure

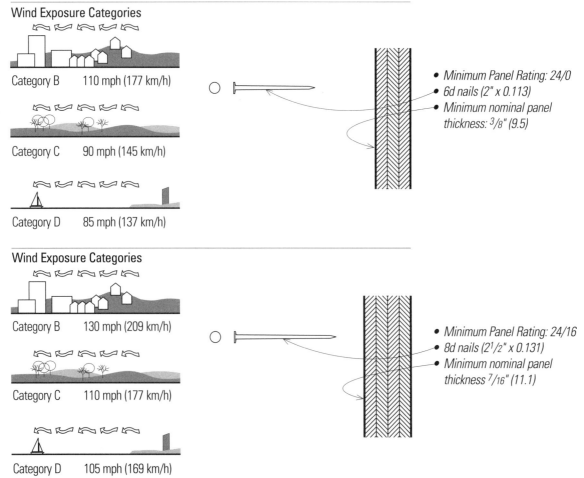

Wind Exposure Categories

Category B   110 mph (177 km/h)

Category C   90 mph (145 km/h)

Category D   85 mph (137 km/h)

- *Minimum Panel Rating: 24/0*
- *6d nails (2" x 0.113)*
- *Minimum nominal panel thickness: $^3/_8$" (9.5)*

Wind Exposure Categories

Category B   130 mph (209 km/h)

Category C   110 mph (177 km/h)

Category D   105 mph (169 km/h)

- *Minimum Panel Rating: 24/16*
- *8d nails (2$^1/_2$" x 0.131)*
- *Minimum nominal panel thickness $^7/_{16}$" (11.1)*

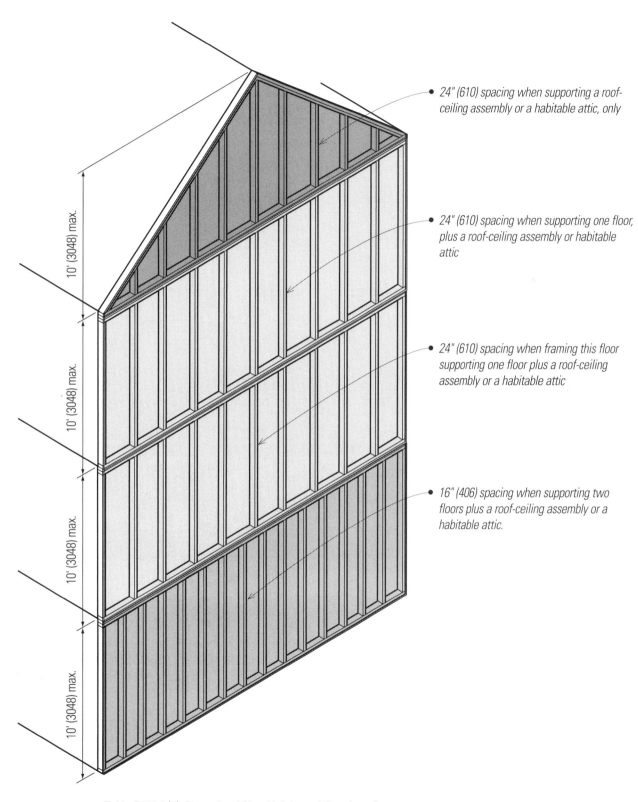

10' (3048) max.

10' (3048) max.

10' (3048) max.

10' (3048) max.

- 24" (610) spacing when supporting a roof-ceiling assembly or a habitable attic, only

- 24" (610) spacing when supporting one floor, plus a roof-ceiling assembly or habitable attic

- 24" (610) spacing when framing this floor supporting one floor plus a roof-ceiling assembly or a habitable attic

- 16" (406) spacing when supporting two floors plus a roof-ceiling assembly or a habitable attic.

Table R602.3.(5) Example of Size, Height and Spacing of Wood Studs at 2x6 (51 x 152) Bearing Walls

Wood Wall Components

Wall components are to be assembled per the directions of the code sections illustrated in Figures R602.3(1) and R602.3(2).

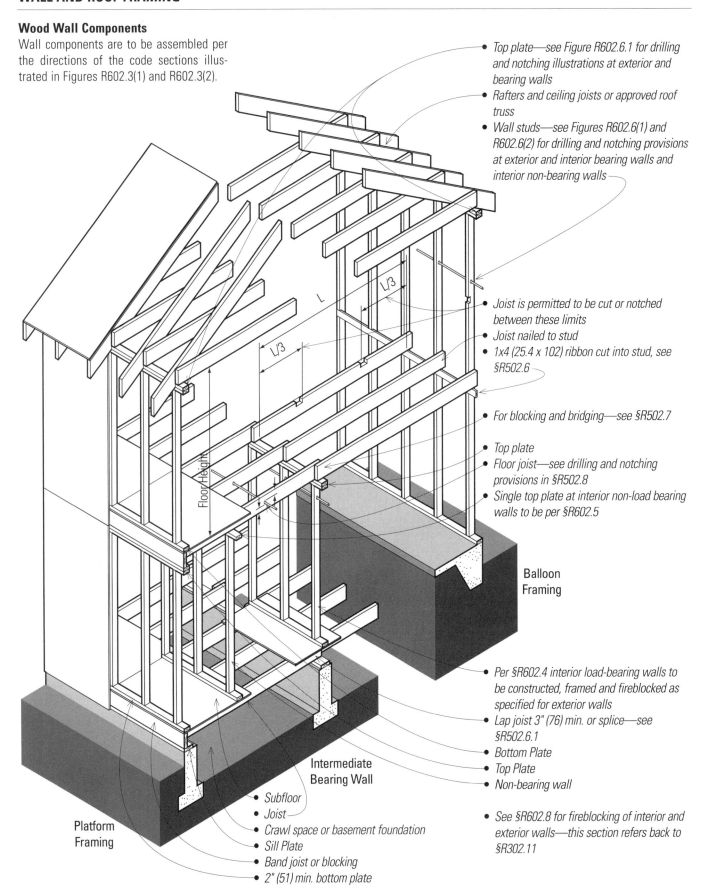

- Top plate—see Figure R602.6.1 for drilling and notching illustrations at exterior and bearing walls
- Rafters and ceiling joists or approved roof truss
- Wall studs—see Figures R602.6(1) and R602.6(2) for drilling and notching provisions at exterior and interior bearing walls and interior non-bearing walls

- Joist is permitted to be cut or notched between these limits
- Joist nailed to stud
- 1x4 (25.4 x 102) ribbon cut into stud, see §R502.6

- For blocking and bridging—see §R502.7

- Top plate
- Floor joist—see drilling and notching provisions in §R502.8
- Single top plate at interior non-load bearing walls to be per §R602.5

Balloon Framing

- Per §R602.4 interior load-bearing walls to be constructed, framed and fireblocked as specified for exterior walls
- Lap joist 3" (76) min. or splice—see §R502.6.1
- Bottom Plate
- Top Plate
- Non-bearing wall

- See §R602.8 for fireblocking of interior and exterior walls—this section refers back to §R302.11

Floor Height

L/3

L

L/3

Intermediate Bearing Wall

- Subfloor
- Joist
- Crawl space or basement foundation
- Sill Plate
- Band joist or blocking
- 2" (51) min. bottom plate

Platform Framing

Figure R602.3.(1) Typical Wall Floor and Roof Framing

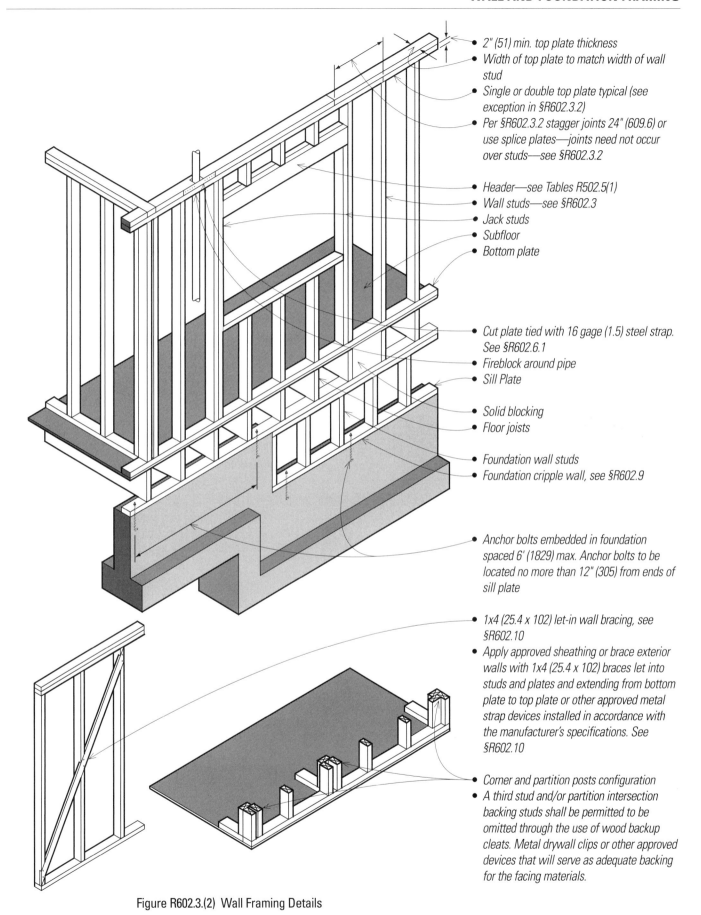

- 2" (51) min. top plate thickness
- Width of top plate to match width of wall stud
- Single or double top plate typical (see exception in §R602.3.2)
- Per §R602.3.2 stagger joints 24" (609.6) or use splice plates—joints need not occur over studs—see §R602.3.2

- Header—see Tables R502.5(1)
- Wall studs—see §R602.3
- Jack studs
- Subfloor
- Bottom plate

- Cut plate tied with 16 gage (1.5) steel strap. See §R602.6.1
- Fireblock around pipe
- Sill Plate

- Solid blocking
- Floor joists

- Foundation wall studs
- Foundation cripple wall, see §R602.9

- Anchor bolts embedded in foundation spaced 6' (1829) max. Anchor bolts to be located no more than 12" (305) from ends of sill plate

- 1x4 (25.4 x 102) let-in wall bracing, see §R602.10
- Apply approved sheathing or brace exterior walls with 1x4 (25.4 x 102) braces let into studs and plates and extending from bottom plate to top plate or other approved metal strap devices installed in accordance with the manufacturer's specifications. See §R602.10

- Corner and partition posts configuration
- A third stud and/or partition intersection backing studs shall be permitted to be omitted through the use of wood backup cleats. Metal drywall clips or other approved devices that will serve as adequate backing for the facing materials.

Figure R602.3.(2) Wall Framing Details

Maximum Stud Height

Maximum stud heights are limited as per Table R602.3.1 based on spacing, size and building configuration. Walls are assumed to be exposed to less than 100 mph (44 m/s) winds or Seismic Design Categories A, B, C, D0, D1, D2.

Legend

| Maximum stud height

▌ *Maximum stud height with conventional framing of 16" (406) o.c.*

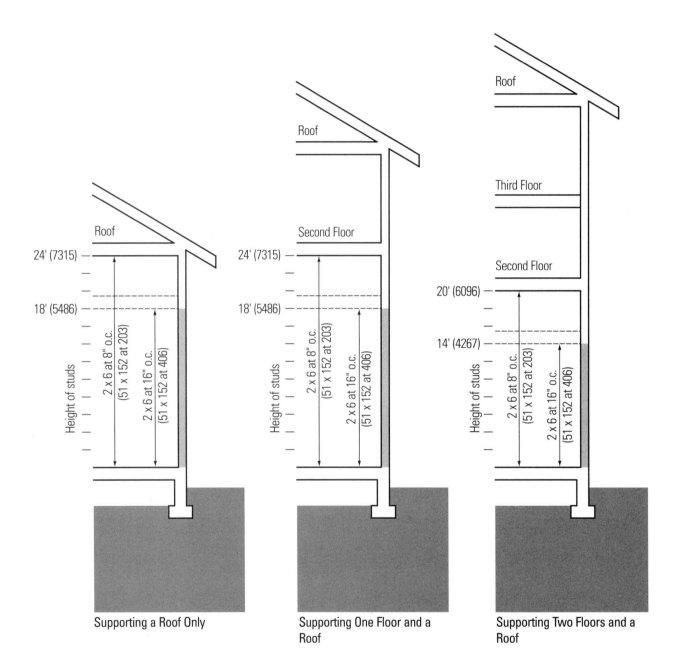

Supporting a Roof Only

Supporting One Floor and a Roof

Supporting Two Floors and a Roof

Maximum Stud Height From Table R602.3.5

Drilling and Notching of Studs

Drilling and notching wood studs and plates weakens their bearing capacity so the number, size and spacing of notches for such things as plumbing lines or electrical conduits are limited by §R602.6. The requirements vary depending on whether the wall is load bearing or non load bearing, whether the hole or notch occurs in the edge or center of a stud, which determines the continuity of how gravity or lateral loads are transmitted from the plate through the stud to a bearing plate at the bottom of the wall. We have included the two illustrations for bearing and nonbearing walls on this and the following page to show a comparison of the variation in the allowable dimensions of notches and drilled holes, depending on whether the wall is bearing or not. We recommend that if the work is taking place in an existing wall, or if it is unclear whether the wall is bearing or nonbearing, that the more stringent bearing wall criteria be applied when drilling or notching such a wall.

Where pipes or conduits pass through plates at exterior walls or interior bearing walls and the notch in the plate exceeds 50% of the width of the plate, they are to be reinforced per the requirements illustrated in Figure R602.6.1. Note that wall sheathing located on the side of the wall where the notch occurs is seen as accomplishing the same reinforcing for the gap in the plate as the metal tie.

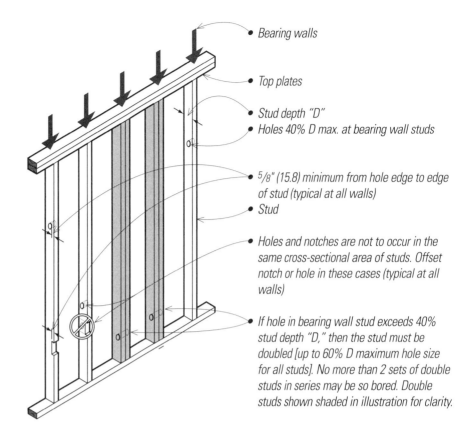

- Bearing walls
- Top plates
- Stud depth "D"
- Holes 40% D max. at bearing wall studs
- 5/8" (15.8) minimum from hole edge to edge of stud (typical at all walls)
- Stud
- Holes and notches are not to occur in the same cross-sectional area of studs. Offset notch or hole in these cases (typical at all walls)
- If hole in bearing wall stud exceeds 40% stud depth "D," then the stud must be doubled [up to 60% D maximum hole size for all studs]. No more than 2 sets of double studs in series may be so bored. Double studs shown shaded in illustration for clarity.

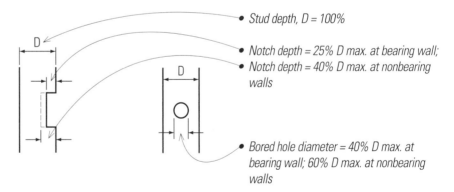

- Stud depth, D = 100%
- Notch depth = 25% D max. at bearing wall;
- Notch depth = 40% D max. at nonbearing walls
- Bored hole diameter = 40% D max. at bearing wall; 60% D max. at nonbearing walls

Figure R602.6.(1) Notching and Bored Hole Limitations for Exterior Walls and Bearing Walls

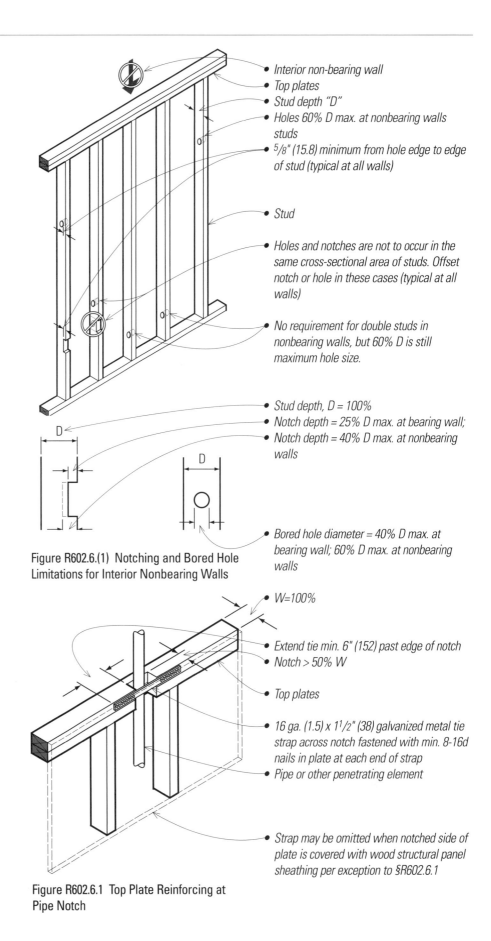

- Interior non-bearing wall
- Top plates
- Stud depth "D"
- Holes 60% D max. at nonbearing walls studs
- ⁵/₈" (15.8) minimum from hole edge to edge of stud (typical at all walls)

- Stud

- Holes and notches are not to occur in the same cross-sectional area of studs. Offset notch or hole in these cases (typical at all walls)

- No requirement for double studs in nonbearing walls, but 60% D is still maximum hole size.

- Stud depth, D = 100%
- Notch depth = 25% D max. at bearing wall;
- Notch depth = 40% D max. at nonbearing walls

- Bored hole diameter = 40% D max. at bearing wall; 60% D max. at nonbearing walls

Figure R602.6.(1) Notching and Bored Hole Limitations for Interior Nonbearing Walls

- W=100%

- Extend tie min. 6" (152) past edge of notch
- Notch > 50% W

- Top plates

- 16 ga. (1.5) x 1¹/₂" (38) galvanized metal tie strap across notch fastened with min. 8-16d nails in plate at each end of strap
- Pipe or other penetrating element

- Strap may be omitted when notched side of plate is covered with wood structural panel sheathing per exception to §R602.6.1

Figure R602.6.1 Top Plate Reinforcing at Pipe Notch

Headers

Headers are required over openings in walls where the load must be transferred from the structure above to the members supporting the wall. Headers over openings may be of solid lumber or built up of smaller members or built up in a box-like configuration. Wood member headers are to sized per the girder and header spans shown in Table R502.5(1) and (2). Table (1) is to be used for headers at exterior bearing walls; Table (2) is to be used for headers in interior bearing walls. The size of the header is dependent on the tributary area of load which is in turn dependent on the width of the building, the number of stories supported and exterior loads such as snow for exterior bearing walls. The sizes of headers may be interpolated from the tables based on loads and building widths. Note that the number of jack studs at the header are to be per these tables. Where a single jack stud is noted, the code permits the use of approved framing anchors attached to the adjacent stud and the omission of an additional jack stud extending from the plate to the underside of the header.

Header may also be constructed as boxed made up of wood structural panels over wood framing members. These constructed headers are to be made as illustrated in Figure R602.7.2. The depth of such headers is to be either 9" (229) or 15" (381) with the depth and spans based upon the overall width of the house, which contributes loading to the header. Table R602.7.2 assumes that these headers support a single story with a trussed roof or that a multiple story building has interior bearing walls so that the built up header is not supporting two stories of load.

Since they do not support a load from above per §R602.7.2 openings in nonbearing walls that are less than 8' (2438) in width do not need headers other than a single flat 2 x 4 (51 x 100). If the opening height is less than 24" below the horizontal framing above then no blocking or cripple studs are required either.

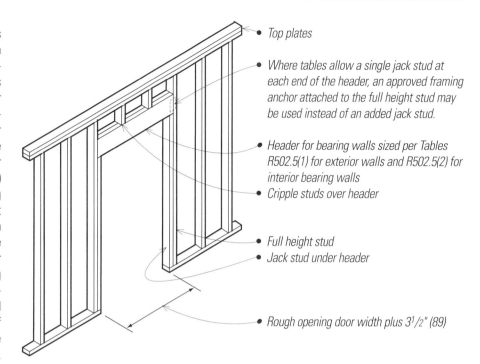

- Top plates
- Where tables allow a single jack stud at each end of the header, an approved framing anchor attached to the full height stud may be used instead of an added jack stud.
- Header for bearing walls sized per Tables R502.5(1) for exterior walls and R502.5(2) for interior bearing walls
- Cripple studs over header
- Full height stud
- Jack stud under header
- Rough opening door width plus 3¹/₂" (89)

§R602.7 Header at Exterior Walls and Interior Bearing Walls

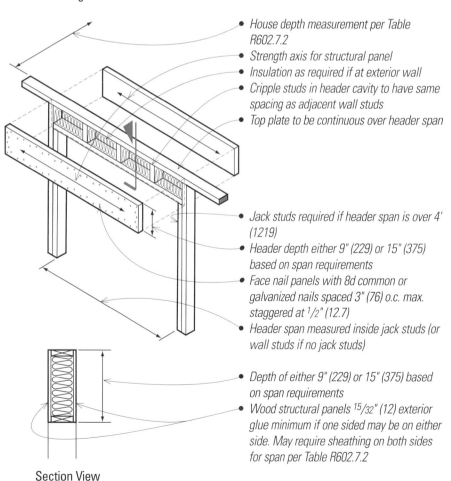

- House depth measurement per Table R602.7.2
- Strength axis for structural panel
- Insulation as required if at exterior wall
- Cripple studs in header cavity to have same spacing as adjacent wall studs
- Top plate to be continuous over header span
- Jack studs required if header span is over 4' (1219)
- Header depth either 9" (229) or 15" (375) based on span requirements
- Face nail panels with 8d common or galvanized nails spaced 3" (76) o.c. max. staggered at ¹/₂" (12.7)
- Header span measured inside jack studs (or wall studs if no jack studs)
- Depth of either 9" (229) or 15" (375) based on span requirements
- Wood structural panels ¹⁵/₃₂" (12) exterior glue minimum if one sided may be on either side. May require sheathing on both sides for span per Table R602.7.2

Section View

Fireblocking

Fireblocking is required as prescribed in §R302.11. See that section for a description of fireblocking at combustible construction.

Cripple Walls

Per §R602.9 Cripple walls are to be framed of studs at least as large as the studs in the walls above them. When cripples walls exceed 4' (1219) in height they are to be framed of stud sizes as required for an additional story. Short cripple walls that are tall enough to allow nailing of sheathing as for a typical wall are required to be sheathed on at least one side or made of solid blocking as they must be for shorter walls where there is not sufficient space to nail sheathing to the cripples studs. Cripple walls less than 14" (536) in height are to be sheathed on at least one side with structural sheathing panels nailed per Table R602.3(1). Cripple walls are considered part of foundation walls and are thus to be supported on continuous foundations. See Figure R602.3(2) showing location of the cripple wall in relation to other wall elements.

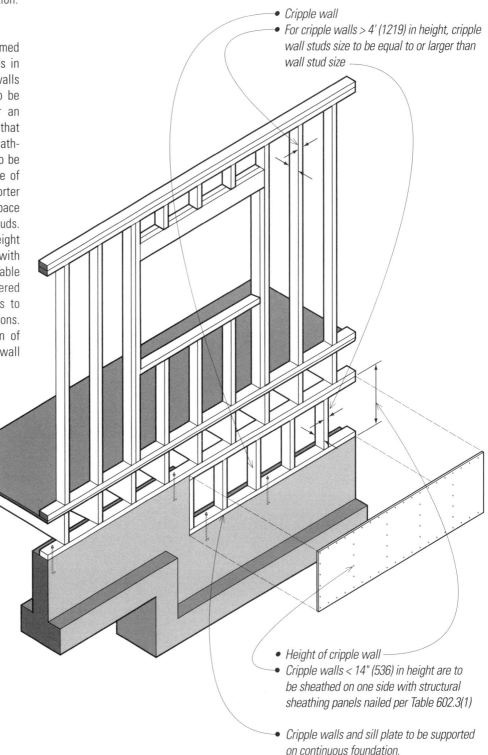

- Cripple wall
- For cripple walls > 4' (1219) in height, cripple wall studs size to be equal to or larger than wall stud size

- Height of cripple wall
- Cripple walls < 14" (536) in height are to be sheathed on one side with structural sheathing panels nailed per Table 602.3(1)

- Cripple walls and sill plate to be supported on continuous foundation.

Wall Bracing

Wall bracing to resist wind and seismic induced lateral loads is an essential part of the load path of any building. These forces, which can push over or overturn a building, must be resisted and transferred safely into the foundation system. §R602.10 describes wall bracing requirements. When the prescriptive requirements of this section cannot be met, then a load path must be designed per the requirements of §R301.1. In order to know which levels of wind or seismic forces must be resisted and designed to accommodate, the building designer must determine what wind or seismic zone the building is in. Once the design parameters for bracing have been determined, the designer must then decide what type of bracing system is most appropriate for the residence being designed. Once the desired system has been selected then the configuration of the building can be determined. After the size and shape of the building are decided upon, then the tables and figures in the code may be utilized to determine bracing requirements.

The basic bracing concept is that of lines of bracing that resist forces such as wind loads or seismic loads parallel to their long direction. A Braced Wall Line is defined in Chapter 2 of the IRC. It is a straight line though the building plan that represents a line of lateral resistance provided by wall bracing panels or a continuously sheathed wall, both of which are also defined terms. The length of bracing panels is determined by the spacing between bracing lines. Thus a building with many parallel bracing lines can have bracing panels of shorter lengths and lower lateral force resistance. Bracing lines may be designed as intermittent panels per the requirements of §R602.10.2 or be designed as continuously sheathed panels per §R602.10.4 or §R602.10.5. Intermittent bracing systems are designated with initials in the various tables in this section. The systems are described in detail and illustrated in Table R602.10.2. Continuously sheathed panels are designated at "CS-xx" panels as illustrated in Table R602.10.4.1.

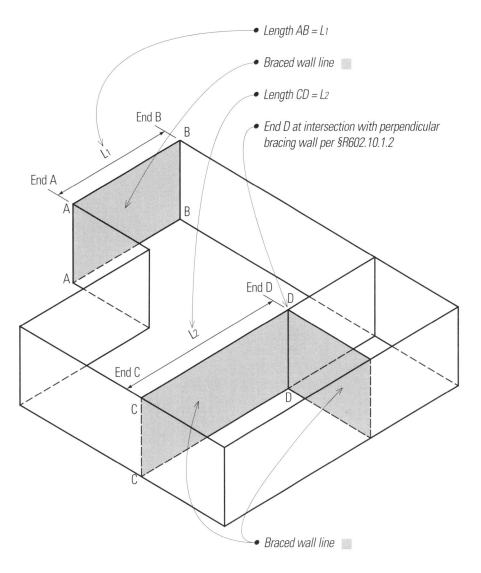

- Length $AB = L_1$
- Braced wall line ▨
- Length $CD = L_2$
- End D at intersection with perpendicular bracing wall per §R602.10.1.2
- Braced wall line ▨

Braced Wall Line Lengths per §R602.10.1

Wall Bracing

Mixing of bracing panels is allowed from story to story per §602.10.1.1.1, but panels may be mixed in the same wall bracing line only in Seismic Design Categories A and B (or C for detached dwellings). Where panel types are mixed in those conditions the highest length requirements for the various systems as required by Table R602.10.1.2(1) or (2) shall govern. All factors for loading, wind, seismic, and number of stories are to be taken into account and the most stringent are to govern per §R602.10.1.1.

Bracing requirements are based on the configuration of the building and on the location of the bracing wall in relation to the number of stories. The design criteria are broken into two sets of criteria—one for wind and one for seismic design. The building design should be evaluated against both sets of criteria, as determined by the location of the building, to determine which one will govern. For example, a residence in the southeastern United States is much more likely to have wind design as the governing design factor for lateral force resistance to hurricane force winds while a building in California will likely have seismic design criteria governing lateral force resistance design. Bracing requirements are based on the configuration of the building and on the location of the bracing wall in relation to the number of stories.

See the comparative illustration of how design per Table R602.10.1.2(1) for wind and per Table R602.10.1.2(2) for seismic design are related to an example building. Note that for these two tables wind design criteria are a function of bracing wall spacing and seismic design criteria are a function of the length of bracing walls. The two tables thus take into account how the two types of lateral forces effect buildings in differing ways that require different design responses.

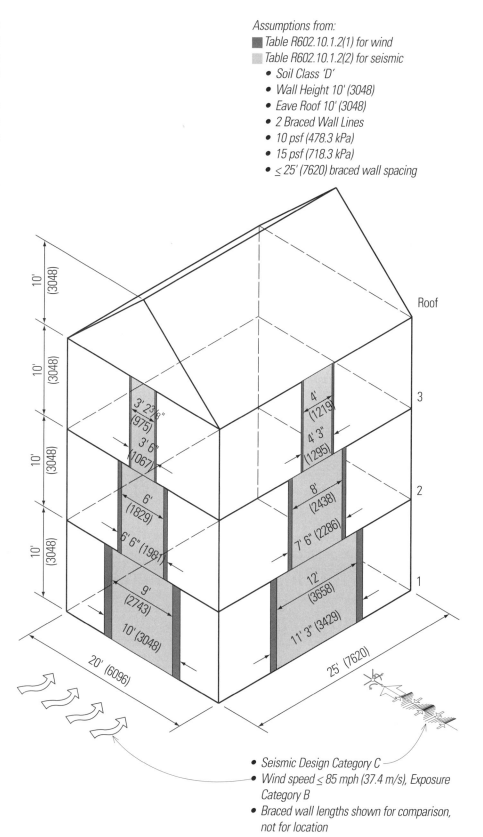

Assumptions from:
- ■ Table R602.10.1.2(1) for wind
- ■ Table R602.10.1.2(2) for seismic
- • Soil Class 'D'
- • Wall Height 10' (3048)
- • Eave Roof 10' (3048)
- • 2 Braced Wall Lines
- • 10 psf (478.3 kPa)
- • 15 psf (718.3 kPa)
- • ≤ 25' (7620) braced wall spacing

- • Seismic Design Category C
- • Wind speed ≤ 85 mph (37.4 m/s), Exposure Category B
- • Braced wall lengths shown for comparison, not for location

Example per Table R602.10.1.2(1) and Table R602.10.1.2(2)
3-Story, 20' x 25' (6096 x 7620) Building with WSP Wood Structural Panel Wall Bracing for Wind and Seismic Loads

§R602.10.1.2.1 Braced Wall Panel Uplift Load Path

Exterior wall bracing panels that support roof rafters or trusses are to be designed to provide a load path from the roof members through the wall into the foundation. Where the building meets the configuration and wind load criteria of §R602.10.1.2.1 then the roof members may be fastened to the wall bracing with typical connections as described by Table R602.3(1). Where the loadings are higher than 100 plf (146 N/mm), then approved uplift framing connectors are to be installed to provide the necessary load path, or the system is to be designed using accepted engineering practice to resist uplift and shear forces.

§R602.10.1.3 Wall Brace Lines at Angled Corners

The basic assumption about wall bracing is that only walls parallel to the bracing line direction can be counted as contributing to the bracing requirements for that line. In no case can the sum of all adjusted bracing lengths be less than 48" (1219) for a line to be considered as a bracing line. However the code recognizes that wall bracing lines may be placed at an angle to the rest of the building. Such diagonal walls do contribute to the wall bracing in the building, but the angle in relation to other walls determines which direction the wall line is to be counted on for resistance to lateral forces. Per §R602.10.1.3 braced wall lines at corners may angle out of the plane of the braced wall line for a distance of up to 8' (2438). The effective length of the bracing walls is to be determined per the criteria shown in the illustration in Figure R602.10.1.3.

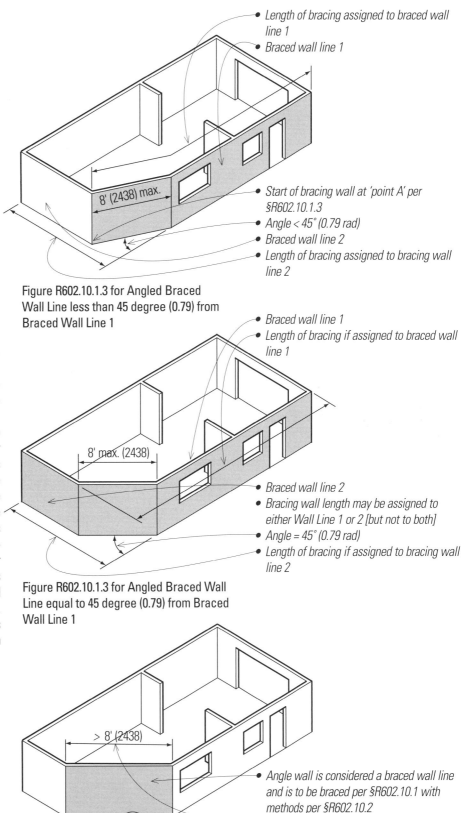

- Length of bracing assigned to braced wall line 1
- Braced wall line 1

8' (2438) max.

- Start of bracing wall at 'point A' per §R602.10.1.3
- Angle < 45˚ (0.79 rad)
- Braced wall line 2
- Length of bracing assigned to bracing wall line 2

Figure R602.10.1.3 for Angled Braced Wall Line less than 45 degree (0.79) from Braced Wall Line 1

- Braced wall line 1
- Length of bracing if assigned to braced wall line 1

8' max. (2438)

- Braced wall line 2
- Bracing wall length may be assigned to either Wall Line 1 or 2 [but not to both]
- Angle = 45˚ (0.79 rad)
- Length of bracing if assigned to bracing wall line 2

Figure R602.10.1.3 for Angled Braced Wall Line equal to 45 degree (0.79) from Braced Wall Line 1

> 8' (2438)

- Angle wall is considered a braced wall line and is to be braced per §R602.10.1 with methods per §R602.10.2
- Condition depends on wall length of angled wall, not on angle of wall to other walls

Figure R602.10.1.3 for Angled Braced Wall Line where the Length of the Angled Wall is greater than 8' (2438)

WALL BRACING

Braced wall panels are to be located per §R602.10.1.4 as illustrated in Figures R602.10.1.4(1) and R602.10.1.4(2). Per §R602.10.1.4.1 and §R602.10.1.5, buildings located in Seismic Design Categories D0, D1 and D2 have additional requirements for braced wall panel locations and braced wall line spacing, as noted in the illustrations. Braced wall panels may be offset from the designated braced wall line location as illustrated in Figures R602.10.1.4(3) and (4). The designer can gain flexibility in locations of braced wall panels by carefully considering where the braced wall line location is designated on the permit drawings.

Braced wall panels are to be fastened to framing at their base and top per the requirements of §R602.10.6. This section also contains requirements for bracing details for buildings in Seismic Design Categories D0, D1 and D2.

- Braced wall line spacing per Tables R602.10.2(1) and R602.10.2(2) [25' (7620) max. in Seismic Design Categories D0, D1, D2]

Braced wall line C

Braced wall line B

Braced wall line A

- See exception for spacing per §R602.10.1.5 single-room spacing
- Braced wall panel spacing, 25' (7620) o.c. max. from centerlines of wall brace panels

- Braced wall panel length

- In Seismic Design Categories D0, D1, and D2, wall bracing panels are to be located at each end of the braced wall line, per §R602.10.1.4.1. There are exceptions to this requirement as illustrated in Figure R602.10.1.4.1.

- 4' (1219)

- Braced wall panel
- Braced wall line

- 1

- End of wall

- Braced wall panel
- Designated braced wall line. Braced wall panels may be offset from this designated line by up to 4' (1219) on either side of the designated braced wall line or a total of 8 (2438) between wall panels.
- Extent of braced wall line runs from end to end of wall

- End distance max. 12' 6" (3810). Sum of end distances 1 and 2 may not exceed 12' 6" (3810)

Braced Wall Panel Locations from Figures
R602.10.1.4(1), R602.10.1.4(2), R602.10.1.4(3)

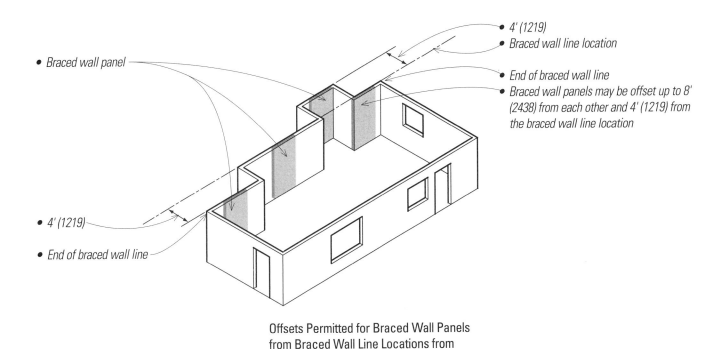

- Braced wall panel
- 4' (1219)
- End of braced wall line

- 4' (1219)
- Braced wall line location
- End of braced wall line
- Braced wall panels may be offset up to 8' (2438) from each other and 4' (1219) from the braced wall line location

Offsets Permitted for Braced Wall Panels from Braced Wall Line Locations from Figure R602.10.1.4(3)

- Braced wall line C
- Braced wall line B
- Braced wall line A
- 4' (1219)
- 4' (1219) offset in each direction from braced wall line. Maximum 8' (2438) total separation between braced wall panels.

- Braced wall line spacing for bracing wall line C
- Braced wall line spacing for bracing wall line A
- Bracing wall line spacing for bracing wall line B is the greater of distance X and distance Y
- Designated braced wall line for building interior for this example
- Designated braced wall line for building exterior for this example

Braced Wall Line Spacing from Figure R602.10.1.4(4)

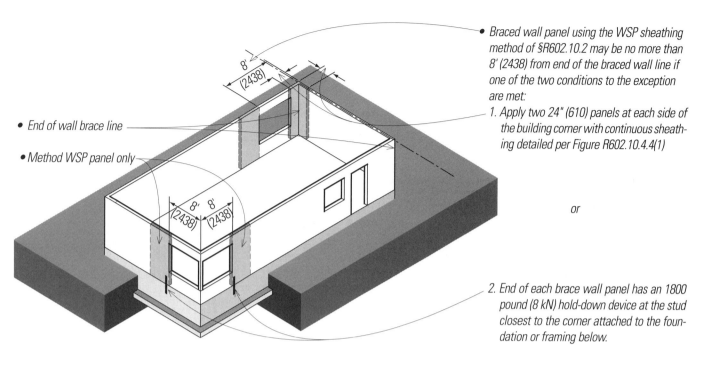

- End of wall brace line
- Method WSP panel only

8'
(2438)

8' 8'
(2438) (2438)

- Braced wall panel using the WSP sheathing method of §R602.10.2 may be no more than 8' (2438) from end of the braced wall line if one of the two conditions to the exception are met:
1. Apply two 24" (610) panels at each side of the building corner with continuous sheathing detailed per Figure R602.10.4.4(1)

or

2. End of each brace wall panel has an 1800 pound (8 kN) hold-down device at the stud closest to the corner attached to the foundation or framing below.

Figure R602.10.1.4.1 Braced Wall Panel Alternate Locations in Seismic Design Categories D0, D1, D2 per Exceptions to §R602.10.4.1

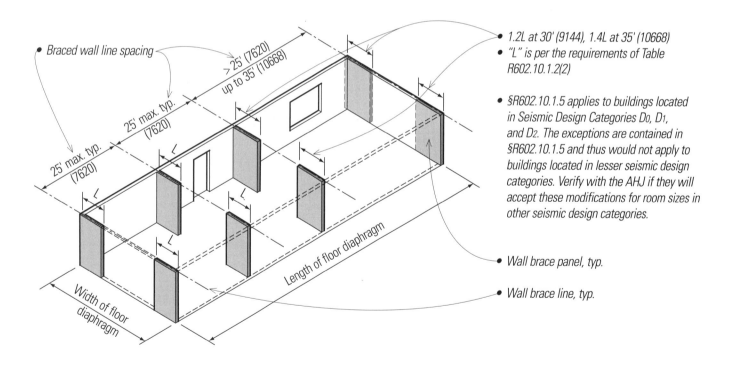

- Braced wall line spacing

> 25' (7620)
up to 35' (10668)

25' max. typ.
(7620)

25' max. typ.
(7620)

Length of floor diaphragm

Width of floor diaphragm

- 1.2L at 30' (9144), 1.4L at 35' (10668)
- "L" is per the requirements of Table R602.10.1.2(2)

- §R602.10.1.5 applies to buildings located in Seismic Design Categories D0, D1, and D2. The exceptions are contained in §R602.10.1.5 and thus would not apply to buildings located in lesser seismic design categories. Verify with the AHJ if they will accept these modifications for room sizes in other seismic design categories.

- Wall brace panel, typ.
- Wall brace line, typ.

Adjustments for Braced Wall panel Lengths Based on Braced Wall Line Spacing per §R602.10.1.5 and Table R602.10.1.5

Intermittent Braced Wall Panel

Intermittent braced wall panels are to be constructed as shown in Table R602.10.2 as illustrated on subsequent pages. The illustrations are organized in the same order as those in the IRC. Note that the panels in the code are not in alphabetical order. They are identified by method descriptors made up of the names assigned to the various types of bracing systems.

These panels are required by §R602.10.2.1 to have $1/2$" (12.7) gypsum board applied to the side opposite the bracing. This may be assumed to be on the interior side, since gypsum board is not an exterior finish, but that is not stated in §R602.10.1.2.1. There are exceptions to this requirement for certain panel types that are noted in the following illustrations. Also, other interior materials may be substituted for gypsum board if the materials are approved by the AHJ as having equivalent in-plane shear resistance to gypsum board. Also, certain panel types may have the gypsum board deleted if the length of the braced wall panels required by Tables R602.10.1.2(1) and (2) are increased to compensate for the loss of the in-plane shear resistance of the gypsum board. Note that adhesive attachment of wall sheathing is not permitted in Seismic Design Categories D_0, D_1 and D_2. Per §R602.10.3 braced wall panels are to be a minimum length for certain types of wall panels described in the relevant illustrations. Moreover, where story heights exceed the standard 10' (3048) assumed in the tables, adjustment factors are to be applied for certain bracing types. Also, where alternate braced wall panels [Methods ABW, PFH and PFG] are used, these panels may be substituted for other panel types as illustrated.

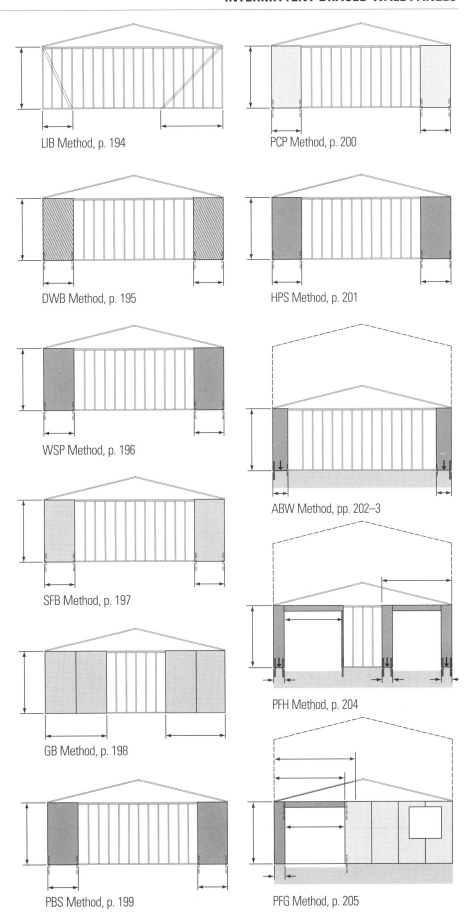

LIB Method, p. 194

PCP Method, p. 200

DWB Method, p. 195

HPS Method, p. 201

WSP Method, p. 196

ABW Method, pp. 202–3

SFB Method, p. 197

PFH Method, p. 204

GB Method, p. 198

PBS Method, p. 199

PFG Method, p. 205

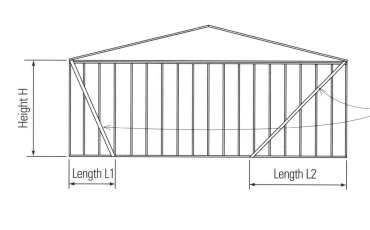

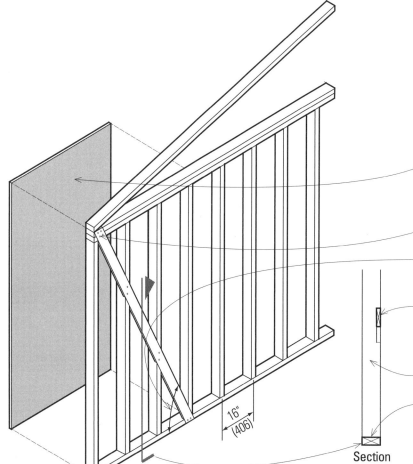

Wall Brace Panel LIB Method

- *Intermittent Wall Bracing per Table R602.10.2*
  - *Bracing Method Name: LIB*
  - *Bracing Type: Let In Bracing*
  - *Restrictions: While not spelled out clearly, let-in bracing is allowed for very limited uses. "LIB" is not mentioned in allowable length text or exceptions in §R602.10.3. Also "LIB" is not listed in Table R602.10.3.1 regarding minimum panel lengths for braced wall panels for wind and seismic design.*
- *Per Table R602.10.1.2(1) Footnote f, "L" adjustment factor of 1.8 applies if no gypsum board sheathing is used.*
- *Also see notes on illustrations.*
- *Commentary: Diagonal brace may be either wood or metal. If metal is used the connections are to be per manufacturer's recommendations.*

- *Min. total length of wall bracing in any braced wall line is to be 48" (1219) per §R602.10.1.2*

- *Gypsum Board sheathing typical at interior, per §R602.10.2.1, attached per GB requirements per Footnote g to Table R602.10.1.2(1)*
- *2-8d nails per member intersection, typical at each stud and plate at let-in wood bracing*
- *Angle 45–60° (0.785–1.047)*

- *1x4 (19 x 89) brace let-in [notched] into stud or metal strap applied to the stud per the strap manufacturer's application instructions*

- *Stud*

- *Bottom plate*

Section View

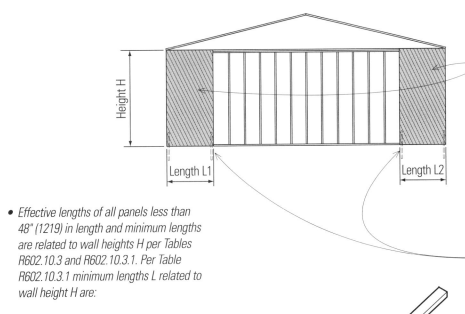

- Intermittent Wall Bracing per Table R602.10.2
  - *Bracing Method Name:* DWB
  - *Bracing Type:* Diagonal Wood Boards
  - *Restrictions:* Per Table R602.10.1.2(1) Footnote f, "L" adjustment factor of 1.4 applies if no gypsum board sheathing is used.
  - Also see notes on illustrations.
  - *Commentary:* Per §R602.10.1.4.1 in Seismic Design Categories D_0, D_1, and D_2. DWB braced wall lines at exterior walls shall have a braced wall panel located at each end of the braced wall line.

- Per Footnote i to Table R602.10.1.2(1) the required bracing length in one-story buildings and in the top story of two- or three-story buildings may be 0.80L when hold-down device with a minimum uplift design value of 800 pounds (363 kg) is fastened to the end studs of each braced wall panel in the braced wall line and to the foundation or framing below.

- For Method DWB each braced wall panel shall be at least 48" (1219) in length, covering a minimum of three stud spaces where studs are spaced 16" (406) on center and covering a minimum of two stud spaces where studs are spaced 24" (610) on center.

- L of each panel 48" (1219) min. per §R602.10.3, but per Exception 4, in Seismic Design Categories A, B, and C; panels between 36" (914) and 48" (1219) in length may count toward the required length of bracing in Tables R602.10.1.2(1) and R602.10.1.2(2) and the effective contribution shall comply with Table R602.10.3.

- $^3/_4$" (19) [1 inch nominal] diagonal wood boards with 2-8d nails or two $1^3/_4$" (44.5) staples per stud.

- Maximum 24" (609) stud spacing

- Gypsum board sheathing typical at interior per §R602.10.2.1, may be omitted if L per Tables R602.10.1.2(1) and R602.10.1.2(2) is increased by a factor of 1.5 per Exception 3 to §R602.10.2.1

- Effective lengths of all panels less than 48" (1219) in length and minimum lengths are related to wall heights H per Tables R602.10.3 and R602.10.3.1. Per Table R602.10.3.1 minimum lengths L related to wall height H are:

Wall Height H		Min. Length L	
8'	(2538)	4' 0"	(1219)
9'	(2743)	4' 0"	(1219)
10'	(3048)	4' 0"	(1219)
11'	(3353)	4' 5"	(1346)
12'	(3658)	4' 10"	(1473)

Wall Brace Panel DWB Method

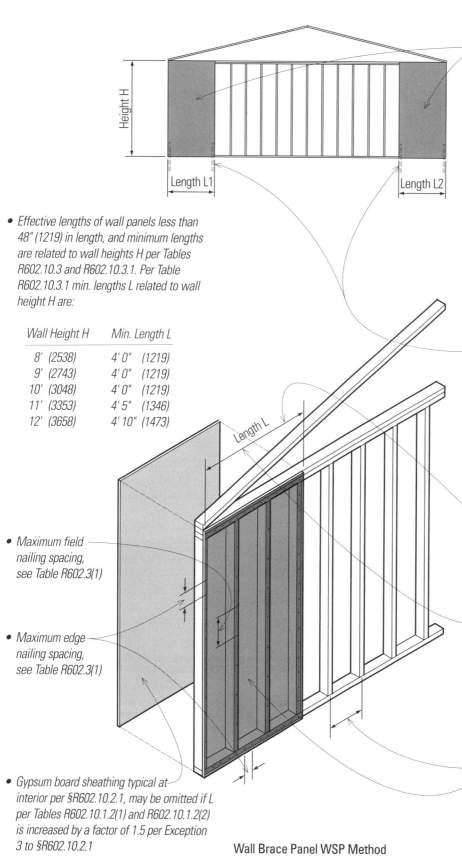

- Effective lengths of wall panels less than 48" (1219) in length, and minimum lengths are related to wall heights H per Tables R602.10.3 and R602.10.3.1. Per Table R602.10.3.1 min. lengths L related to wall height H are:

Wall Height H	Min. Length L
8' (2538)	4' 0" (1219)
9' (2743)	4' 0" (1219)
10' (3048)	4' 0" (1219)
11' (3353)	4' 5" (1346)
12' (3658)	4' 10" (1473)

- Maximum field nailing spacing, see Table R602.3(1)

- Maximum edge nailing spacing, see Table R602.3(1)

- Gypsum board sheathing typical at interior per §R602.10.2.1, may be omitted if L per Tables R602.10.1.2(1) and R602.10.1.2(2) is increased by a factor of 1.5 per Exception 3 to §R602.10.2.1

Wall Brace Panel WSP Method

- Intermittent Wall Bracing per Table R602.10.2
  - Bracing Method Name: WSP
  - Bracing Type: Wood Panel Sheathing
  - Restrictions: Per Table R602.10.1.2(1) Footnote f, the "L" adjustment factor of 1.4 applies if no gypsum board sheathing is used.
- Also see notes on illustrations.
- Commentary: See §R604 for further information on Wood Structural Panel. Per §R602.10.1.4.1 in Seismic Design Categories D_0, D_1, and D_2, braced wall lines at exterior walls shall have a braced wall panel located at each end of the braced wall line. However, per exception to this section, WSP braced wall panels are permitted to begin no more than 8' (2438) from each end of the braced wall line provided one of the construction criteria shown in Figure R602.10.1.4.1 are satisfied.
- Per Footnote i to Table R602.10.1.2(1) the required bracing length in one-story buildings and in the top story of two- or three-story buildings may be 0.80 L when hold-down device with a minimum uplift design value of 800 pounds (363 kg) is fastened to the end studs of each braced wall panel in the braced wall line and to the foundation or framing below.

- For Method WSP each braced wall panel shall be at least 48" (1219) in length, covering a minimum of three stud spaces where studs are spaced 16" (406) on center and covering a minimum of two stud spaces where studs are spaced 24" (610) on center.

- L of each panel 48" (1219) min. per §R602.10.3, but per Exception 4, in Seismic Design Categories A, B, and C, panels between 36" (914) and 48" (1219) in length may count toward the required length of bracing in Tables R602.10.1.2(1) and R602.10.1.2(2) and the effective contribution shall comply with Table R602.10.3.

- Maximum 24" (609) stud spacing
- Wall panel sheathing $^3/_8$" (9.5) minimum thickness for exterior sheathing connection criteria see Table R602.3(3); for interior sheathing connection criteria see Table R602.3(1)

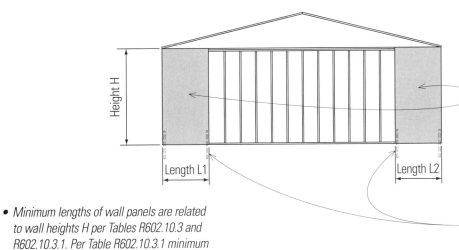

- Intermittent Wall Bracing per Table R602.10.2
  - **Bracing Method Name:** SFB
  - **Bracing Type:** Structural Fiberboard Sheathing
  - **Restrictions:** Per Table R602.10.1.2(1) Footnote f, the "L" adjustment factor of 1.4 applies if no gypsum board sheathing is used.
  - Also see notes on illustrations.

- Minimum lengths of wall panels are related to wall heights H per Tables R602.10.3 and R602.10.3.1. Per Table R602.10.3.1 minimum lengths for SFB panels related to wall height H are:

Wall Height H	Min. Length L
8' (2538)	4' 0" (1219)
9' (2743)	4' 0" (1219)
10' (3048)	4' 0" (1219)
11' (3353)	4' 5" (1346)
12' (3658)	4' 10" (1473)

- Per Footnote i to Table R602.10.1.2(1), the required bracing length in one-story buildings and in the top story of two- or three-story buildings may be 0.80 L when hold-down device with a minimum uplift design value of 800 pounds (363 kg) is fastened to the end studs of each braced wall panel in the braced wall line and to the foundation or framing below.

- For Method SFB each braced wall panel shall be at least 48" (1219) in length, covering a minimum of three stud spaces where studs are spaced 16" (406) on center

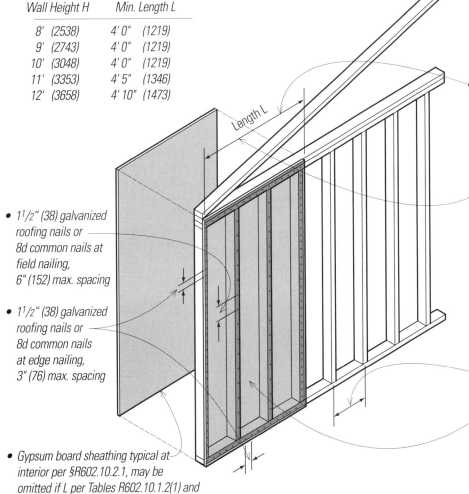

- 1$\frac{1}{2}$" (38) galvanized roofing nails or 8d common nails at field nailing, 6" (152) max. spacing

- 1$\frac{1}{2}$" (38) galvanized roofing nails or 8d common nails at edge nailing, 3" (76) max. spacing

- Gypsum board sheathing typical at interior per §R602.10.2.1, may be omitted if L per Tables R602.10.1.2(1) and R602.10.1.2(2) is increased by a factor of 1.5 per Exception 3 to §R602.10.2.1

- L of each panel 48" (1219) min. per §R602.10.3, but per Exception 4, in Seismic Design Categories A, B, and C; panels between 36" (914) and 48" (1219) in length may count toward the required length of bracing in Tables R602.10.1.2(1) and R602.10.1.2(2) and the effective contribution shall comply with Table R602.10.3.

- Maximum 16" (406) stud spacing

- Structural fiberboard sheathing thickness $\frac{1}{2}$" (12.7) or $\frac{25}{32}$" (19.8)

Wall Brace Panel SFB Method

- Lengths to be doubled when gypsum board is applied to only one side of braced wall panel

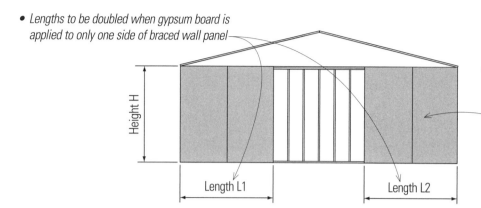

Height H

Length L1   Length L2

- Minimum lengths of wall panels are related to wall heights H per Tables R602.10.3 and R602.10.3.1. Per Table R602.10.3.1 minimum lengths for GB panels related to wall height H are:

Wall Height H	Double-Sheathed Min. Length L		Single-Sheathed Min. Length L	
8' (2538)	4' 0"	(1219)	8' 0"	(2538)
9' (2743)	4' 0"	(1219)	8' 0"	(2538)
10' (3048)	4' 0"	(1219)	8' 0"	(2538)
11' (3353)	4' 5"	(1346)	8' 10"	(2692)
12' (3658)	4' 10"	(1473)	9' 8"	(2946)

- Per §R602.10.3 panel length is 96" (2438) minimum for one sided panels and 48" (1219) min. for panels with gypsum board both sides.

- Intermittent Wall Bracing per Table R602.10.2
  - Bracing Method Name: GB
  - Bracing Type: Gypsum Board sheathing
  - Restrictions: Per Table R602.10.1.2(1) Footnote g, bracing lengths for Method GB are based on the application of gypsum board on both faces of a braced wall panel. When Method GB is provided on only one side of the wall, the required bracing amounts shall be doubled. When Method GB braced wall panels installed in accordance with §R602.10.2 are fastened at 4" (102) on center at panel edges, including top and bottom plates, and are blocked at all horizontal joints, multiplying the required bracing percentage for wind loading by 0.70 shall be permitted.
  - Also see notes on illustrations.
  - Commentary: As noted, the basic requirements for GB panels assume that they are sheathed on both sides with gypsum board. When sheathed on only one side the basic wall panel lengths are to be doubled. Note also that several of the other panel types assume gypsum board being installed on the interior face of exterior walls that are braced with other methods. These assumptions are based on conventional construction practices that assume interior finishes will be applied over gypsum board walls.

- Gypsum board sheathing, 1/2" (12.7) minimum thickness

- Typical screw or nail spacing at panel edges including at top and bottom plates. For nail or screw size at inside of exterior sheathing see Table R602.3(1). For nail or screw size at interior gypsum board sheathing see Table R702.3.5.

Wall Brace Panel GB Method

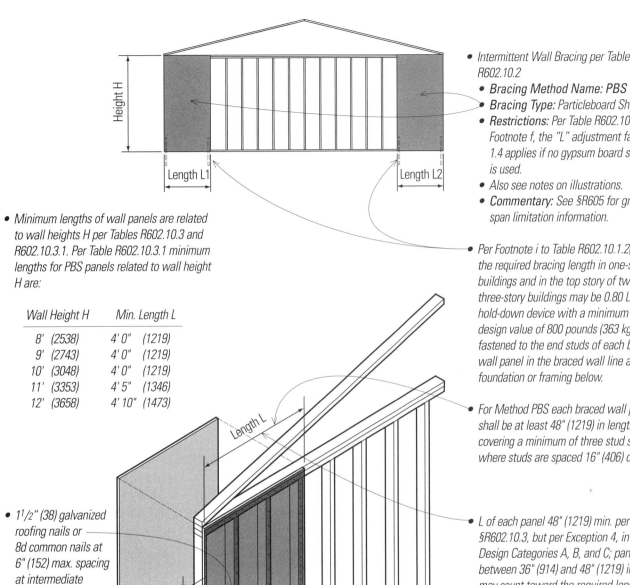

- *Intermittent Wall Bracing per Table R602.10.2*
  - **Bracing Method Name:** *PBS*
  - **Bracing Type:** *Particleboard Sheathing*
  - **Restrictions:** *Per Table R602.10.1.2(1) Footnote f, the "L" adjustment factor of 1.4 applies if no gypsum board sheathing is used.*
  - *Also see notes on illustrations.*
  - **Commentary:** *See §R605 for grading and span limitation information.*

- *Per Footnote i to Table R602.10.1.2(1), the required bracing length in one-story buildings and in the top story of two- or three-story buildings may be 0.80 L when hold-down device with a minimum uplift design value of 800 pounds (363 kg) is fastened to the end studs of each braced wall panel in the braced wall line and to the foundation or framing below.*

- *For Method PBS each braced wall panel shall be at least 48" (1219) in length, covering a minimum of three stud spaces where studs are spaced 16" (406) on center*

- *L of each panel 48" (1219) min. per §R602.10.3, but per Exception 4, in Seismic Design Categories A, B, and C; panels between 36" (914) and 48" (1219) in length may count toward the required length of bracing in Tables R602.10.1.2(1) and R602.10.1.2(2) and the effective contribution shall comply with Table R602.10.3.*

- *Maximum 16" (406) stud spacing*

- *Particleboard sheathing ³/₈" (9.5) or ¹/₂" (12.7) thickness , conforming with §R605 and Table R602.3(4)*

- *Minimum lengths of wall panels are related to wall heights H per Tables R602.10.3 and R602.10.3.1. Per Table R602.10.3.1 minimum lengths for PBS panels related to wall height H are:*

Wall Height H		Min. Length L	
8'	(2538)	4' 0"	(1219)
9'	(2743)	4' 0"	(1219)
10'	(3048)	4' 0"	(1219)
11'	(3353)	4' 5"	(1346)
12'	(3658)	4' 10"	(1473)

- *1¹/₂" (38) galvanized roofing nails or 8d common nails at 6" (152) max. spacing at intermediate supports*

- *1¹/₂" (38) galvanized roofing nails or 8d common nails at 3" (76) max. spacing at panel edges*

- *Gypsum board sheathing typical at interior, per §R602.10.2.1, may be omitted if L per Tables R602.10.1.2(1) and R602.10.1.2(2) is increased by a factor of 1.5 per Exception 3 to §R602.10.2.1*

Wall Brace Panel PBS Method

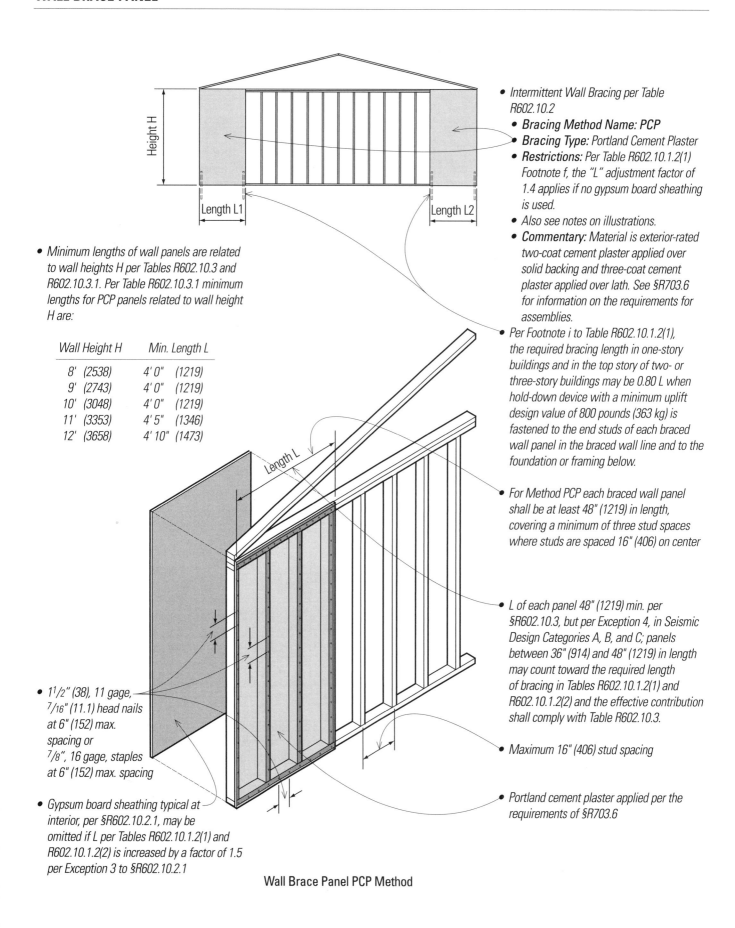

- Intermittent Wall Bracing per Table R602.10.2
  - **Bracing Method Name:** PCP
  - **Bracing Type:** *Portland Cement Plaster*
  - **Restrictions:** *Per Table R602.10.1.2(1) Footnote f, the "L" adjustment factor of 1.4 applies if no gypsum board sheathing is used.*
- *Also see notes on illustrations.*
- **Commentary:** *Material is exterior-rated two-coat cement plaster applied over solid backing and three-coat cement plaster applied over lath. See §R703.6 for information on the requirements for assemblies.*
- *Per Footnote i to Table R602.10.1.2(1), the required bracing length in one-story buildings and in the top story of two- or three-story buildings may be 0.80 L when hold-down device with a minimum uplift design value of 800 pounds (363 kg) is fastened to the end studs of each braced wall panel in the braced wall line and to the foundation or framing below.*
- *For Method PCP each braced wall panel shall be at least 48" (1219) in length, covering a minimum of three stud spaces where studs are spaced 16" (406) on center*
- *L of each panel 48" (1219) min. per §R602.10.3, but per Exception 4, in Seismic Design Categories A, B, and C; panels between 36" (914) and 48" (1219) in length may count toward the required length of bracing in Tables R602.10.1.2(1) and R602.10.1.2(2) and the effective contribution shall comply with Table R602.10.3.*
- *Maximum 16" (406) stud spacing*
- *Portland cement plaster applied per the requirements of §R703.6*

- *Minimum lengths of wall panels are related to wall heights H per Tables R602.10.3 and R602.10.3.1. Per Table R602.10.3.1 minimum lengths for PCP panels related to wall height H are:*

Wall Height H	Min. Length L
8' (2538)	4' 0" (1219)
9' (2743)	4' 0" (1219)
10' (3048)	4' 0" (1219)
11' (3353)	4' 5" (1346)
12' (3658)	4' 10" (1473)

- *1¹/₂" (38), 11 gage, ⁷/₁₆" (11.1) head nails at 6" (152) max. spacing or ⁷/₈", 16 gage, staples at 6" (152) max. spacing*

- *Gypsum board sheathing typical at interior, per §R602.10.2.1, may be omitted if L per Tables R602.10.1.2(1) and R602.10.1.2(2) is increased by a factor of 1.5 per Exception 3 to §R602.10.2.1*

Wall Brace Panel PCP Method

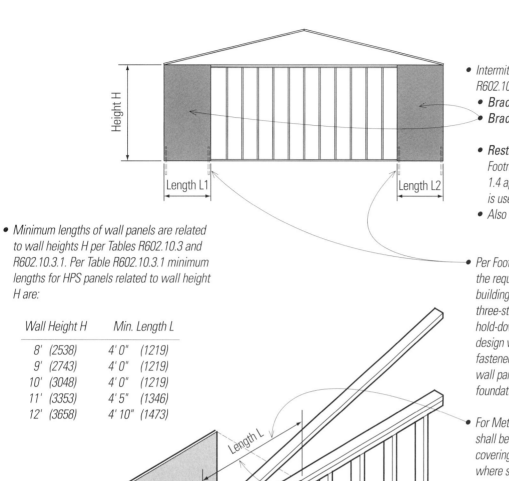

- Intermittent Wall Bracing per Table R602.10.2
  - **Bracing Method Name:** HPS
  - **Bracing Type:** Hardboard Panel Sheathing
  - **Restrictions:** Per Table R602.10.1.2(1) Footnote f, the "L" adjustment factor of 1.4 applies if no gypsum board sheathing is used.
  - Also see notes on illustrations.

- Per Footnote i to Table R602.10.1.2(1), the required bracing length in one-story buildings and in the top story of two- or three-story buildings may be 0.80 L when hold-down device with a minimum uplift design value of 800 pounds (363 kg) is fastened to the end studs of each braced wall panel in the braced wall line and to the foundation or framing below.

- For Method HPS each braced wall panel shall be at least 48" (1219) in length, covering a minimum of three stud spaces where studs are spaced 16" (406) on center

- Minimum lengths of wall panels are related to wall heights H per Tables R602.10.3 and R602.10.3.1. Per Table R602.10.3.1 minimum lengths for HPS panels related to wall height H are:

Wall Height H	Min. Length L
8' (2538)	4' 0" (1219)
9' (2743)	4' 0" (1219)
10' (3048)	4' 0" (1219)
11' (3353)	4' 5" (1346)
12' (3658)	4' 10" (1473)

- L of each panel 48" (1219) min. per §R602.10.3, but per Exception 4, in Seismic Design Categories A, B, and C; panels between 36" (914) and 48" (1219) in length may count toward the required length of bracing in Tables R602.10.1.2(1) and R602.10.1.2(2) and the effective contribution shall comply with Table R602.10.3.

- $^7/_{16}$" (11.1) hardboard panel

- Maximum 16" (406) stud spacing

- 0.092" (2.3) diameter, 0.225" (5.7) head nails with length to accommodate $1^1/_2$" (38) penetration into studs
  - 8" (204) max. spacing at intermediate supports
  - 4" (102) max. spacing at panel edges

- Gypsum board sheathing typical at interior, per §R602.10.2.1, may be omitted if L per Tables R602.10.1.2(1) and R602.10.1.2(2) is increased by a factor of 1.5 per Exception 3 to §R602.10.2.1

Wall Brace Panel HPS Method

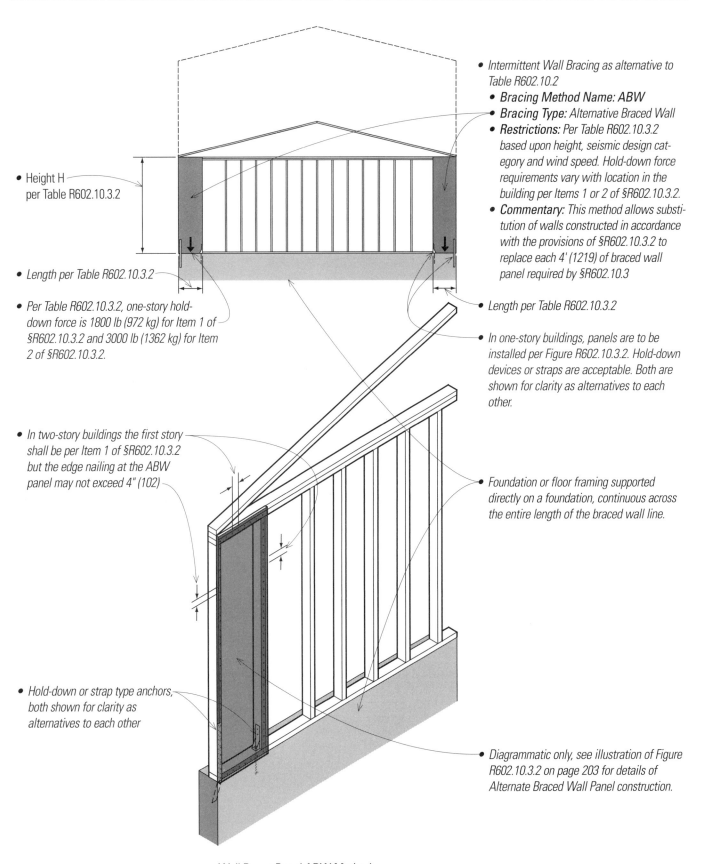

- Height H
  per Table R602.10.3.2

- Length per Table R602.10.3.2

- Per Table R602.10.3.2, one-story hold-down force is 1800 lb (972 kg) for Item 1 of §R602.10.3.2 and 3000 lb (1362 kg) for Item 2 of §R602.10.3.2.

- In two-story buildings the first story shall be per Item 1 of §R602.10.3.2 but the edge nailing at the ABW panel may not exceed 4" (102)

- Hold-down or strap type anchors, both shown for clarity as alternatives to each other

- Intermittent Wall Bracing as alternative to Table R602.10.2
  - **Bracing Method Name:** ABW
  - **Bracing Type:** Alternative Braced Wall
  - **Restrictions:** Per Table R602.10.3.2 based upon height, seismic design category and wind speed. Hold-down force requirements vary with location in the building per Items 1 or 2 of §R602.10.3.2.
  - **Commentary:** This method allows substitution of walls constructed in accordance with the provisions of §R602.10.3.2 to replace each 4' (1219) of braced wall panel required by §R602.10.3

- Length per Table R602.10.3.2

- In one-story buildings, panels are to be installed per Figure R602.10.3.2. Hold-down devices or straps are acceptable. Both are shown for clarity as alternatives to each other.

- Foundation or floor framing supported directly on a foundation, continuous across the entire length of the braced wall line.

- Diagrammatic only, see illustration of Figure R602.10.3.2 on page 203 for details of Alternate Braced Wall Panel construction.

Wall Brace Panel ABW Method

Panel Length per Table R602.10.3.2

Seismic Design Category; Wind Speed < 110 mph (48.4 m/s)

Braced Wall Height H	A, B, C	D0, D1, D2
	Minimum Sheathed Length L	
8' (2440)	2'-4" (711)	2'-8" (813)
9' (2745)	2'-8" (813)	2'-8" (813)
10' (3050)	2'-10" (864)	2'-10" (864)
11' (3355)	3'-2" (966)	NP
12' (3660)	3'-6" (1067)	NP

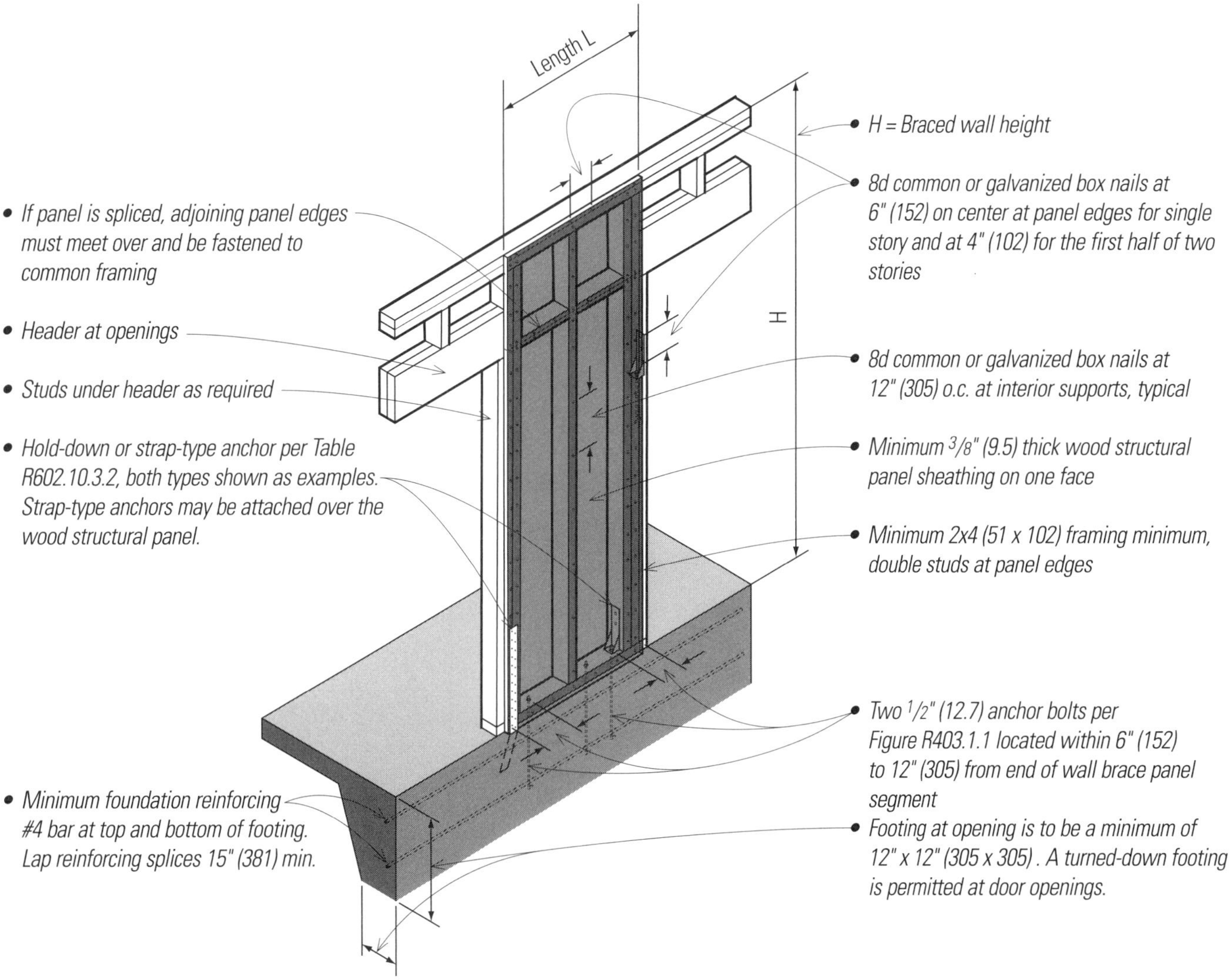

- If panel is spliced, adjoining panel edges must meet over and be fastened to common framing

- Header at openings

- Studs under header as required

- Hold-down or strap-type anchor per Table R602.10.3.2, both types shown as examples. Strap-type anchors may be attached over the wood structural panel.

- Minimum foundation reinforcing #4 bar at top and bottom of footing. Lap reinforcing splices 15" (381) min.

- H = Braced wall height

- 8d common or galvanized box nails at 6" (152) on center at panel edges for single story and at 4" (102) for the first half of two stories

- 8d common or galvanized box nails at 12" (305) o.c. at interior supports, typical

- Minimum $3/8$" (9.5) thick wood structural panel sheathing on one face

- Minimum 2x4 (51 x 102) framing minimum, double studs at panel edges

- Two $1/2$" (12.7) anchor bolts per Figure R403.1.1 located within 6" (152) to 12" (305) from end of wall brace panel segment

- Footing at opening is to be a minimum of 12" x 12" (305 x 305) . A turned-down footing is permitted at door openings.

Figure R602.10.3.2 Alternate Wall Brace Panel

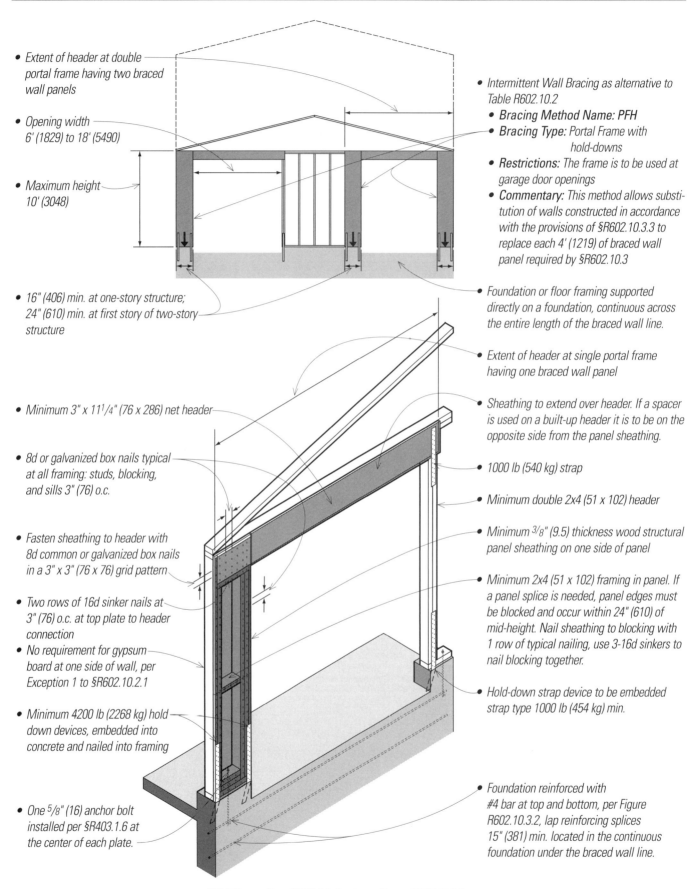

- Extent of header at double portal frame having two braced wall panels

- Opening width 6' (1829) to 18' (5490)

- Maximum height 10' (3048)

- 16" (406) min. at one-story structure; 24" (610) min. at first story of two-story structure

- Minimum 3" x 11 1/4" (76 x 286) net header

- 8d or galvanized box nails typical at all framing: studs, blocking, and sills 3" (76) o.c.

- Fasten sheathing to header with 8d common or galvanized box nails in a 3" x 3" (76 x 76) grid pattern

- Two rows of 16d sinker nails at 3" (76) o.c. at top plate to header connection

- No requirement for gypsum board at one side of wall, per Exception 1 to §R602.10.2.1

- Minimum 4200 lb (2268 kg) hold down devices, embedded into concrete and nailed into framing

- One 5/8" (16) anchor bolt installed per §R403.1.6 at the center of each plate.

- Intermittent Wall Bracing as alternative to Table R602.10.2
  - Bracing Method Name: PFH
  - Bracing Type: Portal Frame with hold-downs
  - Restrictions: The frame is to be used at garage door openings
  - Commentary: This method allows substitution of walls constructed in accordance with the provisions of §R602.10.3.3 to replace each 4' (1219) of braced wall panel required by §R602.10.3

- Foundation or floor framing supported directly on a foundation, continuous across the entire length of the braced wall line.

- Extent of header at single portal frame having one braced wall panel

- Sheathing to extend over header. If a spacer is used on a built-up header it is to be on the opposite side from the panel sheathing.

- 1000 lb (540 kg) strap

- Minimum double 2x4 (51 x 102) header

- Minimum 3/8" (9.5) thickness wood structural panel sheathing on one side of panel

- Minimum 2x4 (51 x 102) framing in panel. If a panel splice is needed, panel edges must be blocked and occur within 24" (610) of mid-height. Nail sheathing to blocking with 1 row of typical nailing, use 3-16d sinkers to nail blocking together.

- Hold-down strap device to be embedded strap type 1000 lb (454 kg) min.

- Foundation reinforced with #4 bar at top and bottom, per Figure R602.10.3.2, lap reinforcing splices 15" (381) min. located in the continuous foundation under the braced wall line.

Wall Brace Panel PFH Method per Figure R602.10.3.3

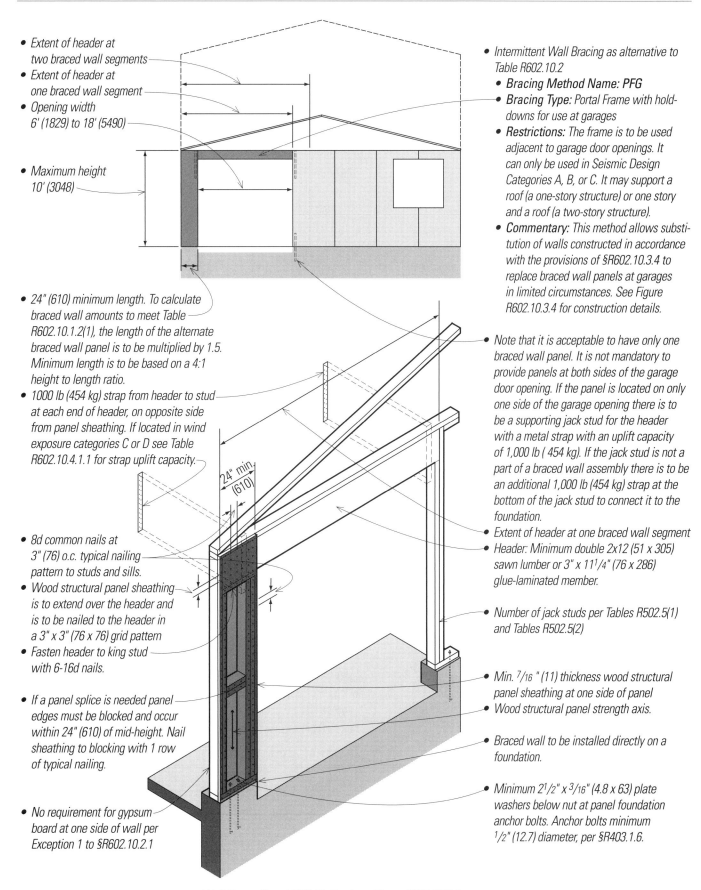

- Extent of header at two braced wall segments
- Extent of header at one braced wall segment
- Opening width 6' (1829) to 18' (5490)

- Maximum height 10' (3048)

- 24" (610) minimum length. To calculate braced wall amounts to meet Table R602.10.1.2(1), the length of the alternate braced wall panel is to be multiplied by 1.5. Minimum length is to be based on a 4:1 height to length ratio.
- 1000 lb (454 kg) strap from header to stud at each end of header, on opposite side from panel sheathing. If located in wind exposure categories C or D see Table R602.10.4.1.1 for strap uplift capacity.

- 8d common nails at 3" (76) o.c. typical nailing pattern to studs and sills.
- Wood structural panel sheathing is to extend over the header and is to be nailed to the header in a 3" x 3" (76 x 76) grid pattern
- Fasten header to king stud with 6-16d nails.

- If a panel splice is needed panel edges must be blocked and occur within 24" (610) of mid-height. Nail sheathing to blocking with 1 row of typical nailing.

- No requirement for gypsum board at one side of wall per Exception 1 to §R602.10.2.1

- Intermittent Wall Bracing as alternative to Table R602.10.2
  - Bracing Method Name: PFG
  - Bracing Type: Portal Frame with hold-downs for use at garages
  - Restrictions: The frame is to be used adjacent to garage door openings. It can only be used in Seismic Design Categories A, B, or C. It may support a roof (a one-story structure) or one story and a roof (a two-story structure).
  - Commentary: This method allows substi-tution of walls constructed in accordance with the provisions of §R602.10.3.4 to replace braced wall panels at garages in limited circumstances. See Figure R602.10.3.4 for construction details.

- Note that it is acceptable to have only one braced wall panel. It is not mandatory to provide panels at both sides of the garage door opening. If the panel is located on only one side of the garage opening there is to be a supporting jack stud for the header with a metal strap with an uplift capacity of 1,000 lb (454 kg). If the jack stud is not a part of a braced wall assembly there is to be an additional 1,000 lb (454 kg) strap at the bottom of the jack stud to connect it to the foundation.
- Extent of header at one braced wall segment
- Header: Minimum double 2x12 (51 x 305) sawn lumber or 3" x 11 1/4" (76 x 286) glue-laminated member.

- Number of jack studs per Tables R502.5(1) and Tables R502.5(2)

- Min. 7/16 " (11) thickness wood structural panel sheathing at one side of panel
- Wood structural panel strength axis.

- Braced wall to be installed directly on a foundation.

- Minimum 2 1/2" x 3/16" (4.8 x 63) plate washers below nut at panel foundation anchor bolts. Anchor bolts minimum 1/2" (12.7) diameter, per §R403.1.6.

24" min (610)

Wall Brace Panel PFG Method per Figure R602.10.3.4

Continuous Sheathing

Wall bracing may be accomplished using continuous sheathing where the walls are all sheathed in the same materials. Per §R602.10.1.1 bracing methods may be mixed between braced wall panels and continuous sheathing under certain circumstances. In Seismic Design Categories A, B and C and where wind speeds are less than 100 mph (44 m/s) the code allows mixing of bracing methods on a single story and between stories. Bracing lengths are to be determined from Table R602.10.2(1) for wind design and Table R602.10.1.2(2) for seismic design. Where bracing is mixed, the higher of the requirements for each type of bracing will govern. Note that mixing of bracing systems is never allowed within the same braced wall line.

Structural panels in continuous sheathing methods are to be provided on all sheathable surfaces on one side of a braced wall line including areas below window and doors openings and at gable ends. Where continuous sheathing alone is used the lengths are determined per Table R602.10.4.2. The required lengths are based on the types of continuous sheathing as described in Table R602.10.4.1 as illustrated on the following pages. The same principals of braced wall lines apply to continuous sheathing as for braced wall lines. The forces to be resisted and the disposition of braced wall lines determine the length of panels required. Note that there are details of how continuous sheathing is to turn exterior corners to provide continuity at the ends of panels and at changes in wall direction. There are three basic types of continuous sheathing as described in Table R602.10.4.1 and a fourth, using structural fiberboard sheathing that is described in §R602.10.5 that we will not discuss here.

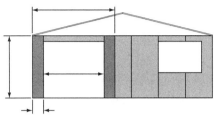

CS-PF Method Detail 1, p. 207

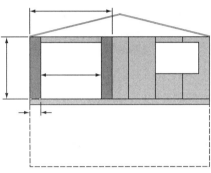

CS-PF Method Detail 2, p. 208

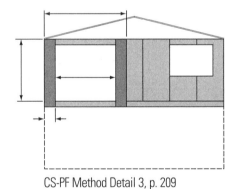

CS-PF Method Detail 3, p. 209

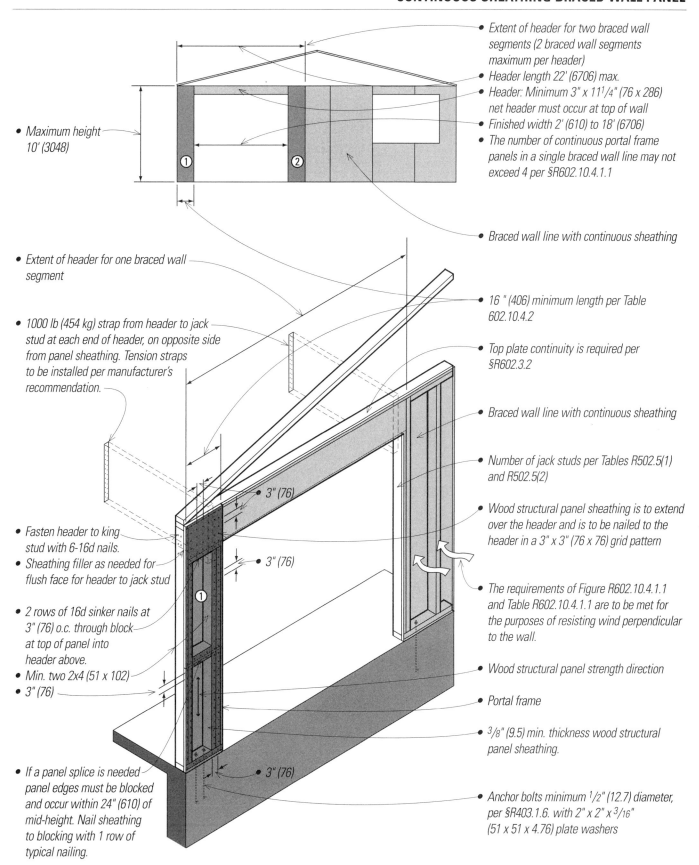

- Extent of header for two braced wall segments (2 braced wall segments maximum per header)
- Header length 22' (6706) max.
- Header: Minimum 3" x 11¼" (76 x 286) net header must occur at top of wall
- Finished width 2' (610) to 18' (6706)
- The number of continuous portal frame panels in a single braced wall line may not exceed 4 per §R602.10.4.1.1

- Braced wall line with continuous sheathing

- 16 " (406) minimum length per Table 602.10.4.2

- Top plate continuity is required per §R602.3.2

- Braced wall line with continuous sheathing

- Number of jack studs per Tables R502.5(1) and R502.5(2)

- Wood structural panel sheathing is to extend over the header and is to be nailed to the header in a 3" x 3" (76 x 76) grid pattern

- The requirements of Figure R602.10.4.1.1 and Table R602.10.4.1.1 are to be met for the purposes of resisting wind perpendicular to the wall.

- Wood structural panel strength direction

- Portal frame

- ³/₈" (9.5) min. thickness wood structural panel sheathing.

- Anchor bolts minimum ¹/₂" (12.7) diameter, per §R403.1.6. with 2" x 2" x ³/₁₆" (51 x 51 x 4.76) plate washers

- Maximum height 10' (3048)

- Extent of header for one braced wall segment

- 1000 lb (454 kg) strap from header to jack stud at each end of header, on opposite side from panel sheathing. Tension straps to be installed per manufacturer's recommendation.

- Fasten header to king stud with 6-16d nails.
- Sheathing filler as needed for flush face for header to jack stud

- 2 rows of 16d sinker nails at 3" (76) o.c. through block at top of panel into header above.
- Min. two 2x4 (51 x 102)
- 3" (76)

- If a panel splice is needed panel edges must be blocked and occur within 24" (610) of mid-height. Nail sheathing to blocking with 1 row of typical nailing.

- 3" (76)
- 3" (76)
- 3" (76)

Continuous Portal Frame Braced Wall Panel CS-PF Method
Detail 1 per Figure R602.10.4.1.1 Condition on Ground Floor at Foundation

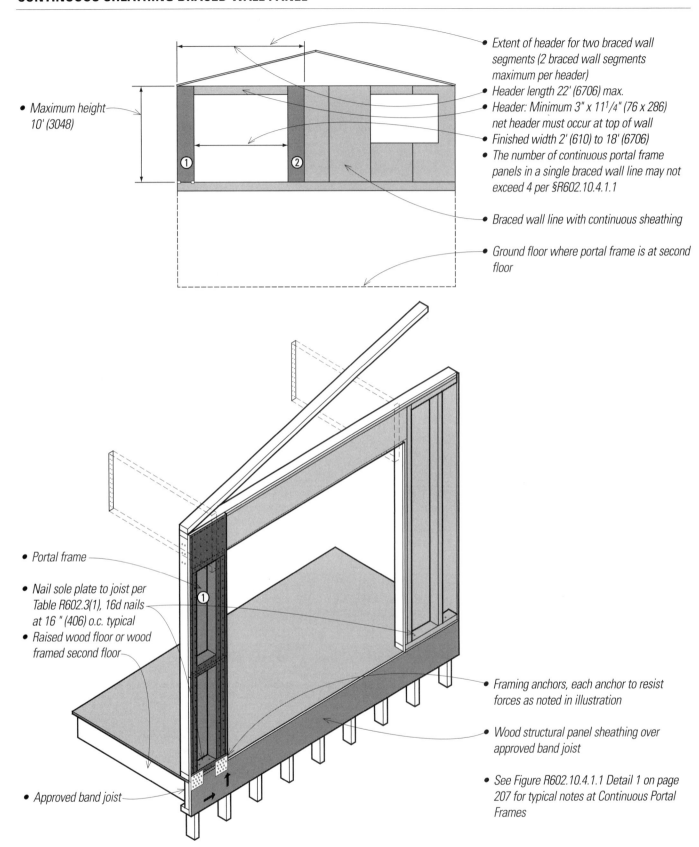

- Maximum height 10' (3048)

- Extent of header for two braced wall segments (2 braced wall segments maximum per header)
- Header length 22' (6706) max.
- Header: Minimum 3" x 11¹/₄" (76 x 286) net header must occur at top of wall
- Finished width 2' (610) to 18' (6706)
- The number of continuous portal frame panels in a single braced wall line may not exceed 4 per §R602.10.4.1.1
- Braced wall line with continuous sheathing
- Ground floor where portal frame is at second floor

- Portal frame
- Nail sole plate to joist per Table R602.3(1), 16d nails at 16 " (406) o.c. typical
- Raised wood floor or wood framed second floor
- Approved band joist

- Framing anchors, each anchor to resist forces as noted in illustration
- Wood structural panel sheathing over approved band joist
- See Figure R602.10.4.1.1 Detail 1 on page 207 for typical notes at Continuous Portal Frames

Continuous Portal Frame Braced Wall Panel CS-PF Method Detail 2 per Figure R602.10.4.1.1 Framing Anchor Option over Raised Wood Floor or at Second Floor

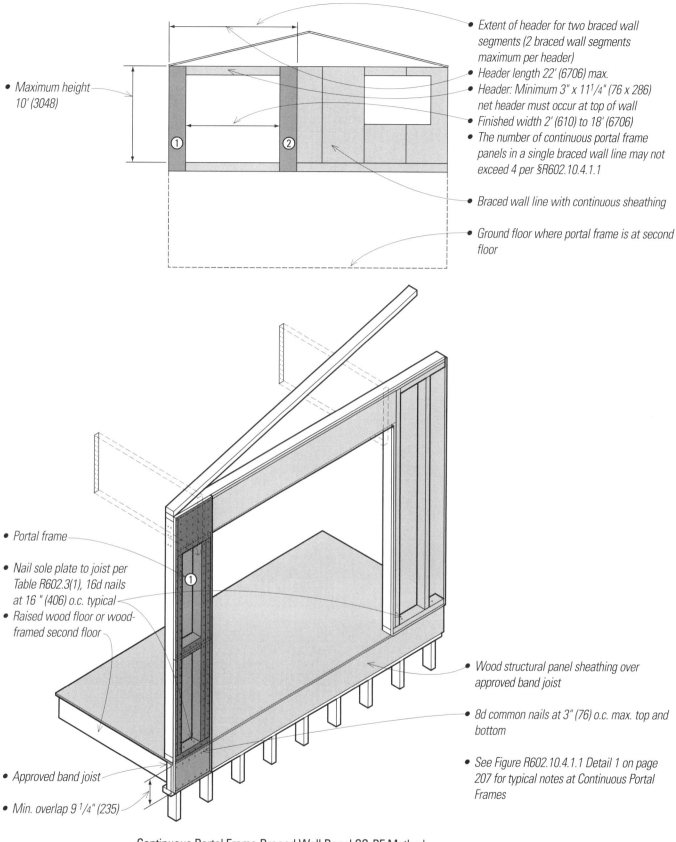

- Maximum height 10' (3048)

- Extent of header for two braced wall segments (2 braced wall segments maximum per header)
- Header length 22' (6706) max.
- Header: Minimum 3" x 11¼" (76 x 286) net header must occur at top of wall
- Finished width 2' (610) to 18' (6706)
- The number of continuous portal frame panels in a single braced wall line may not exceed 4 per §R602.10.4.1.1

- Braced wall line with continuous sheathing

- Ground floor where portal frame is at second floor

- Portal frame

- Nail sole plate to joist per Table R602.3(1), 16d nails at 16 " (406) o.c. typical

- Raised wood floor or wood-framed second floor

- Approved band joist

- Min. overlap 9 ¼" (235)

- Wood structural panel sheathing over approved band joist

- 8d common nails at 3" (76) o.c. max. top and bottom

- See Figure R602.10.4.1.1 Detail 1 on page 207 for typical notes at Continuous Portal Frames

Continuous Portal Frame Braced Wall Panel CS-PF Method
Detail 3 per Figure R602.10.4.1.1 Wood structural Panel Overlap
Option over Raised Wood Floor or at Second Floor

CONTINUOUS SHEATHING FRAMING

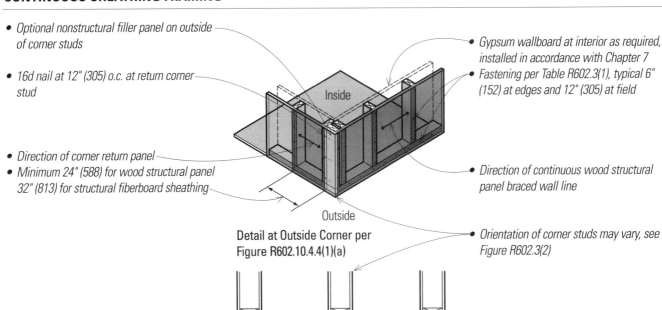

- *Optional nonstructural filler panel on outside of corner studs*
- *16d nail at 12" (305) o.c. at return corner stud*
- *Direction of corner return panel*
- *Minimum 24" (588) for wood structural panel 32" (813) for structural fiberboard sheathing*

- *Gypsum wallboard at interior as required, installed in accordance with Chapter 7*
- *Fastening per Table R602.3(1), typical 6" (152) at edges and 12" (305) at field*
- *Direction of continuous wood structural panel braced wall line*
- *Orientation of corner studs may vary, see Figure R602.3(2)*

Inside

Outside

Detail at Outside Corner per
Figure R602.10.4.4(1)(a)

Corner and Partition Posts Figure R602.3(2)

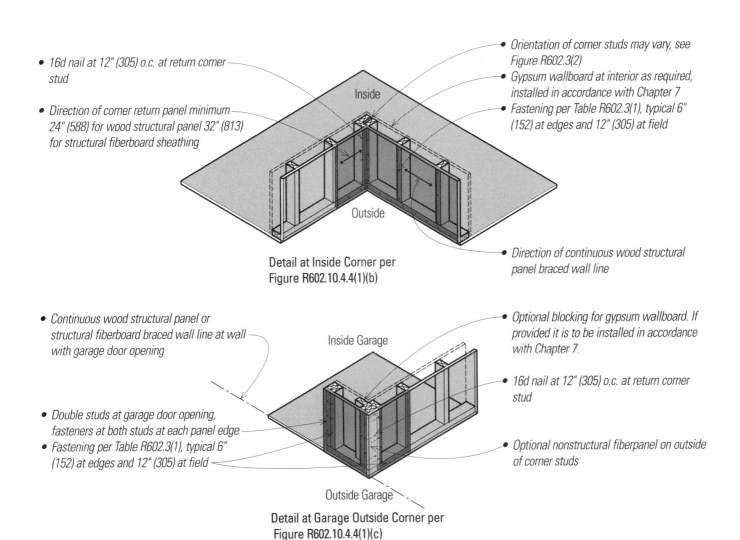

- *16d nail at 12" (305) o.c. at return corner stud*
- *Direction of corner return panel minimum 24" (588) for wood structural panel 32" (813) for structural fiberboard sheathing*

- *Orientation of corner studs may vary, see Figure R602.3(2)*
- *Gypsum wallboard at interior as required, installed in accordance with Chapter 7*
- *Fastening per Table R602.3(1), typical 6" (152) at edges and 12" (305) at field*

Inside

Outside

Detail at Inside Corner per
Figure R602.10.4.4(1)(b)

- *Direction of continuous wood structural panel braced wall line*

- *Continuous wood structural panel or structural fiberboard braced wall line at wall with garage door opening*
- *Double studs at garage door opening, fasteners at both studs at each panel edge*
- *Fastening per Table R602.3(1), typical 6" (152) at edges and 12" (305) at field*

Inside Garage

- *Optional blocking for gypsum wallboard. If provided it is to be installed in accordance with Chapter 7.*
- *16d nail at 12" (305) o.c. at return corner stud*
- *Optional nonstructural fiberpanel on outside of corner studs*

Outside Garage

Detail at Garage Outside Corner per
Figure R602.10.4.4(1)(c)

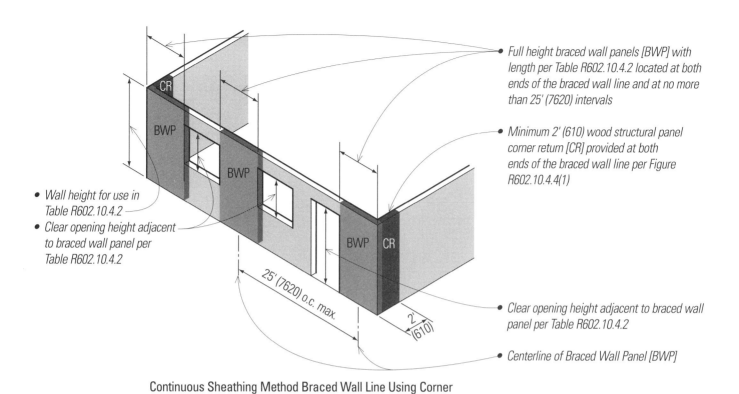

Full height braced wall panels [BWP] with length per Table R602.10.4.2 located at both ends of the braced wall line and at no more than 25' (7620) intervals

Minimum 2' (610) wood structural panel corner return [CR] provided at both ends of the braced wall line per Figure R602.10.4.4(1)

Wall height for use in Table R602.10.4.2

Clear opening height adjacent to braced wall panel per Table R602.10.4.2

Clear opening height adjacent to braced wall panel per Table R602.10.4.2

Centerline of Braced Wall Panel [BWP]

25' (7620) o.c. max.

2' (610)

Continuous Sheathing Method Braced Wall Line Using Corner Return Panels per Figure R602.10.4.4(2)

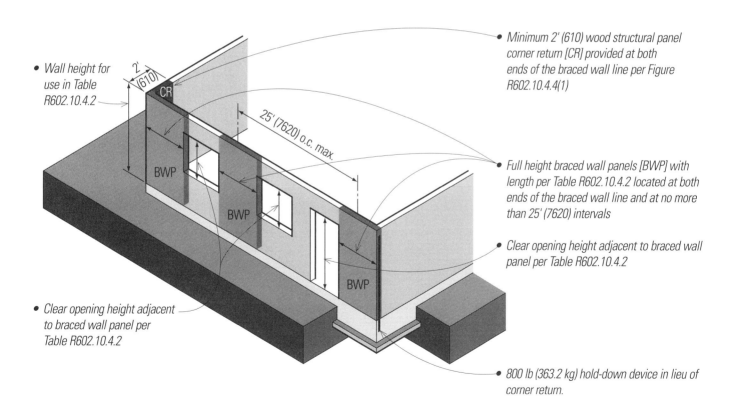

Minimum 2' (610) wood structural panel corner return [CR] provided at both ends of the braced wall line per Figure R602.10.4.4(1)

Wall height for use in Table R602.10.4.2

2' (610)

25' (7620) o.c. max.

Full height braced wall panels [BWP] with length per Table R602.10.4.2 located at both ends of the braced wall line and at no more than 25' (7620) intervals

Clear opening height adjacent to braced wall panel per Table R602.10.4.2

Clear opening height adjacent to braced wall panel per Table R602.10.4.2

800 lb (363.2 kg) hold-down device in lieu of corner return.

Continuous Sheathing Method Braced Wall Line Using Hold-down in lieu of Corner Return Panel per Figure R602.10.4.4(3)

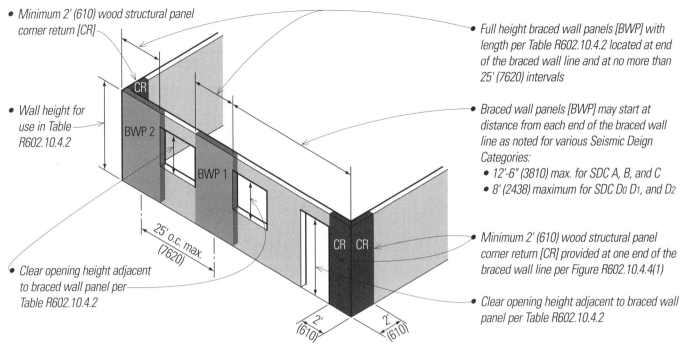

- Minimum 2' (610) wood structural panel corner return [CR]

- Wall height for use in Table R602.10.4.2

- Clear opening height adjacent to braced wall panel per Table R602.10.4.2

CR

BWP 2

BWP 1

25' o.c. max. (7620)

CR CR

2' (610)   2' (610)

- Full height braced wall panels [BWP] with length per Table R602.10.4.2 located at end of the braced wall line and at no more than 25' (7620) intervals

- Braced wall panels [BWP] may start at distance from each end of the braced wall line as noted for various Seismic Deign Categories:
  - 12'-6" (3810) max. for SDC A, B, and C
  - 8' (2438) maximum for SDC D0 D1, and D2

- Minimum 2' (610) wood structural panel corner return [CR] provided at one end of the braced wall line per Figure R602.10.4.4(1)

- Clear opening height adjacent to braced wall panel per Table R602.10.4.2

Continuous Sheathing Method Braced Wall Line with First Braced Wall Panel Located away from End of Braced Wall Line, without Tie-down per Figure R602.10.4.4(4)

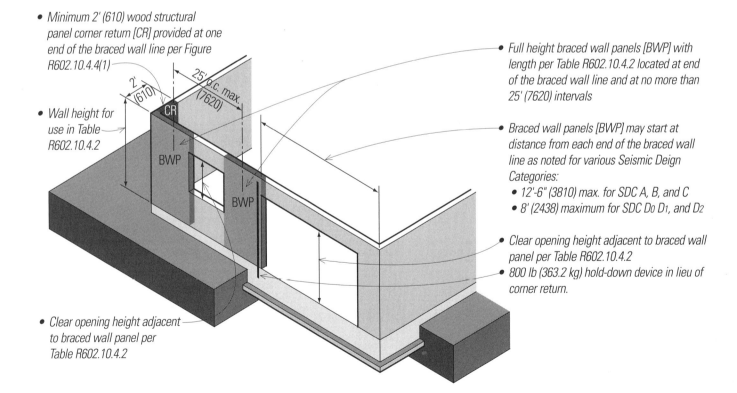

- Minimum 2' (610) wood structural panel corner return [CR] provided at one end of the braced wall line per Figure R602.10.4.4(1)

- Wall height for use in Table R602.10.4.2

2' (610)   25' o.c. max. (7620)

CR

BWP

BWP

- Clear opening height adjacent to braced wall panel per Table R602.10.4.2

- Full height braced wall panels [BWP] with length per Table R602.10.4.2 located at end of the braced wall line and at no more than 25' (7620) intervals

- Braced wall panels [BWP] may start at distance from each end of the braced wall line as noted for various Seismic Deign Categories:
  - 12'-6" (3810) max. for SDC A, B, and C
  - 8' (2438) maximum for SDC D0 D1, and D2

- Clear opening height adjacent to braced wall panel per Table R602.10.4.2
- 800 lb (363.2 kg) hold-down device in lieu of corner return.

Continuous Sheathing Method Braced Wall Line with First Braced Wall Panel Located away from End of Braced Wall Line, with Tie-down per Figure R602.10.4.4(5)

Top and Bottom Connections of Braced Wall Panels

Braced wall panels are to be fastened to framing at their base and top per the requirements of §R602.10.6 to form a complete load path to allow the braced wall panels to do their job in resisting in-plane shear loads. These sections discuss framing connections at the bottom of braced wall panels and foundations for these panels. See the illustrations for a detailed explanation of these requirements.

Connections of exterior braced wall panels to roof framing is to be per the illustrations for Figures R602.10.6(1) and R602.10.6(2). Braced wall panels are to be supported per the requirements of §R602.10.7 as illustrated. Panel joints are to be per §R602.10.8. Cripple walls are relatively short framed walls extending from the top of the footing up to underside of the floor framing for the first story level. Unbraced cripple walls, often found in older residences, are often damaged in seismic events when the house moves laterally and the cripple walls fail. Therefore there are much higher cripple wall bracing requirements in high seismic design categories D_0, D_1 or D_2. Cripple wall bracing is to be per §R602.10.9 as illustrated. Sill conditions at braced wall lines are to be per §R602.11 which requires the panels to be anchored to concrete or masonry foundations. Where steps occur in footings in Seismic Design Categories D_0, D_1 or D_2 at townhouses in Seismic Design Category C, footing steps are to be constructed per the illustration in Figure R602.11.2.

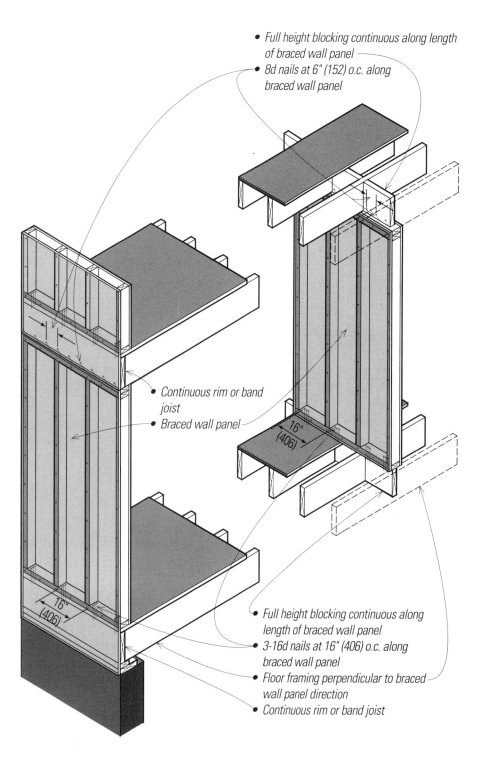

- Full height blocking continuous along length of braced wall panel
- 8d nails at 6" (152) o.c. along braced wall panel

- Continuous rim or band joist
- Braced wall panel

16" (406)

16" (406)

- Full height blocking continuous along length of braced wall panel
- 3-16d nails at 16" (406) o.c. along braced wall panel
- Floor framing perpendicular to braced wall panel direction
- Continuous rim or band joist

Braced Wall Panel Connection when Perpendicular to Floor/Ceiling Framing per Figure R602.10.6(1)

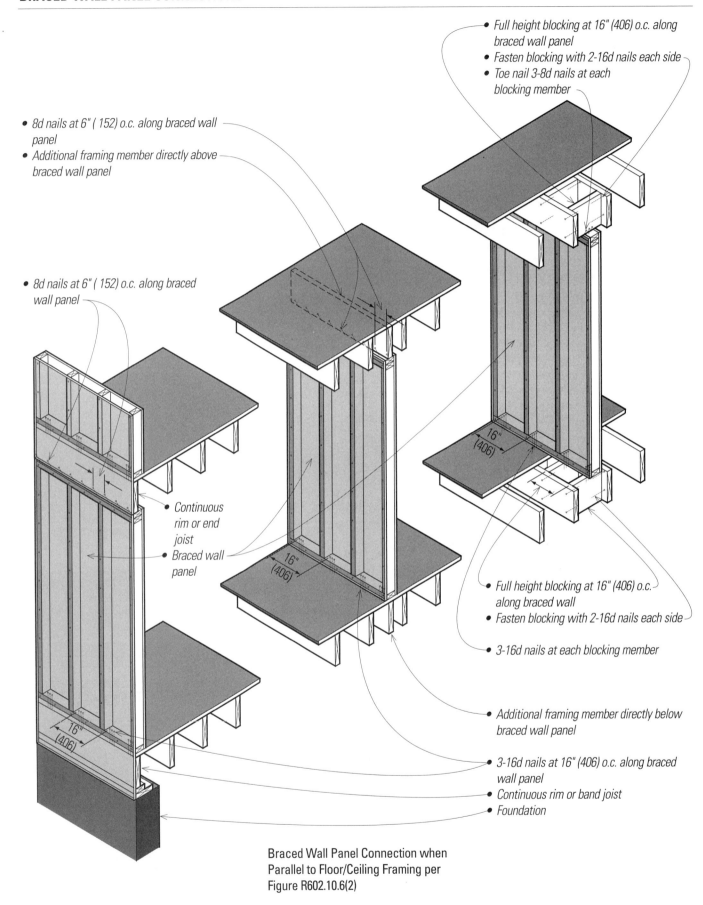

- Full height blocking at 16" (406) o.c. along braced wall panel
- Fasten blocking with 2-16d nails each side
- Toe nail 3-8d nails at each blocking member

- 8d nails at 6" (152) o.c. along braced wall panel
- Additional framing member directly above braced wall panel

- 8d nails at 6" (152) o.c. along braced wall panel

- Continuous rim or end joist
- Braced wall panel

16" (406)

16" (406)

16" (406)

- Full height blocking at 16" (406) o.c. along braced wall
- Fasten blocking with 2-16d nails each side

- 3-16d nails at each blocking member

- Additional framing member directly below braced wall panel

- 3-16d nails at 16" (406) o.c. along braced wall panel
- Continuous rim or band joist
- Foundation

Braced Wall Panel Connection when
Parallel to Floor/Ceiling Framing per
Figure R602.10.6(2)

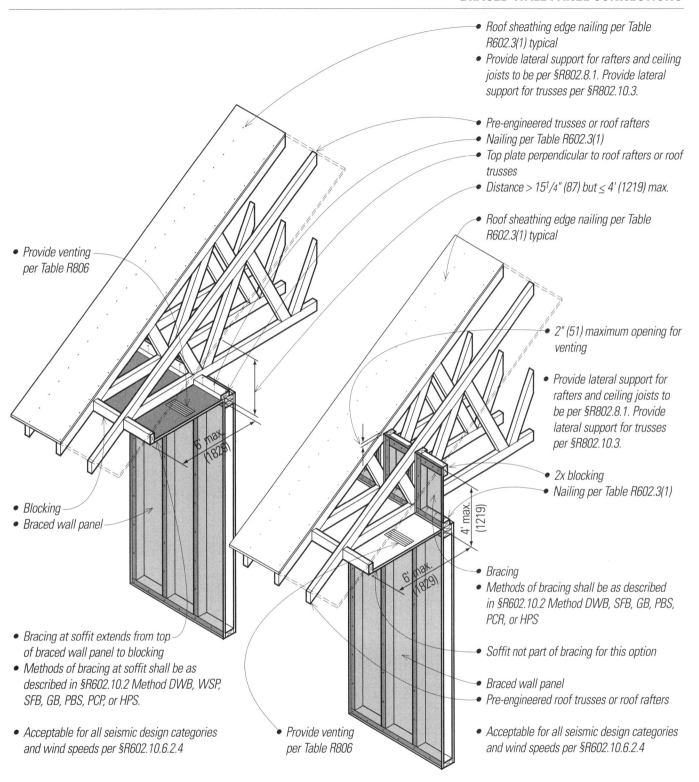

- Roof sheathing edge nailing per Table R602.3(1) typical
- Provide lateral support for rafters and ceiling joists to be per §R802.8.1. Provide lateral support for trusses per §R802.10.3.

- Pre-engineered trusses or roof rafters
- Nailing per Table R602.3(1)
- Top plate perpendicular to roof rafters or roof trusses
- Distance > 15 1/4" (87) but ≤ 4' (1219) max.

- Roof sheathing edge nailing per Table R602.3(1) typical

- Provide venting per Table R806

- 2" (51) maximum opening for venting

- Provide lateral support for rafters and ceiling joists to be per §R802.8.1. Provide lateral support for trusses per §R802.10.3.

- 2x blocking
- Nailing per Table R602.3(1)

- Blocking
- Braced wall panel

6' max. (1829)

4' max. (1219)

6' max. (1829)

- Bracing
- Methods of bracing shall be as described in §R602.10.2 Method DWB, SFB, GB, PBS, PCR, or HPS

- Soffit not part of bracing for this option

- Bracing at soffit extends from top of braced wall panel to blocking
- Methods of bracing at soffit shall be as described in §R602.10.2 Method DWB, WSP, SFB, GB, PBS, PCP, or HPS.

- Braced wall panel
- Pre-engineered roof trusses or roof rafters

- Acceptable for all seismic design categories and wind speeds per §R602.10.6.2.4

- Provide venting per Table R806

- Acceptable for all seismic design categories and wind speeds per §R602.10.6.2.4

Figure R602.10.6.2(2) Braced Wall Panel Connection Option per §R602.10.6.2.4.1 when Perpendicular to Rafters or Roof Trusses

Figure R602.10.6.2(3) Braced Wall Panel Connection Option per §R602.10.6.2.4.2 when Perpendicular to Rafters or Roof Trusses

Wall Bracing at Masonry and Stone Veneer

Per §R602.12 when masonry and stone veneer is to be used on either interior or exterior walls it is to be installed per the requirements of §R703.7. Veneer requires different wall bracing lengths and connections due to the increased weight of the walls resulting from the added materials. See the illustrations taken from the detailed requirements contained in §R602.12.

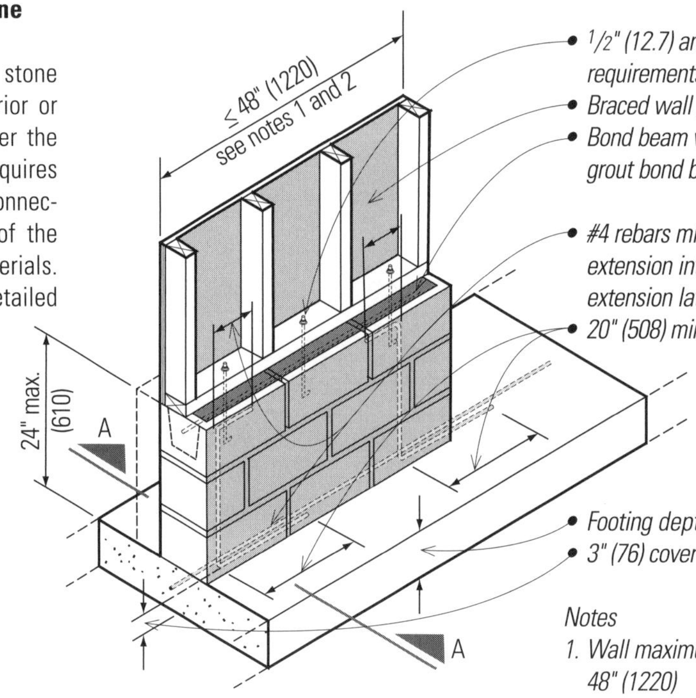

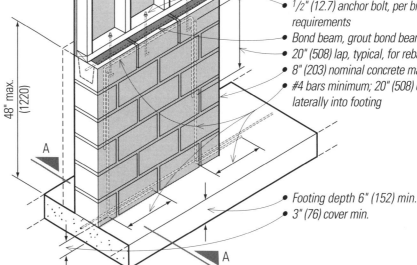

≤ 48" (1220) see notes 1 and 2

24" max. (610)

A

A

- *1/2" (12.7) anchor bolt, per braced wall panel requirements*
- *Braced wall panel, see note 3*
- *Bond beam with one #4 reinforcing bar, grout bond beam*
- *#4 rebars minimum; field blend 6" (152) extension into bond beam and 20" (508) extension laterally into footing*
- *20" (508) min. typical*
- *Footing depth 6" (152) min.*
- *3" (76) cover min.*

Figure R602.10.7-1 Short Stem Wall Reinforcement [see note 5]

Notes
1. *Wall maximum length for these details is 48" (1220)*
2. *Wall supporting braced wall panels > 48" (1220) in length are to be per §R403.1.*
3. *These details may not be used for braced wall panel types ABW (R602.10.3.2) or PFH (R602.10.3.3).*
4. *See Figure R602.10.7.4 on p. 217 for Section A-A.*
5. *Grout bond beams and all cells that contain rebar, threaded rods, and anchor bolts.*

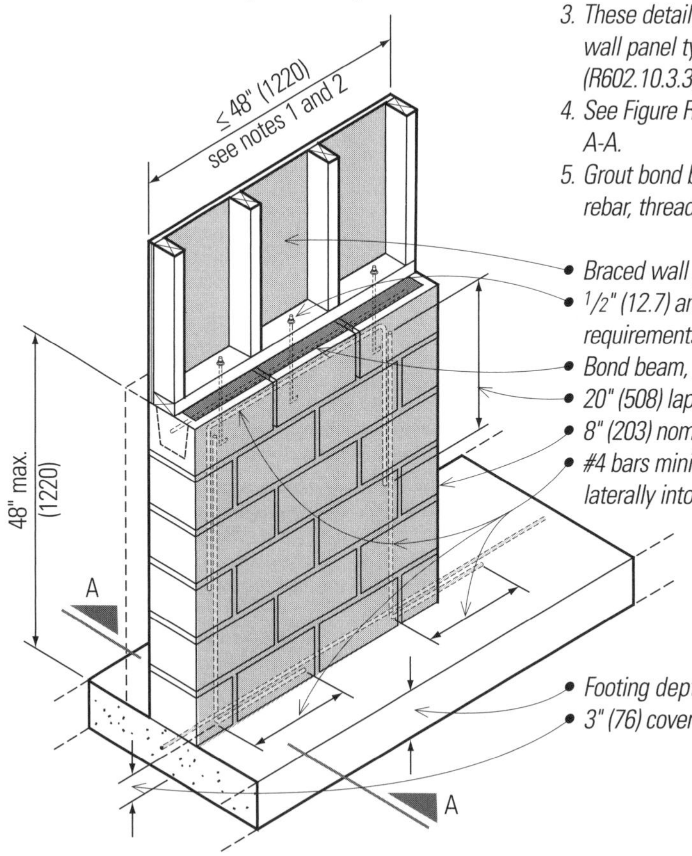

≤ 48" (1220) see notes 1 and 2

48" max. (1220)

A

A

- *Braced wall panel, see note 3*
- *1/2" (12.7) anchor bolt, per braced wall panel requirements*
- *Bond beam, grout bond beam*
- *20" (508) lap, typical, for rebar*
- *8" (203) nominal concrete masonry unit*
- *#4 bars minimum; 20" (508) extension laterally into footing*
- *Footing depth 6" (152) min.*
- *3" (76) cover min.*

Figure R602.10.7-2 Tall Stem Wall Reinforcement [see note 5]

Figure R602.10.7 Masonry Stem Walls Supporting Braced Wall Panels

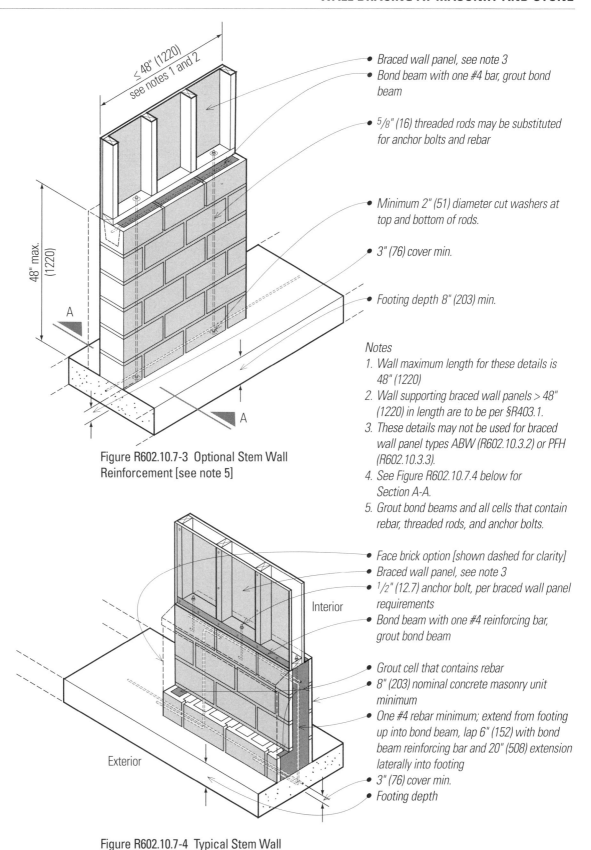

≤ 48" (1220)
see notes 1 and 2

48" max.
(1220)

A

A

- Braced wall panel, see note 3
- Bond beam with one #4 bar, grout bond beam

- ⁵/₈" (16) threaded rods may be substituted for anchor bolts and rebar

- Minimum 2" (51) diameter cut washers at top and bottom of rods.

- 3" (76) cover min.

- Footing depth 8" (203) min.

Notes
1. Wall maximum length for these details is 48" (1220)
2. Wall supporting braced wall panels > 48" (1220) in length are to be per §R403.1.
3. These details may not be used for braced wall panel types ABW (R602.10.3.2) or PFH (R602.10.3.3).
4. See Figure R602.10.7.4 below for Section A-A.
5. Grout bond beams and all cells that contain rebar, threaded rods, and anchor bolts.

Figure R602.10.7-3 Optional Stem Wall Reinforcement [see note 5]

Interior

Exterior

- Face brick option [shown dashed for clarity]
- Braced wall panel, see note 3
- ¹/₂" (12.7) anchor bolt, per braced wall panel requirements
- Bond beam with one #4 reinforcing bar, grout bond beam

- Grout cell that contains rebar
- 8" (203) nominal concrete masonry unit minimum
- One #4 rebar minimum; extend from footing up into bond beam, lap 6" (152) with bond beam reinforcing bar and 20" (508) extension laterally into footing
- 3" (76) cover min.
- Footing depth

Figure R602.10.7-4 Typical Stem Wall Section A-A

Figure R602.10.7 Masonry Stem Walls Supporting Braced Wall Panels

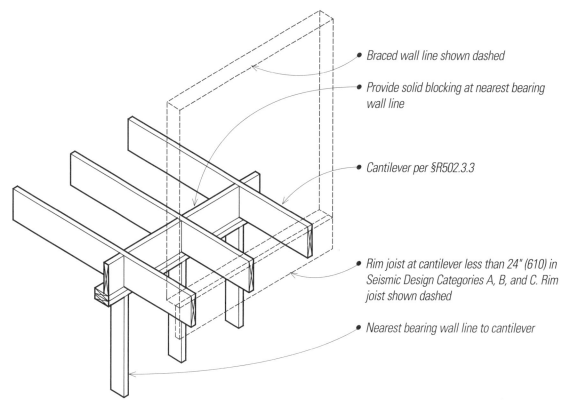

- Braced wall line shown dashed

- Provide solid blocking at nearest bearing wall line

- Cantilever per §R502.3.3

- Rim joist at cantilever less than 24" (610) in Seismic Design Categories A, B, and C. Rim joist shown dashed

- Nearest bearing wall line to cantilever

Figure R602.10.7 Braced Wall Panel Support

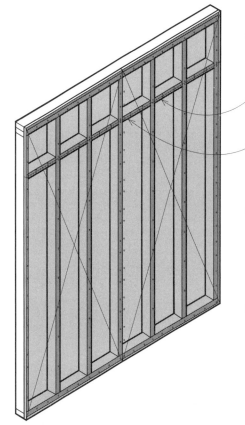

- Sheathing panels shown transparent for clarity.

- All horizontal joints are to be blocked at braced wall panels with certain exceptions

- Blocking to be common for both panels and minimum of 1¹/₂" (38) thickness

- Where the braced length is at least twice the minimum length required by Tables R602.10.1.2(1) or R602.10.1.2(2) blocking is not required in braced wall panels using methods WSP, SFB, GB, PBS, or HPS.

- When method GB panels are applied horizontally, 4' x 8' (1219 x 2438) blocking of horizontal joints is not required.

Figure R602.10.8 Blocking at Panel Joints

Notes

1. *Cripple wall bracing length is to be 1.15 times the aggregate length of WBL1 + WBL2.*
   Thus CWB1 + CWB2 is to equal 1.15 times (WBL1 + WBL2)
2. *See §R602.10.9.1 for additional requirements in Seismic Design Categories D0, D1, and D2.*
3. *Per §R602.10.9.2 cripple walls may be designated as the first story and braced accordingly, but the first floor level is then to be considered as the second "story."*

- *Wall bracing length WBL2*
- *Wall bracing length WBL1*

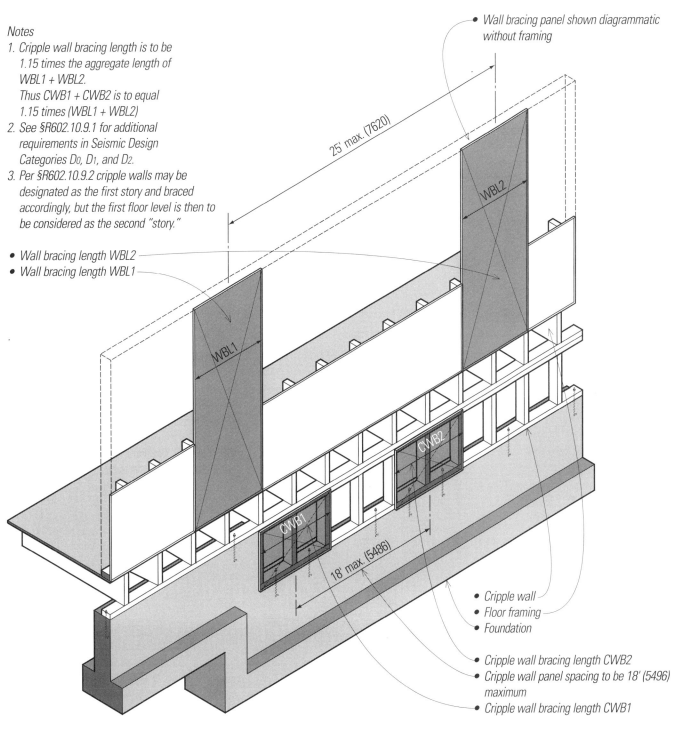

- *Wall bracing panel shown diagrammatic without framing*

25' max. (7620)

WBL2

WBL1

CWB2

CWB1

18' max. (5486)

- *Cripple wall*
- *Floor framing*
- *Foundation*

- *Cripple wall bracing length CWB2*
- *Cripple wall panel spacing to be 18' (5496) maximum*
- *Cripple wall bracing length CWB1*

- *Wall bracing to be per Tables R602.10.1.2(1) or R602.10.1.2(2) with maximum spacing of 25' (7620)*

Figure R602.10.9 Cripple Wall Bracing

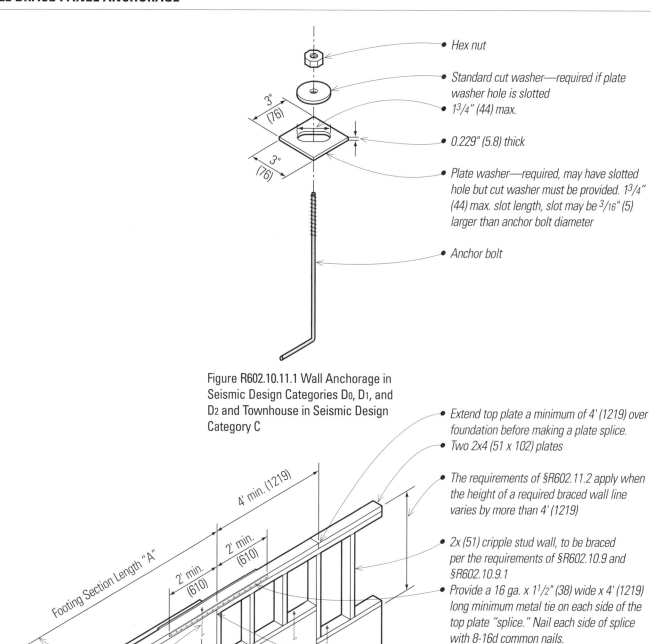

Hex nut

Standard cut washer—required if plate washer hole is slotted

$1^3/4$" (44) max.

0.229" (5.8) thick

3" (76)

3" (76)

Plate washer—required, may have slotted hole but cut washer must be provided. $1^3/4$" (44) max. slot length, slot may be $3/16$" (5) larger than anchor bolt diameter

Anchor bolt

Figure R602.10.11.1 Wall Anchorage in Seismic Design Categories D0, D1, and D2 and Townhouse in Seismic Design Category C

Extend top plate a minimum of 4' (1219) over foundation before making a plate splice.

Two 2x4 (51 x 102) plates

The requirements of §R602.11.2 apply when the height of a required braced wall line varies by more than 4' (1219)

2x (51) cripple stud wall, to be braced per the requirements of §R602.10.9 and §R602.10.9.1

Provide a 16 ga. x $1^1/2$" (38) wide x 4' (1219) long minimum metal tie on each side of the top plate "splice." Nail each side of splice with 8-16d common nails.

Concrete stepped footing

Where lower plate ends is the bottom plate "splice" location per Figure R602.11.2

Anchor bolts at 1' (305) and 3' (914) max. from footing step

Where floor framing rests directly on the sill, if Footing Section Length "A" is more than 8' (2440) then the wall line is considered braced. If Footing Section Length "A" is less than 8' (2440) in a 25' (7625) wall then bracing is required at the cripple stud wall sections.

2x (51) sill plate

4' min. (1219)

2' min. (610)

2' min. (610)

2' min. (610)

Footing Section Length "A"

3' max. (914)

1' (305) max.

Figure R602.10.11.2 Stepped Foundation Construction at Seismic Design Categories D0, D1, and D2

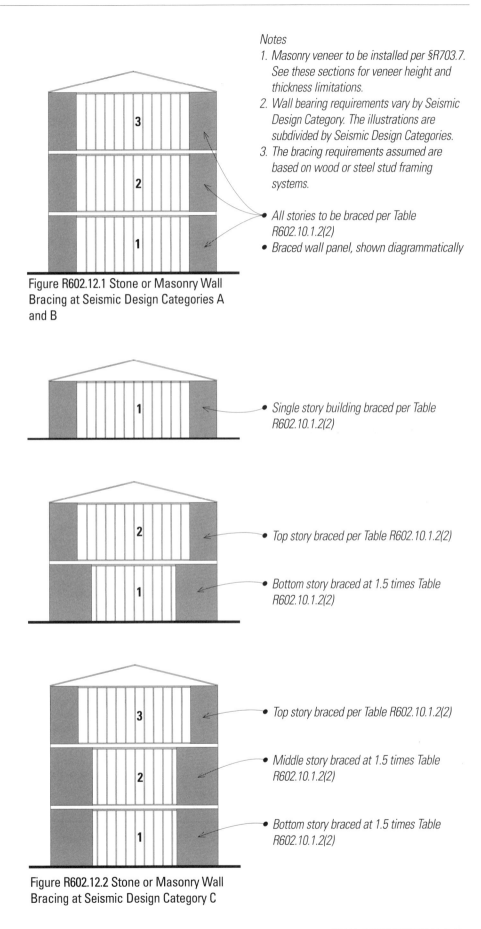

Notes
1. *Masonry veneer to be installed per §R703.7. See these sections for veneer height and thickness limitations.*
2. *Wall bearing requirements vary by Seismic Design Category. The illustrations are subdivided by Seismic Design Categories.*
3. *The bracing requirements assumed are based on wood or steel stud framing systems.*

- *All stories to be braced per Table R602.10.1.2(2)*
- *Braced wall panel, shown diagrammatically*

Figure R602.12.1 Stone or Masonry Wall Bracing at Seismic Design Categories A and B

- *Single story building braced per Table R602.10.1.2(2)*

- *Top story braced per Table R602.10.1.2(2)*

- *Bottom story braced at 1.5 times Table R602.10.1.2(2)*

- *Top story braced per Table R602.10.1.2(2)*

- *Middle story braced at 1.5 times Table R602.10.1.2(2)*

- *Bottom story braced at 1.5 times Table R602.10.1.2(2)*

Figure R602.12.2 Stone or Masonry Wall Bracing at Seismic Design Category C

Key

A. Story values in one-story building

B. Story values in two-story building

C. Story values in three-story building

% = minimum sheathing amount as a percentage of braced wall line length "L", applies to both interior and exterior braced wall lines.

- Panel start 8' (2440) max. from end of braced wall line. Panel spacing 25' (7620) o.c. max.
- Edge nail sheathing to braced wall panel end post with hold-down, typical, see note 2

- Single-story hold-down force—top-story
  - A: NA
  - B: NA
  - C: 0
- Cumulative hold-down force—middle-story
  - A: NA
  - B: 0
  - C: 5400 lb (2452 kg)
- Cumulative hold-down force—bottom-story
  - A: 0
  - B: 5100 lb (2315 kg)
  - C: 8900 lb (4041 kg)

- Braced wall panel, see notes 1, 2, 5, and 6.

Notes

1. Panel sheathing min. $7/16"$ (11) thickness with 8d common nails at 4" (102) o.c. at panel edges and 12" (305) o.c. at intermediate supports.

2. Nailing at braced wall panel end posts with hold-down attached is to be 8d common nails at 4" (102) o.c.

3. Hold-down devices to be per Table R602.12(2).

4. Stud size and spacing to be per Table R602.3(5)

5. Each braced wall panel to be 48" (1219) min. length and cover at least 3 stud spaces when studs are at 16" (406) o.c. and 2 stud spaces when studs are 24" (509) o.c.

6. Alternate braced wall panels per §R602.10.3.2 and continuously sheathed wall bracing per §R602.10.4 are not to be used in place of these wall bracing provisions.

- Option (a) Braced wall panels stacked and align from story to story, use cumulative hold down force from Table R602.12(2)
  - Edges of braced wall panels align and hold-downs align, see note 5

- Option (b) Braced wall panels not stacked, use single-story hold-down force from Table R602.12(2)
  - Edges of braced wall panels do not align. Use option (a) where they align

- Panel start 8' (2440) max. from end of braced wall line. Panel spacing 25' (7620) o.c. max.
- Single-story hold-down force—top-story
  - A: NA
  - B: NA
  - C: 1900 lb (863 kg)

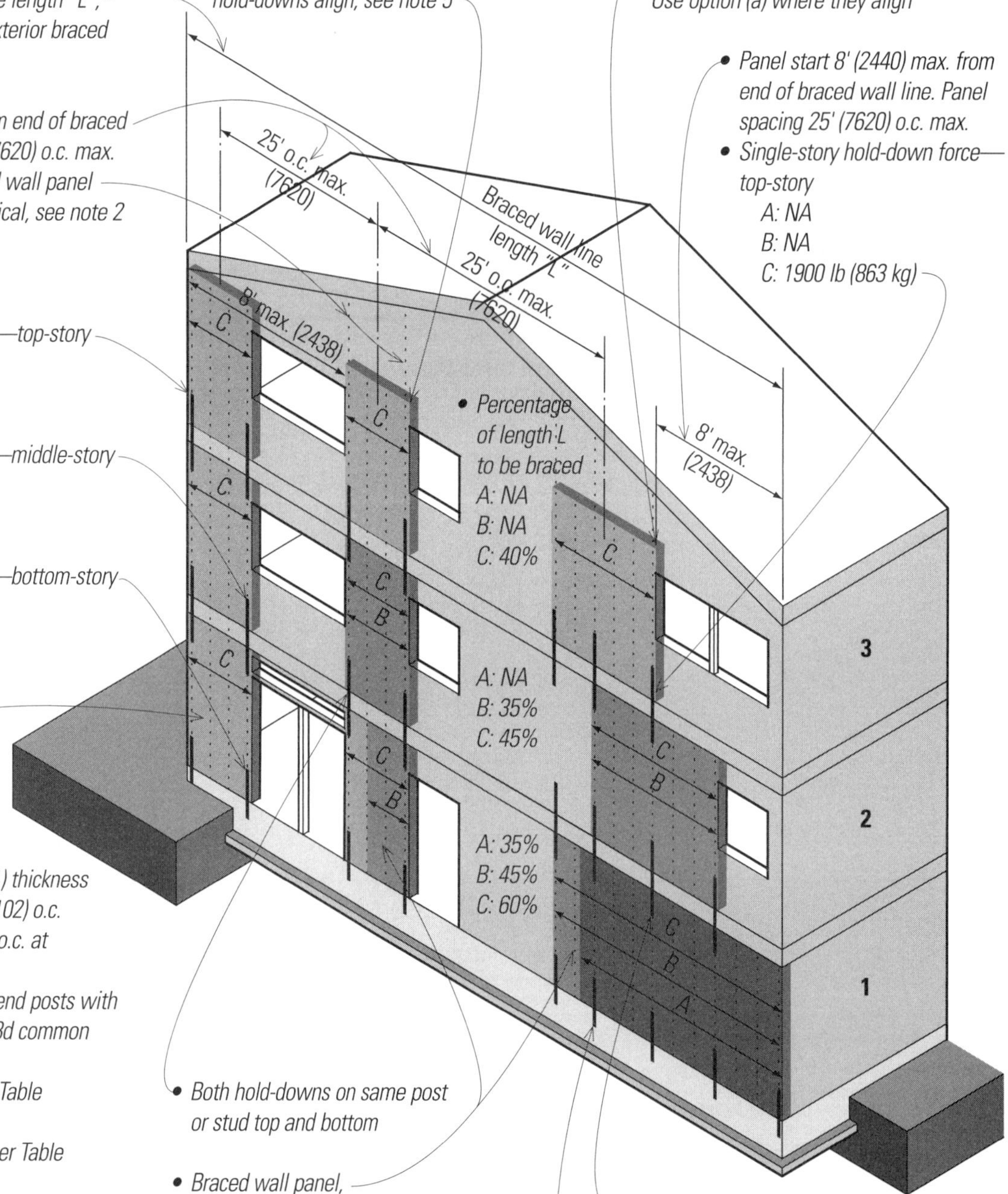

25' o.c. max. (7620)

Braced wall line length "L"

25' o.c. max. (7620)

8' max. (2438)

8' max. (2438)

- Percentage of length L to be braced
  - A: NA
  - B: NA
  - C: 40%

A: NA
B: 35%
C: 45%

A: 35%
B: 45%
C: 60%

3

2

1

- Both hold-downs on same post or stud top and bottom

- Braced wall panel, see notes 1, 2, 5, and 6.

- Hold-down forces per Table R602.12(2) Footnotes c and d

- Single-story hold-down force—middle-story
  - A: NA
  - B: 1900 lb (863 kg)
  - C: 3500 lb (1589 kg)
- Single-story hold-down force—bottom-story
  - A: 0
  - B: 3200 lb (1453 kg)
  - C: 3500 lb (1589 kg)

Figure R602.12 Hold-Downs at Exterior and Interior Braced Wall Panels for Stone or Masonry Wall Bracing at Seismic Design Category D_0

Key

A. Story values in one-story building

B. Story values in two-story building

C. Story values in three-story building

% = minimum sheathing amount as a percentage of braced wall line length "L", applies to both interior and exterior braced wall lines.

- Panel start 8' (2440) max. from end of braced wall line. Panel spacing 25' (7620) o.c. max.
- Edge nail sheathing to braced wall panel end post with hold-down, typical, see note 2

- Single-story hold-down force—top-story
  A: NA
  B: NA
  C: 0
- Cumulative hold-down force—middle-story
  A: NA
  B: 0
  C: 5400 lb (2452 kg)
- Cumulative hold-down force—bottom-story
  A: 0
  B: 5800 lb (2633 kg)
  C: 9500 lb (4313 kg)

- Braced wall panel, see notes 1, 2, 5, and 6.

Notes

1. Panel sheathing min. $^7/_{16}$" (11) thickness with 8d common nails at 4" (102) o.c. at panel edges and 12" (305) o.c. at intermediate supports.
2. Nailing at braced wall panel end posts with hold-down attached is to be 8d common nails at 4" (102) o.c.
3. Hold-down devices to be per Table R602.12(2).
4. Stud size and spacing to be per Table R602.3(5)
5. Each braced wall panel to be 48" (1219) min. length and cover at least 3 stud spaces when studs are at 16" (406) o.c. and 2 stud spaces when studs are 24" (509) o.c.
6. Alternate braced wall panels per §R602.10.3.2 and continuously sheathed wall bracing per §R602.10.4 are not to be used in place of these wall bracing provisions.

- **Option (a)** Braced wall panels stacked and align from story to story, use cumulative hold-down force from Table R602.12(2)
  - Edges of braced wall panels align and hold downs align, see note 5

- **Option (b)** Braced wall panels not stacked, use single-story hold-down force from Table R602.12(2)
  - Edges of braced wall panels do not align. Use option (a) where they align

- Panel start 8' (2440) max. from end of braced wall line. Panel spacing 25' (7620) o.c. max.
- Single-story hold-down force—top-story
  A: NA
  B: NA
  C: 2100 lb (953 kg)

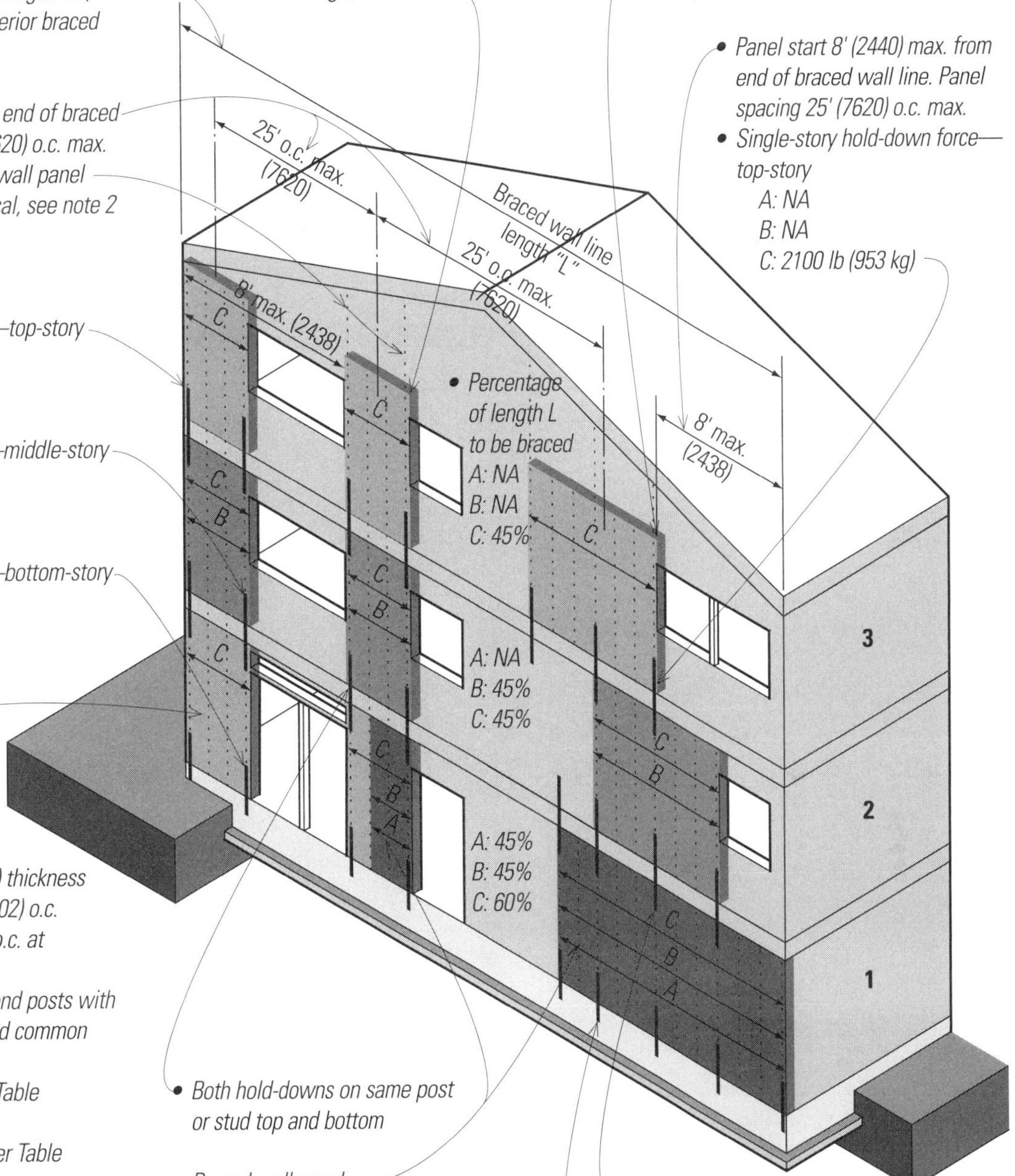

25' o.c. max. (7620)

Braced wall line length "L"

25' o.c. max. (7620)

8' max. (2438)

8' max. (2438)

- Percentage of length L to be braced
  A: NA
  B: NA
  C: 45%

A: NA
B: 45%
C: 45%

A: 45%
B: 45%
C: 60%

3

2

1

- Both hold-downs on same post or stud top and bottom

- Braced wall panel, see notes 1, 2, 5, and 6.

- Hold-down forces per Table R602.12(2) Footnotes c and d

- Single-story hold-down force—middle-story
  A: NA
  B: 2100 lb (953 kg)
  C: 3700 lb (1680 kg)
- Single-story hold-down force—bottom-story
  A: 2100 lb (953 kg)
  B: 3700 lb (1680 kg)
  C: 3700 lb (1680 kg)

Figure R602.12 Hold-Downs at Exterior and Interior Braced Wall Panels for Stone or Masonry Wall Bracing at Seismic Design Category D1

BRACED WALL PANEL HOLD DOWNS

Key
A. Story values in one-story building
B. Story values in two-story building
% = minimum sheathing amount as a
    percentage of braced wall line length "L",
    applies to both interior and exterior braced
    wall lines.

- *Option (a)* Braced wall panels stacked and align from story to story, use cumulative hold-down force from Table R602.12(2)
  - Edges of braced wall panels align and hold downs align, see note 5

- *Option (b)* Braced wall panels not stacked, use single-story hold-down force from Table R602.12(2)
  - Edges of braced wall panels do not align. Use option (a) where they align

  - Panel start 8' (2440) max. from end of braced wall line. Panel spacing 25' (7620) o.c. max.
  - Single-story hold-down force— top-story
    A: NA
    B: 2300 lb (1044 kg)

- Panel start 8' (2440) max. from end of braced wall line. Panel spacing 25' (7620) o.c. max.
- Edge nail sheathing to braced wall panel end post with hold-down, typical, see note 2

- Braced wall panel, see notes 1, 2, 5, and 6.

- Single-story hold-down force—top-story
  A: NA
  B: 0

- Cumulative hold-down force—bottom-story
  A: 0
  B: 6200 lb (2815 kg)

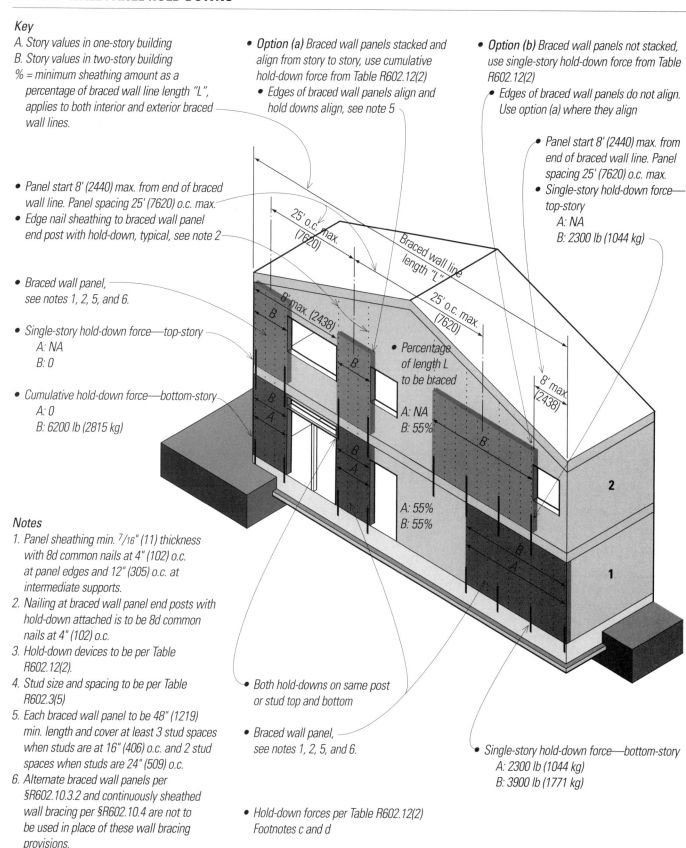

25' o.c. max. (7620)

Braced wall line length "L"

8' max. (2438)

25' o.c. max. (7620)

8' max. (2438)

- Percentage of length L to be braced
  A: NA
  B: 55%

A: 55%
B: 55%

2

1

Notes
1. Panel sheathing min. $^7/_{16}$" (11) thickness with 8d common nails at 4" (102) o.c. at panel edges and 12" (305) o.c. at intermediate supports.
2. Nailing at braced wall panel end posts with hold-down attached is to be 8d common nails at 4" (102) o.c.
3. Hold-down devices to be per Table R602.12(2).
4. Stud size and spacing to be per Table R602.3(5).
5. Each braced wall panel to be 48" (1219) min. length and cover at least 3 stud spaces when studs are at 16" (406) o.c. and 2 stud spaces when studs are 24" (509) o.c.
6. Alternate braced wall panels per §R602.10.3.2 and continuously sheathed wall bracing per §R602.10.4 are not to be used in place of these wall bracing provisions.

- Both hold-downs on same post or stud top and bottom

- Braced wall panel, see notes 1, 2, 5, and 6.

- Single-story hold-down force—bottom-story
  A: 2300 lb (1044 kg)
  B: 3900 lb (1771 kg)

- Hold-down forces per Table R602.12(2) Footnotes c and d

Figure R602.12 Hold-Downs at Exterior and Interior Braced Wall Panels for Stone or Masonry Wall Bracing at Seismic Design Category D2

§R603, Steel Wall Framing

Another method of wall construction using materials other than wood framing is light gage metal framing. The method of construction is similar to wood framing in that the building is constructed of multiple light members used repetitively. These members are formed by bending steel sheets in a cold-forming process. The standards in §R603 are meant to be prescriptive requirements for building up to three stories in height. The requirements are based on a newly adopted steel framing manual developed by the American Iron and Steel Institute (AISI) in 2007. It is *AISI S230 Standard for Cold-Formed Steel Framing —Prescriptive Method for One- and Two-Family Dwellings 2007 Edition*. Note that this covers members that are cold-formed from gage thickness steel sheets. It does not cover heavier steel shapes fabricated by other methods. As noted above, this is a type of "stick framing" using steel members rather than wood ones. The section is arranged similarly to the wood wall framing section with tables relating such variables as member sizes, member spacing, span lengths, number of stories, wind speeds and snow loads. Note that there is an additional variable for metal framing, similar to grades of wood members, which affects the capacities of the members. This is the thickness of the steel sheets from which the members are cold-formed. As would be expected heavier gages of steel sheets result in stiffer members which can support greater loads. To insure that the materials used on site are code-compliant, the steel framing members are to have a legible material and identifying label and information regarding the steel thickness, coatings and yield strength.

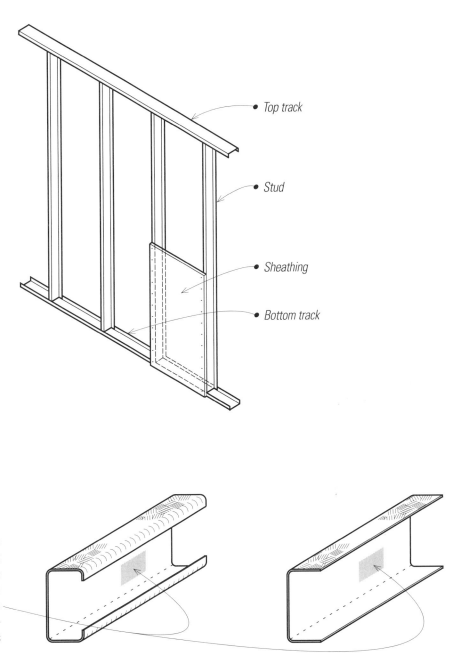

- Top track

- Stud

- Sheathing

- Bottom track

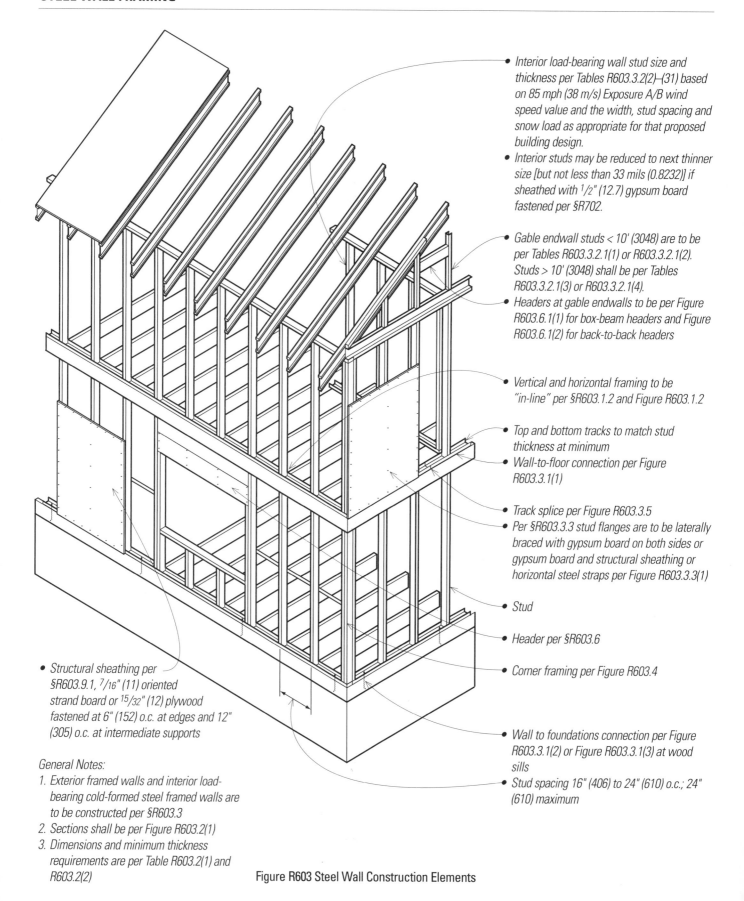

- Interior load-bearing wall stud size and thickness per Tables R603.3.2(2)–(31) based on 85 mph (38 m/s) Exposure A/B wind speed value and the width, stud spacing and snow load as appropriate for that proposed building design.
- Interior studs may be reduced to next thinner size [but not less than 33 mils (0.8232)] if sheathed with ¹/₂" (12.7) gypsum board fastened per §R702.

- Gable endwall studs < 10' (3048) are to be per Tables R603.3.2.1(1) or R603.3.2.1(2). Studs > 10' (3048) shall be per Tables R603.3.2.1(3) or R603.3.2.1(4).
- Headers at gable endwalls to be per Figure R603.6.1(1) for box-beam headers and Figure R603.6.1(2) for back-to-back headers

- Vertical and horizontal framing to be "in-line" per §R603.1.2 and Figure R603.1.2

- Top and bottom tracks to match stud thickness at minimum
- Wall-to-floor connection per Figure R603.3.1(1)

- Track splice per Figure R603.3.5
- Per §R603.3.3 stud flanges are to be laterally braced with gypsum board on both sides or gypsum board and structural sheathing or horizontal steel straps per Figure R603.3.3(1)

- Stud

- Header per §R603.6

- Corner framing per Figure R603.4

- Wall to foundations connection per Figure R603.3.1(2) or Figure R603.3.1(3) at wood sills
- Stud spacing 16" (406) to 24" (610) o.c.; 24" (610) maximum

- Structural sheathing per §R603.9.1, ⁷/₁₆" (11) oriented strand board or ¹⁵/₃₂" (12) plywood fastened at 6" (152) o.c. at edges and 12" (305) o.c. at intermediate supports

General Notes:
1. Exterior framed walls and interior load-bearing cold-formed steel framed walls are to be constructed per §R603.3
2. Sections shall be per Figure R603.2(1)
3. Dimensions and minimum thickness requirements are per Table R603.2(1) and R603.2(2)

Figure R603 Steel Wall Construction Elements

Wall Framing

Per §R603.1.1, buildings using the method described in §R603 are limited to a length of 60' (18288) measured in the direction perpendicular to the joist or truss span, a width of 40' (12192) measured parallel to the joist or truss span and three stories or less in height. Exterior walls are considered as load-bearing walls. These methods may be used on sites with wind speeds of less than 110 miles per hour (49 m/s) with Exposure B or C and maximum ground snow loads of 70 pounds per square foot (3.35 kPa). Wall studs are to be braced per the requirements of §R603.3.3 as illustrated on subsequent pages. All sheathable exterior wall surfaces are to have structural sheathing installed per the requirements of §R603.9 as illustrated.

In-line Framing

Cold-formed steel framing members are to be basically in-line with each other with some tolerances for member arrangements. Thus horizontal framing members are to align with studs below them. Bearing stiffeners are added to the intersections of horizontal and vertical members to facilitate the transfer of forces from horizontal members into vertical supports, as illustrated.

Members are to have profiles as illustrated in Figures R603.2(1) and (2) and have minimum dimensions as noted.

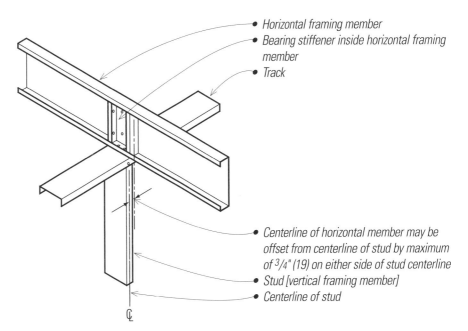

- *Horizontal framing member*
- *Bearing stiffener inside horizontal framing member*
- *Track*

- *Centerline of horizontal member may be offset from centerline of stud by maximum of 3/4" (19) on either side of stud centerline*
- *Stud [vertical framing member]*
- *Centerline of stud*

Horizontal Framing Offset Option A

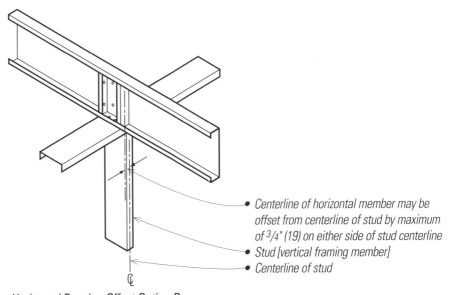

- *Centerline of horizontal member may be offset from centerline of stud by maximum of 3/4" (19) on either side of stud centerline*
- *Stud [vertical framing member]*
- *Centerline of stud*

Horizontal Framing Offset Option B

Figure R603.1.2 In-line Framing with Stiffner Inside Member

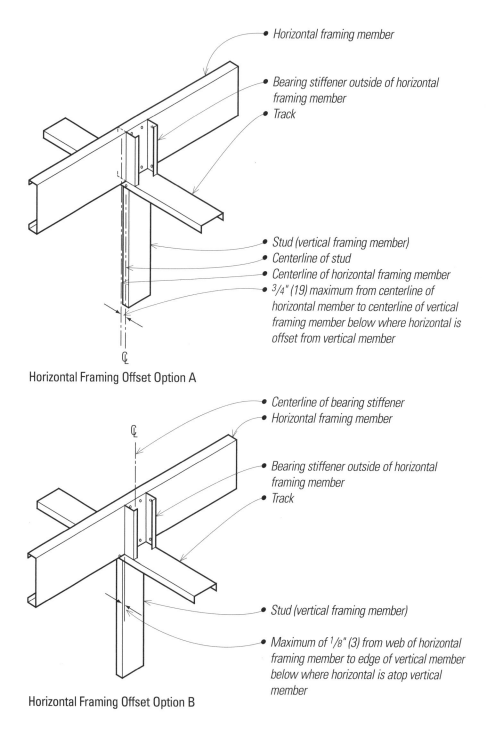

Horizontal framing member

Bearing stiffener outside of horizontal framing member

Track

Stud (vertical framing member)

Centerline of stud

Centerline of horizontal framing member

3/4" (19) maximum from centerline of horizontal member to centerline of vertical framing member below where horizontal is offset from vertical member

Horizontal Framing Offset Option A

Centerline of bearing stiffener

Horizontal framing member

Bearing stiffener outside of horizontal framing member

Track

Stud (vertical framing member)

Maximum of 1/8" (3) from web of horizontal framing member to edge of vertical member below where horizontal is atop vertical member

Horizontal Framing Offset Option B

Figure R603.1.2 In-line Framing with Stiffner Outside Member

Cold-Formed Steel Member Sizes

Steel framing members are to have profiles as illustrated in Figure R603.2(1) and Figure R603.2 (2) and have minimum dimensions as noted.

Member sizes are described in Table R603.2(1) by a numerical system expressed in terms of hundredths of an inch. Thus for "350S162-33" the first set of numbers refers to the member depth in hundredths of an inch 350, or 3.5"(89); the "S" means the member is to be used as a stud or joist; "T" is used for tracks; the second set of numbers is the member flange width in hundredths of an inch [1.62" (41)] and the last set of numbers after the dash is "t", the thickness of the sheet metal in mils [in this example 33 mils or 0.0329" (0.84)].

Members are to be fastened to each other per §R603.2.4. Steel-to-steel connections are based on using a standard #8 self-drilling tapping screw conforming to ASTM 1513. Larger screws may be used and the number of fasteners adjusted per Table R603.2.4. See the illustration for screw locations in members. Note that gypsum board is to be attached to cold-formed steel members using #6 bugle head screws installed per §R702.

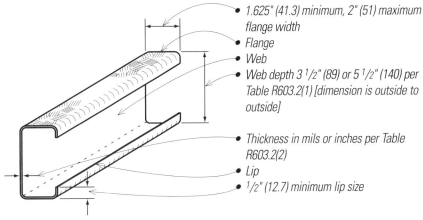

- 1.625" (41.3) minimum, 2" (51) maximum flange width
- Flange
- Web
- Web depth 3 1/2" (89) or 5 1/2" (140) per Table R603.2(1) [dimension is outside to outside]

- Thickness in mils or inches per Table R603.2(2)
- Lip
- 1/2" (12.7) minimum lip size

(1) C-Shaped Section (Stud or Joist)

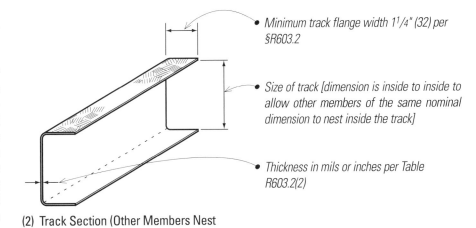

- Minimum track flange width 1 1/4" (32) per §R603.2

- Size of track [dimension is inside to inside to allow other members of the same nominal dimension to nest inside the track]

- Thickness in mils or inches per Table R603.2(2)

(2) Track Section (Other Members Nest Inside)

Figure R603.2 (1) and Figure R603.2(2)

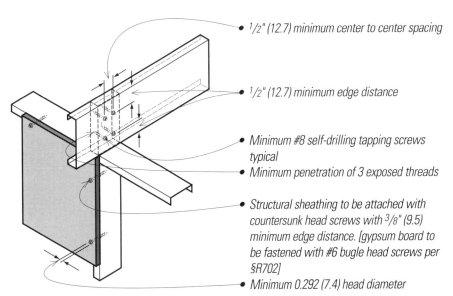

- 1/2" (12.7) minimum center to center spacing

- 1/2" (12.7) minimum edge distance

- Minimum #8 self-drilling tapping screws typical
- Minimum penetration of 3 exposed threads

- Structural sheathing to be attached with countersunk head screws with 3/8" (9.5) minimum edge distance. [gypsum board to be fastened with #6 bugle head screws per §R702]
- Minimum 0.292 (7.4) head diameter

Figure R603.2.4 Fastenings

Holes in Steel Members

Holes in the webs of steel members are allowed for the passage of electrical conduit or plumbing lines. However, there are restrictions on the locations and size of the holes in relation to each other and to the ends of the members. Holes not conforming to the requirements of §R603.2.5.1 are allowed under certain circumstances when located and reinforced as described in §R603.2.5.2 and §R603.2.5.3. Web reinforcing and web hole patching are very similar. The hole patching techniques are illustrated per Figure R603.2.5.3.

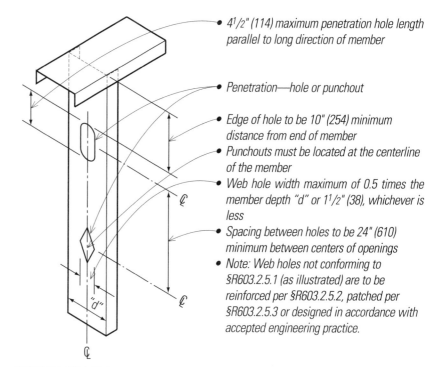

- $4^{1}/_{2}$" (114) maximum penetration hole length parallel to long direction of member

- Penetration—hole or punchout

- Edge of hole to be 10" (254) minimum distance from end of member
- Punchouts must be located at the centerline of the member
- Web hole width maximum of 0.5 times the member depth "d" or $1^{1}/_{2}$" (38), whichever is less
- Spacing between holes to be 24" (610) minimum between centers of openings
- Note: Web holes not conforming to §R603.2.5.1 (as illustrated) are to be reinforced per §R603.2.5.2, patched per §R603.2.5.3 or designed in accordance with accepted engineering practice.

Figure R603.2.5.1 Web Holes

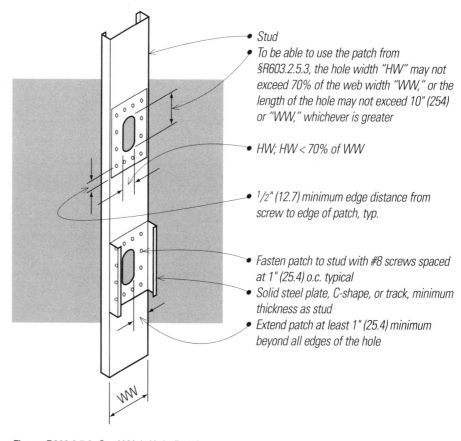

- Stud
- To be able to use the patch from §R603.2.5.3, the hole width "HW" may not exceed 70% of the web width "WW," or the length of the hole may not exceed 10" (254) or "WW," whichever is greater

- HW; HW < 70% of WW

- $^{1}/_{2}$" (12.7) minimum edge distance from screw to edge of patch, typ.

- Fasten patch to stud with #8 screws spaced at 1" (25.4) o.c. typical
- Solid steel plate, C-shape, or track, minimum thickness as stud
- Extend patch at least 1" (25.4) minimum beyond all edges of the hole

Figure R603.2.5.3 Stud Web Hole Patch

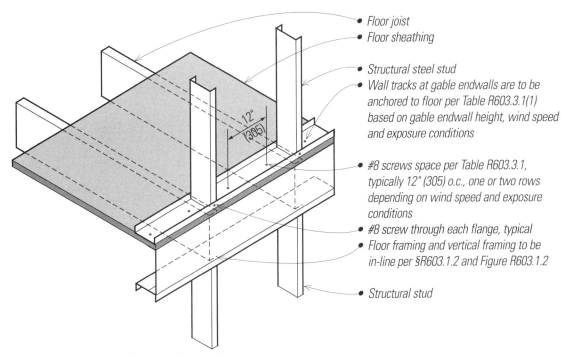

- Floor joist
- Floor sheathing

- Structural steel stud
- Wall tracks at gable endwalls are to be anchored to floor per Table R603.3.1(1) based on gable endwall height, wind speed and exposure conditions

- #8 screws space per Table R603.3.1, typically 12" (305) o.c., one or two rows depending on wind speed and exposure conditions
- #8 screw through each flange, typical
- Floor framing and vertical framing to be in-line per §R603.1.2 and Figure R603.1.2

- Structural stud

12" (305)

Figure R603.3.1(1) Wall-to-Floor Connection

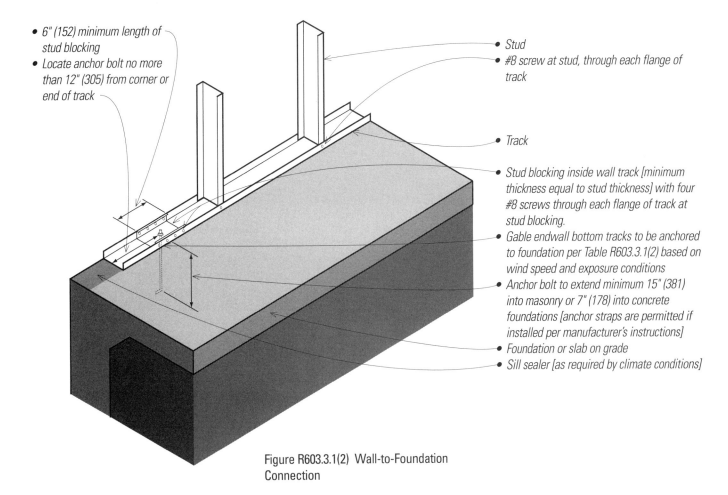

- 6" (152) minimum length of stud blocking
- Locate anchor bolt no more than 12" (305) from corner or end of track

- Stud
- #8 screw at stud, through each flange of track

- Track

- Stud blocking inside wall track [minimum thickness equal to stud thickness] with four #8 screws through each flange of track at stud blocking.
- Gable endwall bottom tracks to be anchored to foundation per Table R603.3.1(2) based on wind speed and exposure conditions
- Anchor bolt to extend minimum 15" (381) into masonry or 7" (178) into concrete foundations [anchor straps are permitted if installed per manufacturer's instructions]
- Foundation or slab on grade
- Sill sealer [as required by climate conditions]

Figure R603.3.1(2) Wall-to-Foundation Connection

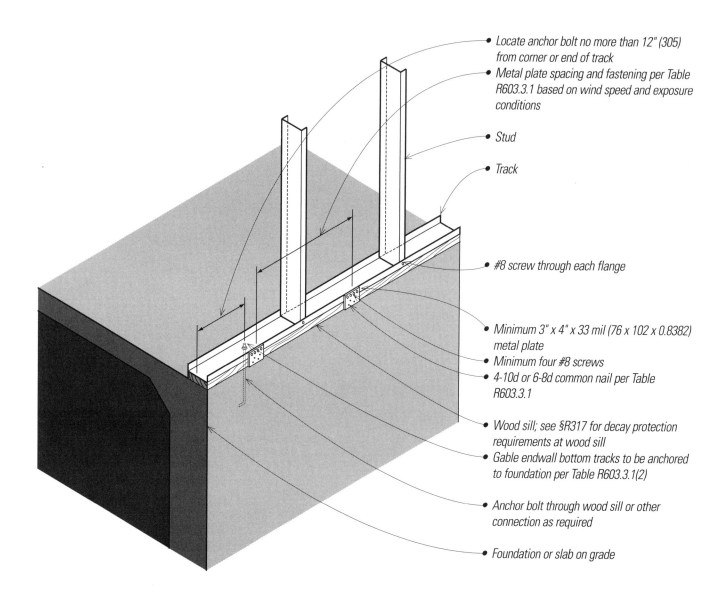

Locate anchor bolt no more than 12" (305) from corner or end of track

Metal plate spacing and fastening per Table R603.3.1 based on wind speed and exposure conditions

Stud

Track

#8 screw through each flange

Minimum 3" x 4" x 33 mil (76 x 102 x 0.8382) metal plate

Minimum four #8 screws

4-10d or 6-8d common nail per Table R603.3.1

Wood sill; see §R317 for decay protection requirements at wood sill

Gable endwall bottom tracks to be anchored to foundation per Table R603.3.1(2)

Anchor bolt through wood sill or other connection as required

Foundation or slab on grade

Figure R603.3.1(3) Wall-to-Wood Sill Connection

Wall Construction

Exterior walls and interior load-bearing walls constructed of cold-formed steel may be constructed using the prescriptive standards contained in §R603.3. This section contains details and tables which, when followed, will result in a code-compliant structural design.

Connections between members at the foundation level or at floor-to-floor connections are described in Figures R603.3.1(1)–(3). See the illustrations for these figures.

Tables R603.3.2(2) through (31) describe the basic framing requirements for cold-formed steel-framed buildings based on the following factors: the number of stories, building width, the steel strength of the framing members, wind speeds, member sizes, stud spacing, stud length and anticipated snow loads. We have illustrated an example using the following criteria:

Stories:	three
Width:	36' (10972)
Steel Strength:	33 ksi (227.53 MPa)
Wind Speed:	85 mph (38 m/s) in Exposure B
Member size:	350S162
Stud Spacing:	16" (406) on-center
Stud length:	9' (2743)
Snow Load:	20 psf (0.958 kPa)

$3^1/2$" (89)

$1^5/8$" (41.2)

Member 350S162

- Maximum snow load = 20 psf (0.958 kPa)
- Gable endwalls less than 10' (3048) 33 mils (0.8382) stud thickness for given design parameters, per Table R603.3.2.1(1)

9' (2743)

- Third floor studs 33 mils (0.8232) thickness for given parameters, per Table R603.3.2(8)

3

- Studs at 16" (406) o.c.

- Second floor studs 33 mils (0.8232) thickness for given parameters, per Table R603.3.2(18)

9' (2743)

2

- First floor studs 43 mils (1.092) thickness for given parameters per Table R603.3.2(28)

9' (2743)

1

Building width 36' (10972)

- Maximum wind speed 85 mph (38 m/s)

Figure R603.3.2(XX) Example of Using Steel Stud Design Tables

Wall Bracing

Per §R603.3.3 studs are to be braced with sheathing per §R603.9 or with horizontal steel strapping per Figure R603.3.3(1). This figure shows horizontal strapping at both sides to the studs. The accompanying figure, R603.3.3(2), is not referenced in the code text, but when the wall bracing and horizontal bracing requirements are read together they result in a configuration as shown in Figure (2) and thus we believe this can be considered code compliant as well.

Stud and header flanges or lips are not to be notched or cut per §R603.3.4. Splices are to be as illustrated in Figure R603.3.5. Corners are to be framed per the illustration in Figure R603.4

Notes per §R603.3.3.1:

1. Wall may be braced with gypsum board on both sides installed with #6 screws per §R702.
2. Walls may have gypsum board on one side installed with #6 screws per §R702 and sheathing on the other installed per §R603.9.1.
3. This illustration is not referenced in the text of §R603.3.3 but is a combination of methods 1 and 2 from that section. See Figure R606.3.3(1) for notes regarding strapping.

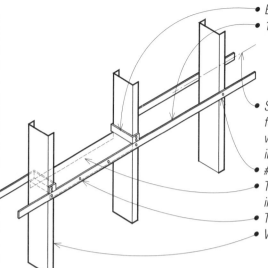

- Bend section or clip flange to form vertical
- 1¹/₂" x 33 mil (38 x 0.84) minimum flat strip

- Strap bracing to be at mid-height of wall for 8' (2438) walls and at one-third points of wall height for walls 9' (2743) or 10' (3048) in height
- #8 screw at each strap to stud
- Track/stud blocking at ends of strap and intermittently every 12' (3658)
- Two #8 screws at strap to blocking
- Wall framing

Figure R603.3.3(1) Stud Bracing with Strapping Only

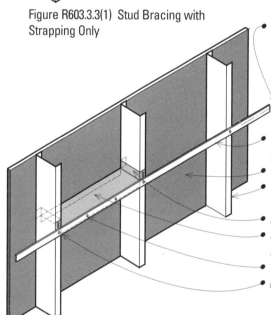

- Strap backing to be at mid-height of wall for 8' (2438) walls and at one-third points of wall height for walls 9' (2743) or 10' (3048) in height

- 1¹/₂" x 33 mil (38 x 0.8232) flat strap (see notes)
- Wall sheathing (see notes)
- Wall framing

- Bend section of clip flange to form vertical
- Stud/track blocking at each end of strap and intermittently every 12' (3658)
- Two #8 screws at strap to blocking
- #8 screw at each strap to stud

Figure R603.3.3(2) Stud Bracing with Strapping and Sheathing Material

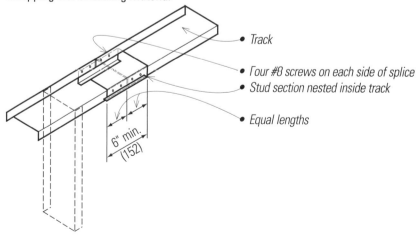

- Track
- Four #8 screws on each side of splice
- Stud section nested inside track
- Equal lengths

6" min. (152)

Figure R603.3.5 Track Splice

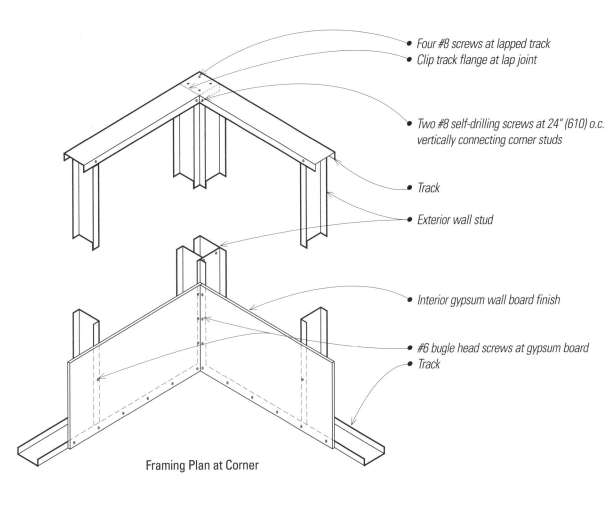

- Four #8 screws at lapped track
- Clip track flange at lap joint

- Two #8 self-drilling screws at 24" (610) o.c. vertically connecting corner studs

- Track

- Exterior wall stud

- Interior gypsum wall board finish

- #6 bugle head screws at gypsum board
- Track

Framing Plan at Corner

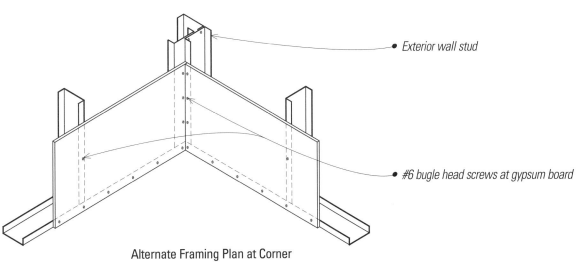

- Exterior wall stud

- #6 bugle head screws at gypsum board

Alternate Framing Plan at Corner

Figure R603.4 Corner Framing at Exterior Walls

Headers

Headers are to be installed over all wall openings in exterior walls and interior load-bearing walls. Headers may be either box beam or back-to-back configurations as illustrated in Figures R603.6(1) or R603.6(2). Headers that occur in gable endwalls may also be either box beam or back-to-back configurations constructed per Figures R603.6.1(1) or R603.6.1 (2). Head and sill tracks are to be designed per Table R603.8. Note that per §R603.8 for small openings with both a head track and a sill track, the allowable spans based on member sizes and thicknesses may be increased. For openings less than 4' (1219) the factor is 1.75 and for openings up to 6'(1829) the factor is 1.5 times the values in Table R603.8.

Structural sheathing is to be per §R603.9. The amount of sheathing required is determined per §R603.9.2 and Tables R603.9.2(1) and R603.9.2 (2). We have illustrated an example of how sheathing lengths are to be determined per these requirements.

Header General Notes:
1. Header to be installed at openings in both exterior wall and interior load-bearing walls.
2. Headers may also be constructed per AISI S100, Section D4, or AISI S230 for L-shaped headers.

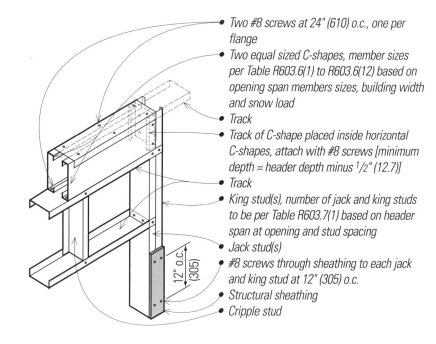

- Two #8 screws at 24" (610) o.c., one per flange
- Two equal sized C-shapes, member sizes per Table R603.6(1) to R603.6(12) based on opening span members sizes, building width and snow load
- Track
- Track of C-shape placed inside horizontal C-shapes, attach with #8 screws [minimum depth = header depth minus ¹/2" (12.7)]
- Track
- King stud(s), number of jack and king studs to be per Table R603.7(1) based on header span at opening and stud spacing
- Jack stud(s)
- #8 screws through sheathing to each jack and king stud at 12" (305) o.c.
- Structural sheathing
- Cripple stud

12" o.c. (305)

Figure R603.6(1) Box Beam Header

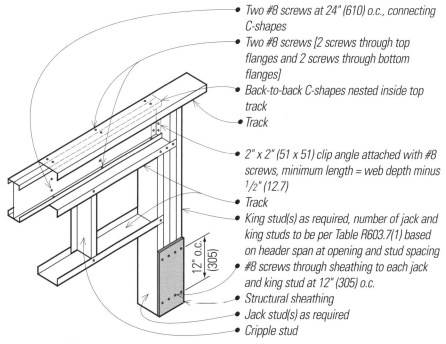

- Two #8 screws at 24" (610) o.c., connecting C-shapes
- Two #8 screws [2 screws through top flanges and 2 screws through bottom flanges]
- Back-to-back C-shapes nested inside top track
- Track
- 2" x 2" (51 x 51) clip angle attached with #8 screws, minimum length = web depth minus ¹/2" (12.7)
- Track
- King stud(s) as required, number of jack and king studs to be per Table R603.7(1) based on header span at opening and stud spacing
- #8 screws through sheathing to each jack and king stud at 12" (305) o.c.
- Structural sheathing
- Jack stud(s) as required
- Cripple stud

12" o.c. (305)

Figure R603.6(2) Back-to-Back Header
[Labeled as Figure R601.6(2) in 2009 IRC]

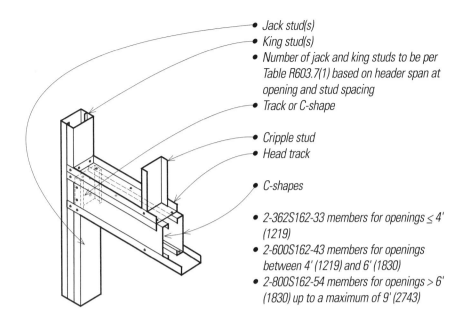

Jack stud(s)

King stud(s)

Number of jack and king studs to be per Table R603.7(1) based on header span at opening and stud spacing

Track or C-shape

Cripple stud

Head track

C-shapes

2-362S162-33 members for openings ≤ 4' (1219)

2-600S162-43 members for openings between 4' (1219) and 6' (1830)

2-800S162-54 members for openings > 6' (1830) up to a maximum of 9' (2743)

Figure R603.6.1(1) Box Beam Header in Gable Endwall

Gable End Header General Notes:
1. Gable end headers may be constructed as permitted for other headers per §R603.6.
2. Alternately the conditions shown in Figures R603.6.1(1) and R603.6.1(2) may be used.

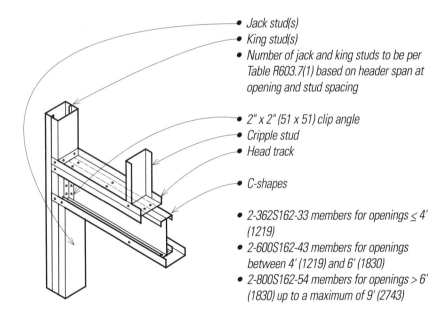

Jack stud(s)

King stud(s)

Number of jack and king studs to be per Table R603.7(1) based on header span at opening and stud spacing

2" x 2" (51 x 51) clip angle

Cripple stud

Head track

C-shapes

2-362S162-33 members for openings ≤ 4' (1219)

2-600S162-43 members for openings between 4' (1219) and 6' (1830)

2-800S162-54 members for openings > 6' (1830) up to a maximum of 9' (2743)

Figure R603.6.1(2) Back-to-Back Header in Gable Endwall

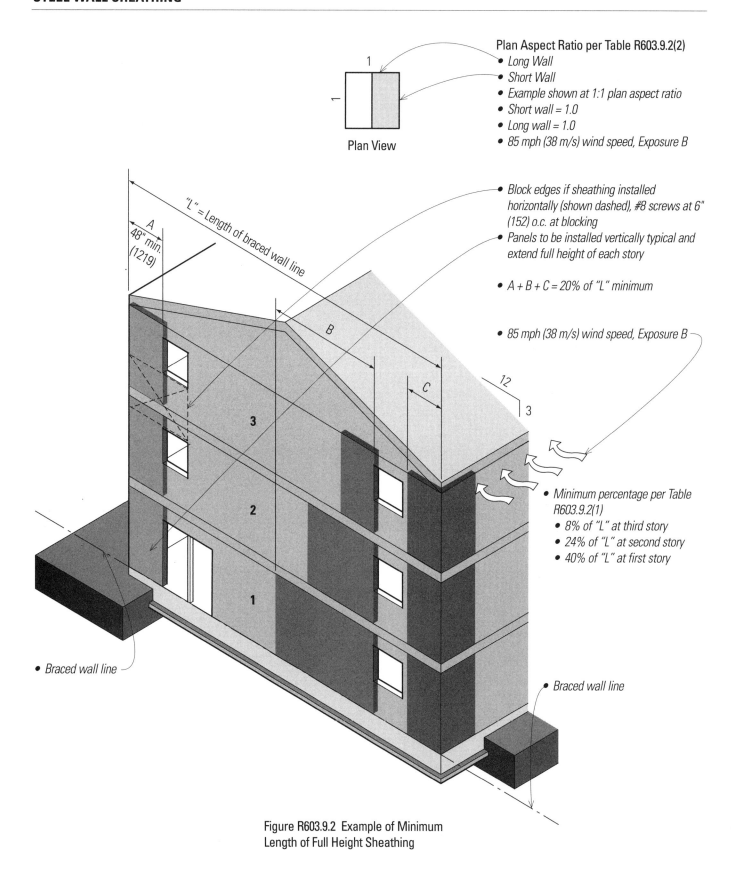

Plan Aspect Ratio per Table R603.9.2(2)
- *Long Wall*
- *Short Wall*
- *Example shown at 1:1 plan aspect ratio*
- *Short wall = 1.0*
- *Long wall = 1.0*
- *85 mph (38 m/s) wind speed, Exposure B*

Plan View

- *Block edges if sheathing installed horizontally (shown dashed), #8 screws at 6" (152) o.c. at blocking*
- *Panels to be installed vertically typical and extend full height of each story*

- *A + B + C = 20% of "L" minimum*

- *85 mph (38 m/s) wind speed, Exposure B*

- *Minimum percentage per Table R603.9.2(1)*
  - *8% of "L" at third story*
  - *24% of "L" at second story*
  - *40% of "L" at first story*

"L" = Length of braced wall line

A
48" min.
(1219)

B

C

12
3

3

2

1

- *Braced wall line*

- *Braced wall line*

Figure R603.9.2 Example of Minimum
Length of Full Height Sheathing

§R604 Wood Structural Panels

Wood structural panels installed over wall framing members are to be in accordance with §R604. This section would seem better located in §R602, but such panels may be used with metal studs as well as wood, so that seems to be the logic for placing this in a separate section. Note that sheathing attachments are to be per the fastener schedule in Table R602.3(1). See the illustration on Page 178 for wood panel nailing and spans over studs taken from Table R602.3(3).

§R605 Particleboard

Particle board used for walls is to be labeled per the requirements of §R605. This section also refers back to §R602 for the allowable spans for particle board on studs. This is to be per Table R602.3(4).

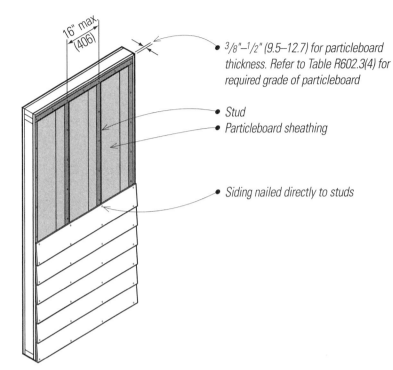

- *3/8"–1/2" (9.5–12.7) for particleboard thickness. Refer to Table R602.3(4) for required grade of particleboard*
- *Stud*
- *Particleboard sheathing*
- *Siding nailed directly to studs*

Siding Nailed Directly to Stud

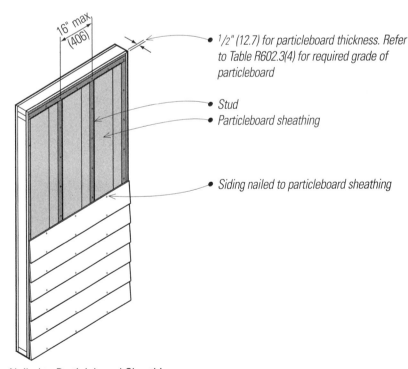

- *1/2" (12.7) for particleboard thickness. Refer to Table R602.3(4) for required grade of particleboard*
- *Stud*
- *Particleboard sheathing*
- *Siding nailed to particleboard sheathing*

Siding Nailed to Particleboard Sheathing

§R606 General Masonry Construction

This section of the code governs masonry wall construction. Alternatively the provisions of the reference standard ACI 530/ASCE 5/TMS 402 may be used for design of masonry walls. When those provisions are used, or the provisions of §R606 are used, the code does not require the use of an architect or engineer unless required by the state laws where the jurisdiction is located. This is similar to the provisions in the IRC for other materials. It is the intent of the IRC that when the prescriptive standards and provisions are followed, a structurally sound building will result.

Wall thicknesses are related to wall heights in feet and the number of stories. Lateral support along either the horizontal or vertical direction is required for masonry walls as illustrated. When masonry walls are corbelled to project the wall face outward, the code has prescriptive requirements for the relationship of the masonry units as illustrated. Bearing and support conditions are also prescribed, as illustrated.

Allowable stresses in masonry are prescribed in Table R606.5. The table describes the several types of masonry covered by the IRC masonry sections. The allowable compressive strengths are related to the type of mortar, whether Type M, S or N. The mortar materials and proportions are listed in Table R607.1. The general description of mortar types is as follows:

- Type M mortar is a high-strength mortar recommended for use in below-grade masonry or in contact with earth or where high lateral or compressive loads are anticipated. It has a compressive strength in a range up to 2500 psi (17250 kPa).
- Type S is high- to medium-strength mortar for general use in above-grade exterior walls where bond and lateral strength may be as important as compressive strengths. It has a compressive strength in the range of 1800 psi (12420 kPa).
- Type N mortar is a medium-strength mortar for general use in exposed masonry where high compressive and lateral strengths are not required. It has a compressive strength in the range of 750 psi (5175 kPa).

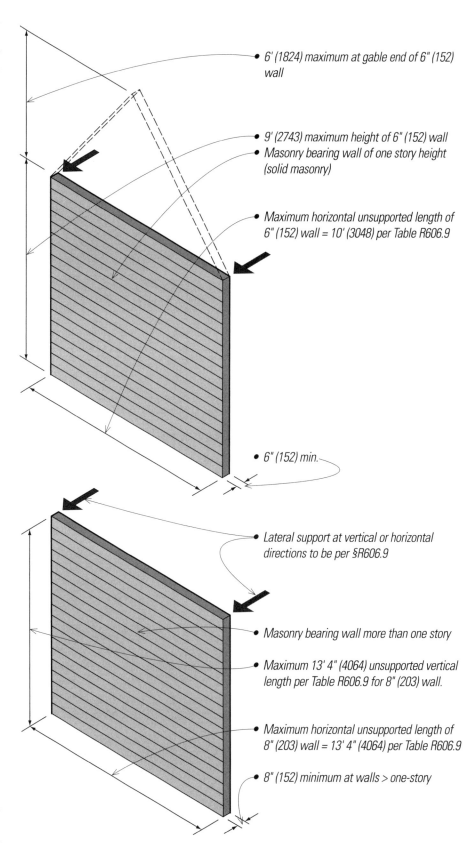

- 6' (1824) maximum at gable end of 6" (152) wall

- 9' (2743) maximum height of 6" (152) wall
- Masonry bearing wall of one story height (solid masonry)

- Maximum horizontal unsupported length of 6" (152) wall = 10' (3048) per Table R606.9

- 6" (152) min.

- Lateral support at vertical or horizontal directions to be per §R606.9

- Masonry bearing wall more than one story

- Maximum 13' 4" (4064) unsupported vertical length per Table R606.9 for 8" (203) wall.

- Maximum horizontal unsupported length of 8" (203) wall = 13' 4" (4064) per Table R606.9

- 8" (152) minimum at walls > one-story

Figure R606.2.1 Minimum Masonry Wall Thickness

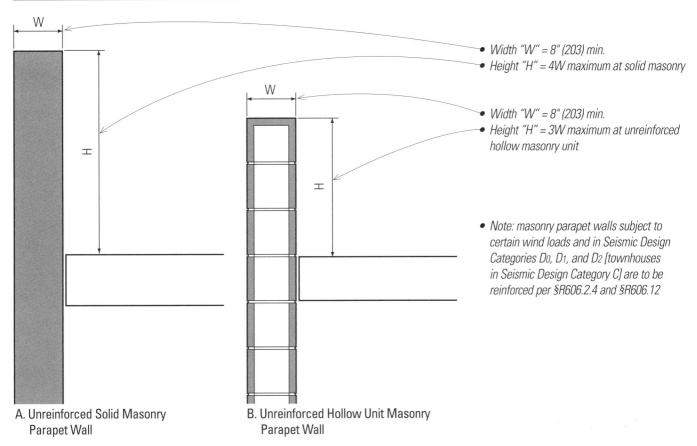

W

H

A. Unreinforced Solid Masonry
Parapet Wall

W

H

B. Unreinforced Hollow Unit Masonry
Parapet Wall

- *Width "W" = 8" (203) min.*
- *Height "H" = 4W maximum at solid masonry*

- *Width "W" = 8" (203) min.*
- *Height "H" = 3W maximum at unreinforced hollow masonry unit*

- *Note: masonry parapet walls subject to certain wind loads and in Seismic Design Categories D$_0$, D$_1$, and D$_2$ [townhouses in Seismic Design Category C] are to be reinforced per §R606.2.4 and §R606.12*

Figure R606.2.4 Parapets at Unreinforced Masonry Walls

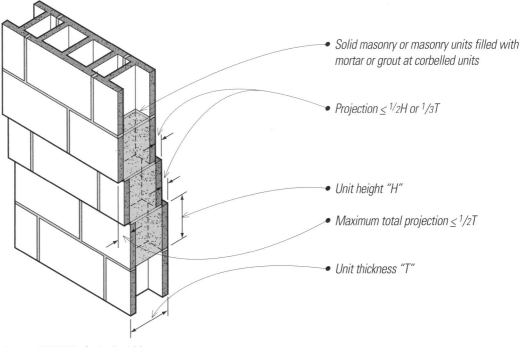

- *Solid masonry or masonry units filled with mortar or grout at corbelled units*

- *Projection ≤ $^{1}/_{2}$H or $^{1}/_{3}$T*

- *Unit height "H"*

- *Maximum total projection ≤ $^{1}/_{2}$T*

- *Unit thickness "T"*

Figure R606.2.3 Corbelled Masonry

Wall and Roof Anchorage

Prescriptive masonry design assumes that floor diaphragms and roof diaphragms are well connected to the masonry walls so they may provide lateral support to the walls. The anchorage requirements are in §R606.9, §R606.11, and §R606.12. The requirements in §R606.9 are general. Those in §R606.11 and §R606.12 as illustrated in Figures R603.11(1), (2) and (3) are subdivided by Seismic Design Category. The reinforced grouted masonry provisions illustrated in Figure R606.11(2) apply to townhouses, per the reference contained in §R606.12.2.

Note that in most cases the detailed structural design requirements related to Seismic Design Categories are more stringent than the general requirements, but not in all cases. They are typically more stringent for higher Seismic Design Categories.

Townhouses located in Seismic Design Category C have seismic design requirements imposed by §R606.12.2 above those required for one- and two-family dwellings in that Seismic Design Category. There are reinforcing requirements for Seismic Design Category C shown in Figure R606.11(2) and minimum solid wall length requirements described in Table R606.12.2.1.

One- and two-family dwellings and townhouses in Seismic Design Categories D_0, D_1 or D_2 are to be designed using the criteria contained in §R606.12.3 for Categories D_0 and D_1 and §R606.12.4 for Category D_2. The requirements for Seismic Design Categories D_0, D_1 and D_2 are shown in Figure R606.11(3). Minimum wall length requirements for Seismic Design Categories C, D_0, D_1 and D_2 are contained in Table R606.12.2.1.

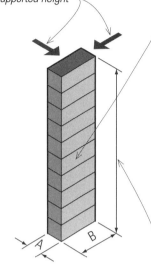

- Masonry pier [see §R606.6 for grouting requirements for various types of masonry]
- Pier lateral support locations determine unsupported height

- Unsupported height = 10A maximum
- Pier least dimensions is A since A < B

Figure R606.6 Masonry Piers

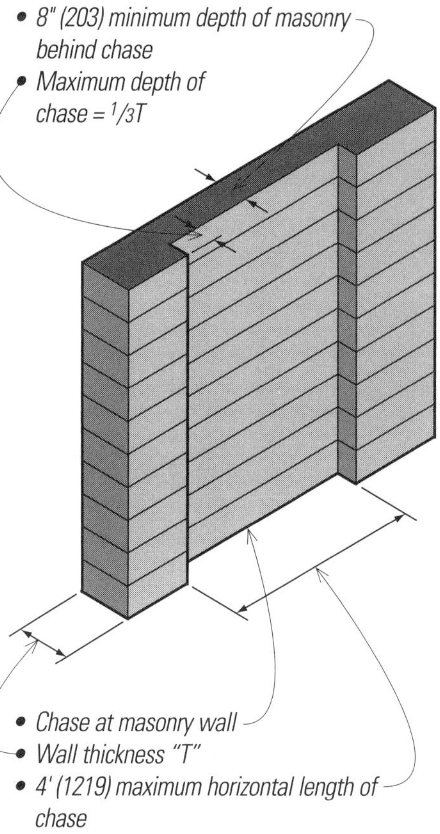

- 8" (203) minimum depth of masonry behind chase
- Maximum depth of chase = $^1/_3T$

- Chase at masonry wall
- Wall thickness "T"
- 4' (1219) maximum horizontal length of chase

Figure R606.7 Chases at Masonry Walls

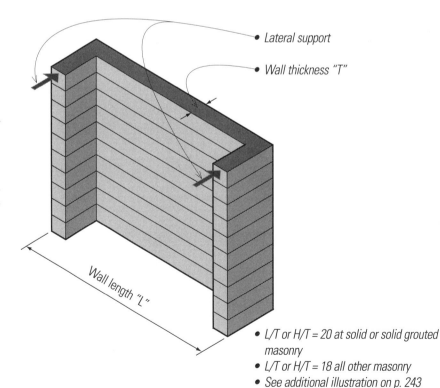

- Lateral support
- Wall thickness "T"

- L/T or H/T = 20 at solid or solid grouted masonry
- L/T or H/T = 18 all other masonry
- See additional illustration on p. 243

Figure R606.9 Lateral Support at Masonry Bearing Wall

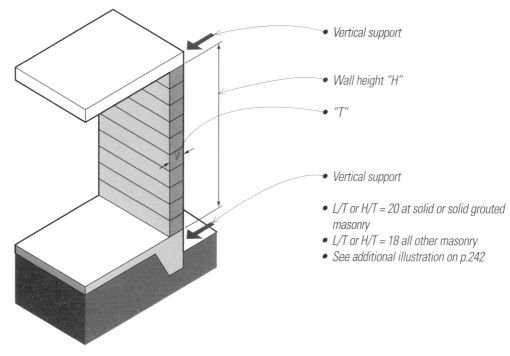

• Vertical support

• Wall height "H"

• "T"

• Vertical support

• L/T or H/T = 20 at solid or solid grouted masonry
• L/T or H/T = 18 all other masonry
• See additional illustration on p.242

Figure R606.9 Lateral Support at Masonry Bearing Wall

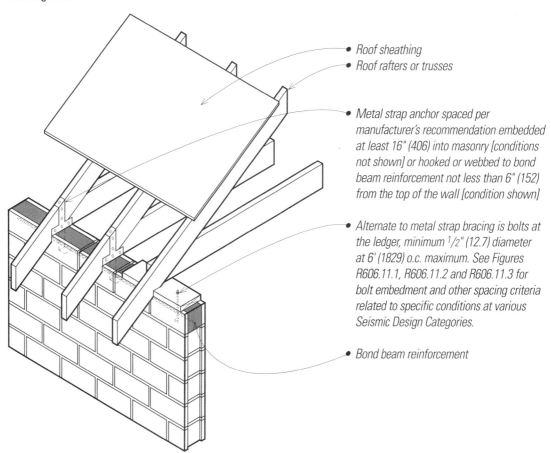

• Roof sheathing
• Roof rafters or trusses

• Metal strap anchor spaced per manufacturer's recommendation embedded at least 16" (406) into masonry [conditions not shown] or hooked or webbed to bond beam reinforcement not less than 6" (152) from the top of the wall [condition shown]

• Alternate to metal strap bracing is bolts at the ledger, minimum 1/2" (12.7) diameter at 6' (1829) o.c. maximum. See Figures R606.11.1, R606.11.2 and R606.11.3 for bolt embedment and other spacing criteria related to specific conditions at various Seismic Design Categories.

• Bond beam reinforcement

Figure R606.9.1 General Requirements for Roof Anchorage to Wall

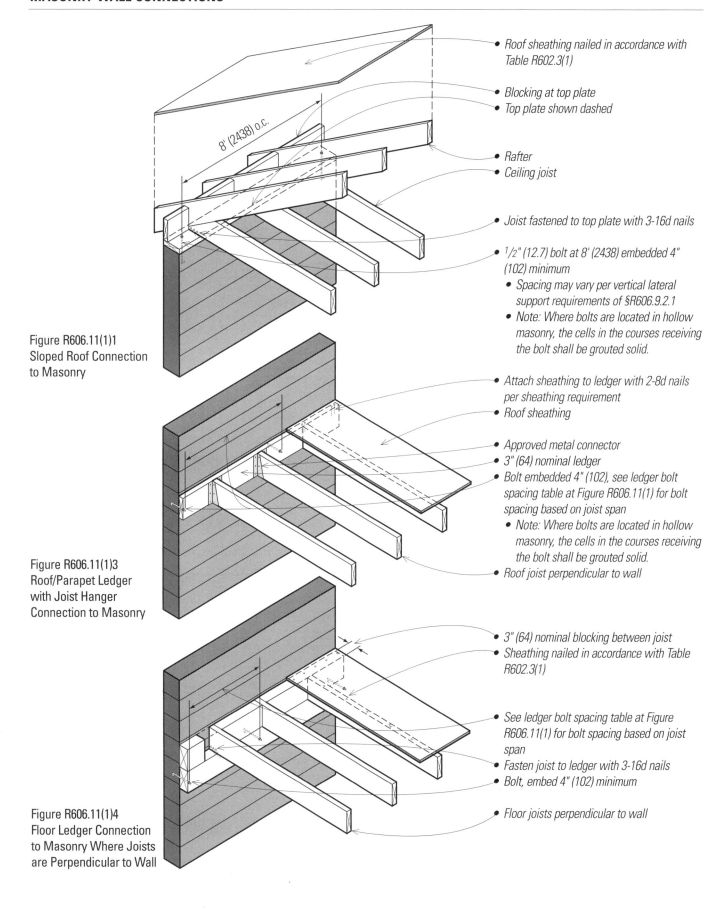

Figure R606.11(1)1
Sloped Roof Connection
to Masonry

Figure R606.11(1)3
Roof/Parapet Ledger
with Joist Hanger
Connection to Masonry

Figure R606.11(1)4
Floor Ledger Connection
to Masonry Where Joists
are Perpendicular to Wall

- Roof sheathing nailed in accordance with Table R602.3(1)

- Blocking at top plate
- Top plate shown dashed

- Rafter
- Ceiling joist

- Joist fastened to top plate with 3-16d nails

- $1/2$" (12.7) bolt at 8' (2438) embedded 4" (102) minimum
  - Spacing may vary per vertical lateral support requirements of §R606.9.2.1
  - Note: Where bolts are located in hollow masonry, the cells in the courses receiving the bolt shall be grouted solid.

- Attach sheathing to ledger with 2-8d nails per sheathing requirement
- Roof sheathing

- Approved metal connector
- 3" (64) nominal ledger
- Bolt embedded 4" (102), see ledger bolt spacing table at Figure R606.11(1) for bolt spacing based on joist span
  - Note: Where bolts are located in hollow masonry, the cells in the courses receiving the bolt shall be grouted solid.
- Roof joist perpendicular to wall

- 3" (64) nominal blocking between joist
- Sheathing nailed in accordance with Table R602.3(1)

- See ledger bolt spacing table at Figure R606.11(1) for bolt spacing based on joist span
- Fasten joist to ledger with 3-16d nails
- Bolt, embed 4" (102) minimum

- Floor joists perpendicular to wall

8' (2438) o.c.

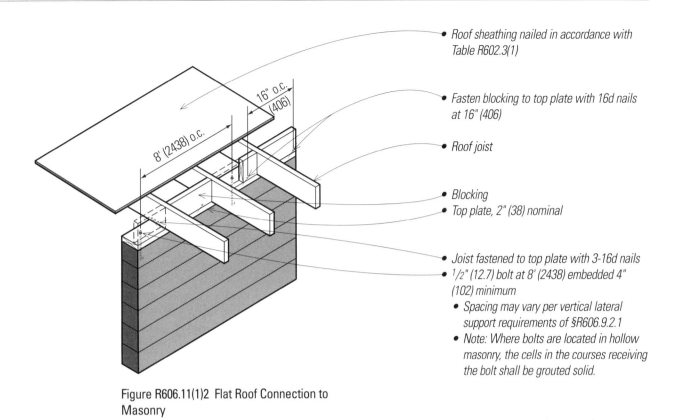

Roof sheathing nailed in accordance with Table R602.3(1)

Fasten blocking to top plate with 16d nails at 16" (406)

Roof joist

Blocking

Top plate, 2" (38) nominal

Joist fastened to top plate with 3-16d nails

$1/2$" (12.7) bolt at 8' (2438) embedded 4" (102) minimum

- Spacing may vary per vertical lateral support requirements of §R606.9.2.1
- Note: Where bolts are located in hollow masonry, the cells in the courses receiving the bolt shall be grouted solid.

16" o.c. (406)

8' (2438) o.c.

Figure R606.11(1)2 Flat Roof Connection to Masonry

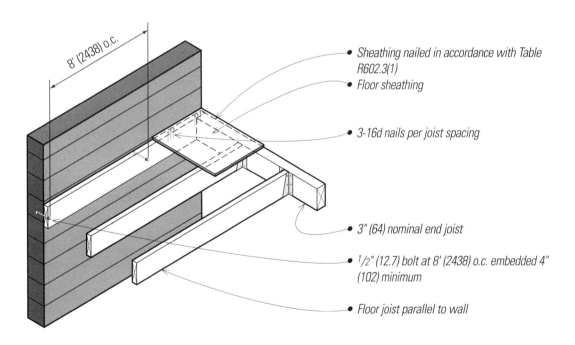

Sheathing nailed in accordance with Table R602.3(1)

Floor sheathing

3-16d nails per joist spacing

3" (64) nominal end joist

$1/2$" (12.7) bolt at 8' (2438) o.c. embedded 4" (102) minimum

Floor joist parallel to wall

8' (2438) o.c.

Figure R606.11(1)5 Floor Ledger Connection to Masonry Where Joists are Parallel to Wall

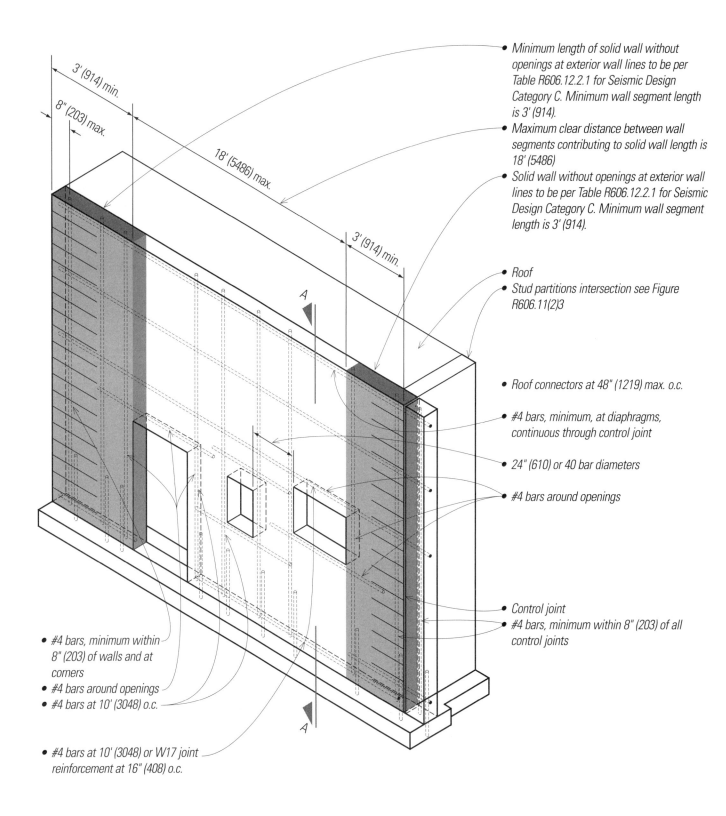

3' (914) min.

8" (203) max.

18' (5486) max.

3' (914) min.

A

A

- Minimum length of solid wall without openings at exterior wall lines to be per Table R606.12.2.1 for Seismic Design Category C. Minimum wall segment length is 3' (914).

- Maximum clear distance between wall segments contributing to solid wall length is 18' (5486)

- Solid wall without openings at exterior wall lines to be per Table R606.12.2.1 for Seismic Design Category C. Minimum wall segment length is 3' (914).

- Roof
- Stud partitions intersection see Figure R606.11(2)3

- Roof connectors at 48" (1219) max. o.c.

- #4 bars, minimum, at diaphragms, continuous through control joint

- 24" (610) or 40 bar diameters

- #4 bars around openings

- Control joint
- #4 bars, minimum within 8" (203) of all control joints

- #4 bars, minimum within 8" (203) of walls and at corners
- #4 bars around openings
- #4 bars at 10' (3048) o.c.

- #4 bars at 10' (3048) or W17 joint reinforcement at 16" (408) o.c.

Figure R606.11(2)1 Minimum Reinforcement for Masonry Walls at Seismic Design Category C for Townhouses

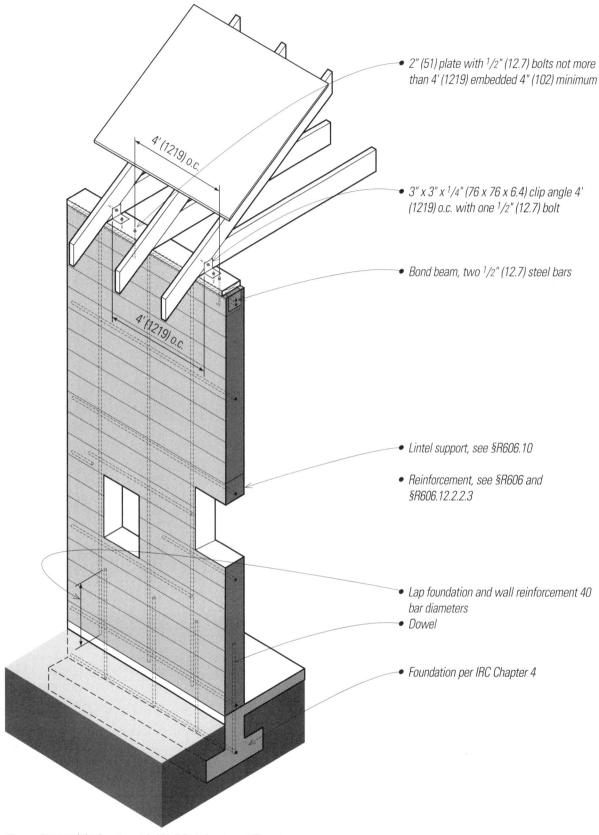

2" (51) plate with $^1/_2$" (12.7) bolts not more than 4' (1219) embedded 4" (102) minimum

3" x 3" x $^1/_4$" (76 x 76 x 6.4) clip angle 4' (1219) o.c. with one $^1/_2$" (12.7) bolt

Bond beam, two $^1/_2$" (12.7) steel bars

Lintel support, see §R606.10

Reinforcement, see §R606 and §R606.12.2.2.3

Lap foundation and wall reinforcement 40 bar diameters

Dowel

Foundation per IRC Chapter 4

Figure R606.11(2)2 Section AA, Wall Reinforcing at Townhouses at Seismic Design Category C

- Roof connectors at 48" (1219) max. o.c.
- #4 bars, minimum, at diaphragms, continuous through control joint
- #4 bars, minimum within 8" (203) of ends of walls and corners

3' (914) min.

18' (5486) max.

A

3' (914) min.

- Minimum length of solid wall without openings at exterior wall lines to be per Table R606.12.2.1 for Seismic Design Category C. Minimum wall segment length is 3' (914).
- Maximum clear distance between wall segments contributing to solid wall length is 18' (5486).
- Roof
- Per §R606.12.3.1, masonry partition walls not part of the lateral force resisting system are required to be designed or to comply with §R606.12.2.2.2 or, if limited to one story and to 9' (2743) between lateral supports, need not be designed if they comply with the minimum reinforcement requirements of §R606.12.3.2 and §R606.12.3.2.1.

9' (2743) max.

One-story height

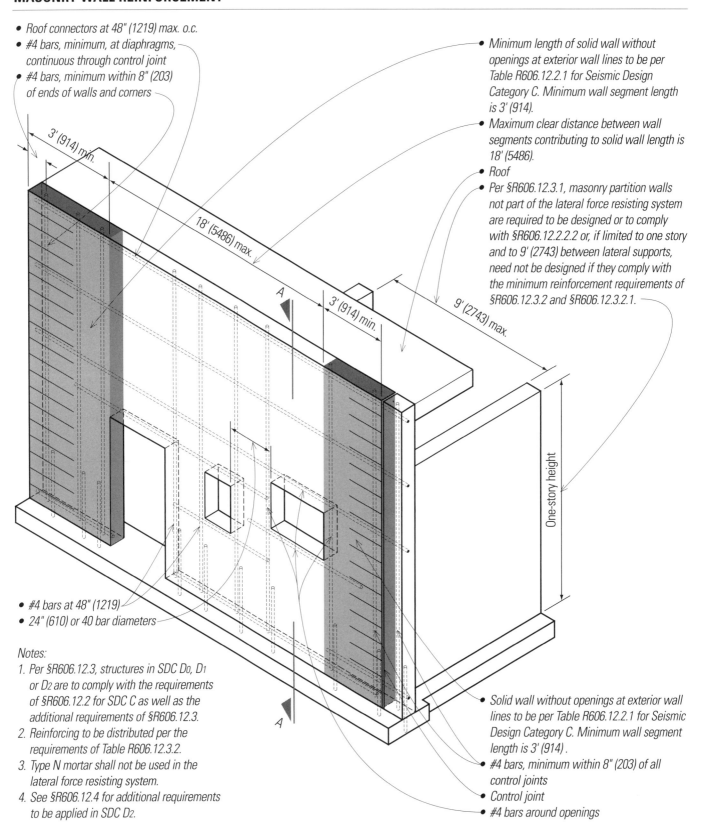

- #4 bars at 48" (1219)
- 24" (610) or 40 bar diameters

Notes:
1. Per §R606.12.3, structures in SDC D0, D1 or D2 are to comply with the requirements of §R606.12.2 for SDC C as well as the additional requirements of §R606.12.3.
2. Reinforcing to be distributed per the requirements of Table R606.12.3.2.
3. Type N mortar shall not be used in the lateral force resisting system.
4. See §R606.12.4 for additional requirements to be applied in SDC D2.

A

- Solid wall without openings at exterior wall lines to be per Table R606.12.2.1 for Seismic Design Category C. Minimum wall segment length is 3' (914).
- #4 bars, minimum within 8" (203) of all control joints
- Control joint
- #4 bars around openings

Figure R606.11(3)1 Minimum Reinforcement for Masonry Walls at Seismic Design Category D0, D1 or D2

Notes:
1. *Provide the reinforcing shown in addition to that required for SDC C per §R606.12.2*
2. *Reinforcing to be distributed per the requirements of Table R606.12.3.2*
3. *See §R606.12.4 for additional requirements to be applied in SDC D2.*

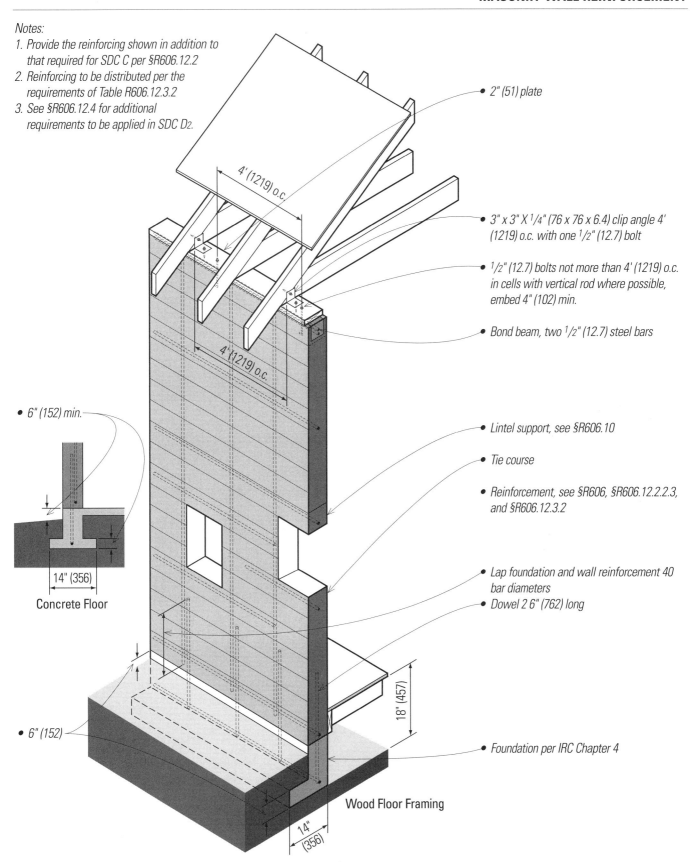

2" (51) plate

3" x 3" X 1/4" (76 x 76 x 6.4) clip angle 4' (1219) o.c. with one 1/2" (12.7) bolt

1/2" (12.7) bolts not more than 4' (1219) o.c. in cells with vertical rod where possible, embed 4" (102) min.

Bond beam, two 1/2" (12.7) steel bars

4' (1219) o.c.

4' (1219) o.c.

Lintel support, see §R606.10

Tie course

Reinforcement, see §R606, §R606.12.2.2.3, and §R606.12.3.2

6" (152) min.

Lap foundation and wall reinforcement 40 bar diameters

Dowel 2 6" (762) long

14" (356)

Concrete Floor

18" (457)

6" (152)

Foundation per IRC Chapter 4

14" (356)

Wood Floor Framing

Figure R606.11(3)2 Section AA, Wall Reinforcing at Seismic Design Category D0, D1 or D2

UNIT MASONRY

§R607 Unit Masonry

This section is a subchapter to the masonry construction requirements. Its title notwithstanding, this section addresses how grout is to be used in masonry construction. Mortar joint thicknesses and tolerances are also discussed in this section as are wall tie installation criteria.

§R608 Multiple Wythe Masonry

Masonry walls that are more than one masonry unit thick are to be constructed in accordance with §R608, which is another expansion of the general masonry requirements in §R606. The multiple walls are to be bonded or tied together so that they will react as a single unit. The walls may be tied with masonry header courses per §R608.1.1, with wall ties or with joint reinforcement per §R608.1.2 or with natural or cast stone per §R608.1.3. See the illustrations for masonry headers and wall ties.

§R609 Grouted Masonry

In grouted masonry the space between multiple wythes is solidly filled with grout (note, grout, not mortar). Both unit masonry and multiple wythe masonry may be constructed with grout in the wall cavities. Table R609.1.2 sets forth the relationships between the consistency of the grout, the grout "pour height" and the width of the grout space between wythes. Typically wider grout spaces allow higher grout pours. Conversely, where the wythe spacing is narrow, the grout pours must be shorter to allow proper consolidation of the grout by rodding or vibrating the mortar to insure a firm grout bond between the two wall wythes. Where hollow unit masonry is to have reinforcing in the cells, the walls are to conform with the requirements of §R609.4 in addition to the requirements of §R609.3. Here too, the intent of the requirements is to ensure that grouted cells are fully filled with well-consolidated grout that is fully in contact with the masonry and the reinforcing within the cells to facilitate the transfer of lateral and vertical forces so that the composite construction acts as a single unit.

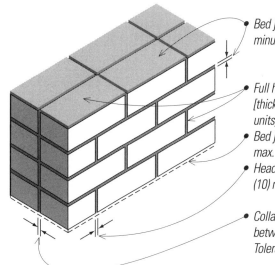

- Bed joint $3/8$" (10) thick, tolerance plus or minus $1/8$" (3)

- Full head and bed joints at solid masonry [thickness of face shell at hollow masonry units]
- Bed joint at foundation $1/4$" (7) min, $3/4$" (19) max.
- Head joint $3/8$" (10) thick tolerance plus $3/8$" (10) minus $1/4$" (7)

- Collar joint [vertical longitudinal space between wythes] dimension varies. Tolerance: plus $3/8$" (10), minus $1/4$" (7)

Figure R607.1 Mortar at Masonry Units

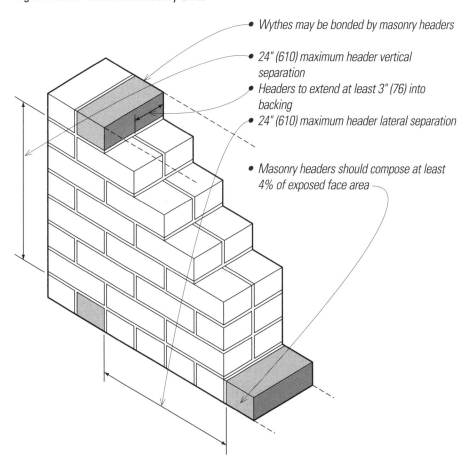

- Wythes may be bonded by masonry headers

- 24" (610) maximum header vertical separation
- Headers to extend at least 3" (76) into backing
- 24" (610) maximum header lateral separation

- Masonry headers should compose at least 4% of exposed face area

Figure R608.1.1 Multiple Wythe Masonry Bonding with Masonry Headers

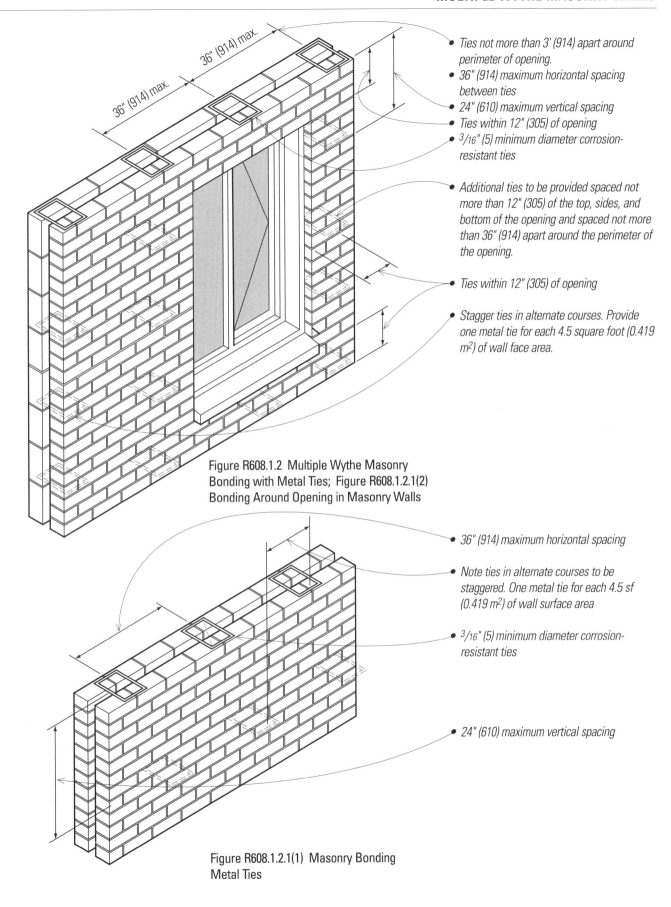

36" (914) max.

36" (914) max.

- Ties not more than 3' (914) apart around perimeter of opening.
- 36" (914) maximum horizontal spacing between ties
- 24" (610) maximum vertical spacing
- Ties within 12" (305) of opening
- ³/₁₆" (5) minimum diameter corrosion-resistant ties

- Additional ties to be provided spaced not more than 12" (305) of the top, sides, and bottom of the opening and spaced not more than 36" (914) apart around the perimeter of the opening.

- Ties within 12" (305) of opening

- Stagger ties in alternate courses. Provide one metal tie for each 4.5 square foot (0.419 m²) of wall face area.

Figure R608.1.2 Multiple Wythe Masonry Bonding with Metal Ties; Figure R608.1.2.1(2) Bonding Around Opening in Masonry Walls

- 36" (914) maximum horizontal spacing

- Note ties in alternate courses to be staggered. One metal tie for each 4.5 sf (0.419 m²) of wall surface area

- ³/₁₆" (5) minimum diameter corrosion-resistant ties

- 24" (610) maximum vertical spacing

Figure R608.1.2.1(1) Masonry Bonding Metal Ties

CONCRETE WALL CONSTRUCTION

§R611 Exterior Concrete Wall Construction

This section covers the construction requirements for all types of exterior concrete walls, whether conventionally formed walls, or those using insulating concrete forms. The chapter makes use of the provisions of the Portland Cement Association (PCA) standard PCA 100 Prescriptive Design of Exterior Concrete Walls for One- and Two-Family Dwellings. Per §R611.1.1, the provisions of this section are based on the assumption that interior walls and partitions—both load-bearing and non-load-bearing as well as floors, floor/ceiling assemblies and roofs—are constructed with "light-frame construction" as defined in Chapter 2 of the IRC. Concrete walls not specifically covered by the IRC, such as interior concrete walls, are to be constructed per ACI 318. See the illustration for the limits contained in §R611.2 regarding when the provisions of §R611 may be used.

- Maximum wind load:
  - 130 mph (58 m/s) Exposure B
  - 110 mph (49 m/s) Exposure C
  - 100 mph (45 m/s) Exposure D
- Seismic Design Category:
  - One- and two-family dwellings and townhouses in Seismic Design Category A or B
  - One- and two-family dwellings only in Seismic Design Category C
- Minimum wall thickness:
  - Flat walls 4" (102)
  - Waffle-grid systems: 6" (152) Core and web per Table R611.3
  - Screen-grid systems: 6" (152) core dimensions per Table R611.3 and Figure R611.3(3)

- Floor/ceiling dead load 10 psf (0.479 kPa) maximum
- Attic dead load 20 psf (0.958 kPa) max.
- Roof/ceiling dead load 15 psf (0.718 kPa) maximum

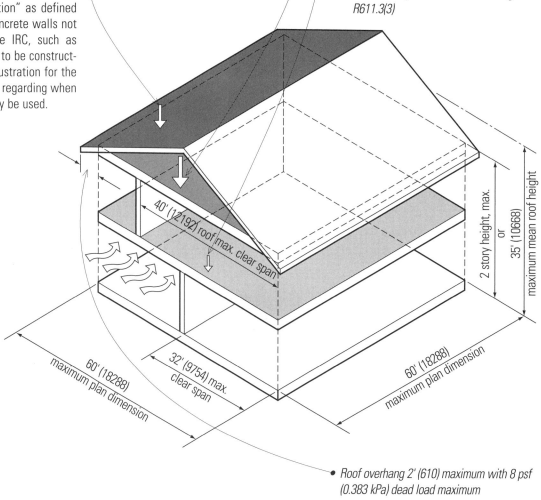

- 40' (12192) roof max. clear span
- 2 story height, max. or 35' (10668) maximum mean roof height
- 60' (18288) maximum plan dimension
- 32' (9754) max. clear span
- 60' (18288) maximum plan dimension
- Roof overhang 2' (610) maximum with 8 psf (0.383 kPa) dead load maximum

Figure R611.1 Exterior Concrete Walls Applicability Limits

§R612 Exterior Windows and Glass Doors

This section contains the performance requirements for windows and doors located in exterior walls. §R612.2, §R612.3, and §R612.4, while not calling attention to the requirements, contain provisions to prevent people, especially children, from falling out of windows. The provisions for window fall protection apply when operable windows are located more than 72" (1829) above the exterior finish grade or an exterior surface. The lowest part of the clear opening of the window is to be a minimum of 24" (610) above the finished floor of the room with some exceptions, as illustrated.

The section also contains references to standards for windows and doors as well as details for attachment of exterior windows and doors to the exterior wall. The manufacturing requirements are primarily related to how the windows and doors will perform under wind loads. The criteria, per §R611.5, are those contained in Table R301.2(2) as adjusted for height and exposure of the openings and walls per Table R301.2(3). The basic criterion for attachment is to follow the published recommendations of the window or door manufacturer for the applicable conditions in the dwelling. The attachment criteria assume that the windows or doors are attached to the main force-resisting system in the exterior walls. The section assumes that the assemblies have been tested by the manufacturer to accepted industry standards, or in accordance with other applicable standards as listed.

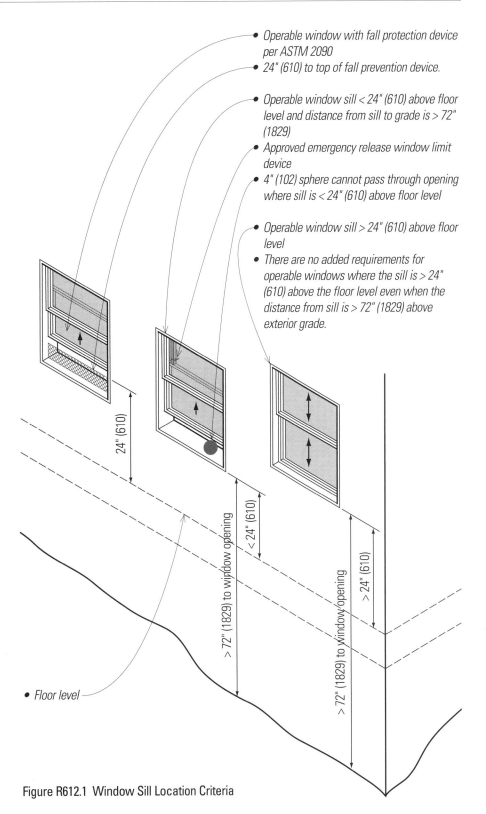

- Operable window with fall protection device per ASTM 2090
- 24" (610) to top of fall prevention device.

- Operable window sill < 24" (610) above floor level and distance from sill to grade is > 72" (1829)
- Approved emergency release window limit device
- 4" (102) sphere cannot pass through opening where sill is < 24" (610) above floor level

- Operable window sill > 24" (610) above floor level
- There are no added requirements for operable windows where the sill is > 24" (610) above the floor level even when the distance from sill is > 72" (1829) above exterior grade.

- Floor level

Figure R612.1 Window Sill Location Criteria

§R613 Structural Insulated Panel Wall Construction

Structural insulated wall panels are defined in Chapter 2 of the IRC as "A structural sandwich panel that consists of a light-weight foam plastic core securely laminated between two thin, rigid wood structural panel facings." The use of these panels is limited to the conditions listed in §R613.2 as illustrated. Materials for the foam core and the facing panels as well as provision of bottom and top plates to facilitate connections between panels are to be as specified in this section.

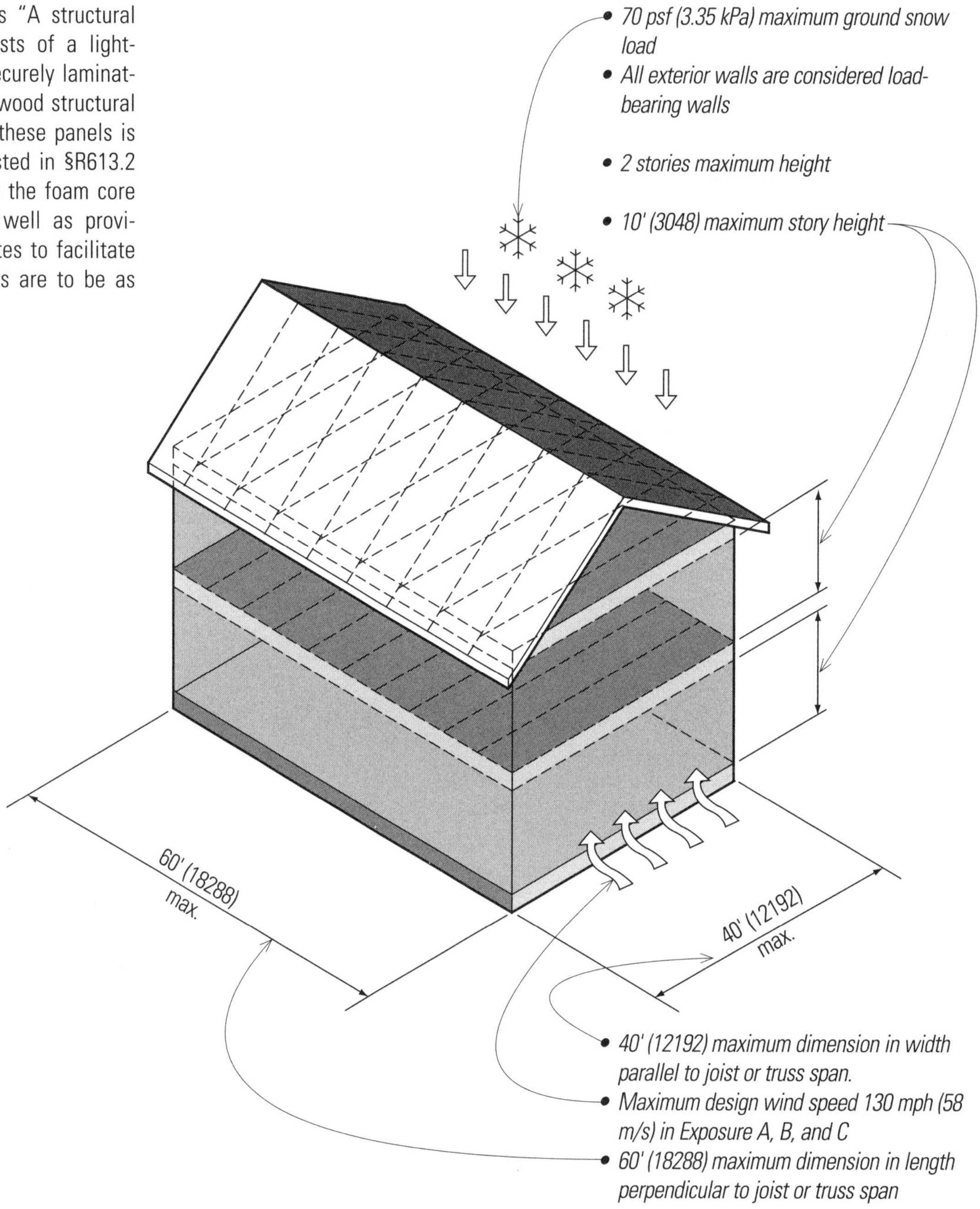

- 70 psf (3.35 kPa) maximum ground snow load
- All exterior walls are considered load-bearing walls

- 2 stories maximum height

- 10' (3048) maximum story height

- 40' (12192) maximum dimension in width parallel to joist or truss span.
- Maximum design wind speed 130 mph (58 m/s) in Exposure A, B, and C
- 60' (18288) maximum dimension in length perpendicular to joist or truss span

60' (18288) max.

40' (12192) max.

Figure R613.1 Structural Insulated Panel Wall Construction Application Units

7
Wall Covering

This chapter covers the design and construction of both interior and exterior wall coverings. It addresses that installation of materials should take into account the impact of moisture on both interior and exterior wall systems so the code requires that adequate weather protection be in place before the installation of interior wall coverings. §R701.2 also requires that exterior sheathing be dry before wall coverings are installed over the sheathing to keep from trapping moisture in the wall system. The systems covered range from interior gypsum board and plaster to exterior wood, plaster, and masonry to exterior insulation finish systems. The chapter contains numerous references to material standards for various materials. Note also that, notwithstanding the title of the chapter, there are some provisions applicable to ceilings in this chapter. Many materials are applied to interior walls and ceilings. A prime example of this is gypsum board. We will highlight those sections where ceiling requirements appear in this chapter instead of Chapter 8, where roof/ceiling assemblies are typically described.

§R702 Interior Covering

The general requirements of this section direct users to the tables relevant to plaster and gypsum board thicknesses as illustrated. Interior masonry uses similar details to those for exterior masonry called out in §R703.7, but without the requirements for an air space since the veneer is not exposed to weather. A reference is given to §R302.9, reminding users that wall and ceiling materials must meet code mandated flame spread and smoke-development criteria.

§R702.2 Interior Plaster

Plaster may be made up of either gypsum-based or cement-based materials. Plaster finishes are to be applied in a minimum of two or three coats, depending on the lathing material used to support them. Veneer plaster is a thin coat of plaster no more than 3/16" (4.76) thick, applied over a smooth substrate. It may be applied in a single coat, assuming the backing material is approved for veneer applications. For cement plaster, each coat is to be allowed to cure before the next coat of plaster can be applied. Coats are to be kept moist for at least 24 hours prior to the application of the next coat. Curing times vary for two- and three-coat cement plaster systems, with the finish coat for both systems being applied no sooner than 48 hours after application of the base coat. The intermediate (or "brown") coat for a three-coat system is to be applied no sooner than 24 hours after the first (or "scratch") coat. See the illustrations for the variations between two- and three-coat systems. Note also that there are no curing times noted for gypsum plaster in the code. The referenced standards and the material information that accompany these products should be consulted to see if there are different curing times noted in that information. The information in the standards is applicable since they are adopted by reference into the code. Note further that per the Exception to §R702.2.2.1, cement plaster installed using the criteria of ASTM C 926 may have a different curing or moistening time than the code requirements, based on criteria contained in that standard.

Support are specified for both metal and gypsum lath. The code language is somewhat confusing, since the maximum support spacing is given only for gypsum lath in terms of its thickness. For 16" (406) o.c. support spacing 3/8" (9.5) minimum thickness gypsum lath is required and for 24" (610) o.c. support spacing 1/2" (12.7)

minimum thickness gypsum lath is required. See the illustrations for examples and for a depiction of how the gypsum sheathing is to be applied in relation to the studs. We believe that the spacing recommendations should be applied to metal lath as well, based on the total thickness of the metal lath and plaster assembly as noted in Table R702.1(1). A thicker finish is required over a wider support spacing since the material assembly is spanning a greater distance between supports.

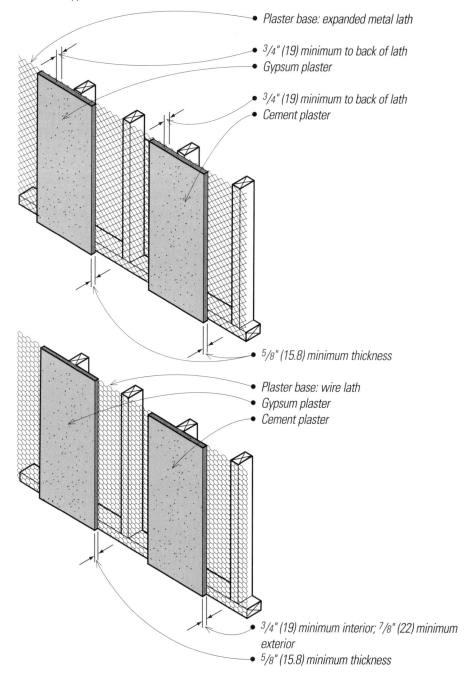

- Plaster base: expanded metal lath
- 3/4" (19) minimum to back of lath
- Gypsum plaster
- 3/4" (19) minimum to back of lath
- Cement plaster
- 5/8" (15.8) minimum thickness
- Plaster base: wire lath
- Gypsum plaster
- Cement plaster
- 3/4" (19) minimum interior; 7/8" (22) minimum exterior
- 5/8" (15.8) minimum thickness

Figure R702.1(1) Plaster Thickness

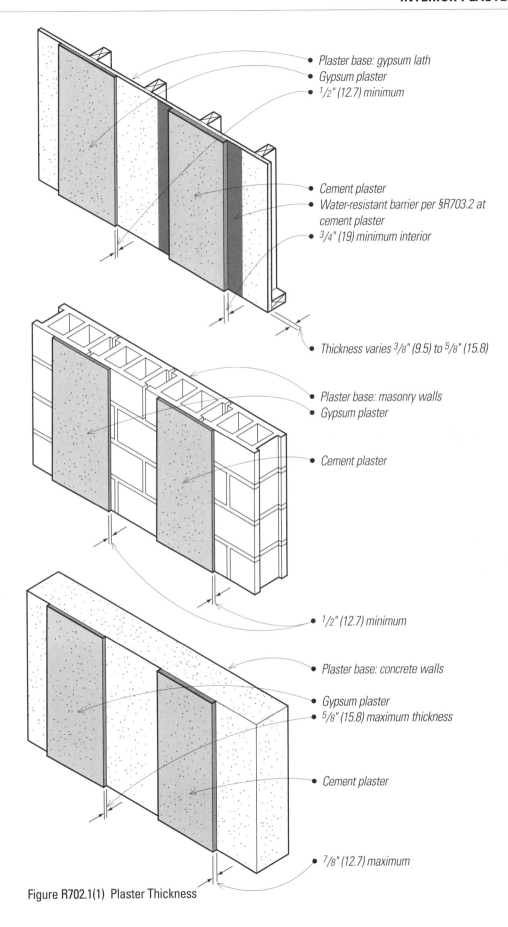

- Plaster base: gypsum lath
- Gypsum plaster
- $^1/_2$" (12.7) minimum

- Cement plaster
- Water-resistant barrier per §R703.2 at cement plaster
- $^3/_4$" (19) minimum interior

- Thickness varies $^3/_8$" (9.5) to $^5/_8$" (15.8)

- Plaster base: masonry walls
- Gypsum plaster

- Cement plaster

- $^1/_2$" (12.7) minimum

- Plaster base: concrete walls

- Gypsum plaster
- $^5/_8$" (15.8) maximum thickness

- Cement plaster

- $^7/_8$" (12.7) maximum

Figure R702.1(1) Plaster Thickness

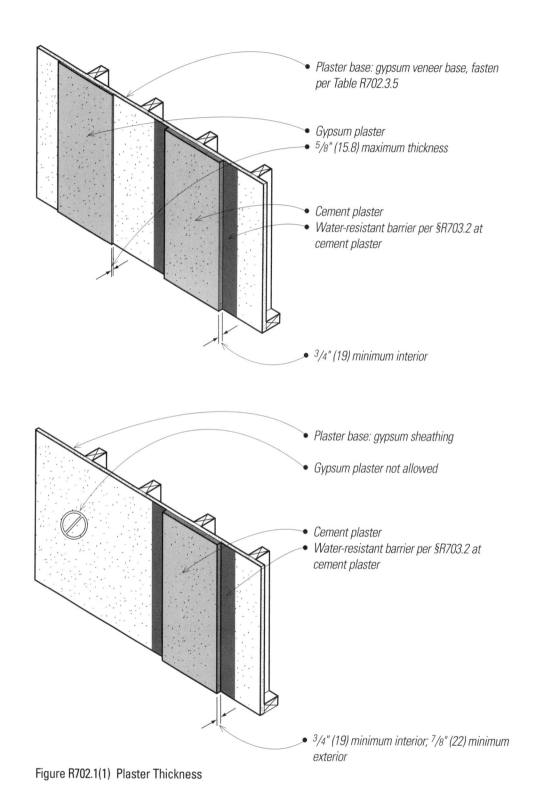

- Plaster base: gypsum veneer base, fasten per Table R702.3.5

- Gypsum plaster
- 5/8" (15.8) maximum thickness

- Cement plaster
- Water-resistant barrier per §R703.2 at cement plaster

- 3/4" (19) minimum interior

- Plaster base: gypsum sheathing

- Gypsum plaster not allowed

- Cement plaster
- Water-resistant barrier per §R703.2 at cement plaster

- 3/4" (19) minimum interior; 7/8" (22) minimum exterior

Figure R702.1(1) Plaster Thickness

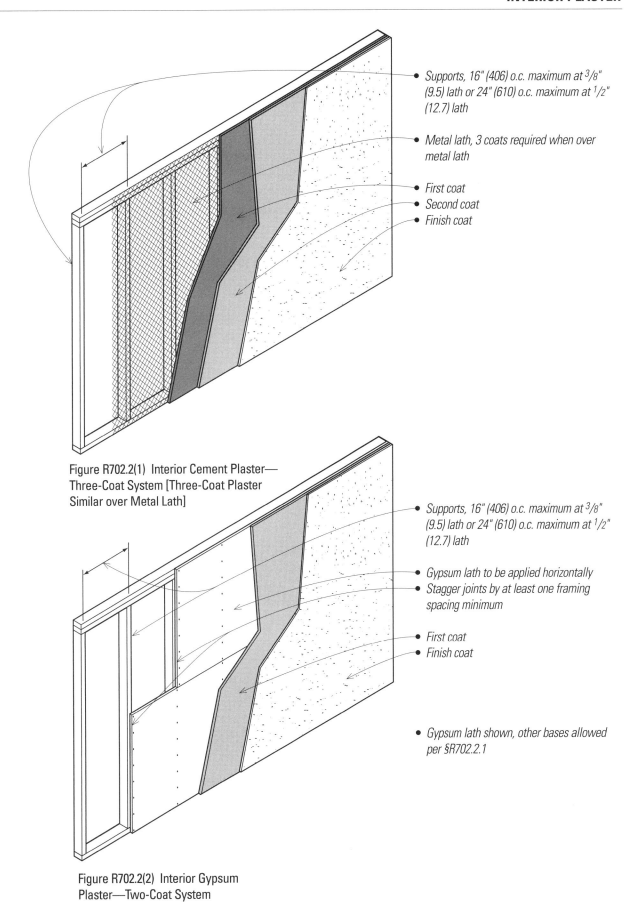

Supports, 16" (406) o.c. maximum at $^3/_8$" (9.5) lath or 24" (610) o.c. maximum at $^1/_2$" (12.7) lath

Metal lath, 3 coats required when over metal lath

First coat
Second coat
Finish coat

Figure R702.2(1) Interior Cement Plaster—Three-Coat System [Three-Coat Plaster Similar over Metal Lath]

Supports, 16" (406) o.c. maximum at $^3/_8$" (9.5) lath or 24" (610) o.c. maximum at $^1/_2$" (12.7) lath

Gypsum lath to be applied horizontally
Stagger joints by at least one framing spacing minimum

First coat
Finish coat

Gypsum lath shown, other bases allowed per §R702.2.1

Figure R702.2(2) Interior Gypsum Plaster—Two-Coat System

GYPSUM BOARD

§R702.3 Gypsum Board

Gypsum board, adhesives and finish materials are to conform to the standards adopted by reference in §R702.3.1. The installation methods are contained in the code. Table R702.3.5 specifies installation methods for gypsum board. Note that this table contains installation criteria for gypsum board at ceilings as well as for walls, notwithstanding the title of the chapter being about wall finishes. See the illustrations for depictions of wall and ceiling gypsum board installations.

- Ceiling framing
- Note: Ceiling fastening criteria occur in wall covering chapter. See Table R702.3.5. See Table footnotes for limitations on gypsum board thickness and application direction under certain conditions.

- Gypsum board to be applied at right angles or parallel to framing, typical, for perpendicular and parallel applications. Ends and edges of gypsum board shall occur at framing members except those ends and edges perpendicular to framing [gypsum board cut away to show framing]
- Wood framing at stud walls to be 2" (51) nominal width in least dimension, cold-formed steel framing to be 1¹/4" (32) in least dimension.
- Gypsum board [parallel to studs]
- Single nailing in adhesive application, double nailing without; see Figure R702.3.5(2) below
- Nailing, typical, ³/8" (9.5) minimum from edges per material standards, refer to Table R702.3.5 for fastener spacing
- Gypsum board [perpendicular to studs]
- Studs

Figure R702.3.5(1) Gypsum Wallboard Application Over Studs

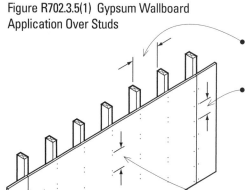

- Support spacing for walls and ceilings per Table R702.3.5

- 8" (203) maximum sidewalls; 7" (178) maximum for ceilings

- 12" (305) o.c. between nail pairs

- 2" (51) minimum, 2 ¹/2" (63.5) maximum double nail spacing
- ³/8" (9.5) minimum edge spacing

Figure R702.3.5(2) Gypsum Wallboard— Double-nailing Application [Allowed per Footnote a to Table R702.3.5 where adhesive is not used]

Gypsum Board Diaphragm Ceilings

Note that §R702.3.7 and Table R702.3.7 contain criteria for gypsum board diaphragms used as ceilings. These should perhaps more properly be in Chapter 8 since the requirements pertain to ceilings, but they are in Chapter 7. See the illustrations for installation criteria and details.

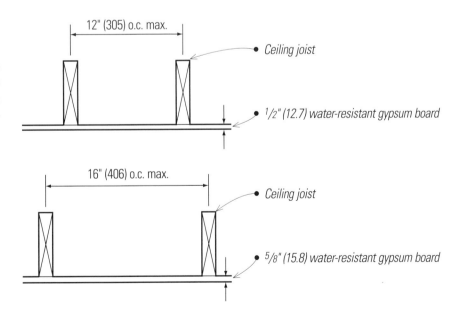

- 16" (406) joist spacing = shear value of 90 plf (134 kg/m)
- 24" (610) joist spacing = shear value of 70 plf (104 kg/m)

- $^1/_2$" (12.7) min. thickness gypsum board installed perpendicular to ceiling joists

- Top plates
- 2x6 (51 x 51) edge blocking, project 2" (51) minimum past top plates for nailing
- Shear wall
- Ceiling may not be used to resist lateral forces imposed by concrete or masonry construction

- Diaphragm proportions between shear resisting element a:b to be $1^1/_2$:1 max.
- Shear wall

Figure R702.3.7 Horizontal Gypsum Board Diaphragm Ceiling

Water-Resistant Gypsum Backing Board at Ceilings

Per §R702.3.8, water-resistant gypsum board may be used at ceilings in damp environments if the support spacing does not exceed 12" (305) for $^1/_2$" (12.7) thick water-resistant gypsum board and 16" (406) for $^5/_8$" (16) thick water-resistant gypsum board.

12" (305) o.c. max.

- Ceiling joist

- $^1/_2$" (12.7) water-resistant gypsum board

16" (406) o.c. max.

- Ceiling joist

- $^5/_8$" (15.8) water-resistant gypsum board

Water-Resistant Gypsum Backing Board

Per §R702.3.8 water-resistant gypsum backing board conforming to the ASTM standards noted in this section may be used as a base or backer for adhesive application of ceramic tile. These materials may be used at ceilings under the conditions described above for ceilings. Note, however, that water-resistant gypsum board may not be used over a Class I or II vapor retarder in a tub or shower compartment. The materials and details for these installations are contained in §R702.4 regarding ceramic tile interior finishes. These conditions are illustrated in the ceramic tile section. Cut edges of water-resistant gypsum board are to be sealed per manufacturer's instructions. Note further that §R702.3.8.1 places limitations on the use of water-resistant gypsum backing board. This material is not to be used where it will be directly exposed to water or in areas subject to continuous high humidity. We recommend that this material be used with great caution in areas where moisture will likely be regularly present, like rooms containing baths, showers, spas, laundries or swimming pools. See §R702.4.2 regarding acceptable backing materials for ceramic tiles for guidance on wall and ceiling materials in moist or damp environments, even if ceramic tile is not to be installed. Examples of tile installations on various backings are illustrated.

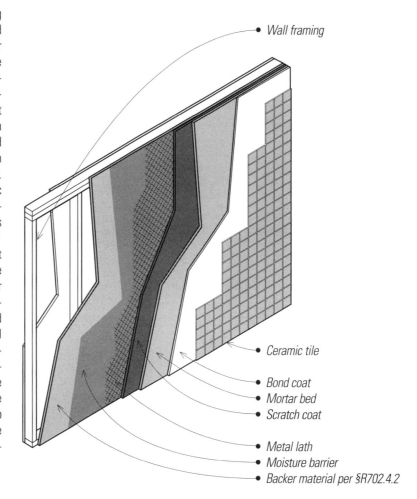

- Wall framing
- Ceramic tile
- Bond coat
- Mortar bed
- Scratch coat
- Metal lath
- Moisture barrier
- Backer material per §R702.4.2

Figure R702.4.1(1) Ceramic Tile Installation at Walls in Tub and Shower Areas

- Note: Mortar-set tile detail is shown. Tile may be thin-set, but backer material must meet the requirements of §R702.4.2 for both conditions. Water-resistant gypsum board may not be used over vapor retarders at tubs or showers per §R702.3.8.

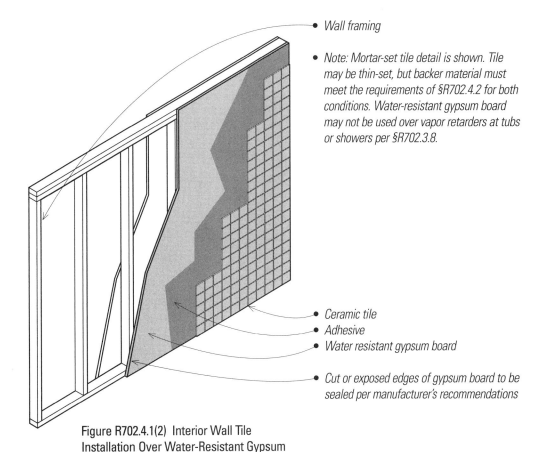

- Wall framing
- Note: Mortar-set tile detail is shown. Tile may be thin-set, but backer material must meet the requirements of §R702.4.2 for both conditions. Water-resistant gypsum board may not be used over vapor retarders at tubs or showers per §R702.3.8.
- Ceramic tile
- Adhesive
- Water resistant gypsum board
- Cut or exposed edges of gypsum board to be sealed per manufacturer's recommendations

Figure R702.4.1(2) Interior Wall Tile Installation Over Water-Resistant Gypsum Board

Other Finishes

Wood paneling and wood shakes or shingles may be installed as interior finish materials. The code requirements, as in those for interior masonry, recognize that there is no need for weather protection in these interior conditions, but there are requirements for adequate substrates to ensure secure fastening of interior finishes. Furring strips are to be 1x2 (25 x 51) or 1x3 (25 x 76) minimum size. The spacing of furring strips for shingles is determined by the exposure of the shingles, with the strips being spaced to allow having two fasteners in the top of each shingle, as illustrated.

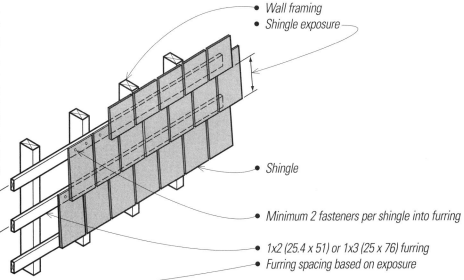

- Wall framing
- Shingle exposure
- Shingle
- Minimum 2 fasteners per shingle into furring
- 1x2 (25.4 x 51) or 1x3 (25 x 76) furring
- Furring spacing based on exposure

Figure R702.6 Interior Shingles at Wall [Over Furring]

§R703 Exterior Covering

The general requirements for this section state that exterior walls are to provide the building with a weather-resistant exterior wall envelope. This includes finish materials, such as siding as well as stone or masonry veneers along with proper flashing. The wall is to be designed and constructed to prevent the accumulation of water in the wall assembly by design and construction and by the incorporation of a water-resistant barrier into the exterior wall envelope. The provisions of this chapter address keeping water out of the supporting structure behind the exterior wall material through the use of membranes and flashing. The code also requires that the envelope provide a backup way of allowing any moisture that may get into the wall via small leaks or condensation a way to drain back out of the wall.

Siding materials are to be attached per the requirements of Table R703.4. Alternative attachment methods other than those listed in the table may be used, but they must be "approved." Approved in this context means per the definition in Chapter 2: "Acceptable to the building official." Alternate attachment methods must be appropriate to the exterior covering materials being fastened and the structure to which attachment is being made. Per §R703.4 the prescriptive attachment methods in Table R703.4 are appropriate for geographic areas where wind speeds are 110 mph (49 m/s) or less. When wind speeds exceed that velocity, the attachment of wall coverings is to be designed to resist the loads specified in Tables R301.2(2) and R301.2(3).

§R703.1 General Water- and Wind-Resistance Requirements

The exterior wall envelope, as illustrated, is to be designed to prevent the accumulation of water within the wall assembly. There is to be a water-resistive barrier incorporated into the building envelope system unless the entire wall system—including joints, penetrations and intersections between dissimilar covering materials—has been tested as an assembly to demonstrate its resistance to penetration by wind-driven rain. The use of approved envelope systems must match their performance in wind-driven rain to the anticipated site climate conditions. The separate water-resistive barrier may be omitted when paperbacked stucco lath

is used if the lath is an approved weather-resistant barrier. In addition exterior water-resistive barrier wall systems are to have appropriate condensation protection as required by §R601.3. Note that the location of the condensation barrier in the wall assembly, while typically on or near the inside face of the wall assembly, may vary based on the characteristics of the barrier material and the climate conditions of the building site.

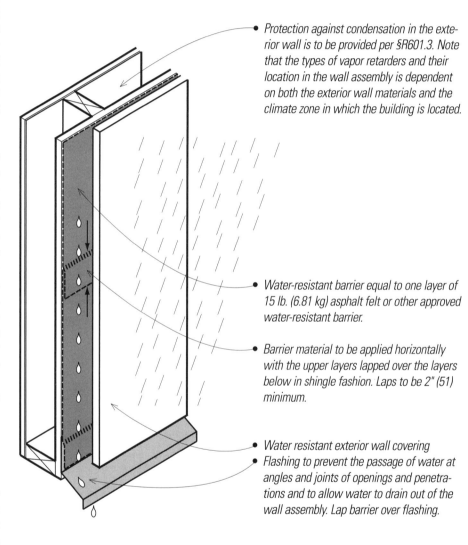

• Protection against condensation in the exterior wall is to be provided per §R601.3. Note that the types of vapor retarders and their location in the wall assembly is dependent on both the exterior wall materials and the climate zone in which the building is located.

• Water-resistant barrier equal to one layer of 15 lb. (6.81 kg) asphalt felt or other approved water-resistant barrier.

• Barrier material to be applied horizontally with the upper layers lapped over the layers below in shingle fashion. Laps to be 2" (51) minimum.

• Water resistant exterior wall covering
• Flashing to prevent the passage of water at angles and joints of openings and penetrations and to allow water to drain out of the wall assembly. Lap barrier over flashing.

Figure R703.1 Water-Resistive Requirements at Exterior Walls

§R703.3 Wood, Hardboard and Wood Structural Siding Requirements

Wood or hardboard siding, whether panels or separate members, is to be detailed for water resistance. Joints, both horizontal and vertical are to be lapped, sealed, covered, or flashed, as illustrated. Horizontal lap siding is to be installed per the manufacturer's recommendations, but if there are no such recommendations, the siding is to lap as illustrated. Corners are to be sealed, battened or flashed for water resistance.

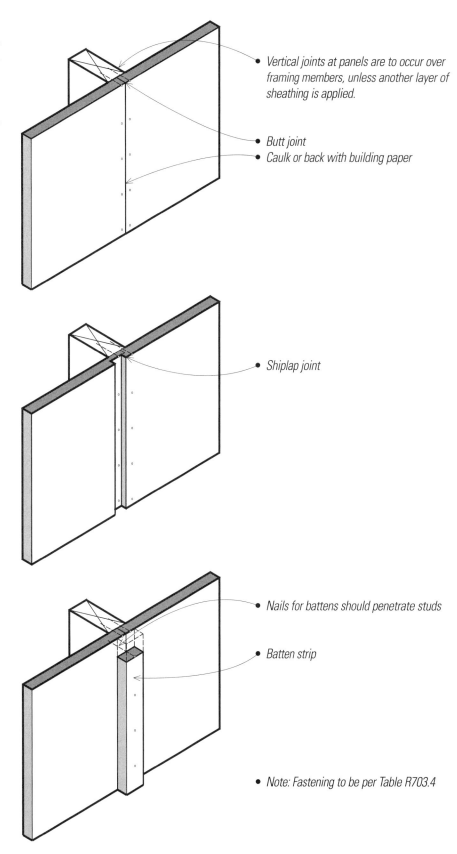

• *Vertical joints at panels are to occur over framing members, unless another layer of sheathing is applied.*

• *Butt joint*
• *Caulk or back with building paper*

• *Shiplap joint*

• *Nails for battens should penetrate studs*

• *Batten strip*

• *Note: Fastening to be per Table R703.4*

Figure R703.3.1(1) Vertical Joints at Panel Siding

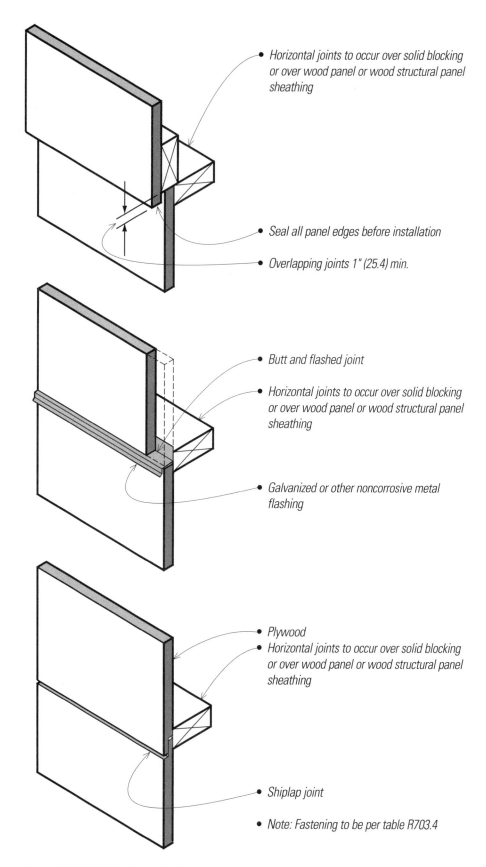

- Horizontal joints to occur over solid blocking or over wood panel or wood structural panel sheathing

- Seal all panel edges before installation

- Overlapping joints 1" (25.4) min.

- Butt and flashed joint

- Horizontal joints to occur over solid blocking or over wood panel or wood structural panel sheathing

- Galvanized or other noncorrosive metal flashing

- Plywood
- Horizontal joints to occur over solid blocking or over wood panel or wood structural panel sheathing

- Shiplap joint

- Note: Fastening to be per table R703.4

Figure R703.3.1(2) Horizontal Joints at Panel Siding

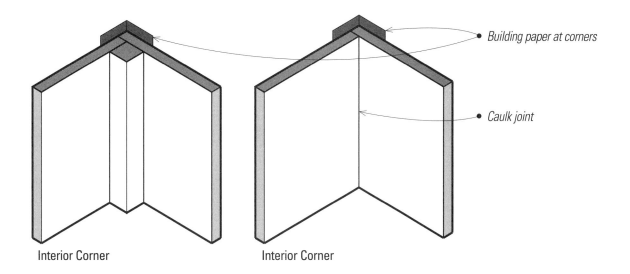

Building paper at corners

Caulk joint

Interior Corner   Interior Corner

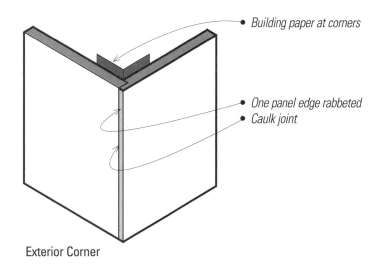

Building paper at corners

One panel edge rabbeted
Caulk joint

Exterior Corner

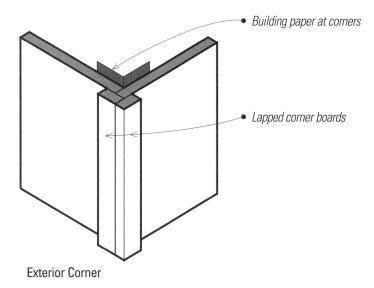

Building paper at corners

Lapped corner boards

Exterior Corner

Figure R703.3.1(3) Corners at Panel Siding

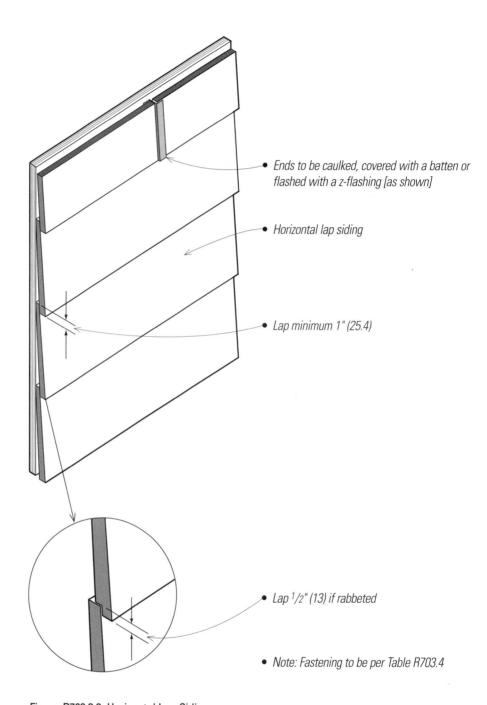

- Ends to be caulked, covered with a batten or flashed with a z-flashing [as shown]

- Horizontal lap siding

- Lap minimum 1" (25.4)

- Lap ¹/₂" (13) if rabbeted

- Note: Fastening to be per Table R703.4

Figure R703.3.2 Horizontal Lap Siding

§R703.5 Wood Shakes and Shingles

Exterior wood shakes and shingles may be applied in single or double courses. They may be fastened directly to wood sheathing since the sheathing presents a broad and uniform nailing surface. When shingles are applied over materials where nails may not be able to penetrate or where nails may not hold in the backing materials, furring strips are to be used. Exposure requirements for various conditions of shingle or shake sizes and single or double exposure are described in Table R703.5.2. The various conditions for shingle exposure, offsets for drainage, joint separations and attachments are shown in the illustration.

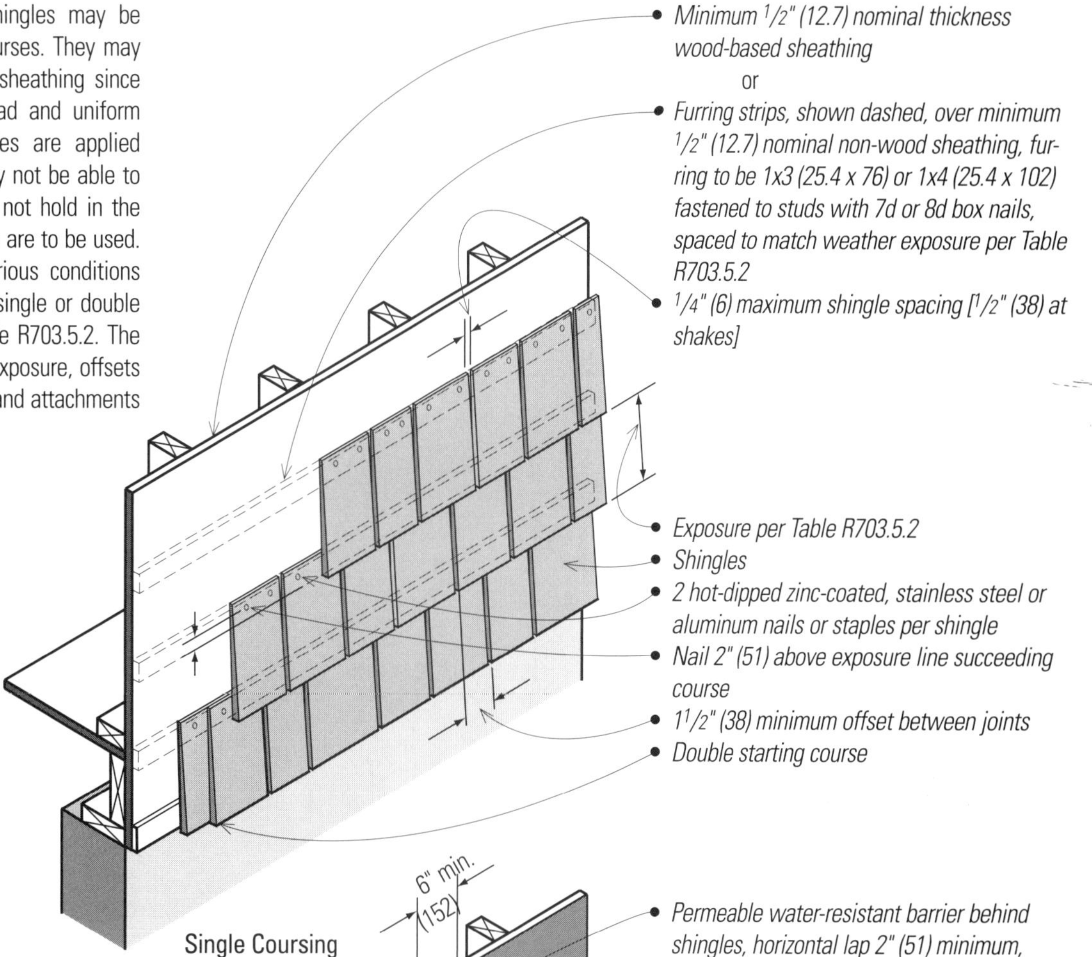

- Minimum $1/2$" (12.7) nominal thickness wood-based sheathing

  or

- Furring strips, shown dashed, over minimum $1/2$" (12.7) nominal non-wood sheathing, furring to be 1x3 (25.4 x 76) or 1x4 (25.4 x 102) fastened to studs with 7d or 8d box nails, spaced to match weather exposure per Table R703.5.2

- $1/4$" (6) maximum shingle spacing [$1/2$" (38) at shakes]

- Exposure per Table R703.5.2
- Shingles
- 2 hot-dipped zinc-coated, stainless steel or aluminum nails or staples per shingle
- Nail 2" (51) above exposure line succeeding course
- $1 1/2$" (38) minimum offset between joints
- Double starting course

Single Coursing Application

6" min. (152)

- Permeable water-resistant barrier behind shingles, horizontal lap 2" (51) minimum, vertical lap 6" (152) minimum, provide for any coursing pattern

- Exposure per Table R703.5.2

- Surface shingles
- Undercourse

- 2" (51) min. lap

- Triple starting course

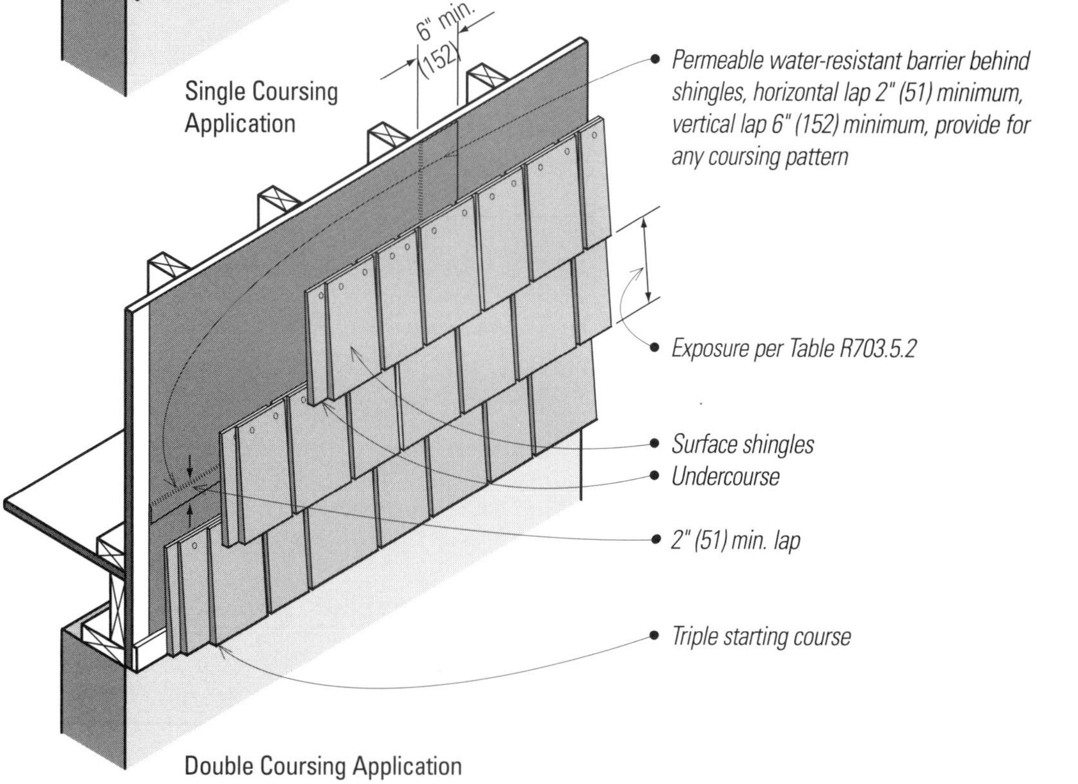

Double Coursing Application

Figure R703.5 Exterior Wood Shake and Shingle Application

§R703.6 Exterior Plaster

Exterior plaster must be portland-cement plaster. Gypsum plaster is not durable under exterior weather exposure. For the purposes of this section, when we use the word "plaster," this is assumed to refer to portland-cement plaster. The requirements for exterior plaster are essentially the same as those for interior cement plaster in §R702. The thickness of finished coats is to be per the requirements of Table R702.1(1). Proportions of plaster mixes are to be per Table R702.1(3). Weep screeds must be provided to meet the water drainage criteria of §R703.1.1 to allow any moisture trapped in the wall assembly to escape. The weep screed is to be located a minimum distance above either paved surfaces or earth to prevent moisture from splashing or wicking up into the wall cavity through the weep screed. A water-resistive barrier is required per §R703.2. Note that over wood-based sheathing, the equivalent of two layers of Grade D building paper is required unless a water-resistive barrier with resistance equal to or greater than 60 minute Grade D paper is provided along with an intervening non-water absorbing layer or a drainage space designed to allow water to escape from the wall assembly. Type I felt paper comes in four grades: A, B, C and D. Grade D is the only vapor permeable paper. Plaster is to be cured by keeping the first coat in a moist condition for at least 48 hours prior to application of the next coat. For two-coat plaster the curing time is in actuality 7 days, since the last coat may not be applied sooner than 7 days after the first coat. The second coat of a three-coat plaster system may be applied 48 hours after the first coat. The last or third coat of a three-coat system cannot be applied until at least 7 days after the second coat. See the illustrations for examples of the plaster systems and their components.

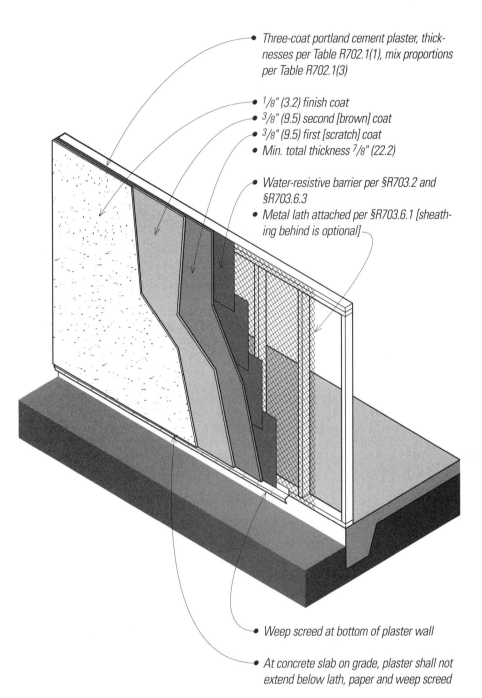

- Three-coat portland cement plaster, thicknesses per Table R702.1(1), mix proportions per Table R702.1(3)

- 1/8" (3.2) finish coat
- 3/8" (9.5) second [brown] coat
- 3/8" (9.5) first [scratch] coat
- Min. total thickness 7/8" (22.2)

- Water-resistive barrier per §R703.2 and §R703.6.3
- Metal lath attached per §R703.6.1 [sheathing behind is optional]

- Weep screed at bottom of plaster wall

- At concrete slab on grade, plaster shall not extend below lath, paper and weep screed

Figure R703.6.1 Three-Coat Cement Plaster on Metal Lath

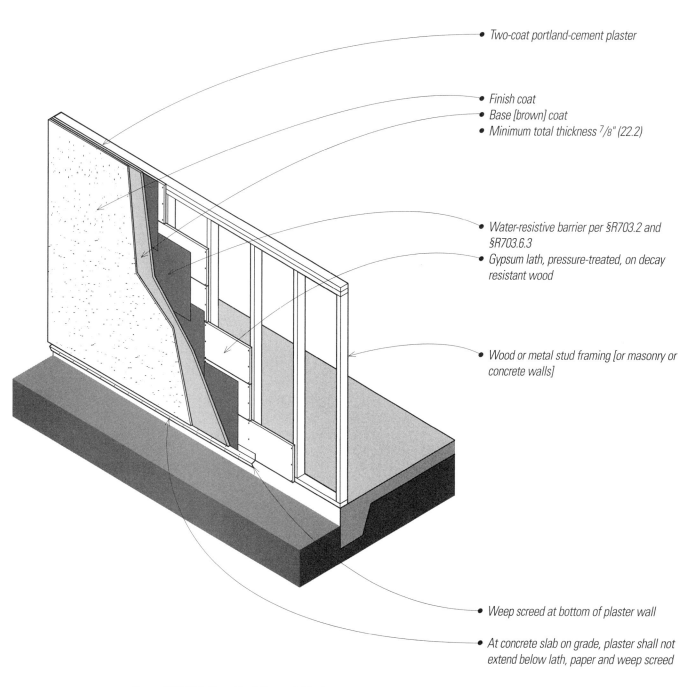

• Two-coat portland-cement plaster

• Finish coat
• Base [brown] coat
• Minimum total thickness $^7/_8$" (22.2)

• Water-resistive barrier per §R703.2 and §R703.6.3
• Gypsum lath, pressure-treated, on decay resistant wood

• Wood or metal stud framing [or masonry or concrete walls]

• Weep screed at bottom of plaster wall

• At concrete slab on grade, plaster shall not extend below lath, paper and weep screed

Figure R703.6.2 Two-Coat Cement Plaster

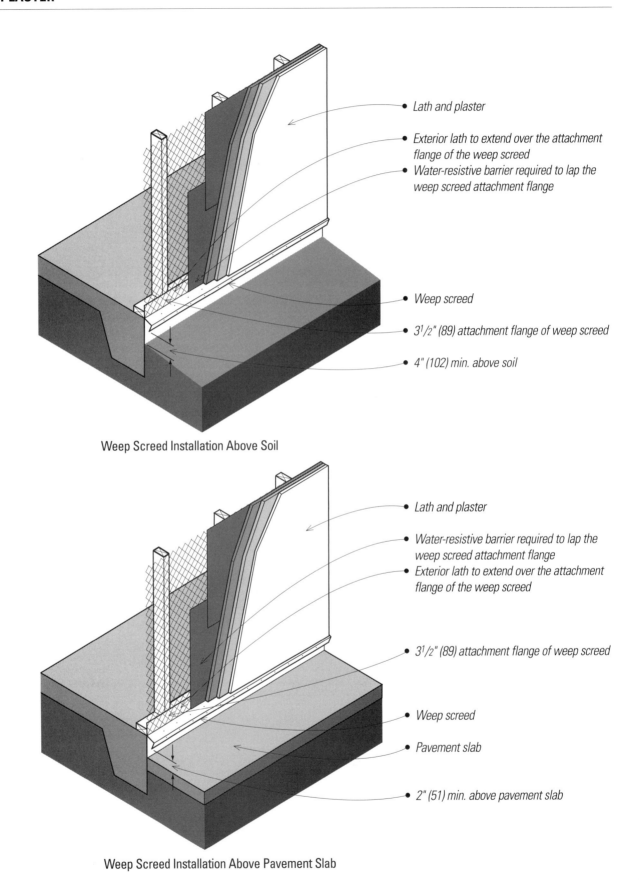

Weep Screed Installation Above Soil

- Lath and plaster
- Exterior lath to extend over the attachment flange of the weep screed
- Water-resistive barrier required to lap the weep screed attachment flange

- Weep screed
- 3¹/₂" (89) attachment flange of weep screed
- 4" (102) min. above soil

Weep Screed Installation Above Pavement Slab

- Lath and plaster
- Water-resistive barrier required to lap the weep screed attachment flange
- Exterior lath to extend over the attachment flange of the weep screed

- 3¹/₂" (89) attachment flange of weep screed

- Weep screed
- Pavement slab

- 2" (51) min. above pavement slab

Figure R703.6.2.1 Weep Screed at Exterior Cement Plaster

§R703.7 Stone and Masonry Veneer

Decorative, non-structural masonry or stone veneer is applied to the exterior of many residences. It may also occur in the interior as part of interior finishes. To be considered as veneer, the materials may not be load-bearing elements and they must not interact structurally with their backing. Veneers are typically applied like other exterior finish materials over a substrate attached to the wall framing system. §R703.7 limits such veneers to a single story when applied over a backing of wood or cold-formed steel. However, the exceptions to this requirement allow much taller veneer applications. The limitations are described further in Tables R703.7(1) for Seismic Design Categories A, B and C. The limitations in this table apply to one- and two-family dwellings and townhouses. Table R703.7(2) applies to only one- and two-family dwellings located in Seismic Design Categories D_0, D_1 and D_2. Note also that the first table applies to both wood and cold-formed steel framing while the second table, in the higher seismic design categories, applies only to wood framing. Recognizing that these materials add weight to the structure, the code limits the thickness and thus the weight of the materials. It also requires analysis of the quantity of wall bracing to resist the increased lateral loads due to the veneer. The added lateral bracing requirements are grouped in Chapter 6, with other wall construction requirements. See §R602.12 for the additional bracing requirements for stone and masonry veneer at wood framed structures. See §R603.9.5 for the wall bracing requirements at veneer for cold-formed steel construction.

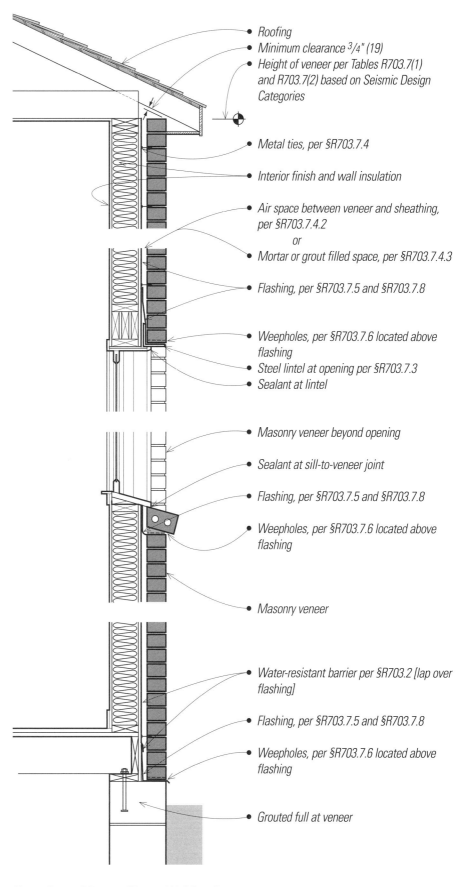

- Roofing
- Minimum clearance $^3/_4$" (19)
- Height of veneer per Tables R703.7(1) and R703.7(2) based on Seismic Design Categories
- Metal ties, per §R703.7.4
- Interior finish and wall insulation
- Air space between veneer and sheathing, per §R703.7.4.2
  or
- Mortar or grout filled space, per §R703.7.4.3
- Flashing, per §R703.7.5 and §R703.7.8
- Weepholes, per §R703.7.6 located above flashing
- Steel lintel at opening per §R703.7.3
- Sealant at lintel
- Masonry veneer beyond opening
- Sealant at sill-to-veneer joint
- Flashing, per §R703.7.5 and §R703.7.8
- Weepholes, per §R703.7.6 located above flashing
- Masonry veneer
- Water-resistant barrier per §R703.2 [lap over flashing]
- Flashing, per §R703.7.5 and §R703.7.8
- Weepholes, per §R703.7.6 located above flashing
- Grouted full at veneer

Figure R703.7 Masonry Veneer Wall Details

STONE AND MASONRY VENEER

§R703.7.1 and §R703.7.2 Interior and Exterior Veneer Support

Interior veneer may be supported on wood or cold-formed steel floors as long as they are designed to support the superimposed load of the veneer materials. Exterior veneer may be supported on wood or cold-formed steel construction instead of concrete, but only under limited conditions per §R703.7.2. The building must be located in Seismic Design Categories A, B or C. Also, the veneer must have an installed weight of less than 40 psf (195 kg/m²). Also, where there are two different support systems for veneers and some veneer is supported by concrete and some by wood or cold-formed steel construction there is to be a movement joint between the two sets of veneer since they are very likely to move differentially and crack if the movement joint is not provided. See the illustrations for typical masonry veneer wall details and details of support conditions for masonry veneer. Veneer above openings is to be supported on lintels of noncombustible construction, typically steel. Lintels over openings at masonry veneer are to be installed per the requirements of §R703.7.3. There are two alternative methods in this section for determining lintel size and allowable spans. The first method, using §R703.7.3.1, makes use of the span tables in Table R703.7.3.1, which relates lintel size and span reinforcing to the horizontal width of the opening and to the number of stories of veneer supported atop the lintel. The second method, noted in §R703.7.3.2, uses a prescriptive approach to the sizing of the lintel and limits the maximum opening width with certain detail conditions as illustrated. Masonry is to be anchored as specified in §703.7.4 as illustrated. Veneer is to have an air space between the back of the veneer and the wall sheathing behind it. This space may be filled solid with mortar or grout, but when this is done an approved water-resistive barrier or other water-resistant system must be provided over studs or sheathing since the cavity will not allow moisture to escape as easily as would the air space. Weepholes located above wall flashing lines to allow moisture to escape are to be provided as shown on the illustrated details.

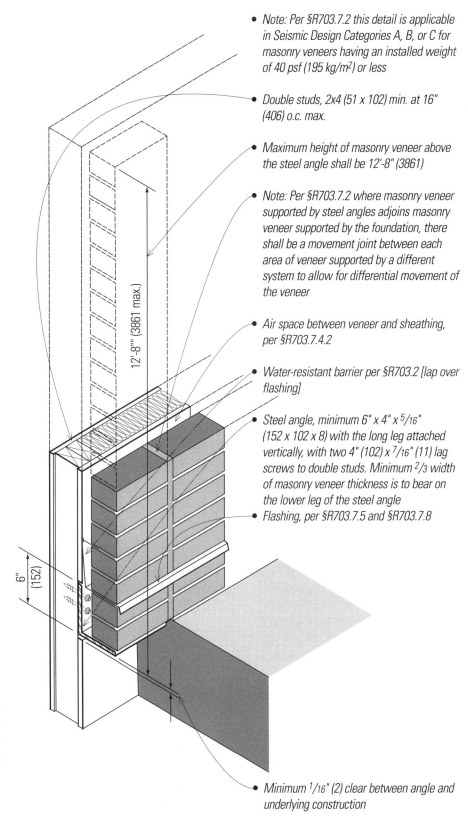

- Note: Per §R703.7.2 this detail is applicable in Seismic Design Categories A, B, or C for masonry veneers having an installed weight of 40 psf (195 kg/m²) or less

- Double studs, 2x4 (51 x 102) min. at 16" (406) o.c. max.

- Maximum height of masonry veneer above the steel angle shall be 12'-8" (3861)

- Note: Per §R703.7.2 where masonry veneer supported by steel angles adjoins masonry veneer supported by the foundation, there shall be a movement joint between each area of veneer supported by a different system to allow for differential movement of the veneer

- Air space between veneer and sheathing, per §R703.7.4.2

- Water-resistant barrier per §R703.2 [lap over flashing]

- Steel angle, minimum 6" x 4" x ⁵⁄₁₆" (152 x 102 x 8) with the long leg attached vertically, with two 4" (102) x ⁷⁄₁₆" (11) lag screws to double studs. Minimum ²⁄₃ width of masonry veneer thickness is to bear on the lower leg of the steel angle

- Flashing, per §R703.7.5 and §R703.7.8

- Minimum ¹⁄₁₆" (2) clear between angle and underlying construction

12'-8"' (3861 max.)

6" (152)

Figure R703.7.2.1 Exterior Masonry Veneer Supported by Steel Angle

- Note: Per §R703.7.2, this detail is applicable in Seismic Design Categories A, B, or C for masonry veneers having an installed weight of 40 psf (195 kg/m²) or less

- Air space between veneer and sheathing, per §R703.7.4.2

- Stud space, shown with insulation

- Sheathing

- Maximum height of masonry veneer above the steel angle shall be 12'-8" (3861)

- Masonry veneer
- Water-resistant barrier per §R703.2 [lap over flashing]
- Flashing, per §R703.7.5 and §R703.7.8

- Metal ties, per §R703.7.4

- Weepholes, per §R703.7.6 located above flashing
- Roof counterflashing over base flashing, lap under wall flashing
- Roof base flashing, extend up under counterflashing
- Roof material

- Steel angle, attach to stud with approved fasteners

- A minimum 2/3 of the masonry veneer thickness is to bear on the lower leg of the steel angle

- Minimum three 2x6 (51 x 152) wood support members attached to wall framing per §R703.7.2.2

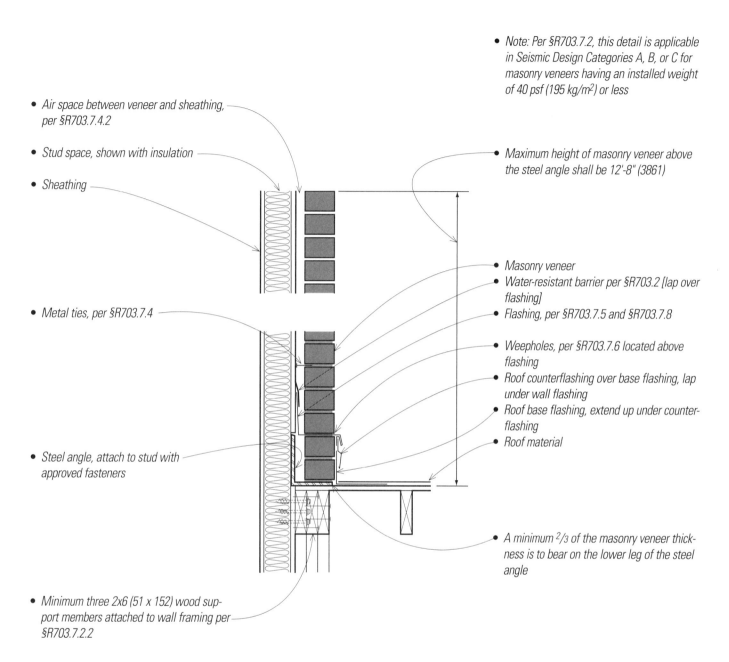

Figure R703.7.2.2 Exterior Masonry Veneer Supported by Roof Members

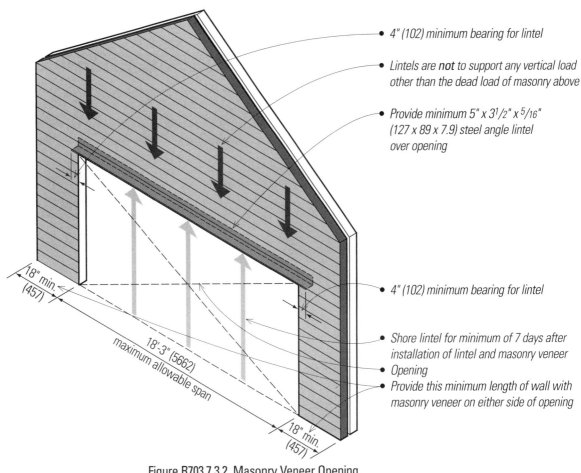

- 4" (102) minimum bearing for lintel

- Lintels are **not** to support any vertical load other than the dead load of masonry above

- Provide minimum 5" x 3$\frac{1}{2}$" x $\frac{5}{16}$" (127 x 89 x 7.9) steel angle lintel over opening

- 4" (102) minimum bearing for lintel

- Shore lintel for minimum of 7 days after installation of lintel and masonry veneer
- Opening
- Provide this minimum length of wall with masonry veneer on either side of opening

18" min. (457)

18'-3" (5662) maximum allowable span

18" min. (457)

Figure R703.7.3.2 Masonry Veneer Opening Lintel, Option Two, per §R703.7.3.2

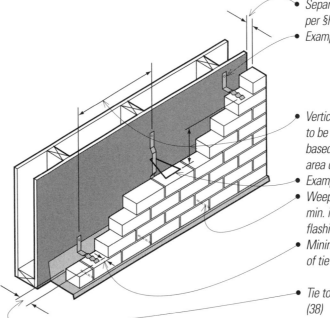

- Separation size is based on anchorage type, per §R703.7.
- Example of corrugated metal tie

- Vertical and horizontal spacing and tie sizes to be per §R703.7.4.1, in addition spacing is based on Seismic Design Category and wind area of building location
- Example of adjustable metal strand wire tie
- Weepholes at 33" (838) max. o.c.; $\frac{3}{16}$" (5) min. in diameter, located immediately above flashing
- Minimum $\frac{5}{8}$" (15.9) mortar cover from end of tie to outside face of veneer

- Tie to extend into veneer minimum of 1$\frac{1}{2}$" (38)

Figure R703.7.4 Exterior Masonry Veneer Anchorage and Weepholes

§R703.8 Flashing

Flashings to control moisture infiltration are to be provided for all exterior wall coverings. See the illustrations on pages 273–276 for examples of flashing required by this section.

§R703.9 Exterior Insulation and Finish Systems

Exterior Insulation and Finish Systems (EIFS) are systems using flexible synthetic plaster finishes over expanded plastic foam to provide an exterior envelope. These systems are typically applied as a system and are to be installed per the manufacturer's installation instructions. There are two sets of criteria for two different types of EIFS systems: those with drainage and those without. This section requires flashings to be installed in all EIFS walls per the requirements of §R703.8. It also requires EIFS to terminate at least 6" (152) above finished ground level to keep ground moisture out of the wall system. Also, trim is not to be face nailed through the EIFS surface finish. This is because these systems rely heavily on the integrity of the surface finish as part of their water resistance. See the illustrations for an example of a typical EIFS system, but be sure to obtain and use the appropriate instructions from the EIFS manufacturer you select when you use EIFS.

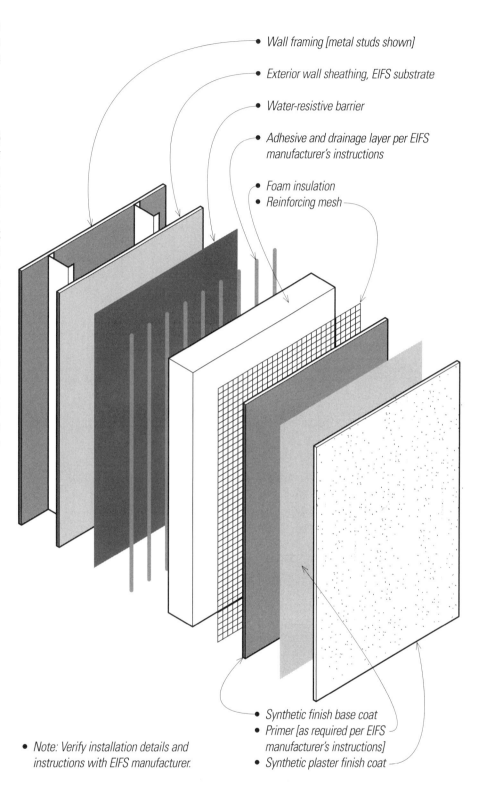

- *Wall framing [metal studs shown]*
- *Exterior wall sheathing, EIFS substrate*
- *Water-resistive barrier*
- *Adhesive and drainage layer per EIFS manufacturer's instructions*
- *Foam insulation*
- *Reinforcing mesh*
- *Synthetic finish base coat*
- *Primer [as required per EIFS manufacturer's instructions]*
- *Synthetic plaster finish coat*

- *Note: Verify installation details and instructions with EIFS manufacturer.*

Figure R703.9 Exterior Insulation and Finish System with Drainage

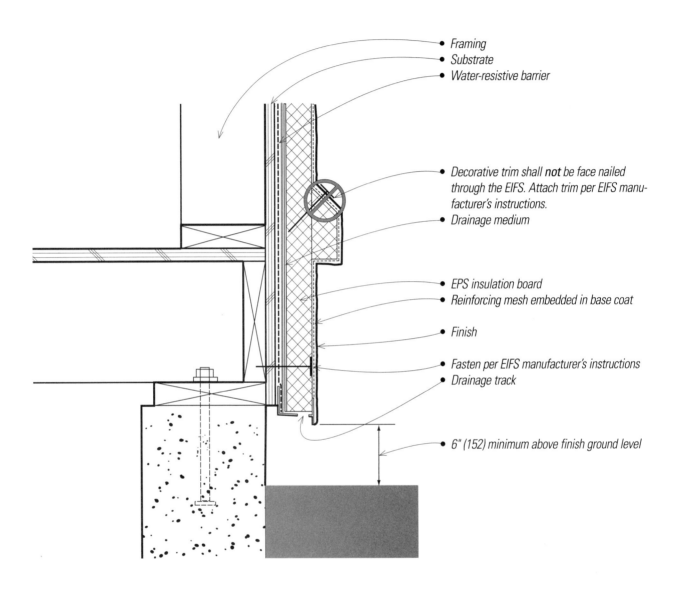

- Framing
- Substrate
- Water-resistive barrier

- Decorative trim shall **not** be face nailed through the EIFS. Attach trim per EIFS manufacturer's instructions.
- Drainage medium

- EPS insulation board
- Reinforcing mesh embedded in base coat

- Finish

- Fasten per EIFS manufacturer's instructions
- Drainage track

- 6" (152) minimum above finish ground level

Figure R703.9.4 Base Detail at EIFS with Drainage

§R703.10 Fiber Cement Siding, §R702.11 Vinyl Siding

Fiber cement materials are made into both panelized and lap siding products. These materials are applied similarly to wood materials of similar configuration. Panels may be applied with their long sides parallel or perpendicular to the wall framing members. Both vertical and horizontal joints are to be weather protected with caulking, battens, or with flashing per §R703.1. Fiber cement lap siding is to have a minimum lap of 1¹/₄" (32). If it does not have tongue and groove end joints, the joints are to be caulked, covered with an H-section joint cover, located over a strip of flashing behind the joint, or otherwise designed to comply with the water-resistance requirements of §R703.1.

Vinyl siding is to be installed per the manufacturer's installation instructions. See the illustrations for typical wall and soffit details. Where applied over foam plastic sheathing, the installation criteria and fastening details are determined by the basic wind speed and exposure categories. The wind loads are to be per the criteria of Table R301.2(2) as adjusted for height of the wall per Table R301.2(3). In wind areas where the basic wind speed exceeds 90 miles per hour (39.6 m/s) or in Exposure Categories C and D, the manufacturer's criteria for installation over solid siding are to be adjusted when installed under certain other conditions such as over foam plastic sheathing per the requirements of §R703.11.2.2. Note that where the manufacturer has an "approved" product specification showing details other than those noted in the code, they are permitted to be used if the materials are installed per the manufacturer's installation instructions.

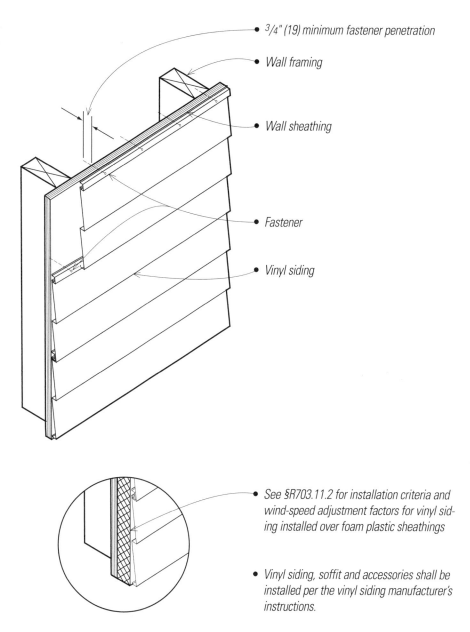

- *³/₄" (19) minimum fastener penetration*
- *Wall framing*
- *Wall sheathing*
- *Fastener*
- *Vinyl siding*

- *See §R703.11.2 for installation criteria and wind-speed adjustment factors for vinyl siding installed over foam plastic sheathings*

- *Vinyl siding, soffit and accessories shall be installed per the vinyl siding manufacturer's instructions.*

Figure R703.11.1 Vinyl Siding Installation

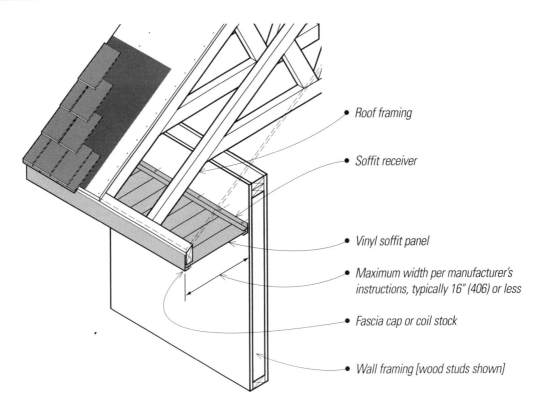

- Roof framing
- Soffit receiver
- Vinyl soffit panel
- Maximum width per manufacturer's instructions, typically 16" (406) or less
- Fascia cap or coil stock
- Wall framing [wood studs shown]

Figure R703.11.2 Vinyl Soffit Panel

§R703.12 Adhered Masonry Veneer

Adhered masonry veneer is usually a cast material that is applied directly to a substrate. The material adds weight to the wall, but the materials are typically thinner than other masonry or stone veneers and typically rely on the adhesive bond to the substrate for support rather than having each material element bear on the one piece below it along with ties to the wall behind, as do other types of veneer. Adhered masonry veneer is a manufactured product and they are to be installed per their manufacturer's installation instructions. See the illustration for an example.

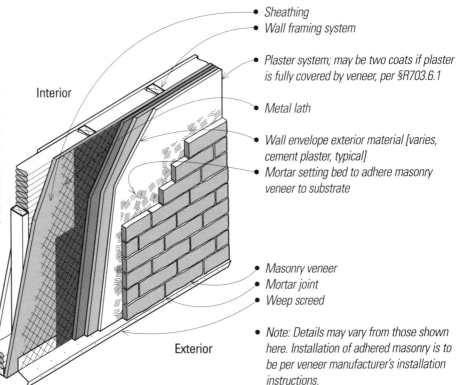

Interior

Exterior

- Sheathing
- Wall framing system
- Plaster system; may be two coats if plaster is fully covered by veneer, per §R703.6.1
- Metal lath
- Wall envelope exterior material [varies, cement plaster, typical]
- Mortar setting bed to adhere masonry veneer to substrate
- Masonry veneer
- Mortar joint
- Weep screed
- Note: Details may vary from those shown here. Installation of adhered masonry is to be per veneer manufacturer's installation instructions.

Figure R703.12 Adhered Masonry Veneer Installation

8
Roof-Ceiling Construction

This chapter covers the design and construction of spanning structures supporting roofs and ceilings. Roof coverings that are applied for weather protection at the exterior of the building are covered in Chapter 9. Also contained in this chapter are requirements for ceiling finishes, ventilation of roof spaces and provision of access to attic spaces. Note that the prescriptive provisions of roof framing contained in §R802 for wood roof framing and §R804 for cold-formed steel roof framing only apply to pitched roofs, not flat roofs. Such pitched roofs must have a roof slope of at least 3:12 (25%). Flat roofs are to be designed in the same manner as for floors since it is possible to have higher dead loads on flat roofs than on pitched roofs.

Roof and ceiling structures are to accommodate anticipated loads per §R301 and transmit them to the structure supporting the roof or ceiling materials. Loads include dead loads of the roof and roofing as well as wind, seismic and snow loads. Wind forces can create uplift conditions, and seismic and wind forces can impart lateral loads to the roof structure, all of which must be resisted. Roof and ceiling sheathing form an integral part of the horizontal system for resisting wind and seismic lateral forces.

Similar to the chapter on wall construction, this chapter is subdivided by material requirements for different construction materials. The two sets of roof framing discussed are wood framing and cold-formed steel framing systems. The language of this chapter often discusses only "roof" framing, but implicit in the requirements is the understanding that they apply to both ceiling and roof assemblies. This may be deduced from the fact that ceilings are usually formed by the bottom parts of roof framing assemblies, as well as from the title of the chapter.

§R801 General

A requirement that could be expected to be found in Chapter 9, relative to roof drainage, is contained in §R801 and illustrated below. In areas where problematic soils exist, which in this case are soils considered prone to either expansion or collapse, drainage is to be provided to control and collect roof drainage water and discharge it to the ground at least 5' (1524) away from foundation walls, or into an approved drainage system.

§R802 Wood Roof Framing
§R802.1 Identification

Members in ceilings and roofs that are load-bearing members are to grade-marked lumber similar to other framing members in floors and walls. Blocking, which is subject to lower forces than other load-bearing members, is allowed to be of lower "utility"-grade lumber. End-jointed lumber, when approved and bearing grade-markings, is considered to be interchangeable with solid-sawn members of the same wood species and lumber grade.

§R802.1.3 Fire-Retardant Treated Wood

Fire-retardant treated wood (FRTW) uses chemicals pressure impregnated in the wood to increase the fire resistance of wood products, which for ceilings and roofs includes dimensional lumber and plywood panels. FRTW materials are to be labeled as such, in addition to those labels used for lumber grading.

Because the treatment of materials to make them fire-retardant involves chemical treatments, heat, pressure and moisture, the treatment process can affect the load bearing capacities of lumber and panels. Accordingly, the code requires that FRTW materials have their strength capacities noted by their manufacturers so that designers may take into account the actual capacities of these materials relative to those of untreated materials when selecting member sizes and panel thicknesses based on design conditions. The applications of FRTW should be tested and approved for the temperatures and climate conditions anticipated at the building location.

When FRTW materials are to be used in exterior or damp conditions the code requires that these materials be identified as suitable for "Exterior" exposure. Where FRTW wood is to be used in interior locations exposed to damp

or moist conditions, those materials should also be tested and approved for installation under those conditions.

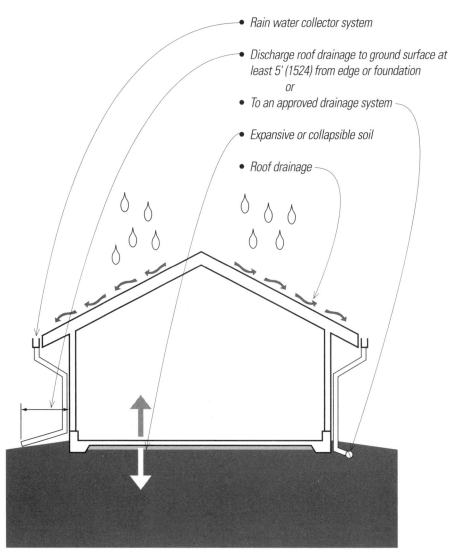

- Rain water collector system

- Discharge roof drainage to ground surface at least 5' (1524) from edge or foundation
  or
- To an approved drainage system

- Expansive or collapsible soil

- Roof drainage

Figure R801.3 Roof Drainage at Expansive or Collapsible Soil

Basic Requirements for Other Roof Framing Members

Structural glued-laminated timbers are to be manufactured and identified per specified criteria drawn from ANSI-AITC A190.1 ASTM D3737. If there is ever any doubt about the quality of materials delivered to a job site, material tags and grade stamps should always be available demonstrating compliance with the stated standards. Structural log members are also to be graded by an approved grading or inspection agency. Since logs are often used for both decorative and structural purposes and often left exposed, a certificate of inspection is acceptable in lieu of having visible grade marks on the material. This is often also the case for glu-lams, which may be left exposed as part of the architectural design. The designer should verify that a certificate of inspection will be acceptable to the AHJ for other timber members such as glu-lams or large timbers so that grade stamps need not be visible in the finished product.

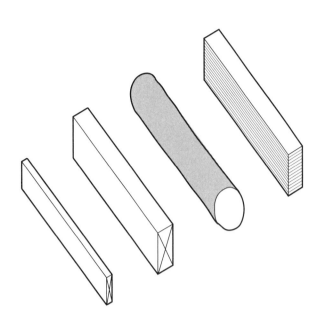

§R802.2. Design and Construction

As noted above, the prescriptive requirements and details contained in §R802 apply only to roofs with a pitch of at least 3 units vertical and 12 units horizontal (25% slope). Per §R802.3 in areas with less than a 3:12 slope, structural members that support rafters and ceiling joists are to be designed as beams. Details for connections and designs of wood roof-ceiling assemblies to wood walls are to be per this section or per the requirements of the AF & PA/NDS. Details for wood roof-ceiling assemblies at masonry walls are to be per details in Figures R606.11.(1), R606.11.(2) and R606.11.(3). Roof-ceiling assemblies, as other wood assemblies, are to be fastened per the master fastening schedule, Table R602.3(1). Note also that there are additional fastening requirements for the heel joints, where rafters and joists come together, contained in Table R802.5.1(9) as illustrated.

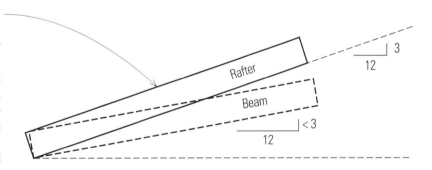

§R802.3 Framing Details

For the purposes of this discussion we have treated rafter and joists according to their generally accepted definitions and as we believe they are intended to be used in the IRC. See the illustration for a description of terms. Thus "rafters" are considered to be the sloping members of a roof framing system and may also be the ceiling framing for sloped ceilings where the rafters are exposed to the room below. "Joists" are considered to be the horizontal members of the roof framing system, which also form the ceiling framing in a triangular roof framing system.

Where rafters come together at the peak of the roof, they are to be framed to a ridge board at the intersection or have a gusset plate provided per the illustrations. Roof valleys and hips are to have valley or hip rafters at least 2" (51) nominal thickness at the intersection of roof rafters. Hip and valley rafters are to be supported at their ridge by a brace to a bearing partition or be otherwise designed to carry and distribute their specific load at the ridge. See the illustration for hip and valley conditions.

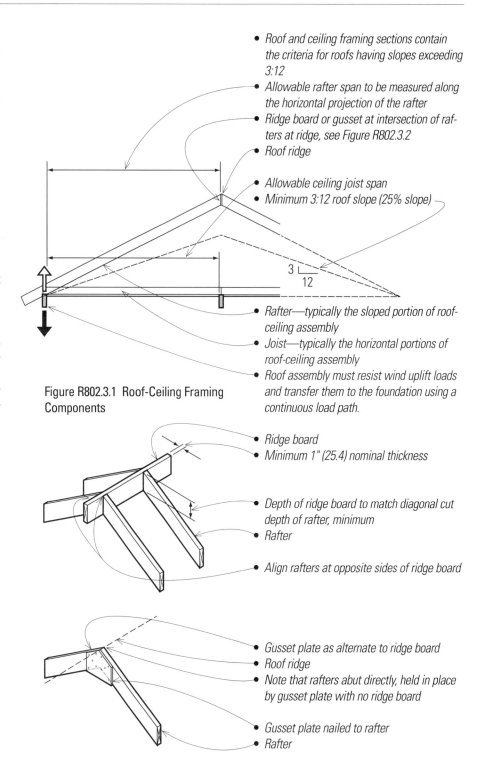

- Roof and ceiling framing sections contain the criteria for roofs having slopes exceeding 3:12
- Allowable rafter span to be measured along the horizontal projection of the rafter
- Ridge board or gusset at intersection of rafters at ridge, see Figure R802.3.2
- Roof ridge

- Allowable ceiling joist span
- Minimum 3:12 roof slope (25% slope)

- Rafter—typically the sloped portion of roof-ceiling assembly
- Joist—typically the horizontal portions of roof-ceiling assembly
- Roof assembly must resist wind uplift loads and transfer them to the foundation using a continuous load path.

Figure R802.3.1 Roof-Ceiling Framing Components

- Ridge board
- Minimum 1" (25.4) nominal thickness

- Depth of ridge board to match diagonal cut depth of rafter, minimum
- Rafter

- Align rafters at opposite sides of ridge board

- Gusset plate as alternate to ridge board
- Roof ridge
- Note that rafters abut directly, held in place by gusset plate with no ridge board

- Gusset plate nailed to rafter
- Rafter

Figure R802.3.2 Roof Ridge Connection Details

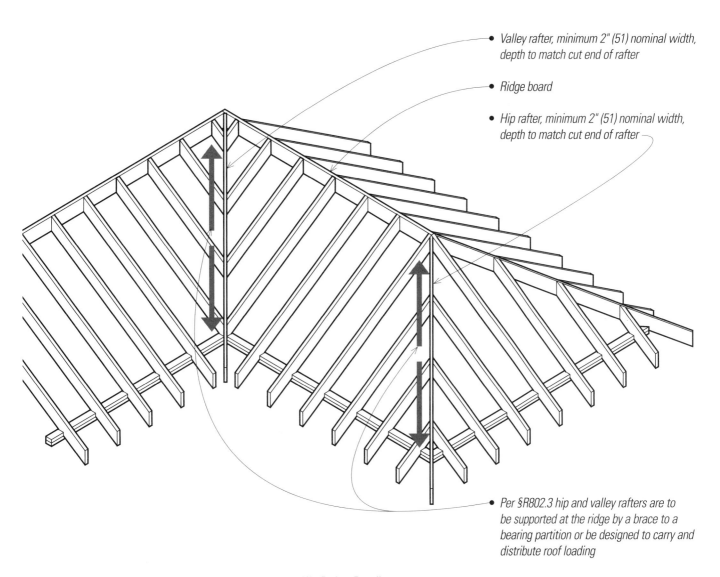

Valley rafter, minimum 2" (51) nominal width, depth to match cut end of rafter

Ridge board

Hip rafter, minimum 2" (51) nominal width, depth to match cut end of rafter

Per §R802.3 hip and valley rafters are to be supported at the ridge by a brace to a bearing partition or be designed to carry and distribute roof loading

Figure R802.3.3 Valley and Hip Rafter Details

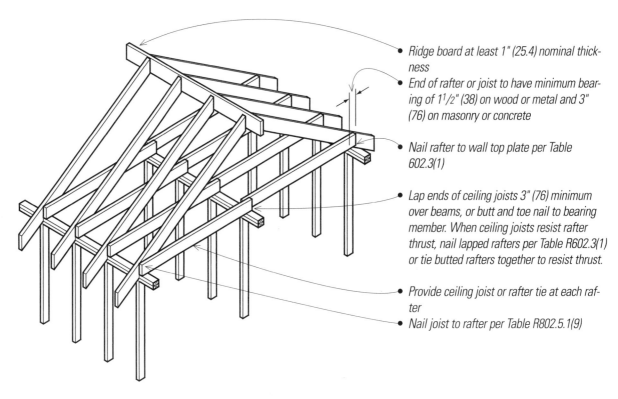

- *Ridge board at least 1" (25.4) nominal thickness*
- *End of rafter or joist to have minimum bearing of 1¹/₂" (38) on wood or metal and 3" (76) on masonry or concrete*

- *Nail rafter to wall top plate per Table 602.3(1)*

- *Lap ends of ceiling joists 3" (76) minimum over beams, or butt and toe nail to bearing member. When ceiling joists resist rafter thrust, nail lapped rafters per Table R602.3(1) or tie butted rafters together to resist thrust.*

- *Provide ceiling joist or rafter tie at each rafter*
- *Nail joist to rafter per Table R802.5.1(9)*

Figure R802.3.4 Ceiling and Rafter Connections and Details; Overlap Joist

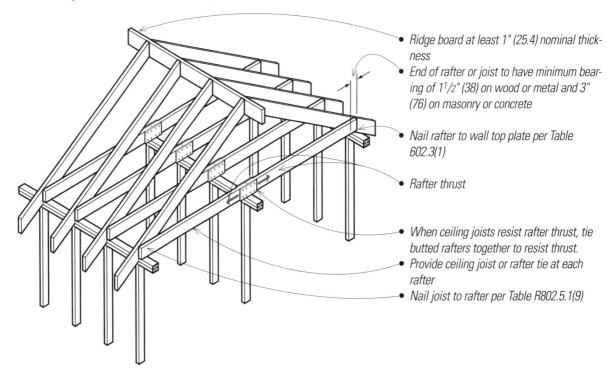

- *Ridge board at least 1" (25.4) nominal thickness*
- *End of rafter or joist to have minimum bearing of 1¹/₂" (38) on wood or metal and 3" (76) on masonry or concrete*

- *Nail rafter to wall top plate per Table 602.3(1)*

- *Rafter thrust*

- *When ceiling joists resist rafter thrust, tie butted rafters together to resist thrust.*
- *Provide ceiling joist or rafter tie at each rafter*
- *Nail joist to rafter per Table R802.5.1(9)*

Figure R802.3.4 Ceiling and Rafter Connections and Details; Butted Ceiling Joist

§R802.3 Framing Details

The prescriptive roof-ceiling framing requirements are based on the assumption that joists or rafter ties are used to resist the outward thrust imposed by gravity loads on sloped roof rafters resting on walls below them. Where ceiling framing is not parallel to the roof rafters, then additional joists or rafter ties are required to resist the horizontal forces on the rafters. Approved connectors may be used to fasten rafters to walls where they provide equivalent lateral force resistance to the horizontal joists or rafter ties. In addition, collar ties are to be installed at the upper portions of roof rafters to resist wind uplift forces on the roof ridge. These collar ties are to be located in the upper third of the attic space and are to be spaced at 4' (1219) o.c. maximum. See the illustrations for typical rafter and joist details.

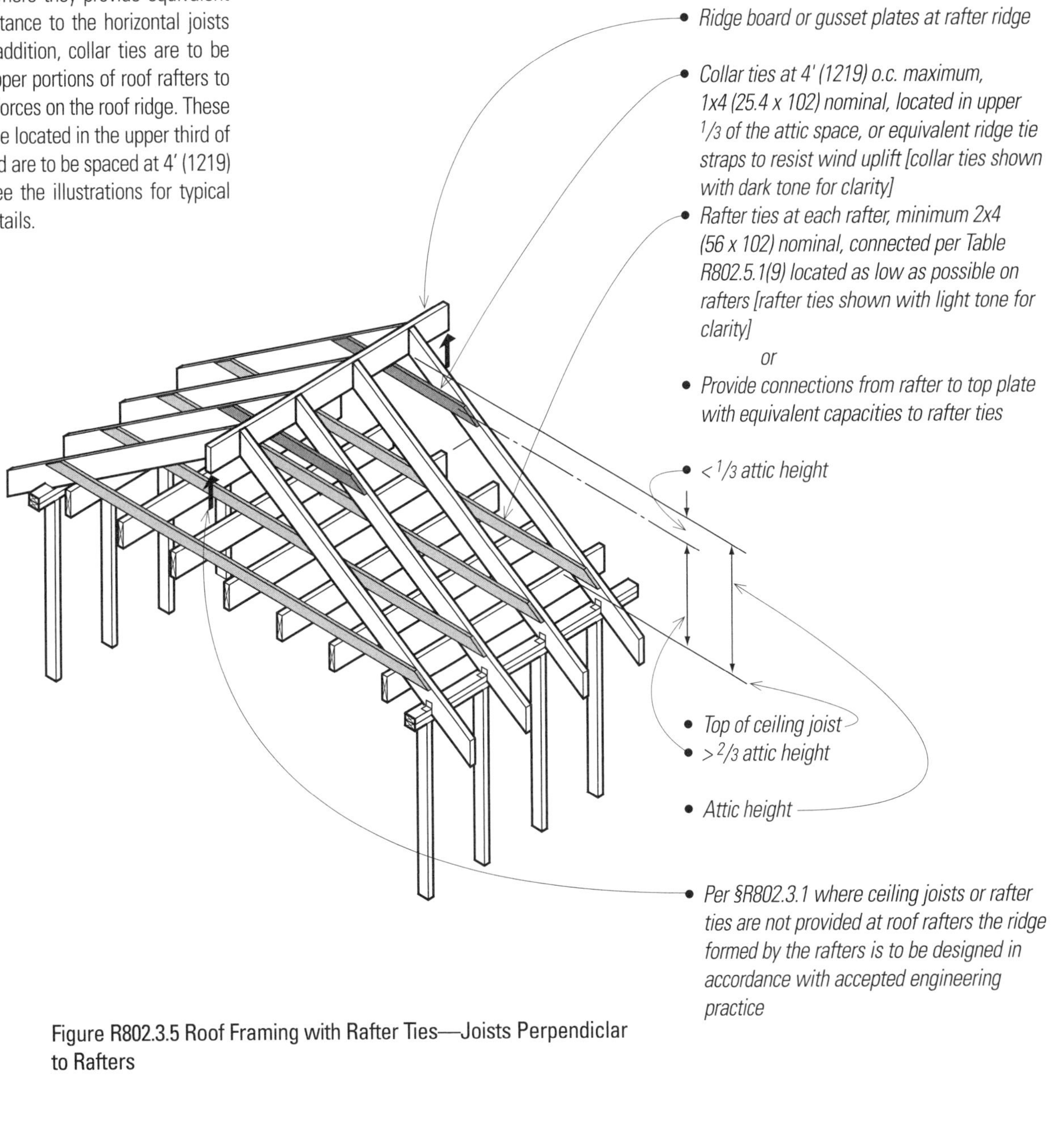

- Ridge board or gusset plates at rafter ridge

- Collar ties at 4' (1219) o.c. maximum, 1x4 (25.4 x 102) nominal, located in upper $1/3$ of the attic space, or equivalent ridge tie straps to resist wind uplift [collar ties shown with dark tone for clarity]

- Rafter ties at each rafter, minimum 2x4 (56 x 102) nominal, connected per Table R802.5.1(9) located as low as possible on rafters [rafter ties shown with light tone for clarity]

  or

- Provide connections from rafter to top plate with equivalent capacities to rafter ties

- $< 1/3$ attic height

- Top of ceiling joist
- $> 2/3$ attic height

- Attic height

- Per §R802.3.1 where ceiling joists or rafter ties are not provided at roof rafters the ridge formed by the rafters is to be designed in accordance with accepted engineering practice

Figure R802.3.5 Roof Framing with Rafter Ties—Joists Perpendiclar to Rafters

§R802.4 and R802.5, Rafter and Joist Span Tables

As noted earlier, the ceiling joist and roof rafter span tables are based on the roof meeting the minimum slope criteria of 3:12. Also, the configuration of the attic area assumes some form of ties between joists and the rafter, or alternatively, installation of rafter ties, or use of framing connectors to provide equivalent lateral force and uplift force resistance capacities in the roof-ceiling assembly. Ceiling joists are sized for two conditions, as illustrated. Both are based on the assumption that the attic area created in the roof-ceiling assembly is uninhabitable space. The distinction between Tables R802.4(1) and (2) is that Table R802.4(1) assumes **no** storage takes place and thus uses a 10 psf (478 Pa) live load for the joists. Table R802.4(2) assumes some **limited** storage will take place in the attic, which we believe should be the basic assumption about how most residential attics will be used. These span tables assume a live load of 20 psf (958 Pa) and thus the joist sizes are larger for a given span and joist, based on the increased live load above the first table. We recommend that Table R802.4(2) typically be used for design of attic joists when there is any likelihood that the attic space will be used for storage.

The assumptions for rafters are that they typically do not have ceiling materials attached to them so that usually their deflection criteria would be $L/\triangle = 180$. In cathedral ceilings, where there are no ceiling joists and the ceiling materials are attached directly to the underside of the roof rafters, the span tables for $L/\triangle = 240$ should be used. This may require deeper rafters for a given span to meet the more stringent deflection limits for such ceilings. The code also assumes that there will be support at each end of rafters that are spanning by themselves with no other lateral-force restraints.

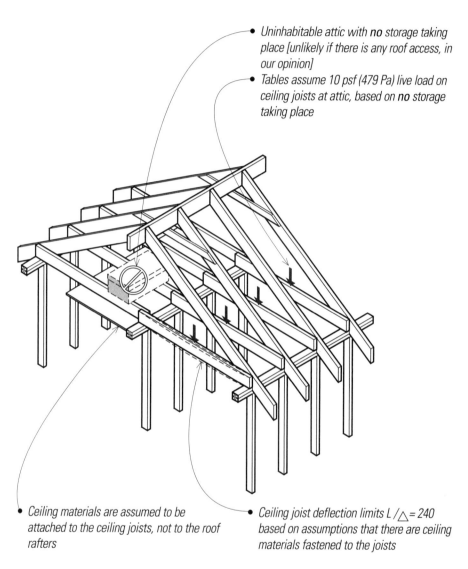

- *Uninhabitable attic with **no** storage taking place [unlikely if there is any roof access, in our opinion]*
- *Tables assume 10 psf (479 Pa) live load on ceiling joists at attic, based on **no** storage taking place*

- *Ceiling materials are assumed to be attached to the ceiling joists, not to the roof rafters*

- *Ceiling joist deflection limits $L/\triangle = 240$ based on assumptions that there are ceiling materials fastened to the joists*

Figure R802.4.1 Joist Span Criteria—Ceiling Not Attached to Rafters, 10 PSF (479 Pa) Live Loads, No Attic Storage [Table R802.4(1)]

The rafter span tables R802.5.1(1) through (8) are subdivided into broad categories:

Conditions	Ceiling Not Attached to Rafters	Ceiling Attached to Rafters
Roof Live Load 20 psf (958 Pa) Tables R802.5.1(1)–(2)	Deflection L $/\triangle$ = 180	Deflection L $/\triangle$ = 240
Ground Snow Loads 30 psf (1437 Pa) through 70 psf (3,353 Pa) Tables R802.5.1(3)–(8)	Deflection L $/\triangle$ = 180	Deflection L $/\triangle$ = 240

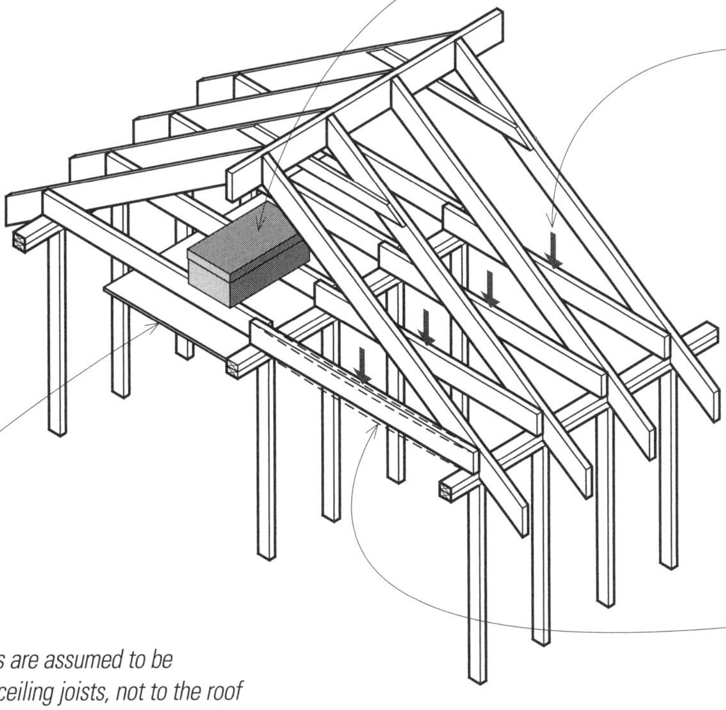

- *Uninhabitable attic with **limited** storage taking place [most likely use scenario, and best design assumption, in our opinion]*
- *Tables assume 20 psf (958 Pa) live load on ceiling joists at attic, based on assumption of some matrials stored atop the joists*

- *Ceiling materials are assumed to be attached to the ceiling joists, not to the roof rafters*

- *Ceiling joist deflection limits L $/\triangle$ = 240 based on assumptions that there are ceiling materials fastened to the joists*

Figure R802.4.2 Joist Span Criteria—Ceiling Not Attached to Rafters, 20 PSF (958)Pa) Live Loads, Limited Attic Storage [Table R802.4(2)]

§R802.5.1 Purlins

When purlins are installed perpendicular to the roof rafter spans they cut down the rafter spans. The installation of purlins is to be as illustrated. The details assume that the purlins are braced back to bearing partitions to provide a stable roof framing assembly.

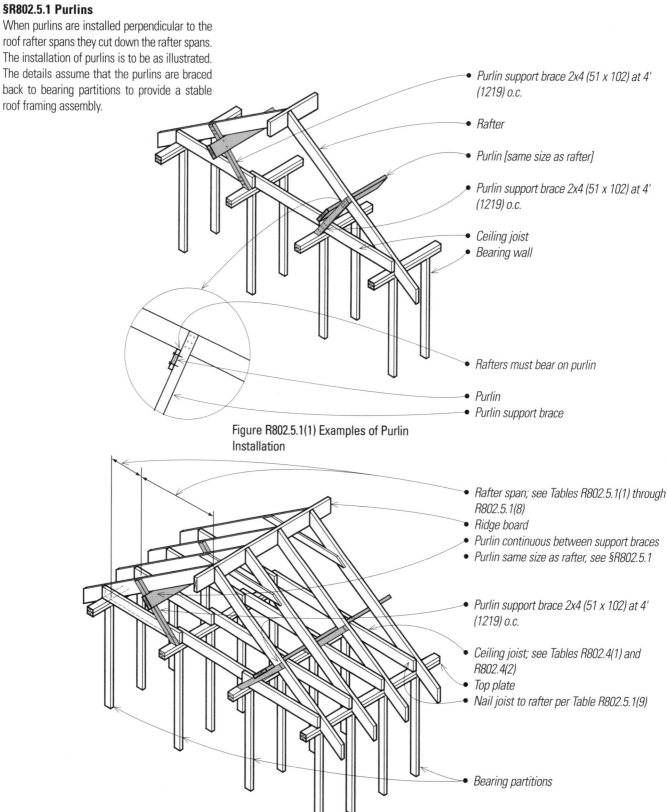

Purlin support brace 2x4 (51 x 102) at 4' (1219) o.c.

Rafter

Purlin [same size as rafter]

Purlin support brace 2x4 (51 x 102) at 4' (1219) o.c.

Ceiling joist

Bearing wall

Rafters must bear on purlin

Purlin

Purlin support brace

Figure R802.5.1(1) Examples of Purlin Installation

Rafter span; see Tables R802.5.1(1) through R802.5.1(8)

Ridge board

Purlin continuous between support braces

Purlin same size as rafter, see §R802.5.1

Purlin support brace 2x4 (51 x 102) at 4' (1219) o.c.

Ceiling joist; see Tables R802.4(1) and R802.4(2)

Top plate

Nail joist to rafter per Table R802.5.1(9)

Bearing partitions

Figure R802.5.1(2) Purlins at Roof Rafters

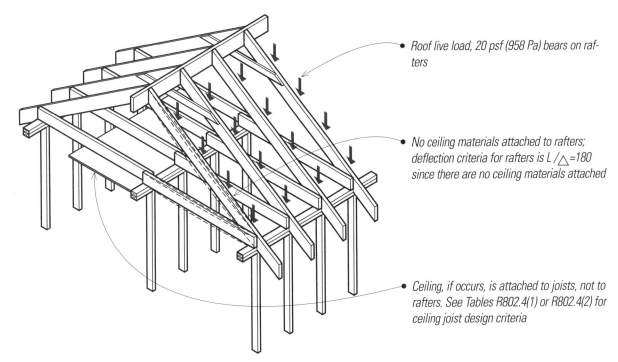

Roof live load, 20 psf (958 Pa) bears on rafters

No ceiling materials attached to rafters; deflection criteria for rafters is $L/\triangle$ =180 since there are no ceiling materials attached

Ceiling, if occurs, is attached to joists, not to rafters. See Tables R802.4(1) or R802.4(2) for ceiling joist design criteria

Figure R802.5.2 Rafter Span Criteria—Ceiling Not Attached to Rafters, 20 PSF (958)Pa) Roof Live Loads, No Snow Loads [Table R802.5.1(1)]

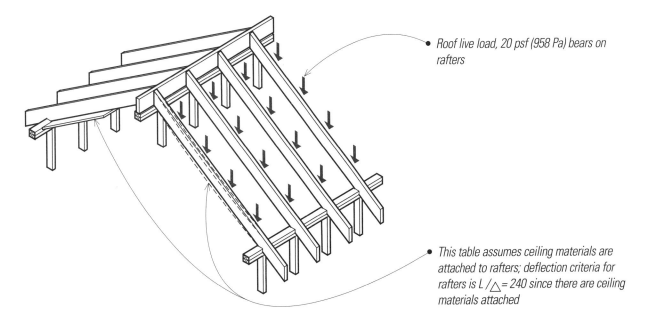

Roof live load, 20 psf (958 Pa) bears on rafters

This table assumes ceiling materials are attached to rafters; deflection criteria for rafters is $L/\triangle$ = 240 since there are ceiling materials attached

Figure R802.5.3 Rafter Span Criteria—Ceiling Attached to Rafters, 20 PSF (958 Pa) Roof Live Loads, No Snow Loads [Table R802.5.1(2)]

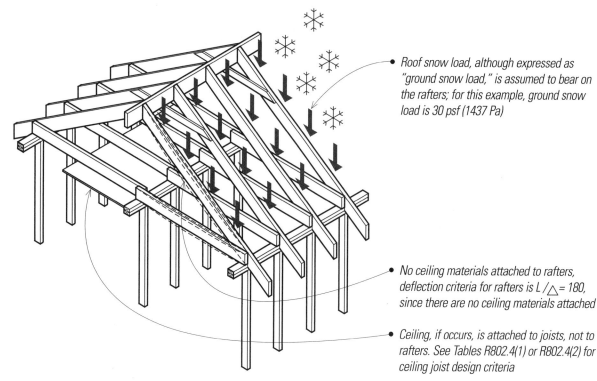

Roof snow load, although expressed as "ground snow load," is assumed to bear on the rafters; for this example, ground snow load is 30 psf (1437 Pa)

No ceiling materials attached to rafters, deflection criteria for rafters is $L/\triangle = 180$, since there are no ceiling materials attached

Ceiling, if occurs, is attached to joists, not to rafters. See Tables R802.4(1) or R802.4(2) for ceiling joist design criteria

Figure R802.5.4 Rafter Span Criteria—Ceiling Not Attached to Rafters, 30 PSF (1437 Pa) Ground Snow Loads [Table R802.5.1(3)]

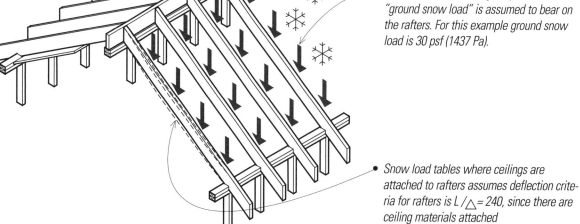

Roof snow load, although expressed as "ground snow load" is assumed to bear on the rafters. For this example ground snow load is 30 psf (1437 Pa).

Snow load tables where ceilings are attached to rafters assumes deflection criteria for rafters is $L/\triangle = 240$, since there are ceiling materials attached

Figure R802.5.5 Rafter Span Criteria—Ceiling Attached to Rafters, 30 PSF (1437 Pa) Snow Loads [Table R802.5.1(5)]

§R802.7 Cutting and Notching

This section sets limits on the cutting or notching of structural roof and ceiling framing elements to insure that they have adequate depths of materials to transmit anticipated dead and live loads to the load path for the roof-ceiling assembly. The requirements are broken into two sections. The first addresses cutting and notching of sawn lumber as illustrated. These requirements are similar to the requirements for drilling and notching of floor joists described in §R502.8 and Figure R502.8.

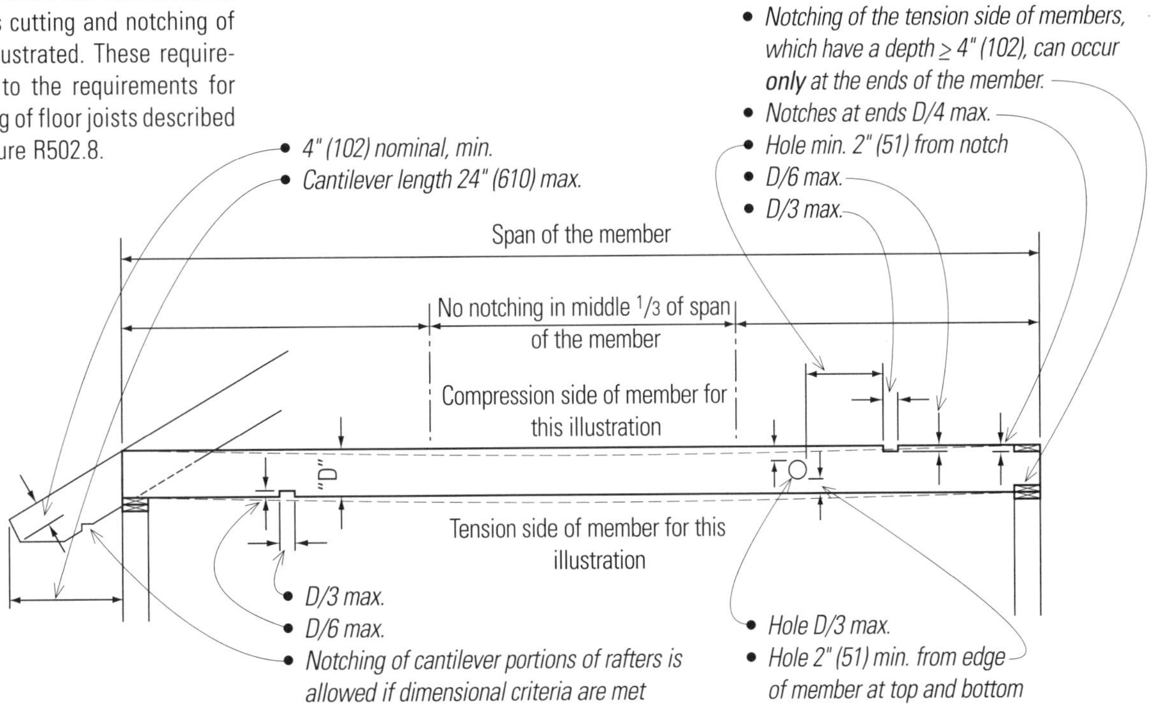

- *4" (102) nominal, min.*
- *Cantilever length 24" (610) max.*

Span of the member

No notching in middle ⅓ of span of the member

Compression side of member for this illustration

"D"

Tension side of member for this illustration

- *D/3 max.*
- *D/6 max.*
- *Notching of cantilever portions of rafters is allowed if dimensional criteria are met*

- *Notching of the tension side of members, which have a depth ≥ 4" (102), can occur only at the ends of the member.*
- *Notches at ends D/4 max.*
- *Hole min. 2" (51) from notch*
- *D/6 max.*
- *D/3 max.*

- *Hole D/3 max.*
- *Hole 2" (51) min. from edge of member at top and bottom*

Figure R802.7 Notching of Sawn Structural Roof Members

The second section addresses engineered wood products such as glued-laminated timbers, manufactured framing lumber, manufactured joists and roof trusses. Here cutting and notching is prohibited except as permitted by the material manufacturer's recommendations or where such alterations are specifically designed for the assembly in question by a registered design professional. For these materials no cutting or notching should be performed without having assurance obtained from the manufacturer's literature that such alterations are permissible in the situation found at the job site. Manufactured elements, especially those made up of compound elements like roof trusses, rely on the integrity of all of their members for their performance, and the structural design calculations done by the manufacturer make assumptions about how much (or how little) that integrity may be compromised by field alterations. The permissible alterations to such systems are so variable and system specific that we have not attempted to illustrate them here. Alterations [cuts, notches, bored holes, gussets, etc.] to engineered trusses should be designed only by a registered design professional.

§R802.8 Lateral Support

Where roof or ceiling framing members have a depth-to-thickness ratio exceeding 5:1 (based on nominal dimensions) they can be prone to rotating under lateral loading. Therefore such members are to be laterally braced at bearing points to prevent rotation from side to side as shown in the illustration. Where roof rafters have ceiling joists attached per the attachment schedule in Table R602.3(1) the depth-thickness ratio is to be determined using the combined thickness of both members as illustrated. Where rafters and ceiling joists have a depth-to-thickness ratio exceeding 6:1 (based on nominal dimensions) they are to have blocking or bridging at 8' (2438) intervals as illustrated, in addition to the blocking at the bearing points as noted above.

§R802.9 Openings in Roof and Ceiling Framing

Openings in roof and ceiling framing are to be framed similarly to those in floors, with header and trimmer joists as illustrated in Chapter 5 for §R502.10. Per the illustrations, framing is to be doubled or framing anchors installed when the opening sizes are large enough to generate added forces on members surrounding the opening, unless additional materials or connection strengths are provided.

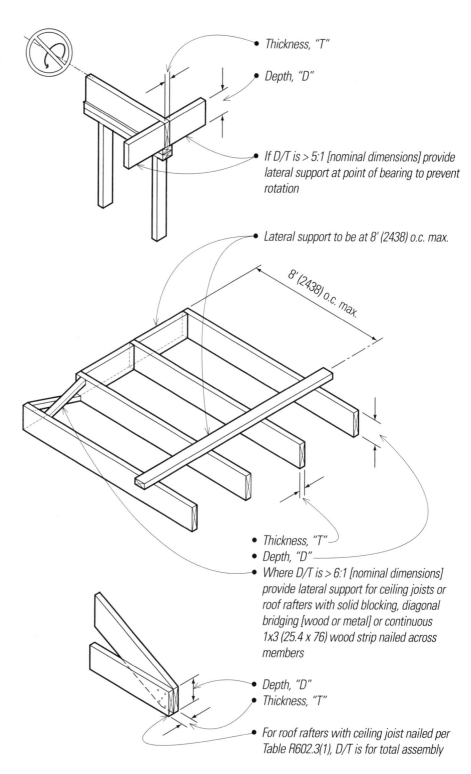

Thickness, "T"

Depth, "D"

If D/T is > 5:1 [nominal dimensions] provide lateral support at point of bearing to prevent rotation

Lateral support to be at 8' (2438) o.c. max.

8' (2438) o.c. max.

Thickness, "T"

Depth, "D"

Where D/T is > 6:1 [nominal dimensions] provide lateral support for ceiling joists or roof rafters with solid blocking, diagonal bridging [wood or metal] or continuous 1x3 (25.4 x 76) wood strip nailed across members

Depth, "D"

Thickness, "T"

For roof rafters with ceiling joist nailed per Table R602.3(1), D/T is for total assembly

Figure R802.8 Lateral Support and Bridging

§R802.10 Wood Trusses

The code recognizes the widespread use of manufactured wood trusses in residential construction. As with floor trusses, wood trusses are to be designed using accepted engineering practice. Many trusses used in residential construction are metal-plate-connected trusses. Such trusses are to be designed in accordance with Standard ANSI/TP1, the National Design Standard for Metal-plate-connected Wood Truss Construction. §R802.10.1 lists the information that is to be furnished on truss design drawings. Trusses are to be braced to prevent rotation and to provide lateral stability. These provisions should be shown in the truss design drawings and referenced in the construction documents. Metal-plate-connected trusses are to be braced per the requirements of the referenced standard: the Building Component Safety Information (BCSI 1-03) "Guide to Good Practice for Handling, Installation & Bracing of Metal Plate Connected Wood Trusses," if more detailed and specific bracing criteria are not included in the truss design drawings. Trusses are to be fastened to wall top plates using approved connectors, as illustrated and also in accordance with the manufacturer's specifications, design drawings and installation instructions.

§R802.11 Roof Tie-Down

Roof assemblies, whether rafters or trusses, which will be subjected to wind uplift pressures of 20 psf (960 Pa) or greater, are to be fastened to their supporting wall assemblies to provide the resistance required by Table R802.11. The relationship between wind speeds, roof spans and anticipated uplift forces is illustrated. The example in the illustration is based on 100 mph (44.7 m/s) wind speeds.

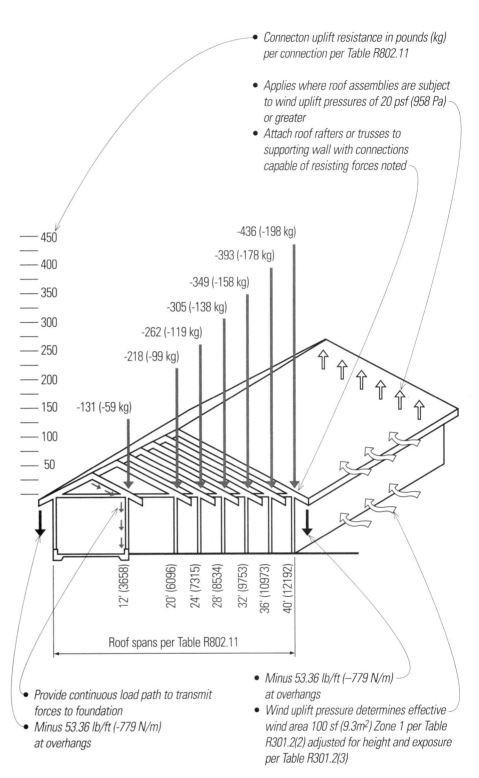

- *Connecton uplift resistance in pounds (kg) per connection per Table R802.11*
- *Applies where roof assemblies are subject to wind uplift pressures of 20 psf (958 Pa) or greater*
- *Attach roof rafters or trusses to supporting wall with connections capable of resisting forces noted*

-436 (-198 kg)
-393 (-178 kg)
-349 (-158 kg)
-305 (-138 kg)
-262 (-119 kg)
-218 (-99 kg)
-131 (-59 kg)

450
400
350
300
250
200
150
100
50

12' (3658)
20' (6096)
24' (7315)
28' (8534)
32' (9753)
36' (10973)
40' (12192)

Roof spans per Table R802.11

- *Provide continuous load path to transmit forces to foundation*
- *Minus 53.36 lb/ft (-779 N/m) at overhangs*

- *Minus 53.36 lb/ft (−779 N/m) at overhangs*
- *Wind uplift pressure determines effective wind area 100 sf (9.3m²) Zone 1 per Table R301.2(2) adjusted for height and exposure per Table R301.2(3)*

Figure R802.11 Uplift Resistance of Roof Assemblies
[100 mph (161 km/h) wind speed used for illustration]

ROOF SHEATHING

§R803 Roof Sheathing

Lumber used as roof sheathing is to conform to the requirements of Table R803.1. When wood sheathing members are spaced to support wood shingles and shakes, they are to conform to the requirements in §R905.7 and §R905.8, as illustrated in Chapter 9 for those roofing materials.

Often roof sheathing uses wood structural panels. These panels are to be manufactured to the standards of DOC PS 1 or PS -2, or CSA 0437 or 0325 when manufactured in Canada. The panels are to have grade marks or certificates of inspection so it can be determined that the panels are rated for the weather exposure and structural application where they are to be used. The relationships between allowable spans over supports versus panel thickness appear in the floor section of the code. Table R503.2.1.1(1) addresses requirements for both floor sheathing and roof sheathing.

While all plywood may be susceptible to moisture damage, fire-retardant-treated plywood may be especially susceptible to moisture damage, depending on the type of fire-retardant treatment. §R803.2.1.2 requires approved methods be used to determine allowable unit stresses and fastener values. It also requires that grading of the FRTW panels be done by an approved agency. Note that all plywood and oriented strand board is to be graded by an approved agency.

Wood structural panel sheathing may be applied with the joints staggered or non-staggered. The panels are to be fastened to support members per the fastening requirements of Table R602.3(1) or APA E30 for wood roof framing members. Footnotes f and g to Table R602.3(1) require nailing in specified patterns and sizes when wind speeds exceed certain values, as illustrated. Where the supporting members are steel roof framing, fastening of roof sheathing panels is to be per Table R804.3.

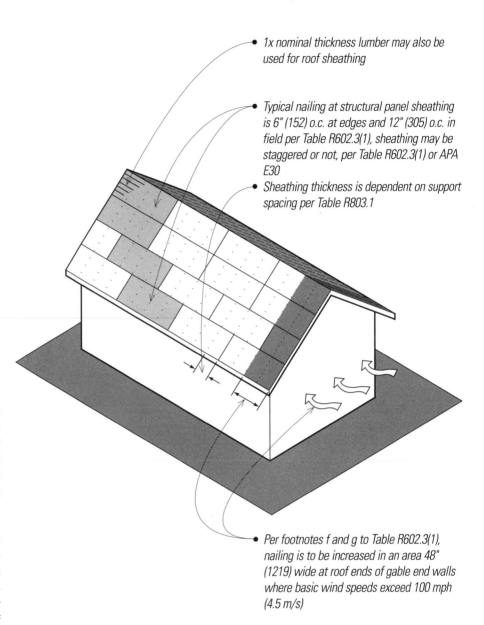

- 1x nominal thickness lumber may also be used for roof sheathing

- Typical nailing at structural panel sheathing is 6" (152) o.c. at edges and 12" (305) o.c. in field per Table R602.3(1), sheathing may be staggered or not, per Table R602.3(1) or APA E30
- Sheathing thickness is dependent on support spacing per Table R803.1

- Per footnotes f and g to Table R602.3(1), nailing is to be increased in an area 48" (1219) wide at roof ends of gable end walls where basic wind speeds exceed 100 mph (4.5 m/s)

Figure R803.1 Fastening at Roof Sheathing

§R804 Steel Roof Framing

This section covers the requirements for using cold-formed steel framing members for roof and ceiling framing. It parallels the requirements for wood framing and covers the same scope of framing members as does the wood framing section of this chapter. The use of these requirements is limited to buildings meeting the criteria for dimensions, heights, wind speeds and snow loads as illustrated. As for wall framing, the rafters and joists are to be in line with framing members below with locations and tolerances as shown in Figure R804.1.2. The framing members are to be of the configurations and dimensions indicated and depicted. Materials are specified in §R804.2.1. Members are to be labeled so that the materials can be field identified as being appropriate for their intended use. The members are to be corrosion protected as specified in §R804.2.3.

This entire section was rewritten and re-illustrated in the 2009 IRC. Although it is not referred to in this chapter, the section was redone to correspond to the new reference standard for cold-formed steel framing: the American Iron and Steel Institute (AISI) *Standard for Cold-Formed Steel Framing—Prescriptive Method for One- and Two-Family Dwellings* (AISI S230). This reference standard is listed in Chapter 44 Reference Standards. It is also listed as acceptable for use as an alternative provision in §R301.1.1. Since the section and the illustrations were done as part of a single code change, they are coordinated and are generally self-explanatory, so we have not repeated many of the illustrations for this chapter. We have added some illustrations to explain items not illustrated in the code.

Screws are used for fastening cold-formed steel members. See the illustration for examples of screw size and location criteria for various parts of roof-ceiling assemblies. As for floor and wall framing, there are criteria for locations and sizes of holes in the members, as shown in the code, as well as criteria for reinforcing of openings that are oversize or that require a "patch" to repair mis-located openings.

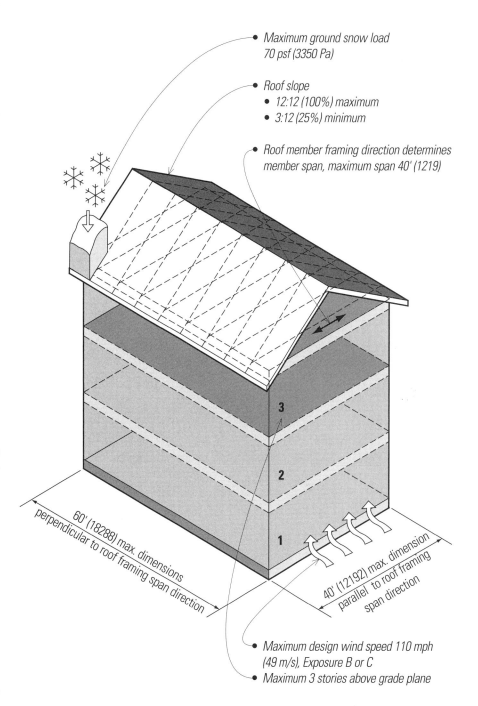

- Maximum ground snow load 70 psf (3350 Pa)
- Roof slope
  - 12:12 (100%) maximum
  - 3:12 (25%) minimum
- Roof member framing direction determines member span, maximum span 40' (1219)
- 60' (18288) max. dimensions perpendicular to roof framing span direction
- 40' (12192) max. dimension parallel to roof framing span direction
- Maximum design wind speed 110 mph (49 m/s), Exposure B or C
- Maximum 3 stories above grade plane

Figure R804.1 Cold-Formed Steel Roof Framing Applicability Limits

§R804.3 Roof Construction

General requirements for roof construction are depicted in Figure R804.3 in the code. We have further annotated the IRC illustration on page 299 with additional code references and detail vignettes.

§R804.3.1 Ceiling Joists

Ceiling joist framing criteria in §R804.3.1 using cold-formed steel members are set out in the span tables; R804.3.1.1(1) through (8). These tables are similar in concept to those for wood members. There are two sets of framing criteria. One set assumes no attic storage and uses a live load of 10 psf (479 Pa). The second set of framing criteria assumes limited attic storage and uses a 20 psf (959 Pa) live load. As for wood framing, we believe it is prudent for the designer to assume that the attic will be used for storage, and design for it, unless the attic space is so small and limited that its use for storage is very unlikely. If the attic meets the dimensional requirements where access is required per §R807 we recommend that such attic areas be designed with storage in mind. The other variables in determining ceiling joist dimensions are of course span, but also include whether lateral support of the top flanges is provided and at what spacing. See the general roof framing illustration for how these criteria are applied.

§R804.3.2 Roof Rafters

Roof rafters are to be sized per the rafter span tables: R804.3.2.1(1) and (2) with the span based on the horizontal projection of the sloped roof rafters. The rafters are assumed to be sloped since this section is only applicable to roofs with a minimum slope of 3:12 (25% slope) and a maximum slope of 12:12 (100% slope). Roof rafters are to have their bottom flanges braced per §R804.3.2.5 as shown on the general roof construction illustration. Eave overhangs of roof rafters are not to exceed 24" (610) with the dimension measured horizontally [parallel to the floor plane]. Gable end overhangs are not to exceed 12" (305) and are to be braced as illustrated in IRC Figure R804.3.2.1.2.

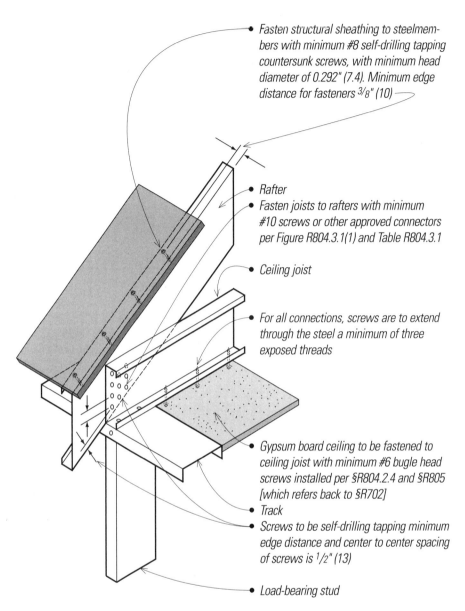

Fasten structural sheathing to steelmembers with minimum #8 self-drilling tapping countersunk screws, with minimum head diameter of 0.292" (7.4). Minimum edge distance for fasteners $^3/_8$" (10)

Rafter

Fasten joists to rafters with minimum #10 screws or other approved connectors per Figure R804.3.1(1) and Table R804.3.1

Ceiling joist

For all connections, screws are to extend through the steel a minimum of three exposed threads

Gypsum board ceiling to be fastened to ceiling joist with minimum #6 bugle head screws installed per §R804.2.4 and §R805 [which refers back to §R702]

Track

Screws to be self-drilling tapping minimum edge distance and center to center spacing of screws is $^1/_2$" (13)

Load-bearing stud

Figure R804.2 Fasteners at Cold-Formed Steel Roof-Ceiling Construction

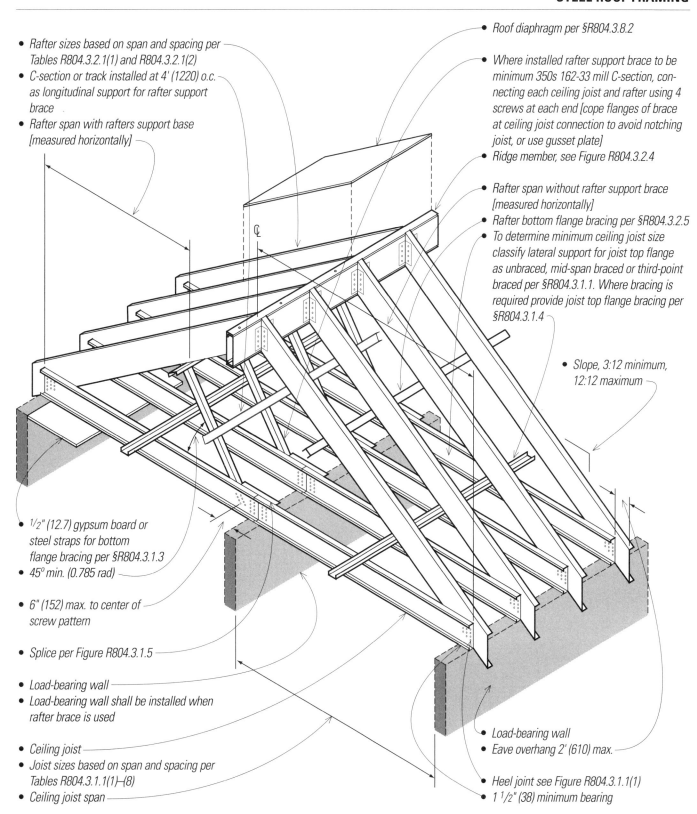

- Rafter sizes based on span and spacing per Tables R804.3.2.1(1) and R804.3.2.1(2)
- C-section or track installed at 4' (1220) o.c. as longitudinal support for rafter support brace
- Rafter span with rafters support base [measured horizontally]

- Roof diaphragm per §R804.3.8.2

- Where installed rafter support brace to be minimum 350s 162-33 mill C-section, connecting each ceiling joist and rafter using 4 screws at each end [cope flanges of brace at ceiling joist connection to avoid notching joist, or use gusset plate]
- Ridge member, see Figure R804.3.2.4

- Rafter span without rafter support brace [measured horizontally]
- Rafter bottom flange bracing per §R804.3.2.5
- To determine minimum ceiling joist size classify lateral support for joist top flange as unbraced, mid-span braced or third-point braced per §R804.3.1.1. Where bracing is required provide joist top flange bracing per §R804.3.1.4

- Slope, 3:12 minimum, 12:12 maximum

- ¹/₂" (12.7) gypsum board or steel straps for bottom flange bracing per §R804.3.1.3
- 45° min. (0.785 rad)

- 6" (152) max. to center of screw pattern

- Splice per Figure R804.3.1.5

- Load-bearing wall
- Load-bearing wall shall be installed when rafter brace is used

- Ceiling joist
- Joist sizes based on span and spacing per Tables R804.3.1.1(1)–(8)
- Ceiling joist span

- Load-bearing wall
- Eave overhang 2' (610) max.

- Heel joint see Figure R804.3.1.1(1)
- 1 ¹/₂" (38) minimum bearing

Figure R804.3 Steel Roof Construction

§R804 Additional Requirements

While holes may be cut in the webs of cold-formed steel roof framing members, cutting and notching of flanges and lips of those members is not allowed at any time. Headers are to be provided where roof framing occurs over wall openings. Per §R804.3.5, headers are to be per the wall requirements in Chapter 6 at §R603.6 and per tables R603.6(1) through (24). Openings in roof and ceiling framing are to be framed as for similar floor openings, using header and trimmer joists. These requirements are illustrated in the code at Figures R804.3.6(1) and R804.3.6(2). Cold-formed steel roof trusses are to be per AISI S100, Section D4 and are to be secured to the load-bearing wall per the requirements of §R804.3.7. Ceiling diaphragms are required at gable end walls. They may be of either $^1/_2$" (12.7) gypsum board or $^3/_8$" (9.5) wood structural panels and are to be fastened to the underside of the ceiling framing and to the bearing walls per Figures R804.3.8(1) and R804.3.8(2) in the code. A roof diaphragm of at least $^3/_8$" (9.5) thick wood structural panels is always required per §R804.3.8.2. As for wood roofs where roof assemblies are subject to wind uplift pressures of greater than or equal to 20 psf (0.96kPa), they are required to have ties per Table 802.11 connecting the rafters to the bearing walls.

§R805 Ceiling Finishes

Ceiling finishes are to be installed per the requirements for wall finishes. This section refers back to §R702 which addresses interior wall coverings.

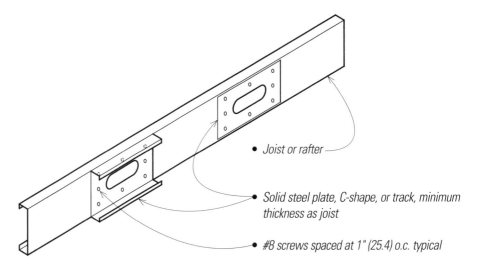

• *Joist or rafter*

• *Solid steel plate, C-shape, or track, minimum thickness as joist*

• *#8 screws spaced at 1" (25.4) o.c. typical*

Figure R804.2.5.3 Web Hole Patch

§R806.1 Ventilation Required

Ventilation of enclosed attic spaces and enclosed rafter spaces is required to allow moisture to escape from these spaces. Trapped moisture can damage structural framing materials and lead to growth of mold or mildew in these spaces if they get damp and remain so. Ventilation openings are to be screened or otherwise be small enough to resist the intrusion of vermin or insects. Openings are to be at least $1/16$" (1.6) wide and no more than $1/4$" (6.4) wide unless they are covered with corrosion-resistant wire cloth screening or similar material with an open pattern at least $1/16$" (1.6) wide between screen elements, but no more than $1/4$" (6.4). Where roof framing members are cut or notched to provide ventilation pathways, the cutting or notching must conform to §R802.

§R806.2 Minimum Ventilation Area

The amount of ventilation to be provided is expressed in terms of "net free area." Any screen or louver placed in a ventilation opening blocks some air. In order to meet the requirements of the code for ventilation area, the net free area of any screening should be taken into account and the rough openings to receive screening should be sized to account for the loss of air movement depending on the net free area of the screen installed in the opening. Consult manufacturer's data to determine the net free area for vent covers. See the illustrations for how to measure the net free areas required by this section. The amount of net free area is dependent on the height of ventilation openings in relationship to each other. When vertical separation of vents can be achieved, this will promote convective air flow and ventilation. Accordingly, the number of vent openings may be reduced. Where insulation is provided in the roof assembly, care in detailing and installation of the insulation must be taken to allow free flow of air at the vent openings and around the insulation, as illustrated.

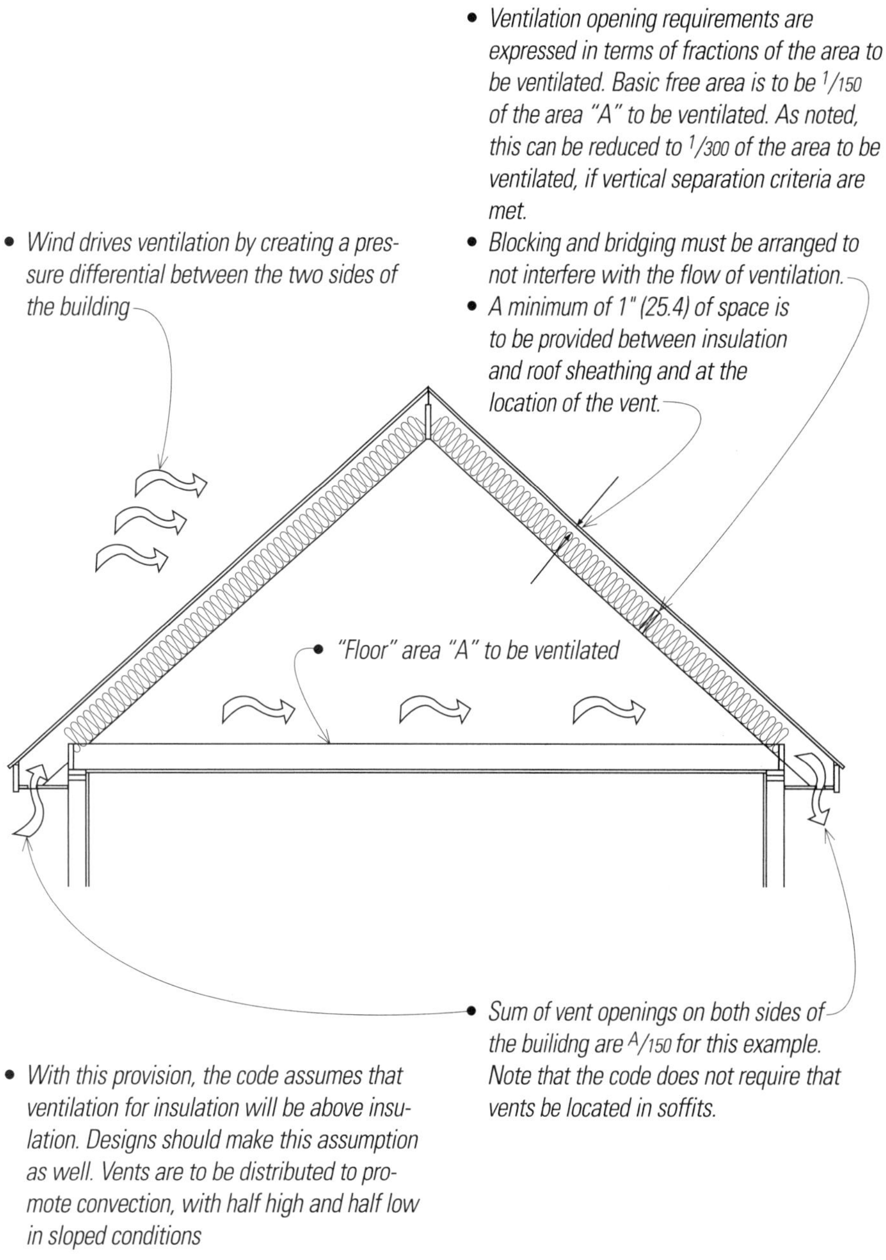

- Wind drives ventilation by creating a pressure differential between the two sides of the building

- Ventilation opening requirements are expressed in terms of fractions of the area to be ventilated. Basic free area is to be $1/150$ of the area "A" to be ventilated. As noted, this can be reduced to $1/300$ of the area to be ventilated, if vertical separation criteria are met.

- Blocking and bridging must be arranged to not interfere with the flow of ventilation.

- A minimum of 1" (25.4) of space is to be provided between insulation and roof sheathing and at the location of the vent.

- "Floor" area "A" to be ventilated

- Sum of vent openings on both sides of the buiildng are $A/150$ for this example. Note that the code does not require that vents be located in soffits.

- With this provision, the code assumes that ventilation for insulation will be above insulation. Designs should make this assumption as well. Vents are to be distributed to promote convection, with half high and half low in sloped conditions

Figure R806.1 Attic Ventilation

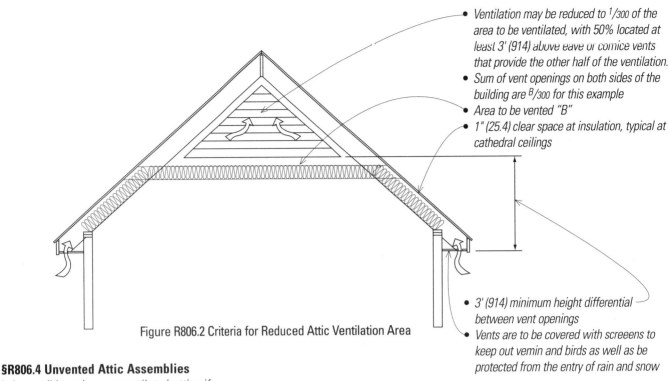

- Ventilation may be reduced to $1/300$ of the area to be ventilated, with 50% located at least 3' (914) above eave or cornice vents that provide the other half of the ventilation.
- Sum of vent openings on both sides of the building are $B/300$ for this example
- Area to be vented "B"
- 1" (25.4) clear space at insulation, typical at cathedral ceilings

Figure R806.2 Criteria for Reduced Attic Ventilation Area

- 3' (914) minimum height differential between vent openings
- Vents are to be covered with screeens to keep out vemin and birds as well as be protected from the entry of rain and snow

§R806.4 Unvented Attic Assemblies

It is possible to have unventilated attics if an interrelated set of requirements are met. It is essential to understand that use of unvented assemblies per §R806.4 depends on meeting all of the criteria. See the illustration for how all of the pieces relate to each other. There is some flexibility in detailing, depending on the air permeability of the insulation at the underside of the roof sheathing, and on the detailing of the installation of various elements of the roof assembly.

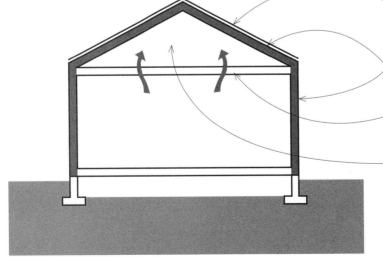

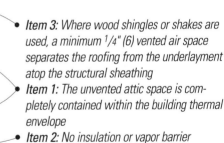

- *Item 3:* Where wood shingles or shakes are used, a minimum $1/4$" (6) vented air space separates the roofing from the underlayment atop the structural sheathing
- *Item 1:* The unvented attic space is completely contained within the building thermal envelope
- *Item 2:* No insulation or vapor barrier between attic and space below top story

- Unvented attic
- Item numbers shown are taken from §R806.4. See that code section and the details on the following page for further criteria.

Figure R806.4 Unvented Attic Conditions and Details

- Conditions for unvented attic. Note that all conditions must be met. These are three options for Item 5 as shown, but one of those must also be met along with other conditions. Item numbers shown are taken from §R806.4.

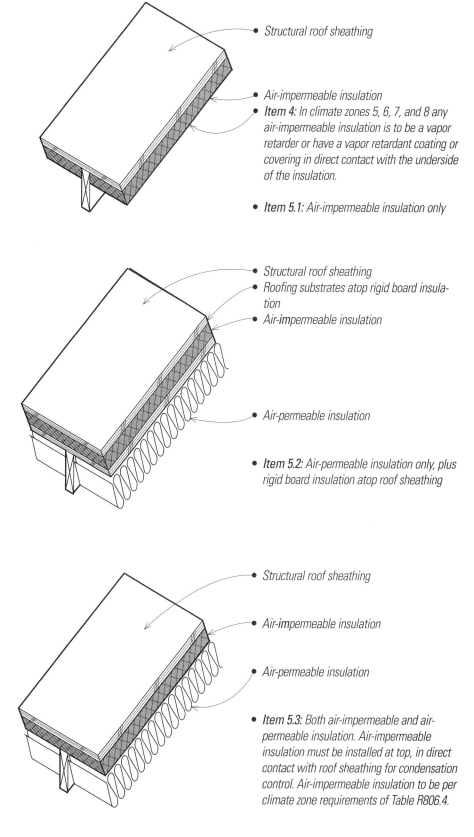

- Structural roof sheathing

- Air-impermeable insulation
- **Item 4:** In climate zones 5, 6, 7, and 8 any air-impermeable insulation is to be a vapor retarder or have a vapor retardant coating or covering in direct contact with the underside of the insulation.

- **Item 5.1:** Air-impermeable insulation only

- Structural roof sheathing
- Roofing substrates atop rigid board insulation
- Air-impermeable insulation

- Air-permeable insulation

- **Item 5.2:** Air-permeable insulation only, plus rigid board insulation atop roof sheathing

- Structural roof sheathing

- Air-impermeable insulation

- Air-permeable insulation

- **Item 5.3:** Both air-impermeable and air-permeable insulation. Air-impermeable insulation must be installed at top, in direct contact with roof sheathing for condensation control. Air-impermeable insulation to be per climate zone requirements of Table R806.4.

Figure R806.4 Unvented Attic Conditions and Details

§R807 Attic Access

In buildings with combustible ceiling construction where sufficient space occurs in the attic, as defined in the code and illustrated, then access must be provided to that space. The dimensional criteria given are for the clear height inside the attic space and for the "floor" area of the attic space. Where attic access is provided, the size of the access opening is specified, as illustrated. Note that the access door is to be located in a readily accessible location for use by the owner and potentially for use by first responders in an emergency. The attic opening is to be located to allow sufficient headroom above the opening to minimize the chance that users will bump their heads when moving up through the access panel.

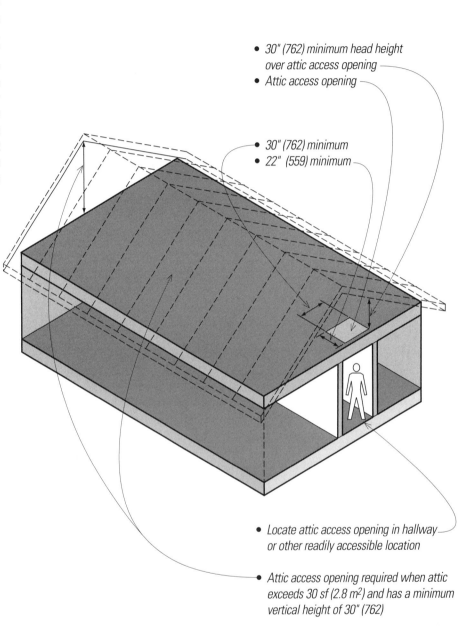

- *30" (762) minimum head height over attic access opening*
- *Attic access opening*

- *30" (762) minimum*
- *22" (559) minimum*

- *Locate attic access opening in hallway or other readily accessible location*

- *Attic access opening required when attic exceeds 30 sf (2.8 m²) and has a minimum vertical height of 30" (762)*

- *When located in wall, attic access opening is to be 22" (559) by 30" (762) minimum in size*

9
Roof Assemblies

This chapter covers the design, materials, construction and quality of roof assemblies. These assemblies sit atop the roof construction covered in Chapter 8 and provide protection for the building from weather. As part of their role in providing weather protection, there are requirements that roof coverings remain in place during high winds and other severe weather in geographic locations where such weather is likely to occur. There are general requirements for all roofing systems called out in the first few sections of the chapter. The chapter then calls out materials and components for various roofing systems on a system-by-system basis. There is a section on roof insulation that occurs above the roof deck. The insulation under the deck is covered by Chapter 8 and insulation above the deck is covered by §R906 in this chapter. The final section of this chapter, §R907, has provisions for re-roofing of existing buildings.

§R902 Roof Classification

Roof covering materials are to meet the material criteria of §R904 and are to be installed per §R905 as called out for each roofing material. Roofing materials are often required by local adoptions to be classified as "A", "B" or "C". Roof classes are determined by fire testing for exposure to a fire outside of the structure per ASTM E108, the "Standard Test Methods for Fire Tests of Roof Coverings" or the similar UL 790 test. These are pass-fail tests with the length of time that the roof resists a pre-determined intensity fire setting the classification. If the roof meets one of the three time standards it is classified as either A, B or C based on the time of resistance. If the material fails to meet the time criteria it does not receive a classification. Class A has the longest resistance time with B and C resisting the fire for shorter times. The code itself only requires Class A, B or C roofing be used on roofs that are closer than 3' (914) to the property line in order to protect the building from exposure from fire from the adjacent property. In other situations unclassified roof materials may be used per the IRC. The code mentions that Class A, B or C roofing is to be installed "where required by law," thus acknowledging that many local jurisdictions adopt these standards for residential construction in those locales. The exceptions to §R902.1 include certain roofing materials by reference as meeting Class A standards. These materials are those which by observation and convention can be considered to be non-combustible roofing materials installed on noncombustible decks. The designer should verify local roofing material requirements early in the construction document preparation process. The code also addresses the use of fire-retardant-treated wood shingles and shakes. Such materials are to be pressure impregnated per Standard AWPA C1. Bundles are to be labeled to identify the roof classification of these materials.

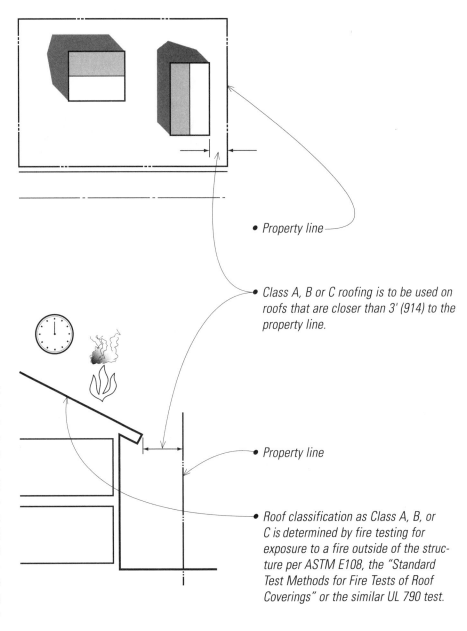

• *Property line*

• *Class A, B or C roofing is to be used on roofs that are closer than 3' (914) to the property line.*

• *Property line*

• *Roof classification as Class A, B, or C is determined by fire testing for exposure to a fire outside of the structure per ASTM E108, the "Standard Test Methods for Fire Tests of Roof Coverings" or the similar UL 790 test.*

§R903 Weather Protection

Roof decks are to be covered with approved materials and the roofing is to be secured to the structure. The code assumes there is a significant role for the manufacturer's instructions to guide installation of various roofing materials. The code recognizes that roofing assemblies have many component parts. See the illustrations for examples of each of these components. Flashing is to be installed to prevent moisture from entering the walls and roofs. Flashing is required at the intersections of walls and roofs and where vents penetrate the roofing. Where items such as chimneys or other items wider than 30" (762) perpendicular to the roof slope abut or penetrate the roofing, crickets and saddles, which can be considered as a type of flashing, are required. Parapets are to have copings on top. Roof drainage is required, either using sloping roofs with drainage over the roof edge, or using roof drains. Where roof drains are provided, overflow drains or scuppers are to be provided to allow water to drain if the main drain is obstructed. This prevents accumulation of ponded water on the roof which could overload the roof structure if not drained. See the illustration showing location and size criteria for roof drains.

§R904 Materials

Roof assemblies are to comply with the requirements of this section and with the manufacturer's installation instructions. Materials for roof assemblies are to be compatible. This requirement applies to items such as flashings and sealants and with the structure supporting the roofing assembly. The building official has the right to ask for testing or other verification of the compatibility of roofing materials when in doubt. Roofing materials are to be delivered to the site in packages or with certificates or bills of lading for bulk materials, to allow verification of who manufactured or supplied the materials and that they comply with all required material and testing standards.

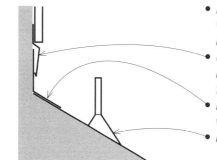

Figure R903.2 Flashing Requirements

- Base and cap flashings are to be installed at wall/roof intersections or at changes in roof direction
- Cap flashing is to be corrosion-resistant metal of the same gauge as the base flashing.
- Flashing extends over roof below to prevent water infiltration
- Provide flashing at roof penetrations

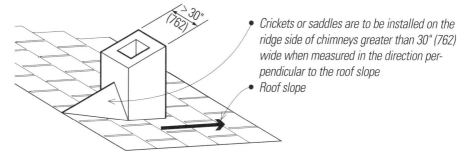

Figure R903.2.2 Chimney Crickets and Saddles

- Crickets or saddles are to be installed on the ridge side of chimneys greater than 30" (762) wide when measured in the direction perpendicular to the roof slope
- Roof slope

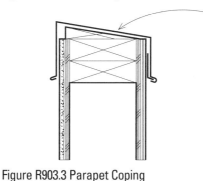

Figure R903.3 Parapet Coping

- The tops of parapet walls are to be topped with coping of noncombustible weatherproof materials. The width of this material [typically sheet metal] is to be no less than the width of the parapet.

- 2" (51) max. above roof low point
- 4" (102) min. opening height

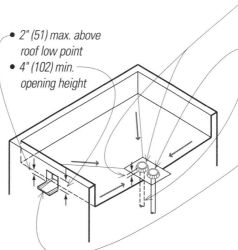

Figure R903.4 Roof Drains, Overflow Drains and Scuppers

- Overflow drain with inlet flow line 2" (51) above low point of roof [or provide scuppers as alternative, see note below]
- Main roof drain, located at or near the low point of roof
- Overflow drain lines to discharge to an approved location and to be piped separately from roof drain for entire piping run. Pipe sizing and installation to be per the International Plumbing Code
- As an alternative to roof overflow drains, overflow scuppers through parapet wall adjacent to the roof drain may be provided. Scuppers are to be 3 times the size of roof drains, with inlet flow line 2" (51) maximum above the low point of the roof area served by the scupper. The height of the scupper opening is to be 4" (102) min.

§R905 Requirements for Roof Coverings

Roof assemblies are to be fastened to install the loads set forth in Tables R301.2(2) and R301.2(3). These loads are produced by winds acting on the structure as determined by the mean height of the roof, the roof area, and the roof slope as adjusted for the classification of wind exposure. This section describes the detailed requirements for various types of roofing materials as listed and as illustrated.

§R905.2 Asphalt Shingles

Asphalt shingles may be used only on roofs with a minimum slope of 2:12 or greater. Where shallow roof slopes of between 2:12 and 4:12 are used, double underlayment is required per §R905.2.7. Asphalt shingles are to be tested and labeled with wind speed classifications to verify that they comply with Tables R905.2.4.1(1) and Tables R905.2.4.1 (2) depending on the appropriate test standard for the asphalt shingles being used. See the illustrations for information about shingle application, underlayment, fastenings and flashings.

- *§R905.2.1 specifies that asphalt shingles are to be installed over solidly sheathed decks.*

- *Typical shingles are to have at least 2 nails per individual shingle or 4 per shingle strip, unless more nailing is called for in the manufacturer's installation instructions.*

- *Minimum roof slope for asphalt shingles is 2:12.*

- *In areas subject to high winds [above 110 mph (49 m/s)] underlayment shall be fastened with corrosion-resistant fasteners per the manufacturer's installation instructions. Fasteners are to be installed along the overlap not further apart than 36" (914) o.c.*

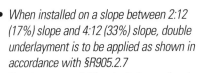

- *When installed on a slope between 2:12 (17%) slope and 4:12 (33%) slope, double underlayment is to be applied as shown in accordance with §R905.2.7*

- *For slopes over 4:12 a single layer of underlayment is acceptable. Single underlayment is to be laid parallel to and starting at eaves, applied in shingle fashion and lapped a minimum of 2" (51).*

- *Asphalt shingles are to have self-seal strips or be interlocking.*

- *They are to be nailed with galvanized steel, stainless-steel, aluminum or copper roofing nails with 12 gage shanks and $^{3}/_{8}$" (19) minimum diameter heads per ASTM F 1667 that must penetrate into the sheathing at least $^{3}/_{4}$" (19.1 mm), or through sheathing of lesser thickness.*

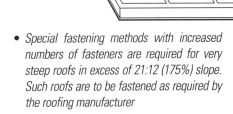

- *Special fastening methods with increased numbers of fasteners are required for very steep roofs in excess of 21:12 (175%) slope. Such roofs are to be fastened as required by the roofing manufacturer*

- *Eaves and gables of shingle roofs may receive drip edge flashings extending below the roof sheathing and extending back under the roof. This would be based on the manufacturer's instructions. This is not explicitly required in the code.*

Figure R905.2.1 Asphalt Shingle Roofing Requirements

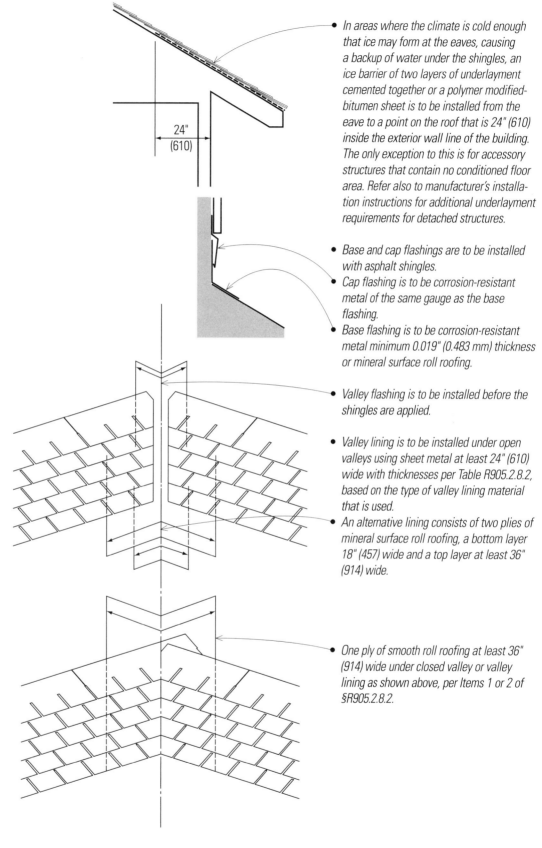

In areas where the climate is cold enough that ice may form at the eaves, causing a backup of water under the shingles, an ice barrier of two layers of underlayment cemented together or a polymer modified-bitumen sheet is to be installed from the eave to a point on the roof that is 24" (610) inside the exterior wall line of the building. The only exception to this is for accessory structures that contain no conditioned floor area. Refer also to manufacturer's installation instructions for additional underlayment requirements for detached structures.

Base and cap flashings are to be installed with asphalt shingles.

Cap flashing is to be corrosion-resistant metal of the same gauge as the base flashing.

Base flashing is to be corrosion-resistant metal minimum 0.019" (0.483 mm) thickness or mineral surface roll roofing.

Valley flashing is to be installed before the shingles are applied.

Valley lining is to be installed under open valleys using sheet metal at least 24" (610) wide with thicknesses per Table R905.2.8.2, based on the type of valley lining material that is used.

An alternative lining consists of two plies of mineral surface roll roofing, a bottom layer 18" (457) wide and a top layer at least 36" (914) wide.

One ply of smooth roll roofing at least 36" (914) wide under closed valley or valley lining as shown above, per Items 1 or 2 of §R905.2.8.2.

24"
(610)

Figure R905.2.2 Asphalt Shingle Roofing Requirements

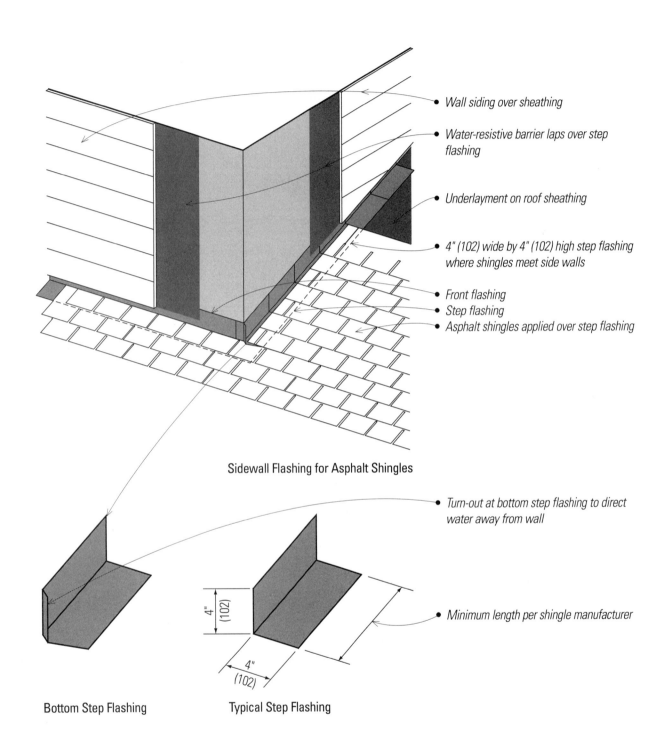

- Wall siding over sheathing

- Water-resistive barrier laps over step flashing

- Underlayment on roof sheathing

- 4" (102) wide by 4" (102) high step flashing where shingles meet side walls

- Front flashing
- Step flashing
- Asphalt shingles applied over step flashing

Sidewall Flashing for Asphalt Shingles

- Turn-out at bottom step flashing to direct water away from wall

- Minimum length per shingle manufacturer

4" (102)

4" (102)

Bottom Step Flashing

Typical Step Flashing

§R905.3 Clay and Concrete Tiles

These relatively heavy roofing materials are to be installed only over solid sheathing or spaced structural sheathing boards arranged to adequately support the tiles. Tiles may not be installed on slopes less than 2^1/$_2$:12. Where shallow roof slopes of between 2^1/$_2$:12 and 4:12 are used for tiles, double underlayment is required per §R905.3.3.1. Tiles are to be installed taking into account the climatic conditions at the building site, roof slopes, the type of underlayment system and the type and configuration of tiles being installed. See the illustrations for information about tile application, underlayment, fastenings and flashings.

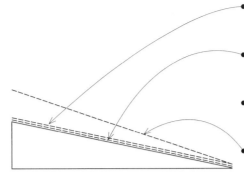

- The slope of the roof deck is to be at least 2^1/$_2$ units vertical in 12 units horizontal (21% slope).
- When the slope is less than 4:12, double underlayment is to be installed per §R905.3.3.1
- Unless otherwise noted, underlayment is to be mineral surface roll roofing conforming to the ASTM requirements cited in §R905.3.3
- At slopes greater than 4:12, one layer of interlayment, installed shingle fashion per §R905.3.3.2, is acceptable.
- In areas subject to high winds [above 110 mph (49 m/s)] underlayment shall be fastened with corrosion-resistant fasteners per the manufacturer's installation instructions. Fasteners are to be installed along the overlap not further apart than 36" (914) o.c.

- Fasteners for these tiles are to be corrosion-resistant with 11 gage shanks and ^{5}/$_{16}$" (11) minimum head diameter and of a length to penetrate at least ^{3}/$_4$" (19.1 mm) into or through the sheathing, whichever is less.
- The number and configuration of fasteners is spelled out in Table R905.3.7. The fastening criteria are dependent on sheathing and roof slope.
- Tile is to be installed in accordance with the manufacturer's installation instructions based on climatic conditions, roof slope, underlayment system and the type of tile being installed.

- Per §R905.3.7, perimeter tiles are to be fastened with at least one fastener per tile. Tiles with weight less than 9 psf (0.4 kg/m^2) require fasteners at every tile regardless of roof slope. In areas where the roof is subject to snow, a minimum of two fasteners per tile shall be used.
- §R905.3.1 requires concrete and clay tiles to be installed over solid or spaced structural board sheathing.

- Flashings are to be corrosion resistant and at least 26 galvanized sheet gage, 0.022" (0.56).
- Flashings are to be installed at the juncture of roof tiles to vertical surfaces, and at valleys.
- Flashing to extend 11" (280) to each side of valley centerline and have a splash diverter rib 1" (25.4) high.
- Overlap flashing 4" (102) at ends.
- 36" (914) wide underlayment for roof slopes of 3:12 and over.
- In cold climates with average daily temperatures in January of 25°F (-4°C) or less, where there is a possibility of ice forming along the eaves, causing backups of water, and the roof is under 7:12 slope, the metal valley flashing underlayment is to be solidly cemented to the roofing underlayment. As an alternative, self-adhering polymer modified bitumen sheet may also be used.

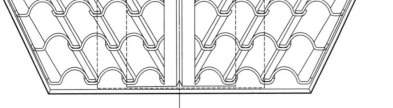

Figure R905.3 Clay and Concrete Tile Roofing Requirements

§R905.4 Metal Roof Shingles

Metal roof shingles are typically made of relatively light gage metal and are required to be installed only over solid decking. They may be installed over spaced sheathing boards if the roofing is specifically designed for that type of application. Metal shingles may not be installed on slopes less than 3:12. See the illustrations for information about shingle application, underlayment, fastenings and flashings. Note that metals for these shingles are to be naturally corrosion resistant, or made so, per the requirements in Table R905.10.3(2). Flashings for metal shingles are to be of the same materials as the shingles or meet the standards of Table R905.10.3(1) to avoid having dissimilar materials interact poorly with each other.

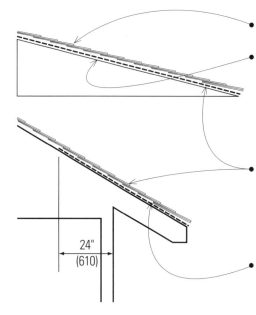

- *Minimum roof slope for metal roof shingles is 3:12 (25%) slope*
- *Metal roof shingles are to be applied to solid decks or closely fitted decks unless the shingles are specifically designed to be applied to spaced sheathing.*

- *This roofing material, being shingles, with more joints than panels, requires underlayment.*

24" (610)

- *An ice barrier is also required in cold climates, similar to that for other types of shingle roofing.*

- *Metal roof shingles are to be attached to the roof per the requirements of Chapter 8 and per the manufacturer's installation instructions.*

- *Flashings are to be of the same material as the shingles or meet the standards for roof materials and corrosion resistance in Tables R905.10.3(1) and (2).*

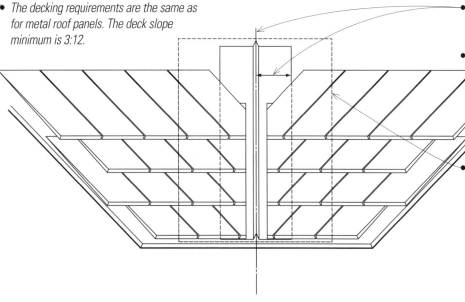

- *The decking requirements are the same as for metal roof panels. The deck slope minimum is 3:12.*

- *Valley flashing to extend 8" (203) to each side of valley centerline and have a splash diverter rib not less than 3/4" (19.1 mm) high.*
- *Lap end joints at least 4" (102).*

- *36" (914) wide underlayment directly under the valley flashing, consisting of one layer of underlayment running the entire length of the valley in addition to the overall roofing underlayment. Where the average daily temperature in January is 25°F (–4°C) or lower, the valley flashing underlayment shall be solid cemented to the roofing underlayment below it when roof slopes are more than 7:12 (58%) slope. As an alternative, self-adhering polymer modified bitumen sheet may also be used.*

Figure R905.4 Metal Roof Shingle Roofing Requirements

§R905.5 Mineral-Surfaced Roll Roofing

Mineral-surface roll roofing may only be used on solidly sheathed roofs. The material does not have any ability to span openings in spaced sheathing. Asphalt shingles may be used only on roofs with a minimum slope of 1:12 (8%) or greater. See the illustrations for information about roll roofing application, underlayment, fastenings and flashings.

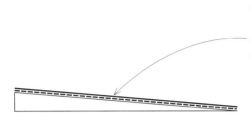

- *Mineral-surfaced roll roofing is to be applied only over solidly sheathed roofs.*
- *The roof slope must be at least 1:12.*
- *A single layer of underlayment is typically required.*

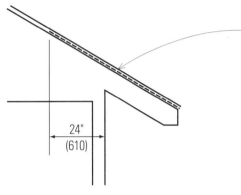

24"
(610)

- *In areas where the climate is cold enough that ice may form at the eaves, causing a backup of water under the shingles, an ice barrier of two layers of underlayment cemented together or a polymer modified-bitumen sheet is to be installed from the eave to a point on the roof that is 24" (610) inside the exterior wall line of the building.*

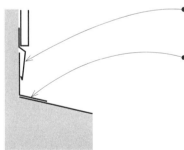

- *Cap flashing is to be corrosion-resistant metal of the same gauge as the base flashing.*
- *Base flashing is to be corrosion-resistant metal minimum 0.019" (0.483 mm) thickness or mineral surface roll roofing.*

Figure R905.5 Mineral-Surfaced Roll Roofing Requirements

§R905.6 Slate and Slate-type Shingles

Natural slate shingles or manufactured materials with a similar profile may only be used on solidly sheathed roofs. The materials do not have any ability to span openings in spaced sheathing. Slate and slate-type shingles may only be used on roofs with a minimum slope of 4:12 or greater. See the illustrations for information about shingle application, underlayment, fastenings and flashings.

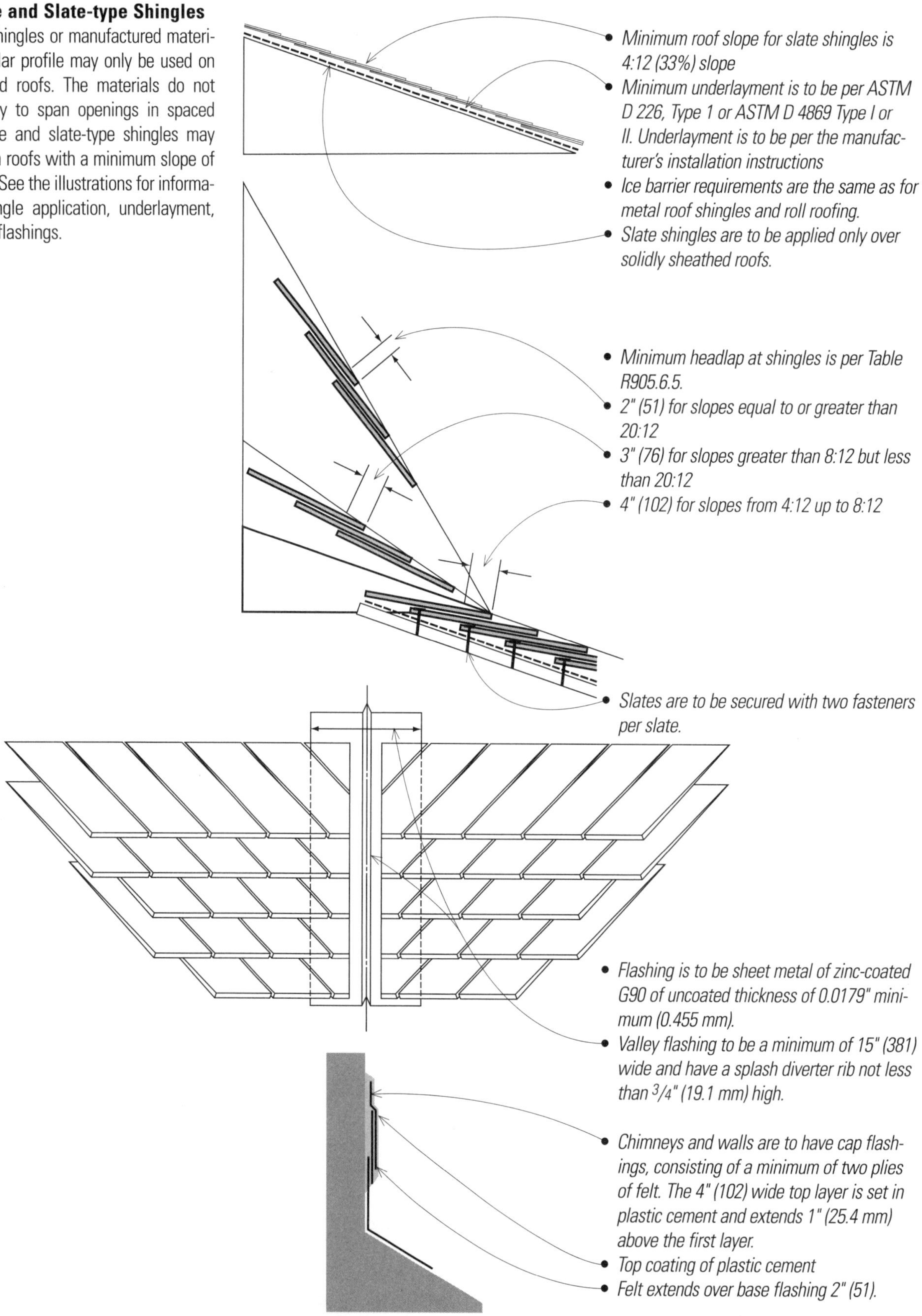

- Minimum roof slope for slate shingles is 4:12 (33%) slope
- Minimum underlayment is to be per ASTM D 226, Type 1 or ASTM D 4869 Type I or II. Underlayment is to be per the manufacturer's installation instructions
- Ice barrier requirements are the same as for metal roof shingles and roll roofing.
- Slate shingles are to be applied only over solidly sheathed roofs.

- Minimum headlap at shingles is per Table R905.6.5.
- 2" (51) for slopes equal to or greater than 20:12
- 3" (76) for slopes greater than 8:12 but less than 20:12
- 4" (102) for slopes from 4:12 up to 8:12

- Slates are to be secured with two fasteners per slate.

- Flashing is to be sheet metal of zinc-coated G90 of uncoated thickness of 0.0179" minimum (0.455 mm).
- Valley flashing to be a minimum of 15" (381) wide and have a splash diverter rib not less than 3/4" (19.1 mm) high.

- Chimneys and walls are to have cap flashings, consisting of a minimum of two plies of felt. The 4" (102) wide top layer is set in plastic cement and extends 1" (25.4 mm) above the first layer.
- Top coating of plastic cement
- Felt extends over base flashing 2" (51).

Figure R905.6 Slate and Slate-type Shingle Roofing Requirements

§R905.7 Wood Shingles

Wood shingles are sawn from wood logs where "shakes" are typically formed by splitting logs. The requirements are similar for the two materials, but they are not identical and are listed separately. The requirements of the appropriate section are to be applied specifically to each material. Wood shingles may be used on solidly sheathed roofs or over spaced sheathing. Wood shingles may only be used on roofs with a minimum slope of 3:12 (25%) or greater. Wood shingles are to be naturally durable wood and are to meet the grading requirements of Table R905.7.4, which lists the applicable grading rules as being those published by the Cedar Shake and Shingle Bureau. Bundles of shingles are to be labeled showing compliance with grading requirements. See the illustrations for information about shingle application, underlayment, fastenings and flashings. The material requirements for wood shingles are summarized in Table R905.7.4.

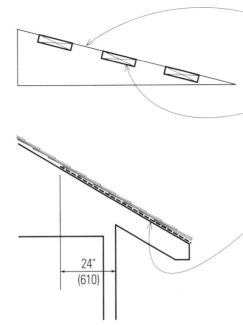

- Minimum roof slope for wood shingles is 3:12 (25%) slope
- Minimum underlayment is to be per ASTM D 226, Type 1 or ASTM D 4869 Type I or II.
- Wood shingles may be installed over either spaced or solid sheathing.
- Spaced sheathing shall not be less than 1×4 (25 x 102) [nominal] boards, spaced equal to exposure of shingles.
- Solid sheathing is required in areas where the average daily temperature in January is 25°F (–4°C) or lower in the area where ice barrier is to be installed.
- In areas where the climate is cold enough that ice may form at the eaves, causing a backup of water under the shingles, an ice barrier of two layers of underlayment cemented together or a polymer modified-bitumen sheet is to be installed from the eave to a point on the roof that is 24" (610) inside the exterior wall line of the building.

24" (610)

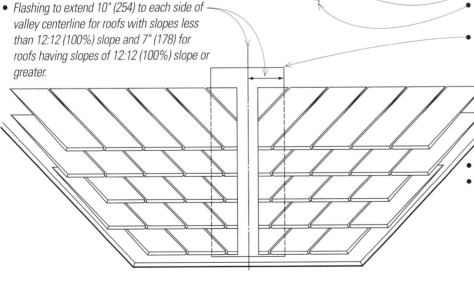

- Course line
- Flashing to extend 10" (254) to each side of valley centerline for roofs with slopes less than 12:12 (100%) slope and 7" (178) for roofs having slopes of 12:12 (100%) slope or greater.

- Wood shingles are to be fastened to the roof with at least two fasteners per shingle.
- Fasteners 3/4" (19) max. from edge of shingle
- Fasteners no more than 1" (25.4) above the exposure line
- Shingles are to have exposures in relation to roof slopes per Table R905.7.5.
- Corrosion-resistant fasteners should penetrate at least 1/2" (13) into, or through the sheathing where it is less than 1/2" (13) thick.
- 1 1/2" (38) minimum sidelap
- Joints in alternate courses should not align.
- 1/4" to 3/8" (6.4 to 9.5) spacing between shingles
- Flashings are to be corrosion-resistant and at least 26 galvanized sheet gage, 0.019" (0.48)

- Overlap flashing 4" (102) at ends.
- In cold climates where there is a possibility of ice forming along the eaves, causing backups of water, and the roof is under 7:12 slope, the metal valley flashing underlayment is to be solidly cemented to the roofing underlayment.

Figure R905.7 Wood Shingle Roofing Requirements

§R905.8 Wood Shakes

As noted previously, wood shakes are typically formed by splitting logs, but they may also be produced by taper-sawing. Wood shakes may be used on solidly sheathed roofs or over spaced sheathing. See the illustration accompanying wood shingle application for the criteria for sheathing boards in spaced applications for wood shakes. Wood shakes may only be used on roofs with a minimum slope of 3:12 (25%) or greater. Wood shakes are to be naturally durable wood and are to meet the grading requirements of Table R905.8.5, which lists the applicable grading rules for various wood materials. As for wood shingles, bundles of wood shakes are to be labeled showing compliance with grading requirements. See the illustrations for information about shake application, underlayment, fastenings and flashings. Note that the maximum exposure of shakes as described in Table R905.8.6 is dependent on the shake material, the length of the shake, the grade of the shake and the roof pitch. Note also that the major distinction between shake and shingle application is the requirement for an application of not less than No. 30 felt as interlayer between courses of shakes as illustrated.

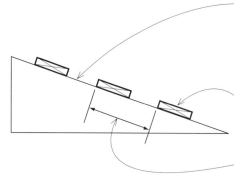

- *Minimum roof slope for wood shakes is 4:12.*
- *While wood shingles are sawn, wood shakes are formed by splitting a short log into a number of tapered radial sections, resulting in at least one texture face.*
- *Wood shakes may be installed over either spaced or solid sheathing.*

- *Spaced sheathing shall not be less than 1×4 (25 × 102) [nominal] boards, spaced equal to weather exposure. Where 2x4 (25 x 102) boards are installed at 10" (254) on center, additional 1x4 (25 x 102) boards are to be installed between the sheathing boards.*
- *Solid sheathing is required in areas where the average daily temperature in January is 25°F (-4°C) or lower in the area where ice barrier is to be installed.*

- *See Figure R905.7 for installation criteria of ice barrier at wood shakes [similar to requirements for wood shingles]*

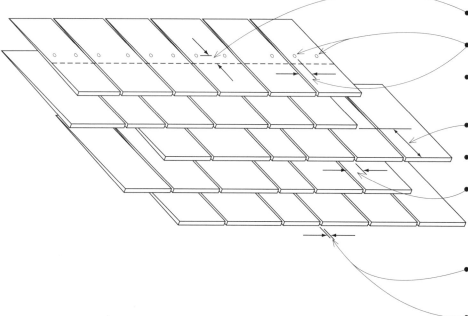

- *Fasteners no more than 2" (51) above the exposure line*
- *2 fasteners per shake, minimum; fastenings 1" (25.4) maximum from each edge of shake*
- *Fasteners to penetrate 1/2" (12.7) into sheathing or through sheathing less than 1/2" (12.7) thick*
- *For weather exposure see Table R905.8.6*

- *Fastening, sidelap and flashing requirements are similar to those of wood shingles.*
- *1 1/2" (38) minimum sidelap*

- *3/8" to 5/8" (9.5 to 15.9) spacing between shakes and tapersawn shakes of naturally durable wood.*
- *1/4" to 3/8" (6.4 to 9.5) spacing between preservative-treated tapersawn shakes*

Figure R905.8(1) Wood Shake Roofing Requirements

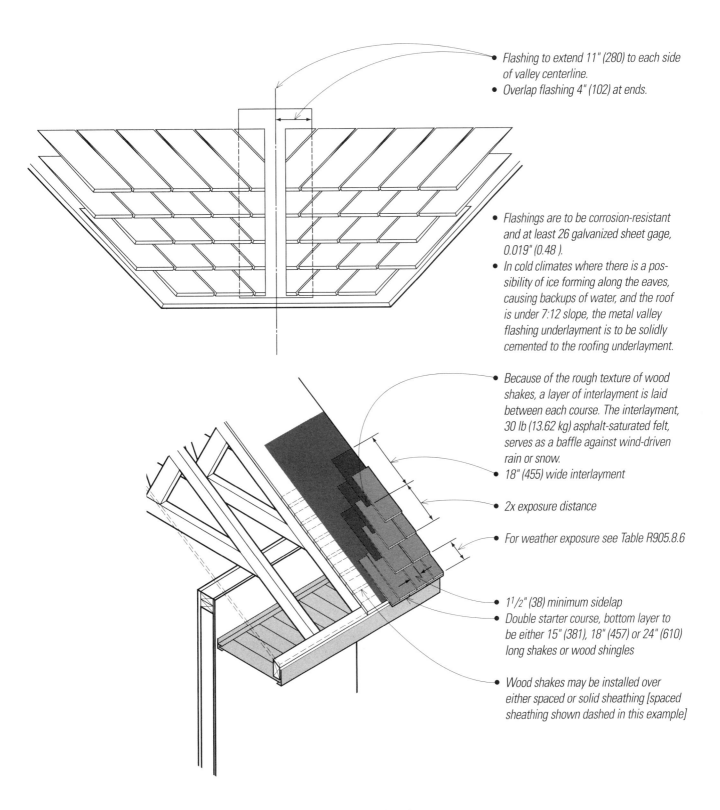

- Flashing to extend 11" (280) to each side of valley centerline.
- Overlap flashing 4" (102) at ends.

- Flashings are to be corrosion-resistant and at least 26 galvanized sheet gage, 0.019" (0.48).
- In cold climates where there is a possibility of ice forming along the eaves, causing backups of water, and the roof is under 7:12 slope, the metal valley flashing underlayment is to be solidly cemented to the roofing underlayment.

- Because of the rough texture of wood shakes, a layer of interlayment is laid between each course. The interlayment, 30 lb (13.62 kg) asphalt-saturated felt, serves as a baffle against wind-driven rain or snow.
- 18" (455) wide interlayment

- 2x exposure distance

- For weather exposure see Table R905.8.6

- 1¹/₂" (38) minimum sidelap
- Double starter course, bottom layer to be either 15" (381), 18" (457) or 24" (610) long shakes or wood shingles

- Wood shakes may be installed over either spaced or solid sheathing [spaced sheathing shown dashed in this example]

Figure R905.8(2) Wood Shake Roofing Requirements

§R905.9 Built-up Roofs

Built-up roofs are used for low-slope roofing conditions where other types of roofing are not allowed. They are constructed on site from materials applied in layers. A typical built-up roof consists of several plies of roofing paper bonded together and waterproofed using hot bitumen or liquefied coal-tar. These roofs may have a solid cap sheet or be topped with gravel ballast depending on the system design. While not noted in this section, one should assume that built-up roofs should only be used on solidly sheathed roofs. The material does not have any ability to span openings in spaced sheathing. Built-up roofing may be used on roofs with a shallow slope, but there must be a minimum slope to allow water to drain without ponding. Built-up roofs are to have a minimum slope of $1/4$:12 (2%). Roofs using coal-tar for coatings may have a minimum slope of $1/8$:12 (1%). Table R905.9.2 lists the ASTM materials standards that the components of a built-up roof are to meet. Built-up roofs have a wide variety of components that are dependent on the manufacturer. Although not stated in the code, the intent of this section is that materials for such roofs must be complementary and work together in accordance with the manufacturer's written installation instructions. The designer should verify the compatibility of the various components of such roofs to be certain they work together chemically and mechanically in accordance with the test criteria and standards cited in §R905.9 and §R905.11.

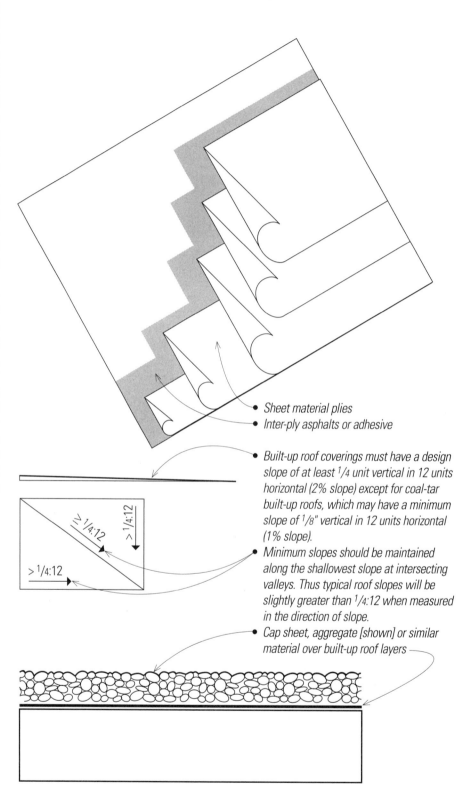

- Material standards for built-up roofs are specified in Table R905.9.2.

- Sheet material plies
- Inter-ply asphalts or adhesive

- Built-up roof coverings must have a design slope of at least $1/4$ unit vertical in 12 units horizontal (2% slope) except for coal-tar built-up roofs, which may have a minimum slope of $1/8$" vertical in 12 units horizontal (1% slope).

- Minimum slopes should be maintained along the shallowest slope at intersecting valleys. Thus typical roof slopes will be slightly greater than $1/4$:12 when measured in the direction of slope.

- Cap sheet, aggregate [shown] or similar material over built-up roof layers

Figure R905.9 Built-up Roofing Requirements

§R905.10 Metal Roof Panels

Metal roofs are applied in panelized sections that are joined together at their seams by various methods of crimping, fastening or soldering. They may be applied to solid or spaced sheathing, but not to spaced supports unless specifically designed for such applications. Where metal panel roofs use support structures, they are to be designed per the International Building Code. The minimum slopes depend on the types of seams, as illustrated. Materials are to conform to Table R905.10.3(1) and be naturally corrosion resistant or protected from corrosion per Table R905.10.3.(2). Unless otherwise specified in the manufacturer's installation instructions, attachments are to be per §R905.10.4. Fasteners for steel roofs are to be galvanized, those for copper roofs are to be copper, brass, bronze, copper alloy or "three hundred series" stainless steel. Stainless steel fasteners are noted as being "acceptable for metal roofs" without specifying any limitations on metal material or the type of stainless steel to be used. However, the requirements of Table R905.10.3(2) are applicable to the roofing materials, which will help define the types of fasteners acceptable for various metal roof panels. Underlayments are to be per the manufacturer's installation instructions.

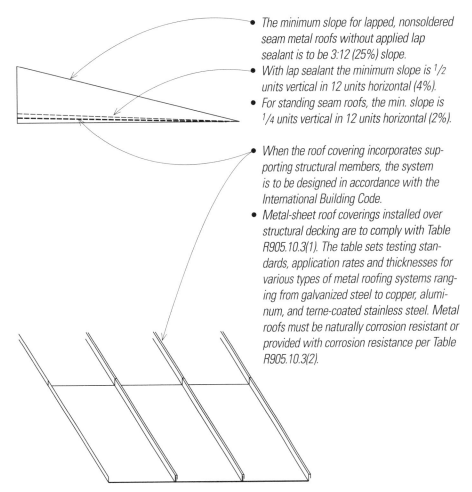

- The minimum slope for lapped, nonsoldered seam metal roofs without applied lap sealant is to be 3:12 (25%) slope.
- With lap sealant the minimum slope is $1/2$ units vertical in 12 units horizontal (4%).
- For standing seam roofs, the min. slope is $1/4$ units vertical in 12 units horizontal (2%).

- When the roof covering incorporates supporting structural members, the system is to be designed in accordance with the International Building Code.
- Metal-sheet roof coverings installed over structural decking are to comply with Table R905.10.3(1). The table sets testing standards, application rates and thicknesses for various types of metal roofing systems ranging from galvanized steel to copper, aluminum, and terne-coated stainless steel. Metal roofs must be naturally corrosion resistant or provided with corrosion resistance per Table R905.10.3(2).

- Fastenings must match the type of metal to avoid corrosion caused by galvanic electrical activity between dissimilar metals.
- Panels are to be installed per the manufacturer's instructions. In the absence of such instructions, the fastenings are to be galvanized fasteners for galvanized roofs and hard copper or copper alloy for copper roofs. Stainless-steel fasteners are acceptable for all types of metal roofs.

- Note that underlayment requirements are not spelled out in the code for metal roof panel installations. Many manufacturers recommend the use of underlayment. This is a reminder that the code is only the minimum standard for construction quality, not the maximum standard. The code says that underlayment is to be installed per the manufacturer's installation instructions.

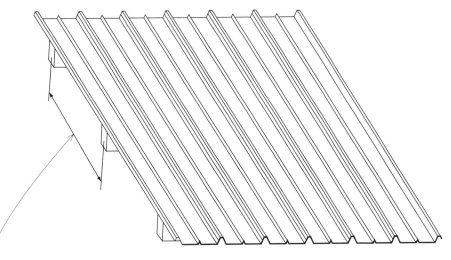

- Metal roof panels are to be installed over solid or closely spaced decking unless specifically designed to be installed over spaced supports.

§R905.11 Modified Bitumen Roofing

Modified bitumen roofs are a variant of built-up roofing and consist of one or more layers of polymer modified asphalt sheets. They use a bitumen with polymer additives for better flexibility then unmodified bitumen. They are used for similar low-slope roofing conditions as built-up roofs where other types of roofing are not allowed. They are constructed on site from materials applied in layers. While not noted in this section, one should assume that built-up roofs should only be used on solidly sheathed roofs. The material does not have any ability to span openings in spaced sheathing. Modified bitumen roofs, as for built-up roofs, are to have a minimum slope of $^1/_4$:12 (2%). Table R905.11.2 lists the ASTM materials standards that each of the components of a modified bitumen roof are to meet. Built-up roofs have a wide variety of components that are dependent on the manufacturer. Thus they rely heavily on manufacturer's installation instructions. See the illustrations for information about typical modified bitumen roofing application and flashings.

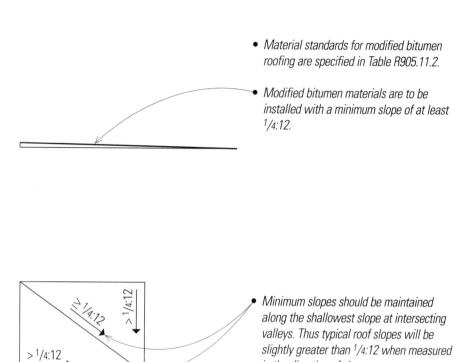

- *Material standards for modified bitumen roofing are specified in Table R905.11.2.*

- *Modified bitumen materials are to be installed with a minimum slope of at least $^1/_4$:12.*

- *Minimum slopes should be maintained along the shallowest slope at intersecting valleys. Thus typical roof slopes will be slightly greater than $^1/_4$:12 when measured in the direction of slope.*

- *Modified bitumen roofing is similar to built-up roofing in application. The sheets are fully adhered or mechanically attached to the substrate or held in place with a layer of ballast.*

- *Cap sheet, aggregate [shown] or similar material over built-up roof layers*

Figure R905.11 Modified Bitumen Roofing Requirements

Monolithic Low Slope Roofing

There are several roofing systems for low-slope roofs that have been gaining in popularity over the last several years. Among these are different types of single-ply roofing systems as well as spray applied and liquid applied coatings. Single-ply roofing membranes are field applied using one layer of a homogeneous or composite material rather than multiple layers.

Single-ply roofing membranes come to the site as large rolls of membrane. They are relatively easy to apply and do not require the use of hot materials applied to the top of the building as do bitumen and coal tar systems. Single-ply systems fall into two basic categories as described in the code: thermoset membranes; typically rubber polymers and thermoplastic membranes; and typically plastic polymers. Roof types are categorized by their material, such as plastic or rubber and whether their fabrication uses heat treating as part of the process. They are further categorized by how the seams are to be fastened together; by heat, chemical welding or mechanically. The flashings used in single-ply roofing have much different details and manufacturer's requirements than other more traditional roofing materials. The manufacturer's installation instructions must be followed with great care when installing single-ply roofing. Also, materials, underlayments, seam attachment methods and adhesives must be compatible with the systems being installed and should not be interchanged between roofing systems, even those from the same manufacturer.

§R905.12 Thermoset Single-ply Roofing

Single-ply membranes classified as "thermoset" are typically made from rubber polymers. They are heated to "set" the polymer chains during the manufacturing process, thus the name. "EPDM" roofing is a typical descriptor for these roofs. Seaming methods vary by material type and are typically by either chemical or heat welding. They may be applied on roofs with a minimum slope of $1/4$:12 (2%) or greater. They are to meet the material standards of §R905.12.2 and be installed per the manufacturer's installation instructions. See the illustration for more details.

§R905.13 Thermoplastic Single-ply Roofing

Single-ply membranes classified as "thermoplastic" are typically made from plastic polymers such as polyvinyl chloride (PVC). Their seams may be chemically welded or heat welded. They may be applied on roofs with a minimum slope of $1/4$:12 (2%) or greater. They are to meet the material standards of §R905.13.2 and be installed per the manufacturer's installation instructions. See the illustration for more details.

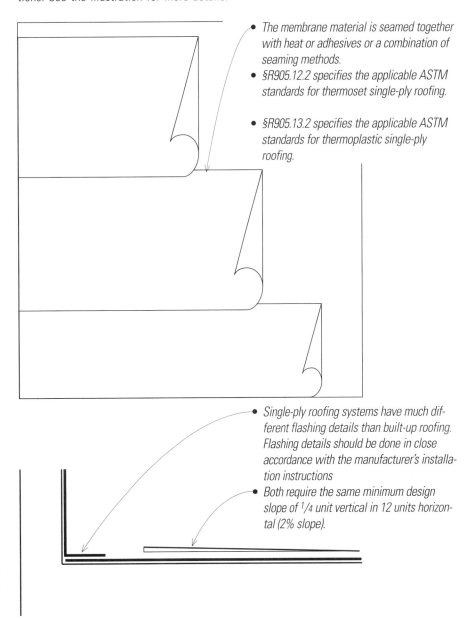

- *The membrane material is seamed together with heat or adhesives or a combination of seaming methods.*
- *§R905.12.2 specifies the applicable ASTM standards for thermoset single-ply roofing.*

- *§R905.13.2 specifies the applicable ASTM standards for thermoplastic single-ply roofing.*

- *Single-ply roofing systems have much different flashing details than built-up roofing. Flashing details should be done in close accordance with the manufacturer's installation instructions*
- *Both require the same minimum design slope of $1/4$ unit vertical in 12 units horizontal (2% slope).*

Figure R905.12 and R905.13 Single-ply Roofing Requirements

Monolithic Low Slope Roofing

Another type of roofing that may be used is sprayed polyurethane foam roofing. This material is applied to the roof substrate using a spray gun. The roofing material then expands to form a waterproof roofing membrane. It is often applied to complex roof shapes such as arched or domed roofs where other materials, even single-ply membranes, would not conform to the roof shape. It must be used with a liquid-applied top coating.

Liquid-applied coatings are polymer-based roof toppings that form a waterproof barrier similar to a thick paint after they are applied. Since they are applied as a liquid, and cure into a membrane conforming to the roof structure below, these coatings can also be used on complex roof shapes similarly to foam roofing.

§R905.14 Sprayed Polyurethane Foam Roofing

As noted by its name this material is sprayed on the roof. It is typically a two-component material that, when applied, expands through a chemical reaction to fill cracks and crevices, and provides a thick membrane with some insulating value. This roof must also use a liquid-applied membrane complying with §R905.15. This coating is to be applied no sooner than 2 hours after foam installation to allow the foam to fully expand, but no more than 72 hours after application of the foam. The material may be applied on roofs with a minimum slope of $1/4$:12 (2%) or greater. Foam plastic materials are also to conform to the requirements for foam plastics contained in §R316 of the IRC. Similar to other innovative roofing materials, it is to be installed in strict accordance with the manufacturer's installation instructions. See the illustration for more details.

This type of system is often used on roofs with unusual or complex profiles. Note that such vaults do not have the minimum slopes at the peak of the vault. Code compliance and durability at this condition should be verified with the AHJ and the roofing manufacturer.

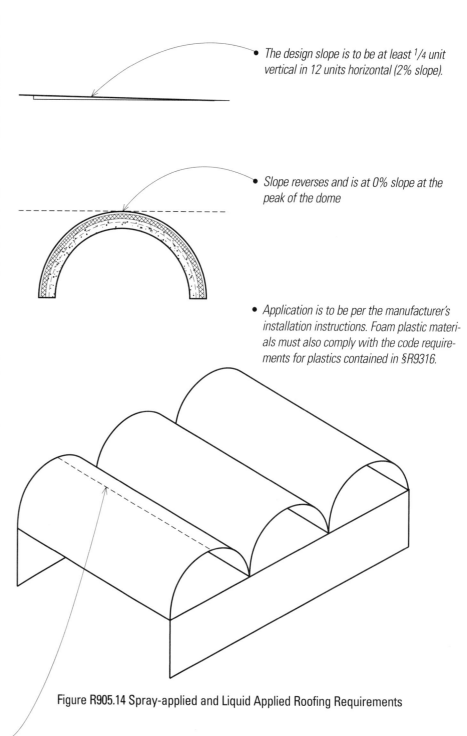

- The design slope is to be at least $1/4$ unit vertical in 12 units horizontal (2% slope).

- Slope reverses and is at 0% slope at the peak of the dome

- Application is to be per the manufacturer's installation instructions. Foam plastic materials must also comply with the code requirements for plastics contained in §R9316.

Figure R905.14 Spray-applied and Liquid Applied Roofing Requirements

§R905.15 Liquid-Applied Coatings as Roofing

Materials that are applied as a liquid on the roof structural substrate and then cure or dry to form a waterproof membrane are covered by this code section. The material may be applied on roofs with a minimum slope of $1/4$:12 (2%) or greater. They are to meet the material standards of §R905.15.2. As for other similar innovative roofing materials, it is to be installed in strict accordance with the manufacturer's installation instructions. Note that liquid-applied coatings are to be the last coat applied to spray foam insulation. As such, this roofing material is to be applied over spray-applied foam roofing installed per §R905.14. See the illustration on the facing page for more details.

● *Liquid-applied roofing must have a minimum design slope of $1/4$ unit vertical in 12 units horizontal (2% slope).*

R906 Roof Insulation

Insulation placed on top of the roof structural deck is covered by this section, as illustrated. The insulation materials, which are typically rigid boards, must meet the fire-resistance requirements of FM 4450 or UL 1256. These tests measure the flame spread potential of roof structural parts, insulation and roofing materials from fires inside the structure. The section also requires that this insulation be covered by roofing materials. This protects the insulation from weathering and from fire exposure. Materials are to meet the standards of Table R906.2

● *Thermal insulation may be installed above the roof decking if it is covered by a roof covering complying with the fire-resistance ratings of FM 4450 or UL 1256.*
● *Foam plastic insulation shall conform to the requirements of Table R906.2.*

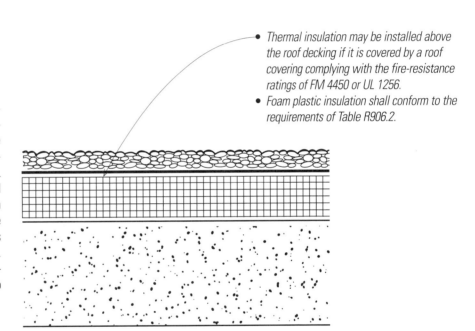

Figure R906 Above-Deck Roof Insulation

§R906 Reroofing

This section of the code addresses work to be done on an existing building. The code section recognizes that some existing flat roof structures may not meet the minimum slope criteria of $1/4$" per foot and exempts roof coverings from the minimum slope requirements. Even though not a code requirement, we recommend that reroofing materials match the slope requirements for new construction as closely as possible.

A key issue to be addressed in reroofing is whether the existing roofing materials should be removed. If too many old roofing layers are left in place the dead load on the roof may exceed the design limits for the roof structure. Also, irregularities in the old roof underlying a new roof may compromise the ability of the new roof to remain waterproof. §R907.3 provides a checklist for determining whether roofing materials must be removed or can be covered with a new roof. Note that if any of the conditions noted in this section occur, then the existing roof must be removed. The exceptions allow certain systems to be installed without removal of the old roofing if certain measures are provided for the new roofing installation. Note especially the requirements of §R907.4 for installation of gypsum board or other approved materials in the roof assembly when the new roof creates a concealed space with combustible materials within it.

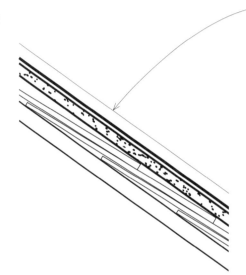

- *Existing roofing must be removed when any of the following conditions occur:*

  1. *The roof or roof covering is water-soaked or deteriorated such that the existing roof is not an adequate base for added roofing.*

  2. *If the existing roof covering is wood shakes, slate, clay, cement or asbestos-cement tile.*

  - *Note that an exception allows metal or tile roofs to be applied over wood shakes if combustible concealed spaces are avoided by applying gypsum board, mineral fiber or glass fiber over the shakes.*

  3. *Where there are already two or more roof applications of any type of roof covering. This is to avoid overloading the roof structure with multiple layers of roofing.*

  4. *For asphalt shingles, when the building is located in an area subject to moderate or severe hail exposure per Figure R903.5*

10
Chimneys and Fireplaces

The naturally drafted chimneys and fireplaces work on physics that have been observed and perfected for thousands of years, with thousands of fires over that time to assist builders in honing the art of their safe construction. Generally, modern fireplaces are no longer used for heat so the current code requirements are related to protecting the adjacent combustible framing and finishes from also being part of the fire, and to provide the time-tested configurations needed for the smoke to draft. Violation of the code is a violation of the physics of proper drafting and is readily observed by smoke-filled rooms.

§1001 Masonry Fireplaces

§R1001.1 through §R1001.5 are related to providing sufficient structural design. Note that the footings must be at least 12" thick, regardless of soil capacity, and that chimneys cannot be used to support the building structure unless the masonry has specifically been designed for the added weight. Limitations on the chimney to support framing is also related to controlling the conductive heat transfer as noted in other sections of the chapter.

- Flue lining
- Effective flue area, based on area of fireplace opening per §R1003.15
- In Seismic Design Categories D0, D1, or D2 provide four #4 full length bars for chimneys up to 40" (1016) wide. Add two additional #4 bars for each additional 40" (1016), or fraction of width, or for each additional flue located in chimney per §R1001.3.1
- In Seismic Design Categories D0, D1, or D2 provide 1/4" (6) horizontal reinforcing ties at 18" (457) o.c. minimum. Provide two horizontal reinforcing ties at each bend in vertical bars per §R1001.3.2
- In Seismic Design Categories D0, D1, or D2 provide anchors at each floor per §R1001.4 unless completely inside exterior walls.
- Throat, 4" (102) deep, min.
- Per §R1001.7.1 ferrous damper at throat, 8" (203) above top of fireplace opening, operable from the room containing the fireplace.
- 10" (254) solid brick firebox wall thickness
  - Where a firebrick lining is used in the firebox, the wall thickness can be reduced to 8" (203). Joints in firebrick are limited to 1/4" (6) maximum per §R1001.5.
- Not more than 45° (0.78 rad) for rolled or sloped chamber walls; not more than 30° (0.52 rad) for corbelled masonry per §R1001.8.1
- Hearth slab thickness 4" (102) per §R1001.9.1
- Provide an exterior air intake or mechanical ventilation at masonry or factory-built fireplaces per §R1006 for combustion make-up air
- Ash dump optional cleanout per §R1001.2.1; provide metal or masonry closure

- Mortar cap
- Bond beams
- 24" (610) min. above highest point of roof within 10' (3048)

10' (3048) clearance sets min. chimney height

3' (914) min. above highest point at roof where chimney penetrates roof

- Flashing provided at intersection of adjacent roof and chimney flue enclosure
- Bond beam
- In Seismic Design Categories D0, D1, or D2 provide two 3/16" x 1" (5 x 25) strap anchorage embedded into chimney 12" (305) min. hooked around outer bar with 6" (157) extension beyond the bend. Fasten each strap to a minimum of four floor joist with two 1/2" (13) bolts per §R1001.4.1
- Minimum air-space clearance to combustibles of 2" (51) on front and sides, 4" (102) on back
- Smoke chamber of solid masonry, stone or concrete
- Minimum wall thickness on front, sides and back of 6" (157) when a lining of 2" (51) firebrick is provided, 8" (203) min. thickness at unlined walls.
- 8" (203) min.
- Thermal distance 21" (533) min. between opening and combustible materials per Figure R1001.1
- 8" (203) distance from top of opening to throat per §R1001.7.1
- Noncombustible lintel
- Fireplace opening height
- Masonry lined steel fireplace units are permitted when in accordance with §R1001.5.1

18" (457) min.

- Hearth slab reinforced to carry its own weight and all imposed loads
- Footing width to extend 6" (157) beyond each side of fireplace wall. Footing depth 12" (305) minimum footing thickness per §R1001.2
- Provide reinforcing bars in footing

Brick Firebox and Chimney on Wood Floor per Figure R1001.1

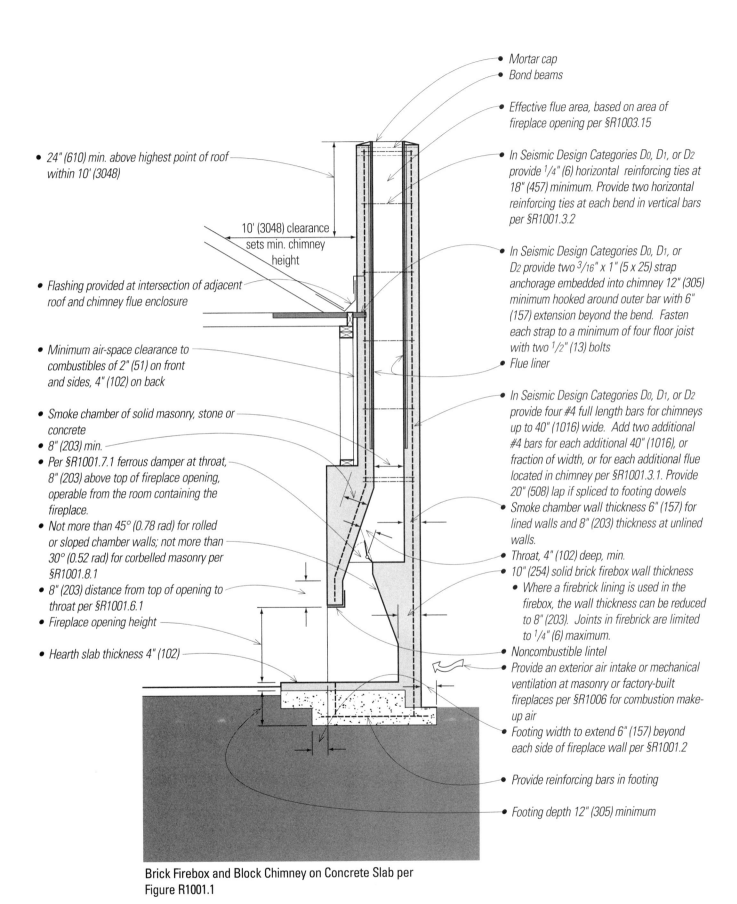

- 24" (610) min. above highest point of roof within 10' (3048)

10' (3048) clearance sets min. chimney height

- Flashing provided at intersection of adjacent roof and chimney flue enclosure

- Minimum air-space clearance to combustibles of 2" (51) on front and sides, 4" (102) on back

- Smoke chamber of solid masonry, stone or concrete
- 8" (203) min.
- Per §R1001.7.1 ferrous damper at throat, 8" (203) above top of fireplace opening, operable from the room containing the fireplace.
- Not more than 45° (0.78 rad) for rolled or sloped chamber walls; not more than 30° (0.52 rad) for corbelled masonry per §R1001.8.1
- 8" (203) distance from top of opening to throat per §R1001.6.1
- Fireplace opening height

- Hearth slab thickness 4" (102)

- Mortar cap
- Bond beams

- Effective flue area, based on area of fireplace opening per §R1003.15

- In Seismic Design Categories D0, D1, or D2 provide 1/4" (6) horizontal reinforcing ties at 18" (457) minimum. Provide two horizontal reinforcing ties at each bend in vertical bars per §R1001.3.2

- In Seismic Design Categories D0, D1, or D2 provide two 3/16" x 1" (5 x 25) strap anchorage embedded into chimney 12" (305) minimum hooked around outer bar with 6" (157) extension beyond the bend. Fasten each strap to a minimum of four floor joist with two 1/2" (13) bolts
- Flue liner

- In Seismic Design Categories D0, D1, or D2 provide four #4 full length bars for chimneys up to 40" (1016) wide. Add two additional #4 bars for each additional 40" (1016), or fraction of width, or for each additional flue located in chimney per §R1001.3.1. Provide 20" (508) lap if spliced to footing dowels
- Smoke chamber wall thickness 6" (157) for lined walls and 8" (203) thickness at unlined walls.
- Throat, 4" (102) deep, min.
- 10" (254) solid brick firebox wall thickness
  - Where a firebrick lining is used in the firebox, the wall thickness can be reduced to 8" (203). Joints in firebrick are limited to 1/4" (6) maximum.
- Noncombustible lintel
- Provide an exterior air intake or mechanical ventilation at masonry or factory-built fireplaces per §R1006 for combustion make-up air
- Footing width to extend 6" (157) beyond each side of fireplace wall per §R1001.2

- Provide reinforcing bars in footing

- Footing depth 12" (305) minimum

Brick Firebox and Block Chimney on Concrete Slab per Figure R1001.1

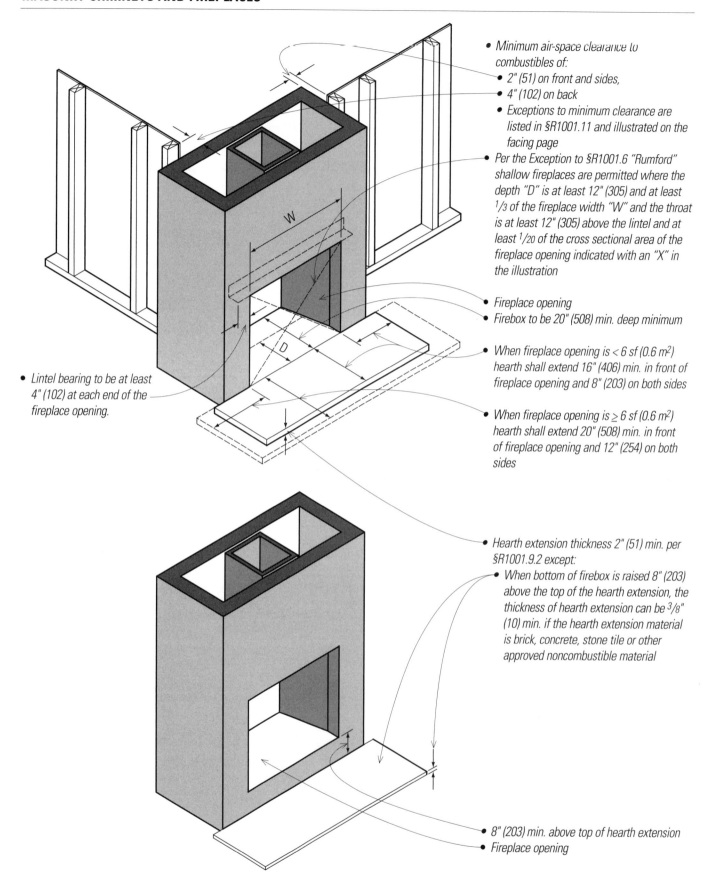

- Minimum air-space clearance to combustibles of:
  - 2" (51) on front and sides,
  - 4" (102) on back
  - Exceptions to minimum clearance are listed in §R1001.11 and illustrated on the facing page
- Per the Exception to §R1001.6 "Rumford" shallow fireplaces are permitted where the depth "D" is at least 12" (305) and at least $1/3$ of the fireplace width "W" and the throat is at least 12" (305) above the lintel and at least $1/20$ of the cross sectional area of the fireplace opening indicated with an "X" in the illustration

- Fireplace opening
- Firebox to be 20" (508) min. deep minimum

- When fireplace opening is < 6 sf (0.6 m²) hearth shall extend 16" (406) min. in front of fireplace opening and 8" (203) on both sides

- When fireplace opening is ≥ 6 sf (0.6 m²) hearth shall extend 20" (508) min. in front of fireplace opening and 12" (254) on both sides

- Lintel bearing to be at least 4" (102) at each end of the fireplace opening.

- Hearth extension thickness 2" (51) min. per §R1001.9.2 except:
  - When bottom of firebox is raised 8" (203) above the top of the hearth extension, the thickness of hearth extension can be $3/8$" (10) min. if the hearth extension material is brick, concrete, stone tile or other approved noncombustible material

- 8" (203) min. above top of hearth extension
- Fireplace opening

Fireplace clearance exceptions per §R1001.11

1. *Masonry fireplaces listed and labeled for use in contact with combustibles may have contact on their exterior surfaces with combustible materials*

2. *When masonry fireplaces are part of masonry or concrete walls, combustible materials in contact with the masonry or concrete walls may abut the masonry side walls if the trim is at least a minimum of 12" (305) from the inside face of the inside surface of the nearest firebox lining.*

3. *Exposed combustible trim and edges of sheathing materials such as wood siding, flooring, and drywall must be located a minimum of 12" (305) from the inside surface of the nearest firebox lining.*

4. *Exposed combustible mantels or trim may be placed directly on the masonry fireplace front surrounding the fireplace opening with the following conditions:*
   - *No combustible mantle or trim is permitted on the fireplace front within 6" (152) of the fireplace opening*
   - *Combustible materials located > 6" (152) but < 12" (305) from the fireplace opening shall not project more than 1/8" (3) from the fireplace front for each 1" (25.4) distance from the fireplace opening.*

• *Extent of fireplace opening*

• *Combustible trim material*

• *3/4" max.*

• *6" (152)*
• *12" (305)*
• *Top of fireplace opening*

6" (152)

12" (254)

Section view

§R1003.5 Corbelling

Corbelling is a technique for horizontally shifting the load of unit masonry utilizing the arching action of its own weight. The corbel is limited to one-half the individual brick height or one-third its depth, whichever is smaller, per course of masonry. The arching action of the brick units works best when the load is symmetrical, so the code allows corbelling with walls less than 12" (305) thick only when it is evenly done on both sides of the chimney.

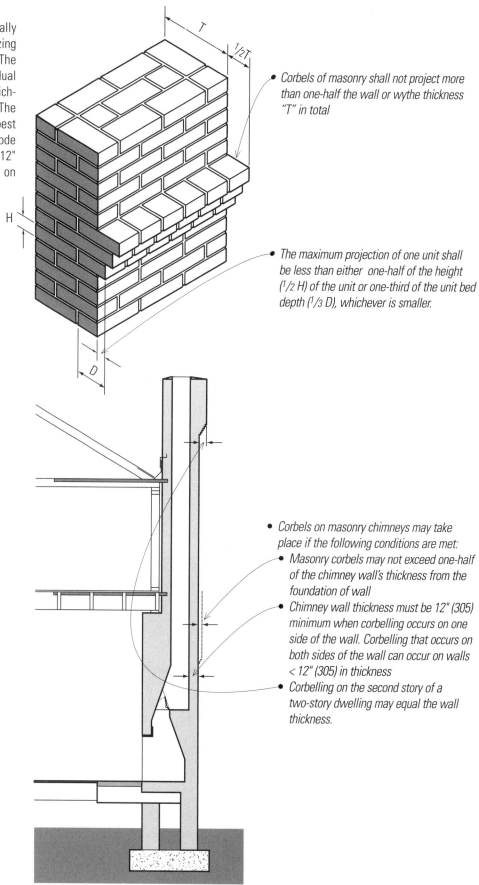

- Corbels of masonry shall not project more than one-half the wall or wythe thickness "T" in total

- The maximum projection of one unit shall be less than either one-half of the height ($^1/_2$ H) of the unit or one-third of the unit bed depth ($^1/_3$ D), whichever is smaller.

- Corbels on masonry chimneys may take place if the following conditions are met:
  - Masonry corbels may not exceed one-half of the chimney wall's thickness from the foundation of wall
  - Chimney wall thickness must be 12" (305) minimum when corbelling occurs on one side of the wall. Corbelling that occurs on both sides of the wall can occur on walls < 12" (305) in thickness
  - Corbelling on the second story of a two-story dwelling may equal the wall thickness.

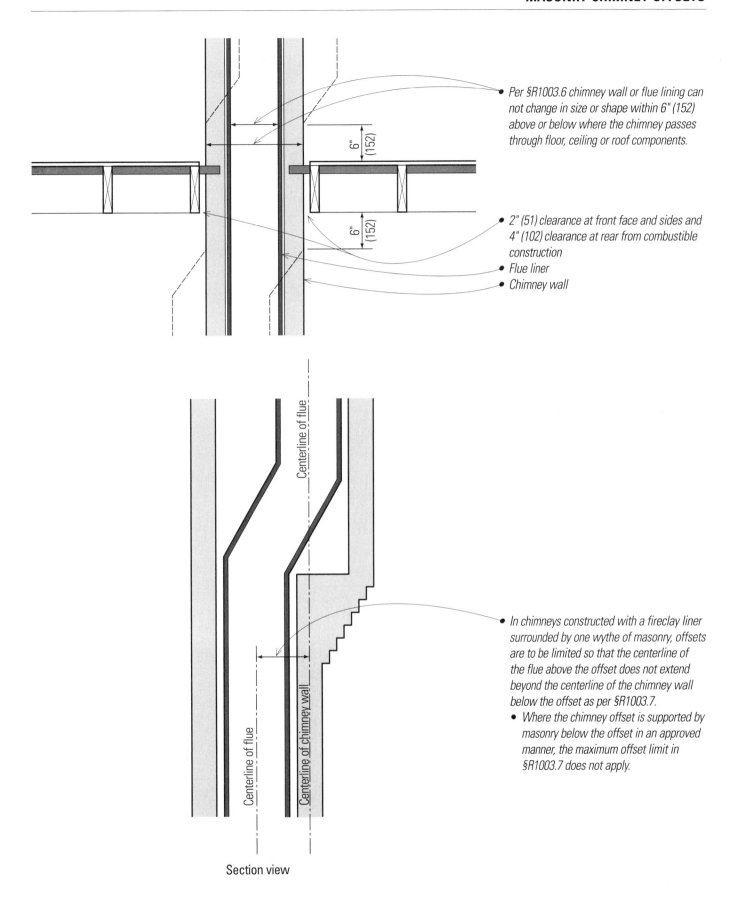

Per §R1003.6 chimney wall or flue lining can not change in size or shape within 6" (152) above or below where the chimney passes through floor, ceiling or roof components.

6" (152)

6" (152)

2" (51) clearance at front face and sides and 4" (102) clearance at rear from combustible construction

Flue liner

Chimney wall

Centerline of flue

In chimneys constructed with a fireclay liner surrounded by one wythe of masonry, offsets are to be limited so that the centerline of the flue above the offset does not extend beyond the centerline of the chimney wall below the offset as per §R1003.7.

Where the chimney offset is supported by masonry below the offset in an approved manner, the maximum offset limit in §R1003.7 does not apply.

Centerline of flue

Centerline of chimney wall

Section view

§R1003.9 Termination

Chimney termination is not structurally related but is a centuries-old relationship of the roof [including dormers, adjacent upper stories, etc.] to the top of the chimney so that wind currents do not prevent the smoke from rising freely.

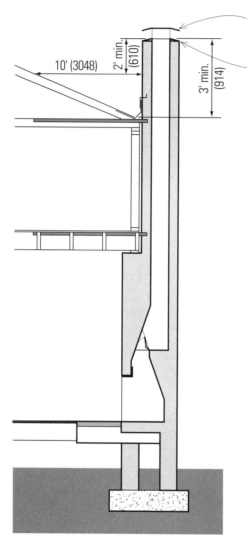

10' (3048)

2' min. (610)

3' min. (914)

• Where spark arrestors are installed they are to meet the requirement of §R1009.3.9.1.

• Chimney shall extend 2' (610) min. higher than any portion of the building within 10' (3048) but must extend a minimum of 3' (914) above the highest point where the chimney passes through the roof, or above the lowest plane of the roof.

Flue Lining of Masonry Chimneys

All masonry chimneys need liners. While this was disputed some decades ago, liners provide the smooth and corrosion-resistant surface that allows easier drafting and also permits the temperature of the liner to be elevated higher than the surrounding and supporting masonry. Note that §R1001.9 requires the liners to have refractory [high-heat] mortar, while the brick surround does not. Constant high heat of bricks and mortar can lead to early failure of the joints. Clay liners are the historic liner of choice, but metal ones may be installed as well. The metal liners are popular for existing chimneys, which were originally designed for multiple fireplaces or other appliances (coal or gas furnaces, etc.).

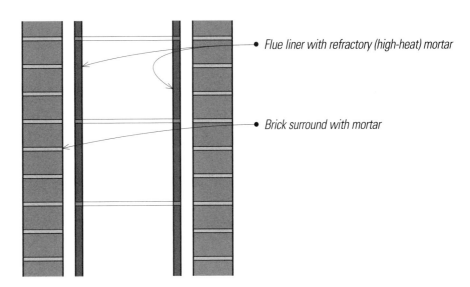

- *Flue liner with refractory (high-heat) mortar*

- *Brick surround with mortar*

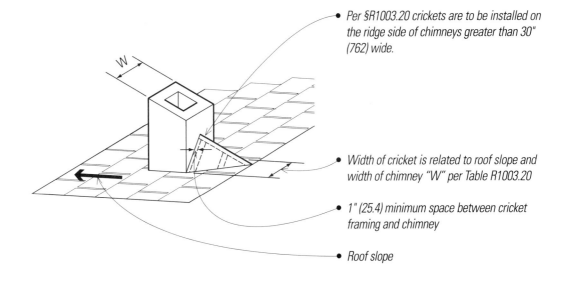

- *Per §R1003.20 crickets are to be installed on the ridge side of chimneys greater than 30" (762) wide.*

- *Width of cricket is related to roof slope and width of chimney "W" per Table R1003.20*

- *1" (25.4) minimum space between cricket framing and chimney*

- *Roof slope*

FACTORY-BUILT CHIMNEYS AND FIREPLACES

§R1004 Factory-Built Fireplaces

Many fireplaces are constructed using prefabricated parts. These fireplaces are described as "factory-built" and typically have spaces and brick linings built into their construction to allow for their placement in close proximity to combustible materials. Factory-built fireplaces are listed for their intended use and should be installed in accordance with the manufacturer's installation instructions and the identified listing.

§R1004 Factory-Built Chimneys

Factory-built fireplaces are typically installed with factory-built chimneys. The chimneys are to be installed per their listing and are to be matched with the type of fireplace or combustion appliance they serve. Chimney segments are to be well supported and any supporting structures are to be designed to support any additional loads imposed by the chimney.

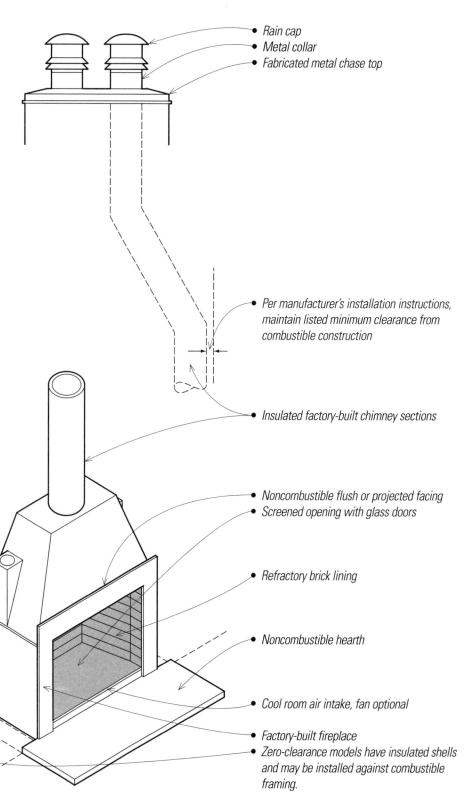

- Rain cap
- Metal collar
- Fabricated metal chase top

- Per manufacturer's installation instructions, maintain listed minimum clearance from combustible construction

- Insulated factory-built chimney sections

- Noncombustible flush or projected facing
- Screened opening with glass doors

- Refractory brick lining

- Noncombustible hearth

- Cool room air intake, fan optional

- Factory-built fireplace
- Zero-clearance models have insulated shells and may be installed against combustible framing.

Bibliography

2009 International Residential Code, International Code Council, 2009.

Significant Changes to the International Residential Code, 2009 Edition, International Code Council, 2009.

2009 International Residential Code Study Companion, International Code Council, 2009.

2006 International Residential Code and Commentary, International Code Council, 2007.

Code Check: An Illustrated Guide to Building a Safe Home, 6th edition, The Taunton Press, 2010.

Crawlspace Construction for Buildings Located in Special Flood Hazard Areas, Technical Manual FIA-TB-11, Federal Emergency Management Agency, 2001.

Empirical Design of Concrete Masonry Walls, TEK 14-8A, National Concrete Masonry Association.

Engineered Wood Construction Guide, APA, The Engineered Wood Association, 2003.

National Design Standard for Metal-plate-connected Wood Truss Construction, Truss Plate Institute, 2002.

Safety Standard for Architectural Glazing Materials, 16CFR1201.1, Consumer Products Safety Commission.

Standard for Cold-formed Steel Framing-prescriptive Method for One- and Two-family Dwellings, American Iron and Steel Institute, 2007.

Standard for the Installation of Sprinkler Systems in One- and Two-family Dwellings and Manufactured Homes, Standard 13D, National Fire Protection Association, 2007.

The Gypsum Construction Handbook, 6th Edition, United States Gypsum, R.S. Means Company, Inc., 2009.

Vinyl Siding Installation Manual, Vinyl Siding Institute, 2007.

Wood Frame Construction Manual for One- and Two-Family Dwellings, ANSI/AF & PA, 2008.

Index

Get Your Free 30-Day Trial of International Code Council's *2009 International Residential Code© (IRC) Premium* **from eCodes—ICC's Electronic Library**

The 2009 IRC© Premium version gives you complete Internet access to the code in electronic format with many helpful features:

- Add notes, graphics, hyperlinks to other websites, and more to your material section by section.
- Key word and highlighting search features.
- Enjoy powerful search and print capabilities.

Available for PC users as well as Mac and Linux users.

Experience the versatility and value of eCodes Premium, ICC's most powerful electronic tool.

To begin your FREE 30-day trial, **visit www.iccsafe.org/wiley2009IRC**
If you have difficulty accessing this online offer, please contact ICC directly at support@ecodes.biz or (888) 422-7233 x33822.